The Expression of Information Structure

The Expression of Cognitive Categories

ECC 5

Editors
Wolfgang Klein
Stephen Levinson

De Gruyter Mouton

The Expression
of Information Structure

edited by

Manfred Krifka
Renate Musan

De Gruyter Mouton

ISBN 978-3-11-026214-8
e-ISBN 978-3-11-026160-8

Library of Congress Cataloging-in-Publication Data

A CIP catalog record for this book has been applied for at the Library of Congress.

Bibliographic information published by the Deutsche Nationalbibliothek

The Deutsche Nationalbibliothek lists this publication in the Deutsche Nationalbibliografie; detailed bibliographic data are available in the Internet at http://dnb.dnb.de.

© 2013 Walter de Gruyter GmbH & Co. KG, Berlin/Boston

Cover design: Frank Benno Junghanns, Berlin
Typesetting: Frank Benno Junghanns, Berlin
Printing: Hubert & Co. GmbH & Co. KG, Göttingen
∞ Printed on acid-free paper

Printed in Germany

www.degruyter.com

To Ursula

Contents

Information structure:
Overview and linguistic issues

Manfred Krifka and Renate Musan

1. What is information structure?[1]

1.1. Common ground and information packaging

While the term *information structure* was introduced by Halliday (1967), the concept itself has its roots in antiquity (see von Heusinger 1999, and below). The term has been used for a number of different phenomena. Here we follow the influential article by Chafe (1976), who introduced the notion of *information packaging*, to refer to how information is presented, in contrast to the information itself. More specifically, with the term information structure we understand aspects of natural language that help speakers to take into consideration the addressee's current information state, and hence to facilitate the flow of communication. The view behind this is that communication can be seen as continuous change of the *common ground,* i.e., of the information that is mutually known to be shared in communication; speakers plan their contributions with respect to the common ground. To take a concrete example, suppose the speaker utters (1).

(1) *I have a cat, and I had to bring my cat to the vet.*

The first clause in (1) introduces the information that the speaker has a cat into the common ground. The noun phrase *my cat* in the second clause presupposes this; the speaker can use this phrase because its referent can be assumed to be salient in the common ground after the first clause was uttered. The second clause adds the information that the speaker had to

---

[1] This chapter relies in large parts heavily on Krifka (2007), who acknowledges support of the DFG in the context of Sonderforschungsbereich 632: Informationsstruktur. The participation of Renate Musan consists in revising the original text and adding sections concerning givenness, historical aspects of information structure, the crosslinguistic inventory of information structural coding, and truth.

bring the cat to the vet to the common ground. The addressee adopts the information. Thus, the common ground is continuously enriched during communication.

The original notion of common ground (cf. Stalnaker 1974, Karttunen 1974, Lewis 1979) allowed for a promising way of modeling the distinction between presuppositions, as requirements for the input common ground, and assertions or the preferred content, as the proposed change in the output common ground. This distinction is relevant for information packaging, a term proposed by Chafe (1976), as the common ground changes continuously, and information has to be packaged in correspondence with the current common ground. For example, it can be explained why (1) is fine but (2) is odd: Here the second sentence introduces the information that the speaker has a cat which is already present in the input common ground at this point (cf. van der Sandt 1988).

(2)   #*I had to bring my cat to the vet, and I have a cat.*

It was pointed out already by Stalnaker, Karttunen and Lewis that speakers can also change the common ground by letting the addressee accommodate a presupposition. Accommodation can be understood as a repair strategy: If a piece of information cannot be interpreted with respect to the current common ground, then the current common ground can minimally be changed in a way that it fits the requirement of the piece of information. Of course, this can only be done if the change is uncontroversial. This is why (3a) is good but (b) is less acceptable:

(3)   a. *I had to bring my cat to the vet because it was sick.*
      b. *I had to bring my gorilla to the vet because it was sick.*

A few words concerning the common ground content are in order. Above we said that the common ground consists of the information that is mutually known to be shared in communication and that the addressee adopts the information provided by the speaker. We do not mean to say that the common ground can only contain true propositions, of course. Consider the following conversation:

(4)   A: *Daddy, what is the earth like?*
      B: *Well, the earth is flat and sits upon the back of a big turtle.*
      A: *Oh, I would like to see the turtle! Can we visit it?*
      B: *No, of course not! We would fall down!*

As a conversation this clearly works fine, and hence, the common ground must be able to contain false propositions. But it does not even have to be the case that all participants believe the propositions in the common ground to be true. Rather, a theory of the common ground has to leave room for hypothetical assumptions and for discussions like the following.

(5)   A: *The earth is flat and sits upon the back of a big turtle.*
       B: *Wow, great!*
       A: *Yes. I wanted to visit it, but my dad said that's too dangerous. We would fall down.*
       B: *Right. But wait: Wouldn't the turtle also fall down? The whole story can't be true!*
       A: *Oh. I see. Well, I guess it's a bird then.*

Since one can obviously refer to propositions one does not believe to be true and negotiate whether propositions are true or not, it must be possible to have such propositions at least temporarily in the common ground. The same holds for presuppositions. They do not have to be true and they may be used temporarily for supporting certain untrue or hypothetical sentences.

The notion of common ground was first applied to factual information, but it was extended soon after that to *discourse referents* (in particular, by Kamp 1981 and Heim 1982, building on ideas of Karttunen 1969). That is, the common ground consists not only of a set of propositions that is presumed to be mutually accepted (or the conjunction of this set, forming one proposition), but also of a set of entities that have already been introduced into the common ground previously. Such entities can be explicitly introduced, e.g., by an indefinite noun phrase, as in the first clause of (1), or they can be accommodated, as in (3a). They can be taken up by pronouns, as in the second clause of (3a), or by definite noun phrases, as in the second clause of (1), which express requirements for the input common ground. The choice of anaphoric expression depends on the recency of the antecedent, again a notion that falls squarely within Chafe's notion of packaging.

Another example of information packaging is shown in (6). Here the preposed expression *as for my cat* gives the addressee a hint as to what the utterance is about.

(6)   *As for my cat, I prefer dry food.*

One problem with Chafe's approach is that there are aspects of optimization of the message that, on the one hand, respond to the temporary state of the addressee, but on the other also affect the message itself, and hence cannot be treated as pure packaging. For example, focus, as expressed by sentence accent in English, can be used for information packaging, as in answers to questions, cf. (7), but can also lead to truth-conditional differences, as it does when it is associated with focus-sensitive particles like *only*, cf. (8).

(7)   a.   A: *What did John show Mary?*
              B: *John showed Mary [the PICtures]$_F$.*
       b.   A: *Who did John show the pictures?*
              B: *John showed [MAry]$_F$ the pictures.*

(8)   a.   *John only showed Mary [the PICtures]$_F$*
       b.   *John only showed [MAry]$_F$ the pictures.*

The truth conditions of B's answers in (7a,b) arguably are the same, whereas the truth conditions of (8) differ. One and the same linguistic device, sentence accent, can be used for packaging as well as for constructing the content.

There are two possible ways of dealing with multiple uses of marking devices such as accent: One is to assume that the two uses of the same device are essentially unrelated, just as the uses of accent in English to express focus and to distinguish words such as *REcord* and *reCORD*. The other is to assume that the device is to be interpreted in a particular way that makes sense for the purposes of information packaging and for building information content. For methodological reasons the second way appears to be more attractive: If it can be shown that one and the same interpretation of a marking device has multiple uses, then only one interpretation should be assumed, instead of multiple interpretations. We will see that focus can indeed be interpreted in this way, as pragmatic focus and as semantic focus.

The properties of the common ground mentioned so far all had to do with the truth-conditional information of the common ground, and so we can subsume them under the heading of *common ground content*. But any ecologically valid notion of common ground must also contain information about the manifest communicative interests and goals of the participants.

For example, questions typically do not add factual information to the common ground, but indicate informational needs on the side of one participant that should be satisfied by a conversational move of the other. We propose to call this dimension of the common ground *common ground management*, as it is concerned with the way in which the common ground content should develop. As with common ground content, common ground management is proposed to be shared, with the understanding that the responsibility for it may be asymmetrically distributed among participants. There is a wide variety of studies that can be captured under the notion of common ground management, some formal such as Merin (1994) or Groenendijk (1999), some less formal such as Clark (1996), and studies of Conversational Analysis such as Sacks, Schegloff and Jefferson (1974). The distinction is important for our purposes, as we can associate those aspects of information structure that have truth-conditional impact with common ground content, and those which relate to the pragmatic use of expressions with common ground management.

It is not surprising that cognitive categories such as the distinction between unfamiliar and familiar discourse referents, the presence of alternatives, and the indication of what an utterance is about, play a role in communication and hence, in languages universally: To a large extent, communication works similarly in all linguistic communities. Hence, all natural languages have developed devices to express these categories. Among these devices are the choice of specific lexical items, word order, specific syntactic constructions, certain particles, and prosodic means. This book will bring together articles that deal with the expression of information structure from various perspectives, and with respect to several languages. The purpose of this introduction is to define and discuss the central notions the book is based on: *focus* (as indicating alternatives) and its various uses, *givenness* (as indicating that a denotation is already present in the common ground), and *topic* (as specifying what a statement is about). It also proposes a new notion, which comprises contrastive topics and frame setters, namely *delimitation*; it indicates that the current conversational move does not satisfy the local communicative needs totally.

1.2. A clarification: Expressions vs. what they stand for

Before we discuss specific notions of information structure, we would like to mention a terminological problem. We often find that the distinction between an expression and what it stands for, its denotatum, is not made. For example, in a sentence like (9), the expression *as for the beans*, or *the beans*, may be called the "topic" of the sentence, but also the beans referred to are called its "topic". After all, the sentence is about the beans, not about *the beans*.

(9)   *As for the beans, John ate them.*

For some reason, this confusion of expression and meaning occurs particularly often with information structural notions. With notions like subject, predicate or direct object it does not arise; no one would claim that John the person is the grammatical subject of (9), it is *John* the noun phrase. The imprecision of information structure terms can be endured if one is aware of it. But in any instance in which it is relevant, it is important to make the intended interpretation clear. For example, we can refer to *(as for) the beans* as the topic constituent of the sentence, or as a *topic expression*, and of the beans that it refers to, or of the discourse referents anchored to them, as the topic referents or *topic denotation*.

2.   Focus

2.1. What is focus?

It is difficult to trace back the history of "focus" as a linguistic notion, because the concept was expressed in different terms, the term was used to express different concepts, and it may be that there was not even a uniform concept in the first place. The term *focus* was used prominently in the Prague School as a complementary notion to topic, and was related to newness (cf. Sgall, Hajičová and Benešová 1973; Sgall, Hajičová and Panenova 1986). Halliday (1967) was instrumental in introducing the term into the anglophone linguistic world. In Generative Grammar, it was used in Chomsky (1970) and Jackendoff (1972) as the complement notion to presupposition – intuitively, what is new in an utterance. Under a different term, *psychological predicate*, a related notion was proposed in the work of von der Gabelentz (1869) and refined by Paul (1880). In that latter work, there is a first systematic discussion of one of the most prominent uses of focus, namely, to identify the part in an answer to a *wh*-question that corresponds to the *wh*-constituent in the question – in a sense, what is new in the answer. Another aspect in language use for which the term *focus* was used is to express contrast; for example, Chafe (1976) referred to the focus of a contrastive statement.

 We will refer to the various uses of focus, and to the various conceptions of focus, later in this chapter. Here we would like to assume a particular idea about focus that was put forward in Rooth (1985, 1992) and subsequent work, and that is able to subsume other notions of focus. It can be phrased in a very general way.

(10) Focus indicates the presence of alternatives that are relevant for the interpretation of linguistic expressions.

Note, however, that alternatives play a role in language all the time, and not only in connection with focus. Thus, in a sentence like *John [MARried]$_F$ Sue*, the verb *married* is focused and hence indicates alternatives to marrying someone – like, for instance, carrying someone, beating someone, or meeting someone. But of course there are also alternatives to John as well as alternatives to Sue that are relevant for the interpretation of the sentence. Thus, the definition in (10) means to say that focus especially stresses and points out the existence of particular alternatives.

The rather general definition in (10) does not say anything about how focus is marked; in fact it is compatible with different ways of marking. It does, however, say that we should use terms like focus marking or focus construction only to indicate that alternatives play a role in interpretation. Even still, it may well be that different ways of focus marking signal different ways of how alternatives are exploited; e.g., focus marking by cleft sentences often signals an exhaustive interpretation that in-situ focus lacks. We can then talk about subtypes of focus, such as cleft focus and in-situ focus, that may employ the alternatives in more specific ways. Also, (10) allows for languages to differ in the ways they mark focus and in the specific interpretational effects of focus. This is in no way different from other linguistic categories, such as time, negation, case, or gender. But it seems reasonable, and consistent with current uses of the term, to use "focus" exactly in those cases that satisfy (10) [2] The following sections will show that all current uses of the term can be subsumed under (10).

2.2. Expression focus and denotation focus

Definition (10) is silent about the nature of the alternatives that are relevant for interpretation. In fact, the alternatives may be alternatives of form or of denotation. We call the first case *expression focus*. The expression

---

[2] Moreover, there are other cases in which alternatives play a role that are not indicated by focus. For example, the standard theory of scalar implicatures assumes that they arise due to alternatives to an expression ordered by a Horn scale, and these alternatives do not have to be focused. For example, *John or Mary will come* implicates that not both will come as *or* has *and* as its alternative, but clearly, *or* does not have to be focused.

alternatives can affect a variety of aspects, like choice of words and pronunciation, and they do not even have to involve constituents or meaningful units. Focus on expressions is typically used for corrections, and it often but not necessarily occurs together with an overt negation (cf. Horn 1985 on metalinguistic negation). Two examples:

(11) *Grandpa didn't [kick the BUCKet]$_F$, he [passed aWAY]$_F$.*

(12) A: *They live in BERlin.*
      B: *They live in [BerLIN]$_F$!*

In (11) the relevant alternatives of both foci are the expressions {*kick the bucket, pass away*}. These alternatives cannot be their denotations, as they are identical, namely the property DIE. The expressions differ among other things in their connotations, which is the feature in which they contrast here, so what is contrasted cannot just be their denotation. In (12) the relevant alternatives are the expressions {*BERlin, BerLIN*} that only differ in their accent, and speaker B corrects speaker A by supplying the form that B thinks has the right accent structure.

Expression focus is typically marked in-situ, not by clefts or other types of movement. It can focus on constituents below the word level, and it can be deeply embedded within a sentence. This follows from the assumption that expression focus affects surface representations of linguistic objects. The typical use of expression focus is the rejection of a string $[\alpha_1 ... \alpha_{i,F} ... \alpha_n]$ in favor of a string $[\alpha_1 ... \alpha_{i,F}' ... \alpha_n]$, where focus identifies the substring to be replaced.

We will call the second case *denotation focus*. Here the relevant alternatives are construed on the level of denotations, leading to alternative denotations of complex expressions. Denotation focus on an expression α with meaning $\|\alpha\|$ leads to the assumption of a set of alternative meanings that play a role in the interpretation of the constituent in which α occurs. The alternative denotations have to be comparable to the denotation of the expression in focus, that is, they have to be of the same type, and often also of the same ontological sort (e.g., persons or times), and they can be more narrowly restricted by the context of utterance. In the rest of the chapter, we will concentrate on denotation focus, which is certainly more important in communication.

To summarize, focus is the property of a string $[\alpha_1 ... \alpha_{i,F} ... \alpha_n]$ to point out the existence of alternatives either to the expression or to its denotation. On the surface this often appears as accent, but this can also be achieved by other means like, for instance, certain syntactic constructions. Similarly to the terminological confusion pointed out in Section 1.2, the term 'focus' is often used for the device that marks the property focus, e.g., the focus accent, for the property, or for the linguistic expression in focus.

2.3. Semantic vs. pragmatic uses of focus: Common ground content vs. common ground management

We now turn to the notion of the interpretation of focused expressions. It is useful to explicate this notion within the general theory of common ground introduced in Section 1.1, where we introduced the distinction between common ground content and common ground management. This differentiation is useful to distinguish between two quite different uses of focus. So-called *pragmatic uses* of focus relate to the public communicative goals of the participants, the common ground management. So-called *semantic uses* of focus relate to the factual information, the common ground content.

The pragmatic use of focus does not have an immediate influence on truth conditions, but it helps in guiding the direction in which communication should develop, and it also aids in building the cognitive representations that are to be constructed by the interlocutors. Here, failing to select the right focus typically results in incoherent communication. The semantic use of focus, on the other hand, affects the truth-conditional content of the common ground. In this case, failing to set focus right will result in transmitting unintended factual information. The two uses of focus cannot always be neatly separated, mostly because the pragmatic use can have truth-conditional side-effects. But there are prototypical cases that clearly belong to the one or to the other category, to which we now turn.

2.4. Pragmatic uses of focus

The classical pragmatic use of focus is to highlight the part of an answer that corresponds to the *wh*-part of a constituent question (Paul 1880). This can be captured straightforwardly within our model of common ground change. A question changes the current common ground in such a way as to indicate the communicative goal of the questioner.[3] The formation of the

---

[3] Following Hamblin (1973), we can model this effect by interpreting a question as a *question set*, i.e., as a set of propositions each of which is the denotation of a congruent answer.

> A: Who stole the cookie?
> Hamblin meaning of the question: $\{STOLE(COOKIE)(x) \mid x \in PERSON\}$

question, as well as the construction of the focus-induced alternatives of the answers, clearly belongs to common ground management, not to common ground content: The question specifies the way in which the common ground should develop in the immediate future; the answer relates an expression to the immediately preceding context. Hence, focus in answers obviously is an information-packaging device in the sense of Chafe, as it corresponds to the current common ground, as prepared by the preceding question. The formation of questions, as a device of common ground management, can be seen as part of information packaging as well.

We might ask at this point why the marking of question-answer congruence exists in the first place. One *raison d'être* is that it allows for the accommodation of the meaning of questions that are not overtly expressed. That is, it allows for the accommodation of common ground management. For example, the accent structure in (13) can be understood in such a way that the second clause leads to the accommodation of a question, such as *what did you do first*.

(13)   *I built a St. Martin's lantern with my kids. First, I [built the BOdy of the lantern with some CARDboard paper]$_F$.*

A variety of theories have assumed that coherent discourse is structured by such implicit questions (e.g., Klein and von Stutterheim 1987, van Kuppevelt 1994, Roberts 1995, Büring 2003), and focus on the answers to such explicit questions may well help the addressee to construct what the intended questions were.[4] With this understanding, all cases of so-called

---

The answer identifies one of these propositions and adds it to the common ground content. This is the job of the "ordinary meaning" of the answer in Alternative Semantics. Focus, however, induces alternatives that correspond to the Hamblin meaning of questions, i.e., focus evokes an alternative set. In the theory of Rooth (1992), the alternative set is a superset of the question set.

    B: *[PEter]$_F$ stole the cookie.*
    Ordinary meaning of the answer: STOLE(COOKIE)(PETER)
    Focus-induced alternatives: {STOLE(COOKIE)(x) | x∈ENTITY}

The focus in the last line is not restricted to PERSON, different from the question above, in which the *wh*-word *who* enforces this restriction.

[4]   It should be stressed that we should not expect this use of focus to be universal; just as some languages use gender information to express pronoun binding and others don't, the use of focus to mark question/answer-coherence may be restricted. Findings about languages such as Hausa (Hartmann and Zimmermann 2007) and Northern Sotho (Zerbian 2006) suggest that this is the case.

"presentational" or "information" focus which claimed that focus expresses the most important part of the utterance, or what is new in the utterance, can be subsumed under the use of alternatives to indicate covert questions suggested by the context. The following examples suggest questions like *What happened?*, *What did she do?* and *What was there?*, respectively. This explains the types of foci suggested for the second clauses in (14a, b).

(14)   a.   *And then something strange happened. [A MEterorite fell down]$_F$.*
       b.   *Mary sat down at her desk. She [took out a pile of NOTES]$_F$.*
       c.   *Once upon a time, there was [a PRINcess]$_F$*

Other pragmatic uses of focus are to correct and confirm information. In cases like (15B, B′) the focus alternatives must include a proposition that has been proposed in the common ground immediately preceding the statement. What this expresses is that the ordinary meaning of the sentence is the only one among the alternatives that holds. This leads to a corrective interpretation for the case in which the context proposition differed, cf. (B), and to a confirmative interpretation for the case in which the context proposition was the same, cf. (B′). In the latter case the wider common ground must be such that other alternatives are under consideration as well, which are then excluded. Again, focus in this use restricts the possible contexts, and presumably aids the interpretation of a sentence.

(15)   A: *Mary stole the cookie.*
       B: *(No,) [PEter]$_F$ stole the cookie!*
       B′: *Yes, [MAry]$_F$ stole the cookie.*

There is a relatively strong need to express contrast, even in languages that use focus marking sparingly, and to express it with more explicit means such as syntactic movement (cf., e.g., Hartmann and Zimmermann 2007 for Hausa, and Asatiani and Skopeteas, this volume, for Georgian). This can be explained by the plausible principle that if something is unexpected, it should be marked explicitly. We find this principle at work in other areas as well, of course. For example, the textual relation of contrast has to be marked (e.g., by *but, nevertheless,* etc.), whereas non-contrastive relations like narration, elaboration, and causation do not have to be expressed explicitly.

Another pragmatic use of focus is its use to highlight parallels in interpretations. This can affect whole clauses as in (16a) or parts of clauses as in (b). As in the previous cases, focus creates alternatives, with the pragmatic requirement that some of these alternatives are also evoked in the immediately surrounding contexts. In addition, the parallel expressions are required to have the same set of alternatives. In the case of (16a), both clauses evoke the set {STOLE(x)(y) | x,y∈ENTITY}. In the case of (b), the alternatives have to be constructed more locally, for which Rooth (1992) introduces an anaphoric operator C, here presumably at the level of the noun phrase or determiner phrase. The noun phrase level alternatives are {P(FARMER) | P∈NATIONALITY}, a set of predicates like AMERICAN(FARMER), CANADIAN(FARMER), etc.

(16) a. *MAry stole the COOkie and PEter stole the CHOcolate.*
      b. *An AMErican farmer talked to a CaNAdian farmer, ...*

The use of focus to express parallel structures is perhaps one of the least understood aspects of focus. Focus appears to be less obligatory here than in the other cases. Presumably focus assists in constructing mental models of the described scene by associating the contrasted meanings. Presumably, it is advantageous to construct such mental models in parallel, where focus indicates the locations where the models differ.

Yet another pragmatic use of focus is to make the addressee aware of a delimitation of the utterance with respect to the constituent which is in focus. This use subsumes, in particular, cases of contrastive topics such as *John* in (17a), but also cases of focus in frame setting expressions as in (17b). We will come back to this in Section 5.

(17) a. *As for JOHN, he was seen in the KITchen.*
      b. *In MY opinion, JOHN stole the cookies.*

With these types (answers, including selections from a list of items specified in the question, corrections, confirmations, parallels, and delimitation), we probably have covered the main pragmatic uses of focus. We now turn to those uses of focus that have an immediate truth-conditional effect, that is, that directly influence common ground content.

2.5. Semantic uses of focus

We say that semantic operators whose interpretational effects depend on focus are *associated with focus*. The best-known cases are focus-sensitive particles like *only, also,* and *even*. There exist a variety of theories for the meaning of such particles, but they generally resort to the notion of alternatives, which was also central for the pragmatic uses of focus. In the case of exclusive particles like *only*, it is stated that the focus denotation is the only one among the alternatives that leads to a true assertion; additive particles like *also* and *too* express the presupposition that the assertion holds for other alternatives; and scalar particles like *even* presuppose that the denotation of the focus constituent is, in some respect, extreme when compared to other alternatives (cf., e.g., Jacobs 1983, König 1991).

But do these particles indeed affect the truth-conditional meaning? It is interesting to note that the focus information of additive and scalar particles does not affect the output common ground, but rather restricts the input common ground, as the alternatives to the focus are used to impose presuppositions. In particular, additive particles have consequences for common ground management, as they indicate that a proposition with an alternative to the item in focus had been expressed before or is part of the common ground.

(18)   *[JOHN]$_F$ stole a cookie, and [PEter]$_P$, TOO[5], stole a cookie.*

For the case in which the first proposition has not been expressed explicitly, it has to be accommodated. Additive particles like *also* and *too* do not just express that the predication also holds for an alternative to the focus, as was pointed out by Kripke (2009). Otherwise, the additive particle in *John had dinner in New York, too* would not be justified, as it is a truism that many people had dinner in New York.

The negation particle *not* has been analyzed as a focus-sensitive particle as well. In the following example, the proposition that Fred studied linguistics at Stanford is negated, with the presupposition being made that Fred studied something at Stanford.

(19)   *Fred didn't study lingGUIStics$_F$ at Stanford, but phiLOsophy.*

We can capture this by assuming a structure NEG$[...\alpha_F...]$, which presupposes that there is an x such that $[...x...]$ is the case, and negates that $[...\alpha...]$ is the case (cf. Jackendoff 1972).

Other cases in which alternatives are used for semantic purposes include reason clauses as in (20), a variation of a counterfactual example of Dretske (1972), and operators like *fortunately* as in (21).

---

[5]   As for a theory that explains accent on *too*, cf. Krifka (1999).

(20) a   *Clyde had to marry [BERtha]$_F$ in order to be eligible.*
     b. *Clyde had to [MARry]$_F$ Bertha for the inheritance.*

(21) *Fortunately, Bill spilled [WHITE]$_F$ wine on the carpet.*

For example, (21) says that among the two alternatives, *John spilled red wine* and *John spilled white wine*, the latter one was more fortunate (but of course that wine was spilled at all was still unfortunate).

Rooth (1985) has suggested that focus helps in determining the restrictor of quantifiers, in particular adverbial quantifiers, in which case it has a truth-conditional impact as well. For example, focus has a truth-conditional impact in (22); focus on *q* instead would result in the different, and false, reading that every u is followed by a q.

(22) *In English orthography, a [U]$_F$ always follows a q.*
     'Whenever an a, b, c, d, … z follows a q, then a u follows a q.'
     i.e., every q is followed by a u.

Focus can also play a role in the interpretation of sentences with adnominal quantifiers, as in the following example from Herburger (1997). As in the case of adverbial quantifiers, the item in focus is interpreted within the nuclear scope, that is, in the part complementary to the restrictor.

(23) *Few [INcompetent]$_F$ cooks applied.*
     'Few of the cooks that applied were incompetent.'

Interestingly, the focus-sensitive reading is restricted to certain adnominal quantifiers; it does not appear, for example, with universal quantifiers like *every*. For general observations concerning the relation between focus and quantification see Partee (1991, 1999).

One important fact about focus-sensitive operators is that they have to be in a position in which they can have scope over their focus. For example, *only* in (24) could associate with *Mary*, with *Sue*, with *introduced* or with the whole verb phrase, but not with *John* as it does not c-command *John* on any level of representation.

(24) *John only introduced Mary to Sue.*

Yet it should be stressed that the notion of focus does not coincide with the notion of scope. For example, while the focus of *only* in (25a) and (b) is the same, their scopes differ, leading to distinct interpretations.

(25) a. *Mary only said that JOHN stole a cookie.*
'Mary didn't say of anyone but John that he stole a cookie.'

b. *Mary said that only JOHN stole a cookie.*
'Mary said that nobody but John stole a cookie.'

2.6. The relation between pragmatic and semantic uses

What we have learned about focus so far results in a somewhat schizo-phrenic overall picture. On the one hand, we have seen that focus is a prag-matic phenomenon. With the help of focus, we can indicate that the propo-sition expressed stands in relation to some other, related proposition. This is arguably a packaging phenomenon, and thus belongs to information struc-ture. On the other hand, we have seen that focus, in the context of operators like *only*, *always*, or *fortunately*, can have a role in determining the proposi-tion itself. This is clearly not just a packaging phenomenon, but is part of the content of what is expressed itself.

If we assume that focus basically belongs to pragmatics, then the question arises of how we can account for the apparent truth-conditional, semantic effects of focus. An important subquestion would be, why do we observe this dependency with some semantic operators, but not with others. For example, why do temporal operators like *yesterday* or universal adnom-inal quantifiers like *every* not lead to focus-sensitive interpretations?

This issue was treated in detail in Beaver and Clark (2008). They assume a general Focus Principle, stating that "Some part of a declarative utterance should evoke a set of alternatives containing the propositions of the Current Question", where the assumption is that at each stage of the development of a common ground, a current question can be assumed. This principle – or variations of it that cover, for example, contrastive uses of focus – can explain pragmatic uses of focus, but also uses of focus with truth-condi-tional impact. Beaver and Clark assume that there are three degrees of asso-ciation of focus with semantic operators: quasi-associations, free associa-tions, and conventional associations.

We find quasi-association of focus with negation and with other non-veridical operators, such as *perhaps* or propositional attitude constructions like *John thinks...* These operators turn out not to associate with focus at all; all that we need is the Focus Principle. To see this, consider apparent focus-sensitive negation, cf. (19), and two possible context questions (26a, b).

(26) a. *What didn't Fred study at Stanford?*
b. *What did Fred study at Stanford?*

Context question (a) is invoked by the focus on the whole sentence of (19), and context question (b) is invoked by (19) in case we exclude the negation. Now the accent that realizes focus in (19) can be different: A simple high accent (H*) with falling clause-final accent (L%) indicates a complete answer. This evokes the somewhat special question (a), as it would not be a complete answer to (b). This would normally not be considered a case of focus-sensitive negation. A rising accent (L+H*) with a rising clause-final accent (L–H%) indicates incompleteness. This is compatible with the more regular question (b), for which the proposition 'Fred didn't study linguistics at Stanford' is an incomplete answer, as it excludes only one field of study. This is the case that has been analyzed as focus-sensitive negation. But notice that now we do not have to assume that negation associates with the negation. The context question is evoked by the general Focus Principle, and we predict that we typically continue such sentences with a full answer, like *he studied phiLOsophy*$_F$. (There is a third reading, when the negation and the focus is realized with a low accent L*, resulting in a contradiction to a proposition in the common ground.)

Free association with focus comprises cases that involve apparent association of quantifiers with focus. Beaver and Clark assume that the restrictor of a quantifier introduces a set variable, the value of which typically is determined by contextual factors. The context question invoked by focus plays a role in determining the variable. For example, in (22) focus on *U* evokes, following the Focus Principle, the context question *What follows a q?* This context question defines the domain variable, which is a set of events e (here, letter tokens in texts) in which some letter or other follows a q. The quantificational sentence then says that in every such event, a *u* follows a *q*.

Conventional association with focus is the case closest to real association with focus. This comprises, among others, cases of focus-sensitive particles like *only*. Beaver and Clark assume that the Focus Principle is active in this case as well, and that the operator associates conventionally with the evoked context question. For example, in *John only introduced MAry*$_F$ *to Sue*, the evoked context question is 'Who did John introduce to Sue?', and *only* conventionally states that the proposition is the complete answer to this question. The fact that operators associate with the evoked context question, and not with the focus directly, explains why focus only plays a limited role in semantics.[6]

---

[6] For example, Rooth (1992) pointed out that there is no verb **tolfed* that works like *told* except that it identifies the direct object by way of association with focus within the sentential complement, such that *John tolfed that he will*

It should be mentioned here that there have also been attempts to explain the pragmatic use of focus as instances of association with focus. Jacobs (1984) argued that instances of "free", that is, apparently non-associated focus are actually cases in which focus associates with the illocutionary operator of a sentence. For example, in case of an assertion like *John introduced MAry$_F$ to Sue*, the assertion operator associates with *Mary*, triggering a presupposition that it is currently at stake who John introduced to Mary. Obviously, this is exactly what Beaver and Clark's Focus Principle would do in this case, and so it would not have to be stipulated explicitly.

2.7. Comparison with alternative notions of focus

The notion of focus has been explicated in a variety of ways, in particular as highlighting the most important or new information in an utterance. While such explications are intuitively appealing and may make sense for a majority of cases, we consider them unsatisfactory as definitions. The notion of highlighting is a particularly unclear one that is hardly predictive as long as we do not have a well drawn out theory of what highlighting is. We are also not aware of any well drawn out theory of communication that has made clear what "importance" means, let alone one that has introduced a graded notion of importance. Even on an intuitive level, the notion of importance is difficult to apply. In which sense is *John* the most important part in (27)? Isn't the most important thing the fact that someone else stole the cookie?

(27) *It wasn't JOHN who stole the cookie.*

As for the third explication, the notion of newness has been defended most often in quite different frameworks, ranging from Halliday's information focus (cf. Halliday 1967) to the Prague school (Sgall, Hajičová and Panenova 1986) and to Jackendoff (1972). But it clearly gives us wrong predictions. There are many cases in which a constituent that refers to something mentioned previously is in focus. One might say that what is new in (28) is not John, or the expression *John,* but the information that John satisfies the description *x stole the cookie.*

---

introduce MARY$_F$ to Sue means 'John told Mary that he will introduce her (i.e., Mary) to Sue'. This verb could not be expressed as dependent on a context question induced by focus on *Mary.*

(28)   A: *Who stole the cookie, John or Mary?*
       B: *JOHN stole the cookie.*

Following Jackendoff's (1972) definition of information focus as the information that is not shared by speaker and addressee, we must say something
like the following: It is shared information in (28) that John or Mary stole
the cookie. The difference to what the sentence says, that John stole the
cookie, is a more specific proposition. But not just any more specific proposition would do; it must be one that is more specific in a particular dimension, indicated by the focus. This leads to the idea that focus indicates an
existential presupposition (cf. Geurts and van der Sandt 2004). If we have a
sentence with a focus, $[...\alpha_F...]$, then this sentence comes with the presupposition $\exists x[...x...]$, where x replaces the denotation of α in the representation of the denotation of $[...\alpha_F...]$. For example, (27) and (28) presuppose
that someone stole the cookie, and in many other types of uses of focus we
can plausibly assume existence presuppositions. But existence presuppositions do not arise with every use of focus, as in the following examples:

(29)   *Not even MAry$_F$ managed to solve the problem.*

(30)   A: *Who, if anyone, has solved this problem?*
       B: *NOone$_F$ solved this problem.*

If focus indicates the presence of alternatives, as suggested here, we can see
why the other explanations made sense to some degree. The focus denotation typically feels highlighted because it is contrasted with the other alternatives; the selection of this denotation over alternative ones is often felt to
be the most important contribution in a sentence; and the selected alternative is often new (not mentioned previously) as well. Also, in many cases it
is already established in the common ground content that the proposition
applies to one alternative, but it is still open to which specific one it applies.
But this does not mean that highlighting, importance, newness, or presupposition of existence should be figured in the definition of focus. These are
statistical correlations, not definitional features, of focus. Using them to
define focus is similar to using the notion of definiteness to define subjects:
The great majority of subjects in running text are definite, but in many languages indefinite subjects are allowed.

2.8. Further focus types

We have argued that focus in general indicates the presence of alternatives for interpretation. This very general notion of focus naturally allows for subtypes. So far, we have distinguished between expression focus and denotation focus according to the nature of the items in focus, and we have distinguished between pragmatic focus and semantic focus according to the general ways in which focus-induced alternatives are used – whether they make a truth-conditional difference or not. There are a number of additional criteria that can be applied to classify either the kind of alternatives or their use.[7]

Starting with the type of alternatives, we have seen that constituents of different sizes can be put into focus: whole sentences, subconstituents like verb phrases or determined phrases, parts of determined phrases like adjectives or demonstratives. Sometimes terms like *broad* and *narrow* focus are used (cf. Selkirk 1984, Lambrecht 1994), but it should be clear that these are imprecise terms that can only be applied when different focus readings are under discussion. The position of the focus accent in languages like English or German is determined by rules of *accent percolation* (also known as *focus projection*), which leads to well-known ambiguities of focus marking (cf. Gussenhoven 1983, 1992, and Selkirk 1984, 1995). For example, if a transitive verb phrase is in focus, then accent is realized on the argument, which also would signal narrow focus on the argument. For denotation focus it holds that whatever is in focus must be a meaningful unit, as denotational focus contrasts different meanings. An extreme case is so-called *verum focus*, focus on the truth value of a sentence, which may be expressed by accenting an auxiliary (as in *She DOES like broccoli*, cf. Höhle 1992).

An interesting issue is whether parts of words can be put in focus. Paul (1880) has proposed this for a word like *fahren* 'to move in a land-bound vehicle', where according to him it is possible that only the manner component is in focus, which is phonologically indistinguishable from focus on the whole denotation. We think that cases like this do not force us to lexical decomposition; we can also assume that the alternatives are restricted to denotations of verbs of locomotion like *fahren, gehen, reiten*. Another type of sublexical focus is illustrated in *We only saw stalagMITES in the cave, no stalagTITES*, where accent highlights a part which does not carry meaning. As Artstein (2003) argues, this can be explained by a principle which states

---

[7] Halliday (1967) already distinguished between contrastive focus, focus in answers to questions and purely informative focus, as in simple assertions.

that accent creates a maximally distinct representation between the focus and its alternatives.

It sometimes happens that we find several focus markings within a single clause. In this situation we distinguish two cases: First, sometimes one operator makes use of a combination of foci, resulting in *complex focus*:

(31)   *John also introduced BILL to SUE.*

This says: The pair ⟨x, y⟩ such that John introduced x to y is ⟨BILL, SUE⟩, and there is a distinct pair ⟨x′, y′⟩ such that John introduced x′ to y′. This cannot be reduced to single foci. Cases like this have to be distinguished from cases of *multiple focus*:

(32)   *John also introduced BILL only to SUE.*

Here, in one and the same sentence, one expression introduces alternatives that are exploited in one way, and another expression introduces alternatives that are exploited in a different way. (32) can be paraphrased as: John introduced Bill to Sue and to no-one else, and there is another person x besides Bill such that John introduced x to Sue and to no-one else. Notice that the accent on *Bill* is stronger than the accent on *Sue*, in contrast to the complex focus case of (31), where both accents are felt to be equally strong.

Another distinction relating to types of alternatives concerns the issue of the size of the alternative set. Sometimes this set is limited to a few items, perhaps down to the minimal number of two, the item in focus and one alternative. This is often the case in corrections or contrasts, in polarity questions that expect a positive or a negative answer, or in answers to alternative questions or restricted constituent questions such as the following:

(33)   A: *What do you want to drink, tea or coffee?*
       B: *I want [TEA]$_F$.*

At other times the alternative set is unrestricted, satisfying just the general condition that all the alternatives must be compatible with the focus in their semantic type. It is tempting to call focus with a limited set of alternatives contrastive (as suggested by Chafe 1976), but (33B) doesn't seem to be more contrastive than an answer to the non-restricted question *What do you want to drink?* Instead, we would suggest distinguishing between *closed alternatives* and *open alternatives*, and talking about *closed* vs. *open focus*, when necessary.

The notion of *contrastive focus* should, in our opinion, be restricted to focus used for truly contrastive purposes, which presupposes that the common ground content contains a proposition with which the current utterance can be contrasted, or that such a proposition can be accommodated (cf. Jacobs 1988). In (33), it is common ground management, not common ground content, that contains such a proposition. The typical use of contrastive focus is corrective, but it can also be additive, as in A: *John wants coffee.* B: *MAry wants coffee, TOO.* There is evidence for particular marking strategies for contrastive focus, like the use of particular syntactic positions or of special prosodic patterns, see, e.g., Selkirk (2002), Molnár (2002), and Gussenhoven (2004).

Another type of focus that refers to the specific way of how the contribution by the alternatives is interpreted is *exhaustive focus.* It indicates that the focus denotation is the only one that leads to a true proposition, or rather more generally: that the focus denotation is the logically strongest denotation that does so. É. Kiss (1998) has pointed out that focus movement in Hungarian triggers this specific meaning, and it appears that cleft constructions in English trigger it as well:

(34) *It's [JOHN and BILL]$_F$ who stole a cookie.*

This example says that nobody else stole a cookie but John and Bill. Consequently, exhaustive focus is not compatible with additive particles, like *too.* In addition to exhaustive focus, the notion of identification focus has been introduced, which expresses an identity statement, as in *The ones who stole a cookie are John and Bill* (cf. É. Kiss 1998).

As a final focus type, we would like to mention *scalar focus*, also called emphatic focus. With scalar focus, the alternatives are ordered, and the focus denotation often is the least or greatest element. Scalar particles like *even* or *at least* require scalar focus; the same holds true for strong polarity items such as in *[Wild HORses]$_F$ wouldn't drag me there.*

3. Givenness

3.1. What is givenness?

We now turn to the second important category of information structure, the indication that the denotation of an expression is present in the immediate common ground content. Givenness was treated by Halliday (1967), Chafe

(1976), and many others; under different guises, like *theme* and *rheme*, givenness phenomena were also discussed in other early approaches to information structure. There is ample evidence that human languages have devices with which speakers can make addressees aware that something that is present in the immediate linguistic context, i.e., something that is "given", is being taken up again – or that something that is being mentioned is "new", i.e., has not been present in the immediate linguistic context before. Hence, while the second occurrence of the indefinite noun phrase *a suitcase* in (35a) cannot refer to the same entity as the first one, coreference is acceptable in (35b) and (35c) with the definite noun phrase and the pronoun respectively.

(35) a. **There was [a suitcase]$_1$ on the street. John carried [a suitcase]$_1$ inside.*
      b. *There was [a suitcase]$_1$ on the street. John carried [the suitcase]$_1$ inside.*
      c. *There was [a suitcase]$_1$ on the street. John carried it$_1$ inside.*

Roughly speaking, indefinite noun phrases cannot be used to refer to given entities, whereas definite noun phrases and pronouns can.

A theory of givenness, however, has to distinguish more than the two states "given" and "new". A discourse referent can be completely new and non-identifiable for the hearer if there is no representation of it in his memory. But it may also be the case that there is a representation of it in his memory that is just not activated at the moment because the discourse referent has not been mentioned for a long time. And if the discourse referent has been mentioned in the linguistic context of an utterance, this might have happened in the sentence right before, or the antecedent might have occured several sentences earlier. Differences of this kind have been discussed by Chafe (1976, 1987), Prince (1981, 1992), and Lambrecht (1994).

A definition of givenness must be such that it allows for saying that an expression is given to a particular degree, e.g., whether it is maximally salient in the immediate common ground or just given there, or whether it is given in the general common ground or not given at all. The following attempt at a general definition takes care of that.

(36) A feature X of an expression α is a givenness feature if X indicates whether the denotation of α is present in the common ground or not, and/or indicates the degree to which it is present (its *saliency*) in the immediate common ground.

Within the notion of focus we distinguished between expression focus and denotation focus. It appears that we also have to make this distinction for givenness. In a text like (37) we find deaccenting of *a turtle* even though it does not refer to an introduced discourse referent.

(37)   *Turtles make interesting pets. But it is easy to LOSE a turtle in winter because they often are kept at places that are too warm.*

There are two groups of phenomena that refer to givenness, namely specific anaphoric expressions that have givenness features as part of their lexical specification, and other grammatical devices such as deaccentuation, ordering, and deletion that can mark arbitrary constituents as given. We will deal with them in turn.

3.2. Anaphoric Expressions

These are specific linguistic forms that indicate the givenness status of their denotations, including personal pronouns, clitics, and person inflection, demonstratives, definite articles, but also indefinite articles that indicate that their referent is not given. Definite articles can be used to indicate whether a denotation is given in a common ground in general, whereas clitics and pronouns typically indicate that their denotations are given in the immediate common ground.

There is a large body of literature on anaphoric devices, which we cannot even start to do justice to here. But we want to point out that speakers typically have a hierarchy of distinct linguistic means at their disposal (zero forms, clitics, pronouns, demonstratives, etc.), and that denotations in the immediate common ground are ranked with respect to their givenness status such that simpler anaphoric expressions are used to refer to more salient denotations (cf. Prince 1981; Gundel, Hedberg and Zacharski 1993). This insight has been implemented within Centering Theory, which has developed formal means to model the dynamic change of the saliency of discourse referents in communication (cf. Walker et al. 1998, Poesio et al. 2004).

The givenness status of expressions also plays a role with regard to anaphora resolution, a task the hearer has to fulfill especially with regard to pronouns: Whenever he comes across a pronoun he has to figure out what it is supposed to refer to. Depending on the particular language, there may be morphological factors that help the hearer to find the intended antecedent.

I.e., pronouns usually have to occur in a variant that is compatible with the antecedent as far as gender and number are concerned.

Moreover, types of pronouns may differ with regard to where their antecedent can or has to occur. Thus, reflexive pronouns often need to have an antecedent within their clause. Personal pronouns tend to both allow and require a more distant antecedent. Demonstratives in English and German, however, usually need an antecedent that is close to them but not within the same clause. These phenomena have been investigated in Binding Theory (see Büring 2005).

3.3. Deaccentuation, deletion, and word order

In languages like English and German, there are three other ways to indicate Givenness: Deaccentuation, the reduction of the prosodic realization of expressions that are given in the immediate context; deletion, which can be seen as an extreme form of reduction; and the realization of an expression in a non-canonical position, typically before its canonical position. This is illustrated in the following examples:

(38) a. *Ten years after John inherited an old farm, he SOLD [the shed]$_{Given}$.*
    b. *Bill went to Greenland, and Mary did _ too.*
    c. *Bill showed the boy a girl.*
    d. **Bill showed a boy the girl.*
    e. *Bill showed the girl to a boy.*

In (38a), which corresponds to examples used by Umbach (2003), *the shed* is deaccented, and has to be understood as referring to the farm mentioned before. If it were not deaccented, it would mean something different, like the shed that came with the farm. Example (38b) illustrates verb phrase ellipsis, which refers back to a verb phrase meaning. The examples in (38c, d, e) show that in the double object construction, given constituents precede constituents that are new. This is a rule with high functional load in so-called free word order languages, an insight that goes back to Weil (1844). In particular, languages without articles such as most Slavic languages and many East-Asian languages rely on word order variation to indicate the givenness status of the referents. The ways in which these non-canonical word orders can be achieved may be quite different, in particular scrambling (left-adjunction) or diatheses like passives or object-shifts.

As focus constituents typically are not given, and are realized with greater prosodic prominence, it has been proposed that focus is a complementary notion to givenness, which can ultimately be eliminated from theoretical terminology (cf. Daneš 1970, Sgall, Hajičová and Panenova 1986). But given constituents can be in focus, and in that case they bear an accent in languages like English or German. For example, it is possible to focus on pronouns, as in (39).

(39) *Mary only saw HIM$_F$.*

Schwarzschild (1999) develops a more refined theory of the interaction of givenness and focus, which checks givenness recursively and states that constituents not in focus must be given, and that focus only has to be applied when necessary, that is, to prevent a constituent from being given. But while the role of focus is restricted in Schwarzschild's theory, it cannot be eliminated totally.

We have to assume both focus, the indication of alternatives, which is expressed by accentuation, and rules of marking given constituents, e.g., by deaccentuation. As shown by the case of accented pronouns, focus accentuation overrides deaccentuation of given constituents, in the sense that focus has to be expressed by accent. However, if a larger constituent is focused, then givenness can influence the accent rules: The constituent that normally would bear accent can be deaccented, and accent can be realized on some other constituent within the focus expression (cf. Féry and Samek-Lodovici 2006). For example, while the accent in verb phrase focus is normally realized on the argument, it is realized on the head when the argument is given:

(40) A: *I know that John stole a cookie. What did he do then?*
      B: *He [reTURNED [the cookie]$_{Given}$]$_F$*

This suggests an explanation why accent is normally realized on the argument in cases of wide focus. It is the arguments, not the heads, that are referential, and therefore the need to express whether they refer to something given is more pressing. If the normal accentuation rules state that accent is realized on the argument, then the givenness of an argument can be expressed by deaccenting the argument and accenting the head instead.

4. Topics

4.1. What is topic?

The terms topic and comment are used most frequently to capture the idea that one part of a sentence says something about another part. This idea is by no means new.

In fact, Aristotle's (384 BC–322 BC) description of subjects and predicates was already based on a concept like this. According to *Categories*, the predicate says something about the subject. The subject, however, is grammatically defined by its case. Hence, Aristotle does not have separate concepts of subjecthood and topichood. His intuition with regard to subject and predicate may have been caused by the fact that subjects are in fact often topics. Demetrius Phalereus (around 350 BC–around 280 BC) in his work *On Style* also hints in this direction. As Giuseppe G. A. Celano points out (p.c.), Demetrius' subject is literally called "that about which (the sentence is)", while the predicate is called "that which this is". However, Demetrius, who correlates the distinction with word order, identified the term "that about which (the sentence is)" with the grammatical subject just as Aristotle did.

An early distinction between topichood and subjecthood, however, can be found among Arab grammarians of the middle ages. According to Versteegh (1996: 858), Sibawayhi, an Arab grammarian from Persia who died around 800, analyzed so-called nominal sentences as consisting of *mubtada'* and *ḫabar* (translated as "topic" and "predicate" respectively), while so-called verbal sentences consist of *fiʾl* and *faʾil* ("verb" and "agent"). As Levin (1981: 150–151) points out, in both sentence types, the first element is called *musnad*, i.e., "that part of the sentence upon which the *musnad ʾilayhi* leans", and the second element is called *musnad ʾilayhi*, i.e., "that [part of the sentence] which leans upon it (i.e., upon the *musnad*)". These distinctions played a role throughout the Arabian grammatical tradition, although with terminological variants (cf. Goldenberg 1988, Owens 2000).

In more recent times, Henri Weil (1844) discussed the concept of givenness (*le connu* and *l'inconnu*) and its consequences for word order, but also distinguished between *le point du depart* and *l'énonciacion*: "There is then a point of departure, an initial notion which is equally present to him who speaks and to him who hears, which forms, as it were, the ground upon which the two intelligences meet; and another part of discourse which forms the statement (*l'énonciation*), properly so called. This division is found in almost all we say." (Weil 1844/engl. translation 1978: 29)

Some years later, Georg von der Gabelentz (1869: 378) introduced the notions of psychological subject and psychological predicate (*psychologisches Subjekt* and *psychologisches Prädikat*, respectively). According to him, the psychological subject is the entity the speaker wants the hearer to think about. The psychological predicate is what the speaker wants the hearer to think about the psychological subject. None of the elements has to correspond to the grammatical subject or to the grammatical predicate. However, von der Gabelentz observed that the psychological subject tends to occur at the beginning of a sentence, while the psychological predicate follows it. But he notes that the psychological subject and the grammatical subject do not have to be identical. Hermann Paul in "Prinzipien der Sprachgeschichte" and "Deutsche Grammatik" (1882, 1919) also made use of the distinction between psychological subject and psychological predicate.

Taken up on the one side by Hermann Ammann (1928), who introduced the terms "theme" and "rheme", the distinction became important for the work of the functionalist Prague School, which focused mainly on concepts of givenness. On the other side, Hockett (1958: 201) coined the terms "topic" and "comment", which played an important role among American linguists. He focused on the basic ideas of predication that go back to Aristotle: "The speaker announces a topic and then says something about it."

As we have seen, the early notions related to topic and comment differ somewhat with regard to whether they focus on the perspective of the speaker or on his intentions with respect to the hearer's intentions.

In terms related more closely to communication, topic is the entity that a speaker identifies, about which information, the comment, is then given. This presupposes that information in human communication and memory is organized in such a way that it can be said to be "about" something, hence the term "aboutness topic". This does not follow from a general definition of information. For example, relational databases or sets of possible worlds, both models of information, do not presuppose any relation of aboutness.

Reinhart (1982) has integrated this notion of topic into a theory of communication that makes use of the notion of common ground. According to her, new information is not just added to the common ground content in form of unstructured propositions, but is rather associated with entities – just like information in a file card system is associated with file cards that bear a particular heading. For example, while (41 a, b) express the same proposition, they structure it differently insofar as (a) should be stored as information about Aristotle Onassis, whereas (b) should be stored as information about Jacqueline Kennedy.

(41)   a.   *[Aristotle Onassis]*$_{Topic}$ *[married Jacqueline Kennedy]*$_{Comment}$.
       b.   *[Jacqueline Kennedy]*$_{Topic}$ *[married Aristotle Onasses]*$_{Comment}$.

This leads to the following definition, which presupposes a file card like structure of information storage.

(42)   The topic constituent identifies the entity or set of entities under which the information expressed in the comment constituent should be stored in the common ground content.

Just as with the notion of focus, the notion of topic has not been used in a terminologically clean manner. Chafe (1976) called what is defined in (42) subject, a term that should be reserved for grammatical subjects to avoid confusion.

Vallduví (1992) and Vallduví and Engdahl (1996) have used the term "link". In the Prague School, the notion is called "theme" and conflated with the one of old information (e.g., Daneš 1970). We should refrain from this, even if in most cases, topic constituents are "old" in the sense of being inferable from the context, as there are certainly cases of new topics. The following sentence introduces a new entity into discourse and, at the same time, uses it as the denotation of a topic constituent, which amounts to introducing a new file card in the common ground content.

(43)   *[A good friend of mine]$_{Topic}$ [married Britney Spears last year]$_{Comment}$.*

The notions of topic and comment are sometimes mixed up with the notions of background and focus. However, as we will see in Section 4.2, there are topics that contain a focus. And the comment need not be identical to the focus either:

(44)   A: *Tell me something about Onassis. When did he marry Jacqueline Kennedy?*
       B: *[He]$_{Topic}$ [married her [in 1968]$_{Focus}$]]$_{Comment}$*

The definition in (42) includes the option for a comment to be made about a set of entities. This takes care of the typical way quantified sentences are interpreted, in which two sets are related by a quantifier that can be realized as a determiner (45) or as an adverbial (46):

(45)   a. *Every zebra in the zoo was sick.*
       b. *Most zebras in the zoo were sick.*

(46)   *Zebras in the zoo usually are sick.*

The quantifier in such sentences expresses the extent to which the comment holds for the elements of the set. Assuming that sentences like (45), (46) are about zebras explains why natural language quantifiers are conservative, that is, why the truth value of sentences that contain a quantifier can be checked by looking solely at the restrictor set (here the set of zebras in the zoo). It is important to note that the restrictor of quantifiers is not always topical, but in the majority of cases it is, and the property of conservativity, which is motivated in those cases, is transferred to cases in which quantifiers are not topical.

Sentences typically have only one topic, which can be explained within Reinhart's file card metaphor: The simplest way to add information is to add it to the information on one file card. But under certain circumstances, sentences with two or more topics are possible when a relation between two file cards is expressed, as in *As for Jack and Jill, they married last year*. A possible way to handle such cases is to introduce a new file card that contains information concerning both Jack and Jill.

On the other hand, sentences may have no topic constituent at all, under which condition they are called thetic, following Marty (1884). But as Marty has already indicated, this does not mean that such sentences are about nothing. While they lack a topic constituent, they do have a topic denotation, typically a situation that is given in the context, as in [*The HOUSE is on fire*]$_{Comment}$.

In addition to the notion topic/comment, some theories also assume a structuring into subject and predicate, or predication basis and predicate, cf. Sasse (1987), Jacobs (2001), and Kuroda (2005). We will not go into this distinction here in greater detail, as we doubt that it is a distinction that is to be explained as one of information structure.

But then the question is whether topic and comment should be considered terms relating to information structure to begin with. Without question, topic/comment structure is a packaging phenomenon; (41a) and (b) package the same information differently, so that it is entered on the file card for Aristotle Onassis and for Jacqueline Kennedy, respectively. But Section 1.2 stressed that the packaging must respond to the temporary (recent) common ground, and this restriction certainly is not always satisfied. Assume that two speakers A, B meet, who both know John well, and A says to B: *Did you know? John married last week.* This is an assertion about John; the information will be entered in the file card for John in the common ground content of A and B. But this does not necessarily relate to the recent state of the common ground content, it can also respond to the long-term state, e.g., a long established and known interest of B in John.

Yet we find that topic choice often does respond to properties of the temporary information state. There is a well-documented tendency to keep the topic constant over longer stretches of discourse (so-called topic chains, cf. Givón 1983). Hence, while the notions of topic and comment fail to be information structure terms in the sense that they always relate to the temporary state of the common ground, they quite often do relate to it, as the topic denotation in the preceding utterance is the first choice for the topic denotation of the current utterance.

4.2. Contrastive topics

Contrastive topics are topics with a rising accent, as in B's answer in (47). They arguably do not constitute an information-packaging category in their own right, but represent a combination of topic and focus, as indicated in the example, in the following sense: They consist of an aboutness topic that contains a focus, which is doing what focus always does, namely indicating alternatives. In this case, a contrastive topic indicates alternative aboutness topics.

(47)   A: *What do your siblings do?*
       B: *[My [SISter]$_{Focus}$]$_{Topic}$ [studies MEdicine]$_{Focus}$,*
          and [my [BROther]$_{Focus}$]$_{Topic}$ is [working on a FREIGHT ship]$_{Focus}$.

In the first clause of B's response, focus on *sister* indicates an alternative to the topic *my sister*, namely, *my brother*. The typical reason why the presence of an alternative is highlighted is to indicate that the current clause does not deliver all the information that is expected. This is why we often find contrastive topics to indicate a strategy of incremental answering in the common ground management, as in our example in which an issue is split into sub-issues. This has been assumed to be the function of contrastive topics in Roberts (1996) and Büring (1997, 2003). It is pointed out in this literature that there are accommodation phenomena that affect what we call common ground management. In the following case, the contrastive topic accommodates a more general question, *Who was where?*

(48)   A: *Where were you (at the time of the murder)?*
       B: *[[I]$_{Focus}$]$_{Topic}$ [was [at HOME]$_{Focus}$]$_{Comment}$*

However, it should be noted that we also find contrastive topics in cases in which the idea of a questioning strategy is not easily applicable. In example (49), the answer given does not satisfy the expectations expressed in the question. In combination with a rising intonation in the comment, it indicates that the assertion, while the best one to be made, may not satisfy all needs.

(49) A: *Does your sister speak Portuguese?*
　　B: *[My [BROther]$_{Focus}$]$_{Topic}$ [[DOES]$_{Focus}$]$_{Comment}$*

It should be noted that focus within a topic is interpreted as usual, indicating the presence of alternatives, in this case, alternative topics. Focus is marked by (rising) accent, but it is not the main accent of the sentence, which is on a constituent of the comment.

5. Frame setting and delimitation

5.1. Frame setting

Frame setting, according to Jacobs (2001), is often not clearly differentiated from aboutness topic. And Chafe (1976), who stresses the difference between the two notions, uses the term topic for precisely this function. What is it? Statements like (50) certainly should not be entered under a file card about the health situation, and the topic of (51) is *Daimler-Chrysler,* not *Germany* or *America.*

(50) A: *How is John?*
　　B: *{Healthwise/As for his health}, he is [FINE]$_F$.*

(51) A: *How is business going for Daimler-Chrysler?*
　　B: *[In GERmany]$_{Frame}$ the prospects are [GOOD]$_F$,*
　　　but [in AMErica]$_{Frame}$ they are [losing MOney]$_F$.

It is often said that adverbials like *healthwise* or *in Germany* are frame setters that set the frame in which the following expression should be interpreted; Chafe says that it is used "to limit the applicability of the main predication to a certain restricted domain". It is still unclear how this should be understood more precisely. For cases like (50) which contain an evaluative predicate (*fine*) that is unspecified with respect to the dimension of evaluation (financially, healthwise, spiritually, etc.), this can be made precise by assuming that it is the task of the frame-setting adverbial to specify that dimension. Similarly, (51) has a situation dimension that is specified by the frame setter. But we also have statements like (52), which cannot be explained in this way.

(52)   *As for his health situation, he had a bypass operation recently.*

It appears that frame setters indicate the general type of information that can be given. A possible implementation of this idea is that they systematically restrict the language (the notions that can be expressed) in certain ways: Notions like *he won a lot of money* cannot be interpreted in the scope of *healthwise*, and notions like *he is doing fine* have to be restricted to the indicated dimension.

In any case, in exchanges like (50) *alternative* frames play a role, and hence we can assume that explicit frame setters are always focused in the sense of Section 2.1. They choose one out of a set of frames and state that the proposition holds within this frame. If there is no alternative perspective to be considered, then there is no need for an explicit frame setter either. As explicit frame setters always indicate alternatives, they clearly belong to information structure. More specifically, they relate to common ground management, as they imply that there are other aspects for which other predications might hold. In this respect, they are similar to contrastive topics (Section 4.2), as they too split up a complex issue into sub-issues.

5.2. Delimitation

The similarity between contrastive topics and frame setters mentioned above is worth a closer look. What contrastive topics and frame setters have in common is that they express that, with respect to the communicative needs at the current point in the discourse, the current contribution only gives a limited or incomplete answer. With contrastive topics, the current common ground management contains the expectation that information about a more comprehensive, or distinct, entity is given; contrastive topics indicate that the topic of the sentence diverges from this expectation. With frame setters, the current common ground management contains the expectation that information of a different, e.g., more comprehensive, type is given, and the frame setter indicates that the information actually provided is restricted to the particular dimension specified. This more general view is suggested in Büring's notion of contrastive topics, which do not have to be topics in the sense of aboutness topics.

Büring developed a formal model of this notion within the representation framework of Alternative Semantics: A contrastive topic induces a set of alternatives over and above the set of alternatives that are introduced by the focus within the predication, ending up with sets of sets of alternatives.

(53)   A: *Which subjects do your siblings study?*
       B: *[My SISter]$_{Contrastive\ Topic}$ [$_{Comment}$ studies [PoMOlogy]$_{Focus}$]]*
       ={{x STUDIES y | y ∈{POMOLOGY, OLERICULTURE, …}
       | x ∈{SISTER, BROTHER, …}}
       = {{SISTER STUDIES POMOLOGY, SISTER STUDIES OLERICULTURE, …},
       {BROTHER STUDIES POMOLOGY, BROTHER STUDIES OLERICULTURE, …}}

This incorporates the important observation that contrastive topics always occur in expressions that have another focus outside of the contrastive topic itself, a rule that holds for frame setters as well. But one should distinguish the formal implementation of delimitation from its communicative purpose. The following is an attempt to characterize this in a most general way:

(54)   A Delimitator $α$ in an expression $[…α…β_{Focus}…]$ always comes with a focus within $α$ that generates alternatives $α'$. It indicates that the current informational needs of the common ground are not wholly satisfied by $[…α…β_{Focus}…]$, but would satisfy it by additional expressions of the general form $[…α'…β'_{Focus}…]$.

In this definition, no reference is made to (aboutness) topic or frame setting. This allows for cases like (55) that do not plausibly belong to either category:

(55)   *[An [inGEnious] mathematician]$_{Delimitator}$ he is [NOT]$_{Focus}$.*

The sentence suggests that alternative statements like *He is a mediocre mathematician* hold. The definition (54) is also neutral as to the type of speech act of the expression, which explains why delimitations occur in questions and commands as in (56):

(56)   *And when did you read [DostoYEVSky]$_{Delimitator}$ in school?*

The delimitation indicates that the current question does not express the full communicative needs as there are other questions at issue, such as *When did you read Shakespeare in school?*

   If delimitations do what they are suggested to do here, then this explains why they often help to indicate a certain questioning strategy. If it is explicitly marked that an expression is suboptimal as far as the communicative needs of the moment are concerned, then one important reason for this is that the current communicative move only responds to a local need, and not yet to the global need of the common ground. In this way, delimitations help to structure common ground management by distinguishing between local and more global communicative goals.

6. The coding of information structure

So far we have mainly been concerned with the notions of information structure as they apply to English examples. The languages of the world differ with regard to the linguistic means they choose for expressing certain information structural categories. And the inventory of linguistics devices is huge; languages exploit various lexical, syntactic, morphological as well as prosodic devices (cf., e.g., Drubig 2000 for focus). These devices are often optional. This section provides a brief survey of the breadth of linguistic means used for expressing information structural packaging.

Prosodic devices play an especially important role in the expression of information structure cross-linguistically. *Pitch accent* is used in many languages. In English it marks focus and topic – focus is marked by a falling accent while topics carry a fall-rise accent (Bolinger 1958). Delimitators also tend to carry an accent. Many other languages make use of accent, too, e.g., German and Portuguese. *Deaccenting* is another prosodic strategy. In English and German, it signals givenness. In addition to this, topics may be marked by forming separate *intonation phrases* (e.g., in English, German, and tone languages like Cantonese and Japanese). Focus constituents, on the other hand, often form a phonological phrase, or form a phonological phrase with an adjacent head, like verbs; they often trigger deaccenting in the postfocal part of the utterance.

Sometimes *ellipsis*, i.e., complete phonetic reduction, can be applied to items that are given. This is often applied in coordination structures and question-answer contexts, but some languages also exploit topic drop (e.g., German).

There are also various *syntactic devices*. Some of them may be used in order to provide ideal conditions for information structural accent placement or phonological phrasing, cf. Féry and Krifka 2009. Languages like German use *word order* to signal information packaging. In German given items as well as topics tend to occur on the left side of the *Mittelfeld*, while new items and focus constituents tend to occur on the right side of the clause. Frame setters often occur in the *Vorfeld* or specifier-of-CP position. This position, however, can also be used for other constituents, e.g., for topics or focused elements. Selected *syntactic positions* play a role in the encoding of the information structure in several languages. Generally, the clause initial zone is crucial. Topics, in particular, are realized in this prominent position, but some languages present focus constituents in the sentence initial zone: According to Kiss (1998), Hungarian has a preverbal position for focus. Italian places focus clause-initially (Rizzi 1997) or clause-finally (Samek-Lodovici 2006).

Many languages make use of specific *syntactic constructions* such as cleft constructions or pseudo-cleft constructions, especially in order to mark topics or focus.

Particles of different types are used in many languages, too. In Cantonese, Japanese, and Korean, for instance, topics are marked by particles. These particles do not only signal the topic but also provide the possibility of adding particular boundary tones for forming separate intonation phrases. Such particles can help in this respect, especially in tone languages. Markers for focus are used in the Gur languages Buli and Ditammari (Fiedler et al. 2006).

Determiners are another important lexical device. They signal the difference between given and new discourse referents in many languages, e.g., in English or German. And of course, *anaphoric expressions* such as pronouns or pro-adverbs are used for discourse referents that are given.

Inflectional morphemes can also function as information structural markers. Van Valin (p.c., cited after Klein 2008) argues that some languages mark focus constituents by case.

To sum things up: The languages of the world provide their speakers with a rich inventory of information structural strategies that are typically combined with each other and may interact in complex ways. The next six chapters illustrate this in detail for such different languages as Chinese, English, French, Georgian, Hungarian, and Japanese. They aim at showing with which strategies information structural dimensions can be encoded and how these linguistic devices work together. The chapters to follow take the reader through various issues that shed light on aspects of information structure from very different perspectives. They deal with the prosodic analysis of information structure, with various other empirical methods of investigating it, with psycholinguistic research on information structure, with the acquisition of information structure in first and second language, and finally with its modeling in different theories of grammar and in computational linguistics.

References

Ammann, Hermann
    1928   *Die menschliche Rede 2. Der Satz.* Darmstadt: Wiss. Buchgesellschaft.
Beaver, David I. and Brady Z. Clark
    2008   *Sense and Sensitivity. How Focus determines Meaning.* Malden, MA /
              Oxford: Wiley-Blackwell.
Bolinger, Dwight
    1958   A theory of pitch accent in English. *Word* 14: 109–149.
Büring, Daniel
    1998   *The 59th Street Bridge Accent.* London: Routledge.
Büring, Daniel
    2003   On D-trees, beans, and B-accents. *Linguistics and Philosophy* 26:
              511–545.
Büring, Daniel
    2005   *Binding Theory.* Cambridge: Cambridge University Press.
Chafe, Wallace L.
    1976   Givenness, contrastiveness, definiteness, subjects, topics and point
              of view. In *Subject and Topic*, Charles N. Li (ed.), 27–55. New York:
              Academic Press.
Chafe, Wallace L.
    1987   Cognitive constraints on information flow. In *Coherence and
              Grounding in Discourse*, Russel S. Tomlin (ed.), 21–51. Amsterdam:
              John Benjamins.
Chierchia, Gennaro
    2004   Scalar implicature, polarity phenomena, and the syntax/pragmatics
              interface. In *Structures and Beyond*, Adriana Belletti (ed.), 39–103.
              Oxford: Oxford University Press.
Chomsky, Noam
    1970   Deep structure, surface structure and semantic interpretation. In
              Studies in General and Oriental Linguistics, Roman Jakobson and
              Shigeo Kawamoto (eds.). Tokyo: T.E.C. Corporation.
Clark, Herbert H.
    1996   *Using Language.* Cambridge: Cambridge University Press.
Daneš, Frantisek
    1970   One instance of the Prague school methodology: Functional analysis
              of utterance and text. In *Method and Theory in Linguistics*, Paul L.
              Garvin (ed.), 132–140. Paris / The Hague: Mouton.
Dretske, Fred
    1972   Contrastive statements. *Philosophical Review* 1972: 411–437.
Drubig, Hans Bernhard
    1994   *Island Constraints and the Syntactic Nature of Focus and Association
              with Focus.* Arbeitspapiere des Sonderforschungsbereichs 340: 51.
              Heidelberg: Wissenschaftliches Zentrum der IBM Deutschland.

Drubig, Hans Bernhard
  2003   Toward a typology of focus and focus constructions. *Linguistics* 41:
          1–50.
Féry, Caroline and Vieri Samek-Lodovici
  2006   Discussion notes: Focus projection and prosodic prominence in nested
          foci. *Language* 82: 131–150.
Féry, Caroline and Manfred Krifka
  2008   Information structure. Notional distinctions, way of expression. In
          Unitiy and Diversity of Languages, Piet van Sterkenberg (ed.), 123–
          136. Amsterdam: John Benjamins.
Fiedler, Ines, Katharina Hartmann, Brigitte Reineke, Anne Schwarz and Malte
Zimmermann
  2009   Subject focus in West African languages. In *Information Structure.
          Theoretical, typological, and experimental perspectives*, Zimmermann,
          Malte and Caroline Féry (eds.), 234–257. Oxford: Oxford University
          Press.
Gabelentz, Georg von der
  1869   Ideen zu einer vergleichenden Syntax. *Zeitschrift für Völkerpsycho-
          logie und Sprachwissenschaft* 6: 376–384.
Geurts, Bart and Rob van der Sandt (eds.)
  2004   Interpreting focus. *Theoretical Linguistics* 30: 1–44.
Givón, Talmy (ed.)
  1983   *Topic Continuity in Discourse: A Quantitative Cross-Language Study.*
          Amsterdam: John Benjamins.
Goldenberg, Gideon
  1988   Subject and predicate in Arab grammatical tradition. *Zeitschrift der
          deutschen morgenländischen Gesellschaft* 138: 39–73.
Groenendijk, Jeroen
  1999   The logic of interrogation. In *Proceedings of Semantics and Lin-
          guistic Theory* IX, Tanya Matthews and Devon Strolovitch (eds.),
          109–126. Cornell University: CPC Publications.
Gundel, Jeanette K., Nancy Hedberg and Ron Zacharski
  1993   Cognitive status and the form of referring expressions in discourse.
          Language 69: 274–307.
Gussenhoven, Carlos
  1983   Focus, mode, and the nucleus. *Journal of Linguistics* 19: 377–417.
Gussenhoven, Carlos
  1992   Sentence accents and argument structure. In *Thematic Structure. Its
          Role in Grammar*, Iggy M. Roca (ed.), 79–106. Berlin/New York: Foris.
Gussenhoven, Carlos
  2004   *The Phonology of Tone and Intonation.* Cambridge: Cambridge
          University Press.
Halliday, Michael Alexander Kirkwood
  1967   *Intonation and Grammar in British English.* The Hague: Mouton.

Hamblin, Charles Leonard
    1973   Questions in Montague English. *Foundations of Language* 10: 41–53.
Hartmann, Katharina and Malte Zimmermann
    2007   In place – out of place: Focus in Hausa. In *On Information Structure, Meaning and Form*, Kerstin Schwabe and Susanne Winkler (eds.), 365–403. Amsterdam: John Benjamins.
Heim, Irene
    1982   The semantics of definite and indefinite noun phrases. Ph.D. dissertation, University of Massachusetts at Amherst.
Herburger, Elena
    1997   Focus and weak noun phrases. *Natural Language Semantics* 5: 53–78.
Heusinger, Klaus von
    1999   *Intonation and Information Structure*. Unpublished Habilitationsschrift, University of Konstanz.
              http://elib.uni-stuttgart.de/opus/volltexte/2003/1396/pdf/heusinger.pdf
Hockett, Charles
    1958   *A Course in Modern Linguistics*. New York: McMillan.
Höhle, Tilman
    1992   Über VERUM-Fokus im Deutschen. In *Informationsstruktur und Grammatik*, Joachim Jacobs (ed.), 112–141. Opladen: Westdeutscher Verlag.
Jackendoff, Ray
    1972   *Semantic Interpretation in Generative Grammar*. Cambridge, MA: Massachusetts Institute of Technology Press.
Jacobs, Joachim
    1983   *Fokus und Skalen*. Tübingen: Niemeyer.
Jacobs, Joachim
    1984   Funktionale Satzperspektive und Illokutionssemantik. *Linguistische Berichte* 91: 25–58.
Jacobs, Joachim
    1988   Fokus-Hintergrund-Gliederung und Grammatik. In *Intonationsforschungen*, Hans Altmann (ed.). Tübingen: Niemeyer.
Jacobs, Joachim
    2001   The dimensions of topic-comment. *Linguistics* 39: 641–681.
Kamp, Hans
    1981   A theory of truth and semantic representation. In *Formal Methods in the Study of Language*, Jeroen A. G. Groenendijk, Theo M. V. Janssen and Martin B. J. Stokhof (eds.), 277–322. (Mathematical Centre Tracts 135) Amsterdam: Mathematical Centre.
Karttunen, Lauri
    1969   Discourse referents. Coling Stockholm. Reprinted in *Syntax and Semantics 7. Notes from the Linguistic Underground*, James McCawley (ed.), 363–385. New York: Academic Press.
Karttunen, Lauri
    1974   Presuppositions and linguistic context. *Theoretical Linguistics* 1: 181–194.

Kenesei, István
2006   Focus is identification. In *The Architecture of Focus*, Valeria Molnár
           and Susanne Winkler (eds.), 137–168. Berlin/New York: Mouton de
           Gruyter.
Kiss, Katalin É.
1998   Identificational focus versus information focus. *Language* 74: 245–273.
Klein, Wolfgang and Christiane von Stutterheim
1987   Quaestio und referentielle Bewegung in Erzählungen. *Linguistische
           Berichte* 109: 163–183.
Klein, Wolfgang
2008   The topic situation. In *Empirische Forschung und Theoriebildung.
           Beiträge aus Soziolinguistik, Gesprochene-Sprache- und Zweit-
           spracherwerbsforschung. Festschrift für Norbert Dittmar zum
           65. Geburtstag,* Bernt Ahrenholz, Ursula Bredel, Wolfgang Klein,
           Martina Rost-Roth and Romuald Skiba (eds.), 287–305. Frankfurt
           am Main: Peter Lang.
König, Ekkehart
1991   *The Meaning of Focus Particles. A Comparative Perspective.* London,
           New York: Routledge.
Kratzer, Angelika
1994   The representation of focus. In *Handbook of Semantics*, Arnim von
           Stechow and Dieter Wunderlich (eds.), 825–834. Berlin/New York:
           Mouton de Gruyter.
Krifka, Manfred
1992   A compositional semantics for multiple focus constructions. In
           Informationsstruktur und Grammatik, Joachim Jacobs (ed.), 17–53.
           Opladen: Westdeutscher Verlag.
Krifka, Manfred
2001   For a structured account of questions and answers. In *Audiatur Vox
           Sapientiae. A Festschrift for Arnim von Stechow*, Caroline Féry and
           Wolfgang Sternefeld (eds.), 287–319. Berlin: Akademie-Verlag.
Krifka, Manfred
2006   Association with focus phrases. In *The Architecture of Focus*, Valerie
           Molnár and Susanne Winkler (eds.), 105–136. Berlin/New York:
           Mouton de Gruyter.
Krifka, Manfred
2007   Basic notions of information structure. In *Interdisciplinary Studies
           of Information Structure* 6, Caroline Fery and Manfred Krifka (eds.).
           Potsdam: Universitätsverlag Potsdam. Also in: *Acta Linguistica
           Hungarica* 55 (2008): 243–276.
Kripke, Saul
2009   Presupposition and anaphora: Remarks on the formulation of the
           projection problem. *Linguistic Inquiry* 40: 367–386.

Kuroda, Shige-yuki
  2005   Focusing on the matter of topic. A study of "wa" and "ga" in
              Japanese. *Journal of East Asian Linguistics* 14: 1–58.
Lambrecht, Knud
  1994   *Information Structure and Sentence Form. Topic, Focus, and the
              Mental Representation of Discourse Referents.* Cambridge: Cambridge
              University Press.
Levin, Aryeh
  1981   The grammatical terms "al-musnad", "al-musnad ilahi" and "al-isnâd".
              Journal of the American Oriental Society 101: 145–165.
Levin, Aryeh
  1981   Sibawayhi. In *History of the Language Sciences / Geschichte der
              Sprachwissenschaften. An International Handbook on the Evolution
              of the Study of Language from the Beginnings to the Present / Ein
              internationales Handbuch zur Entwicklung der Sprachforschung
              von den Anfängen bis zur Gegenwart,* Sylvain Auroux, Ernst F. K.
              Koerner, Hans-Josef Niederehe and Kees Versteegh (eds.), 252–263.
              Berlin / New York: Mouton de Gruyter.
Levinson, Stephen C.
  2000   *Presumptive Meanings.* Cambridge, MA: Massachusetts Institute of
              Technology Press.
Lewis, David
  1979   Scorekeeping in a language game. *Journal of Philosophical Logic* 8:
              339–359.
Marty, Anton
  1884   Über subjektslose Sätze und das Verhältnis der Grammatik zu
              Logik und Psychologie. *Vierteljahresschrift für wissenschaftliche
              Philosophie* 8: 56–94.
Merin, Arthur
  1994   Algebra of elementary social acts. In *Foundations of Speech
              Act Theory. Philosophical and Linguistic Perspectives,* Savas L.
              Tsohatzidis (ed.), 234–266. London: Routledge.
Molnár, Valéria
  2001   Contrast from a contrastive perspective. In *European Summer School
              in Logic, Language and Information 2001, Workshop on Information
              Structure, Discourse Structure and Discourse Semantics,* Ivana
              Kruiff-Korbayová and Mark Steedman (eds.). Helsinki.
Owens, Jonathan
  2000   The structure of Arabic grammatical theory. In *History of the Lan-
              guage Sciences. An International Handbook on the Evolution of the
              Study of Language from the Beginnings to the Present,* Sylvain
              Auroux, Ernst F. K. Koerner, Hans-Josef Niederehe and Kees
              Versteegh (eds.), 286–300. Berlin / New York: Mouton de Gruyter.

Partee, Barbara
1991 Topic, focus and quantification. In *Proceedings from Semantics and Linguistic Theory 1*, Steven Moore and Adam Zachery Wyner (eds.), 159–188. Cornell: Working Papers in Linguistics.

Partee, Barbara
1999 Focus, quantification, and semantics-pragmatics issues. In *Focus: Linguistic, Cognitive, and Computational Perspectives*, Peter Bosch and Rob van der Sandt (eds.), 213–231. Cambridge Universitiy Press.

Paul, Hermann
1975 *Prinzipien der Sprachgeschichte*. Leipzig. 9. Auflage, Studien-ausgabe, Tübingen: Niemeyer. First published 1880.

Paul, Hermann
1919 *Deutsche Grammatik*. Band III. Teil IV: Syntax (Erste Hälfte). 3. Auflage, Halle a. d. Saale. 1957.

Poesio, Massimo, Rahul Mehta, Axel Maroudas and Janet Hitzeman
2004 Centering: a parametric theory and its instantiations. *Computational Linguistics* 30: 309–363.

Prince, Ellen F.
1981 Towards a taxonomy of given-new information. In *Radical Pragmatics*, Peter Cole (ed.), 223–256. New York: Academic Press.

Prince, Ellen F.
1992 The ZPG letter: Subjects, definiteness, and information-status. In *Discourse Description: Diverse Linguistic Analyses of a Fundraising Text*, Mann, William C. and Sandra A. Thompson (eds.), 295–326. Amsterdam: John Benjamins.

Reinhart, Tanya
1982 *Pragmatics and Linguistics: An Analysis of Sentence Topics*. Bloomington, Indiana: Indiana University Linguistics Club.

Rizzi, Luigi
1997 The fine structure of the left periphery. In *Elements of Grammar: Handbook in Generative Syntax*, Liliane Haegeman (ed.), 281–337. Dordrecht: Kluwer Academic Publishers.

Roberts, Craige
1996 Information structure in discourse: Towards an integrated formal theory of pragmatics. In *Ohio State University Working Papers in Linguistics 49. Papers in Semantics*, Jae-Hak Yoon and Andreas Kathol (eds.), 91–136. Columbus: The Ohio State University.

Rooth, Mats
1985 Association with focus. Ph.D. dissertation, University of Massachusetts at Amherst.

Rooth, Mats
1992 A theory of focus interpretation. *Natural Language Semantics* 1: 75–116.

Sacks, Harvey, Emanuel A. Schegloff and Gail Jefferson
    1974   A simplest systematics for the organization of turn-taking for con-
            versation. *Language* 50: 696–735.
Samek-Lodovici, Vieri
    2006   When right dislocation meets the left periphery: A unified analysis
            of Italian non-final focus. *Lingua* 116: 836–873.
Sasse, Hans-Jürgen
    1987   The thetic/categorical distinction revisited. *Linguistics* 25: 511–580.
Schwarzschild, Roger
    1999   GIVENness, AvoidF and other constraints on the placement of accent.
            Natural Language Semantics 7: 141–177.
Selkirk, Elisabeth O.
    1984   *Phonology and Syntax: The Relation between Sound and Structure.*
            Cambridge, MA: Massachusetts Institute of Technology Press.
Selkirk, Elisabeth O.
    1995   Sentence prosody: Intonation, stress and phrasing. In *Handbook of
            Phonological Theory*, John Goldsmith (ed.), 550–569. Cambridge,
            MA: Blackwell.
Selkirk, Elisabeth O.
    2002   Contrastive *FOCUS* vs. presentational *FOCUS*: Prosodic evidence
            from English. In *Proceedings of the First International Conference
            on Speech Prosody*, Bernhard Bel and Isabelle Marlien (eds), 643–
            646. Université de Provence, Aix-en-Provence.
Sgall, Peter, Eva Hajičová and Eva Benešová
    1973   *Topic, Focus and Generative Semantics.* Kronberg: Scriptor.
Sgall, Petr, Eva Hajičová and Jarmila Panenova
    1986   *The Meaning of the Sentence and its Semantic and Pragmatic
            Aspects.* Dordrecht: Reidel.
Stalnaker, Robert
    1974   Pragmatic presuppositions. In *Semantics and Philosophy*, Milton
            K. Munitz and Peter K. Unger (eds.), 197–214. New York: New York
            University Press.
Stechow, Arnim von
    1990   Focusing and backgrounding operators. In *Discourse Particles*,
            Werner Abraham (ed.), 37–84. Amsterdam: John Benjamins.
Umbach, Carla
    2004   Cataphoric indefinites. In *Proceedings of "Sinn und Bedeutung"* 8,
            301–316. Konstanz: Linguistics Working Papers.
Vallduví, Enrique and Elisabet Engdahl
    1996   The linguistic realization of information packaging. *Linguistics* 34:
            459–519.
Vallduví, Enrique
    1992   *The Informational Component.* New York: Garland.

van der Sandt, Rob A.
  1988   *Context and Presupposition.* London: Croom Helm.
van Kuppevelt, Jan
  1994   Topic and comment. In *The Encyclopedia of Language and Lin-guistics*, Roland E. Asher (ed.), 4629–4633. Oxford: Pergamon Press.
Walker, Marilyn A., Aravind K. Joshi and Ellen F. Prince (eds.)
  1998   Centering Theory in *Discourse.* Oxford: Clarendon Press.
Weil, Henri
  1844   *The Order of Words in the Ancient Languages, Compared with that of the Modern Languages.* Amsterdam: John Benjamins.
Weil, Henri
  1844   *De l'ordre des mots dans les langues anciennes comparées aux langues modernes.* Paris. Didier Érudition.
Wold, Dag
  1996   Long distance selective binding: The case of focus. In *Proceedings of Semantics and Linguistic Theory* XI, 311–328. Cornell University: CPC Publications.
Zerbian, Sabine
  2006   Expression of information structure in the Bantu language Northern Sotho. Ph.D. dissertation, Humboldt University, Berlin.

The information structure of Chinese

Daniel Hole

1. Introduction

The following survey of information structure in Mandarin Chinese has three major sections. Section 2 deals with focus and background, Section 3 treats aboutness topics and frame-setters, and Section 4, finally, looks at patterns relating to the Given/New-divide.

Writing such a condensed overview on Mandarin Chinese is a challenging task, not because research in this area is scarce or hard to come by, but for the exact opposite reason. Mandarin Chinese has been a major playground for the development and testing of information-structural categories over the past 40 years. Chao's (1968) grammar was written with the topic-comment notion as one of its major overarching themes. Li and Thompson's (1976) typology of subject-prominent and topic-prominent languages centered around Chinese as the prime example of the latter type. In the wake of these influential works, there has been a constant tradition of research in the domain of Chinese patterns expressing information-structural categories. It is impossible to do justice to the wealth of this tradition, and therefore much pertinent work and some phenomena have to be left unmentioned. Hence, when confronted with the necessary choice between two phenomena only one of which could be covered given the available space, I chose the more grammaticalized of the two.

The language treated in this article is Mandarin Chinese, the standard language of China, which is called *pǔtónghuà* 'common language', or *guóyǔ* 'national language', in Chinese. It is based on the dialect of Beijing, with certain dialectal peculiarities removed. The dialect of Beijing belongs to the Mandarin dialect group of Chinese (Sino-Tibetan/Sinitic). In English, the term "Mandarin" may thus refer either to the official language of China, or to the northern dialect group of China. In the present article, the terms "Mandarin", "Mandarin Chinese" and "Chinese" are used interchangeably, with "Mandarin Chinese" frequently used at the beginning of sections and subsections.*

---

* The following abbreviations are used in examples: ASP – aspect marker; CL – classifier; COP – copula; EXP – experiential aspect; PRF – perfective aspect; PRT – particle.

2.   Focus

2.1.   Focus and constituent questions

Mandarin Chinese is a *wh*-in-situ language, and also a focus-in-situ language (cf. Huang 1982 or Soh 2006 for discussion of the overt and covert *wh*-syntax of Chinese). Both the *wh*-word in a constituent question and the focus in a neutral sentential answer to that question surface in the canonical position of the respective syntactic function (cf. §§ 2.2./2.4. for non-canonical sentence patterns with specialized focusing devices). Examples for subjects, objects, VPs, and adjuncts are provided in (1) (cf. §§ 2.5/3.5 on prosodic aspects of focus and topic in Chinese; either subsection also looks at the interaction of the lexical tones of Chinese with information-structural prosody).

(1) a. Question-answer pair: subjects

    Q: *Shéi chī-le   Rìběn liàolĭ?*   A: *[Ākiù]*$_F$ *chī-le   Rìběn liàolĭ.*
       who eat-PRF Japan food   Akiu   eat-PRF Japan food
       'Who ate Japanese food?'   '[Akiu]$_F$ ate Japanese food.'

   b. Question-answer pair: objects

    Q: *Ākiù chī-le   shénme?*   A: *Ākiù chī-le   [Rìběn liàolĭ]*$_F$.
       Akiu eat-PRF what   Akiu eat-PRF Japan food
       'What did Akiu eat?'   'Akiu ate [Japanese food]$_F$.'

   c. Question-answer pair: VPs

    Q: *Ākiù zuò/gàn-le shénme?*   A: *Ākiù [chī-le   Rìběn liàolĭ]*$_F$.
       Akiu do/do-PRF what   Akiu eat-PRF Japan food
       'What's Akiu doing?'   'Akiu is eating Japanese food.'

   d. Question-answer pair: adjuncts

    Q: *Ākiù zài nălĭ   chī-le*   A: *Ākiù zài [Dōngjīng]*$_F$ *chī-le*
       Akiu at where eat-PRF   Akiu at Tokyo   eat-PRF
      Rìběn liàolĭ?   *Rìběn liàolĭ.*
      Japan food   Japan food
      'Where did Akiu eat Japanese   'Akiu ate Japanese food in
      food?'   [Tokyo]$_F$.'

Chinese is an SVO language with circumstantial adjuncts typically following subjects and preceding verbs. The sequences in (1) thus illustrate the *in-situ* property for the respective categories. Note that in (1c), the complete

VP is the question focus, even though the *wh*-word in (1c–Q) occupies just the object position. The light verbs *zuò* and *gàn* (both 'do') are used as dummy verbs here compensating for the non-existence of a *wh*-word for complete VPs. No such question option exists for sequences of subjects and verbs to the exclusion of objects. Most researchers would say that the lack of this option is a consequence of the fact that subjects and verbs do not form a constituent, while verbs and objects do. (2) is an example with an all-new, or thetic, utterance as a reply to a 'what happened?' question. In this case, the complete pronounced material is focal, and the relevant background material ('What happened is that…') is left unexpressed.

(2)   Question-answer pair: complete sentences/thetic utterances

   Q: *Fāshēng-le shénme shì?*   A: [*Ākiù chī-le Rìběn liàolǐ*]_{F.}
   happen-PRF what   affair   Akiu eat-PRF Japan food
   'What happened?'   '[Akiu ate Japanese food]_F.'

In actual conversation, shorter ways of answering constituent questions than those given in (1) are the norm. Two examples are provided in (3) (cf. Li and Thompson 1981: 557–558).

(3) a. Q: *Nǐ jǐ-diǎnzhōng   xià   bān?*   A: [*Wǔ*]_F-*diǎnzhōng.*
        you how.many-o'clock descend work   5-o'clock
        'What time do you get off work?'   'At five o'clock.'

    b. Q: *Tā gēn shéi niàn shū?*   A: *Gēn* [*Lǐsì*]_F (*niàn shū*).
        (s)he with who study book   with Lisi   study book
        'Who does (s)he study with?'   'With Lisi.'

In (3a), the time adverbial alone constitutes the answer turn; in (3b) the topical subject (and the VP) is left out. Without going into detail here concerning the matter of which constituents may or may not be elided in short answers, let us just note the fact that short answers to questions must at least be focus phrases in Drubig's (1994) and Krifka's (2006) sense. Taking (3b-A) as an example, a short answer with the preposition left out ("*Lǐsì*", that is) would not be grammatical, this being a reflection of the fact that prepositional phrases may be focus phrases, but prepositional objects may not.

Since there is no visible *wh*-movement in Chinese, and since the focus in canonical Chinese sentences is realized *in-situ*, multiple constituent questions and their answers raise no issues in the (overt) syntax as demonstrated in the question-answer sequences in (4) with the single-pair answer in (4A) and the pair-list answer in (4A). (I leave it open here whether the pair-list answer in (4A) should more accurately be analyzed as three sequences of a contrastive topic and a focus; cf. §3.3.)

(4) Q: *Shéi măi-le   shénme?*   A: [*Zhāngsan*]_F *măi-le*   [*niúroù*]_F.
       who buy-PRF what   Zhangsan   buy-PRF beef
       'Who bought what?'   '[Zhangsan]_F bought [beef]_F.'

     A: [*Zhāngsān*]_F *măi-le*   [*niúroù*]_F;   [*Lĭsì*]_F *măi-le*   [*jīroù*]_F;
        Zhangsan   buy-PRF beef   Lisi   buy-PRF chicken
        '[Zhangsan]_F bought [beef]_F;   [Lisi]_F bought [chicken]_F;

        [*Wángwŭ*]_F *măi-le*   [*zhūroù*]_F.
        Wangwu   buy-PRF pork
        [Wangwu]_F bought [pork]_F.'

Cf. Liao and Wang (2009) for further discussion of the less obvious complications with such multiple questions and answers, and their interrelations with *wh*-movement.

2.2. Contrastive focus and clefts

The most common patterns to mark contrastive focus and verum focus in Mandarin Chinese involve use of the copula *shì*. In the case of contrastive focus, *shì* precedes the contrastive focus phrase. Following Paul and Whitman (2008), this pattern is called the "Bare *shì* Focus Construction" here. *Shì* in the Bare *shì* Focus Construction immediately precedes the focus phrase, but it never occurs further to the right than at the left edge of the VP. Some examples are found in (5) and (6). (6d) presents negative evidence showing that *shì* may not be used inside the VP.

(5) Bare *shì* Focus Construction: contrastive focus preceding the VP

    a. **Shì** [*Zhāngsān*]_F *zài Běijīng xué   yŭyánxué*…
       COP Zhangsan   at Beijing study linguistics.
       '[Zhangsan] studies linguistics in Beijing…' (and not my brother)

    b. *Zhāngsān* **shì** *zài* [*Běijīng*]_F *xué   yŭyánxué*…
       Zhangsan COP at Beijing   study linguistics.
       'Zhangsan studies linguistics in [Beijing]_F…' (and not in Shanghai)

(6) Bare *shì* Focus Construction: contrastive focus inside the VP

    a. *Zhāngsān zài Běijīng **shì** [xué yǔyánxué]*$_F$ ...
       Zhangsan at Beijing COP study linguistics
       'Zhangsan [studies linguistics]$_F$ in Beijing...'
       (he doesn't teach French there)

    b. *Zhāngsān zài Běijīng **shì** xué [yǔyánxué]*$_F$ ...
       Zhangsan at Beijing COP study linguistics
       'Zhangsan studies [linguistics]$_F$ in Beijing...' (and not French)

    c. *Zhāngsān zài Běijīng **shì** [xué]*$_F$ *yǔyánxué* ...
       Zhangsan at Beijing COP study linguistics
       'Zhangsan [studies]$_F$ linguistics in Beijing...' (he doesn't teach it)

    d. **Zhāngsān zài Běijīng xué **shì** [yǔyánxué]*$_F$ ...
       Zhangsan at Beijing study COP linguistics
       int.: 'Zhangsan studies [linguistics]$_F$ in Beijing...' (and not French)

The Bare *shì* Focus Construction is *not* the canonical cleft construction of Chinese. Canonical clefts in Chinese involve the much discussed *shì...de* construction, exemplified in (7).

(7) *shì...de* cleft

    *Zhāngsān **shì** zài [Běijīng]*$_F$ *xué yǔyánxué **de***
    Zhangsan COP at Beijing study linguistics DE.
    'It's in [Beijing]$_F$ that Zhangsan studies linguistics.'

The major properties of canonical Chinese *shì...de* clefts on which most researchers converge are as follows. First, the linear syntax of *shì...de* clefts is as in (8).

(8) TOPIC (***shì***) [[XP]$_{FocP}$...]$_{COMMENT}$ ***de***.

Second, the functional element *de* of Chinese clefts is an instance of the multiply polysemous attribute markers, linkers, and nominalizers found in East and South East Asian languages (Matisoff 1972; Hole and Zimmermann to appear).

    Third, Chinese *shì...de* clefts are exhaustive. They presuppose the falsity of all alternative sentences with non-entailed focus values. This is illustrated in (9); the lack of exhaustiveness in the Bare *shì* Focus Construction is exemplified in (10) (from Paul and Whitman 2008).

(9)   exhaustiveness of *shì...de* clefts

> #*Tā* **shì** [*zài Běijīng*]$_{FocP}$ *xué   yǔyánxué* **de***, dàn yě*   **shì**
> (s)he COP at   Beijing   study linguistics DE but also COP
> [*zài Shànghǎi*]$_{FocP}$ *xué*   **de***.*
> at Shanghai   study DE
>
> #'It's in Beijing that (s)he studied Chinese, but also in Shanghai.'

(10)   non-exhaustiveness of the Bare *shì* Focus Construction

> *Tā*   **shì** [*zài Běijīng*]$_{FocP}$ *xué-guo   yǔyánxué, dàn yě*   **shì**
> s/he COP at   Beijing   study-EXP linguistics but also COP
> [*zài Shànghǎi*]$_{FocP}$ *xué-guo.*
> at Shanghai   study-EXP
>
> '(S)he studied Chinese in Beijing, but also in Shanghai.'

Despite considerable research efforts no consensus has yet emerged on most of the other properties of Chinese clefts. Areas where researchers disagree concern (i) the exact delimitation of Chinese clefts from other focusing constructions (e.g., the Bare *shì* Focus Construction), (ii) positional requirements for clefted constituents, and (iii) what kinds of movement (if any) should be assumed to analyze Chinese clefts. Recent studies in the area include Simpson and Wu (2002), Lee (2005), Cheng (2008), Paul and Whitman (2008), and Hole (2011).

The copula *shì* and *de* are used in pseudoclefts, too. The contribution of *shì* and *de* and the overall syntax of pseudoclefts is less controversial than that of clefts. *De* certainly partakes in the nominalization of the presuppositional constituent of the pseudocleft construction, and the copula *shì* equates the nominalized referent with the referent denoted by the DP to its right. An example is found in (11).

(11)   Chinese pseudoclefts

> [*Zuótiān lái-de   (rén)*] *shì* [*Zhāngsan*]$_{FocP}$.
> yesterday come-DE person COP Zhangsan
> '[(The one) Who came yesterday] was [Zhangsan]$_{FocP}$.'

2.3. Verum focus

The most general means for expressing verum focus in Chinese is the stressed copula *shì* preceding the VP. Examples are provided in (12).

(12) Copula-supported verum focus

    a. [Q: Zhangsan is eating rice?]

       A: [*Shì*]$_F$ (*zài chī fàn*).
          COP ASP eat rice
          'Yes, he [is]$_F$ eating rice.'

    b. [Q: She will probably go there?]

       A: [*Shì*]$_F$ (*huì qù*).
          COP   will go
          'Yes, she [will]$_F$ probably go there.'

    c. [Q: The rose is (not) red?]

       A: [*Shì*]$_F$ (*hóngde*).
          COP   red.
          'Yes, it [is]$_F$ red.'

In a more general perspective, Mandarin verum foci as in (12) belong in a class together with answers to canonical *yes/no*-questions and to the special kind of tag questions frequently found in Chinese. Two examples of so-called A-not-A *yes/no*-questions (cf. Ernst 1994 among others) and their respective answers are found in (13). (14) covers tag questions.

(13) a. Q: *Zhāngsān shì-bu-shì   lǎoshī?*   A: [*Shì*]$_F$.
          Zhangsan COP-not-COP teacher   COP
          'Is Zhangsan a teacher?'   'Yes(, he is).'

    b. Q: *Zhāngsān qù-bu-qù Běijīng?*   A: [*Qù*]$_F$.
          Zhangsan go-not-go Beijing   go
          'Does Zhangsan go to Beijing?'   'Yes(, he does).'

(14) a. Q: *Zhāngsān qù Běijīng, shì   bu shì?*   A: [*Shì*]$_F$.
          Zhangsan go Beijing COP not COP   COP
          'Zhangsan's going to Beijing, right?' 'Right.'

    b. Q: *Zhāngsān qù Běijīng, duì bu duì?*   A: [*Duì*]$_F$.
          Zhangsan go Beijing right not right   right
          'Zhangsan's going to Beijing, right?' 'Right.'

Both A-not-A questions (13) and tag questions (14) are formed by juxta-posing the positive and the negated verb form. A *yes/no*-question may be answered in the positive by repeating the structurally highest verb of the question; this is the functional equivalent of saying *yes* in Chinese. With tag questions as in (14), the answer repeats the predicate in the tag. Answers in the negative are given by a sequence of a negation marker (*bù* or *méi*) and the highest verb; the verb is frequently dropped, though. (13b), for instance, would receive the negative short answer *Bú qù* 'not go' (the tonal change in the negation particle is unrelated to the issue at hand). In this more general perspective, the verum focus marker *shì* in (12) may be seen as a dummy auxiliary in focus which precedes all other verbs or adjectival predicates that may occur in a verum focus reply to a preceding turn. The other verbs or adjectival predicates may be dropped, thereby assimilating 'yes' or 'no' turns in Chinese to the general pattern of expressing verum focus.

2.4. Focus-sensitive particles

Mandarin Chinese has a complex and – at least in parts – highly grammaticalized system of focus-sensitive particles. The system is divided into two major subsystems. The adverbial subsystem involves adverbial particles in a fixed position preceding the VP, auxiliaries, and negation (*zhǐ* and *shènzhì* in (15a)/(16a); *yě* 'also' has a similar syntactic and semantic potential). The focus must be part of, or comprise, the phrase following the particle. The second subsystem involves ad-focus-phrase particles with focus phrases preceding VPs (*zhǐyǒu* and *lián* in (15b)/(16b)). These ad-focus particles, and their focus phrases, are, in most cases, "doubled" by obligatory particles before the VP and verbal functional categories. Shyu (1995) assumes a designated focus phrase projected by *dōu* as a functional head to accommodate the "doubling" particle in the head position, and the focus (phrase) in its specifier. The same could be postulated for *cái*. This subsystem is called "the partition system" here. (15) and (16) present examples from either subsystem for 'only' foci and 'even' foci.

(15) a. adverbial: *Zhāngsān zhǐ* [*hē   chá*].
          Zhangsan only drink tea
          'Zhangsan only drinks tea.'

      b. partition: *Zhāngsān zhǐyǒu* [*chá*]$_F$ [*(cái) hē*].
          Zhangsan only   tea   only drink
          'Zhangsan drinks only [tea]$_F$.'

(16) a. adverbial: *Zhāngsān shènzhì* [*hē   chá*].
          Zhangsan even   drink tea
          'Zhangsan even drinks tea.'

b. partition: *Zhāngsān **lián*** [*chá*]$_F$ [*(***dōu***) *bù* *hē*].
   Zhangsan even tea   even not drink
   'Zhangsan doesn't even drink [tea]$_F$.'

Hole (2004) analyzes the partition system as a focus-background agreement configuration; Shyu's (1995) focus phrase is thus reinterpreted as a background phrase. In addition to foci triggering the use of *cái* or *dōu* as in (15b)/(16b), Hole (2004) assumes two further general focus-quantificational types which project the complete square of opposition for quantification over focus alternatives: truth of all alternatives/no alternative/some alternative/not all alternatives (cf. Oshima 2005 for a parallel proposal for Japanese). The obligatoriness of the doubling particles in the partition system is particularly noteworthy, because it underlines the degree to which the partition system is grammaticalized. Speakers have no choice but to use a particular marker if a focus is marked by a focus-sensitive particle and precedes the VP and negation.

Hole's (2004) analysis in terms of two different subsystems for adverbial focus marking vs. ad-focus marking with background agreement in a partition system is interesting in light of the long-lasting competition between implementations of focus semantics and syntax in terms of adverbial operators with propositional scope (Jacobs 1983, Rooth 1992, Büring and Hartmann 2000) as opposed to analyses in terms of structured meanings and syntactic partitioning into focus and background (von Stechow 1982, Krifka 1992, 2006, Rooth 1996). The bifurcated system of Mandarin Chinese may provide evidence to the effect that both analyses are needed and that each captures one of two distinct systems of marking focus and quantification over focus alternatives or focus meanings.

An area that requires further research concerns the multitude and multiple polysemy of focus-sensitive particles in Chinese. There is no agreement about the exact range of polysemy of individual particles, and about what should be assumed as their core meanings. *Cái* as used in (15b), for instance, has been analyzed as three-way or four-way polysemous depending on subtle syntactic and contextual distinguishing factors. Alleton (1972), Biq (1984), and with minor deviations, Hole (2004) distinguish (i) an aspectual or temporal use ('only just/a moment ago'), (ii) a "parametric" use as in the background marking pattern of (15b), (iii) an emphatic use as a discourse particle and (iv) a "limiting" use ('only') if the focus follows *cái* – an option which is only available with scalar predicates. Lai (1999) argues for a division of the empirical domain into four different uses as well, but the dividing lines between the uses are drawn differently. According to her view, the basic meaning of *cái* is scalar and evaluational;

the focus value amounts to a lower scalar value than what was expected in a given context. A similarly complex situation holds for *dōu* as in (16b). The major issue with *dōu* is whether the *dōu* in the focus constructions under discussion here is the same *dōu* as the infamous distributive marker in (17) (cf. Lin 1996, 1998 or Huang 1996 for a unifying perspective, and Zhang 1996, Sybesma 1996, and Hole 2004 as opponents of such a unification).

(17) *Tāmen dōu mǎi-le   shū.*
      they   all   buy-PRF book
      'They all bought books.'

Apart from matters of the controversial polysemy of individual focus-sensitive particles, the sheer multitude of different particles from different distribution classes calls for more research. Next to adverbial, ad-focus, and background markers as distinguished above, one more sentence-final class of focus-sensitive particles must be distinguished, at least in the domain of 'only' words. (18) illustrates two different ways of expressing an 'only' semantics in a sentence-final slot. The difference between the two variants is mainly one of style, with *ěryǐ* being rather literary, and *bàle* colloquial.

(18) *Zhāngsān gēn   wǒ shuō-shuō ěryǐ/bàle.*
      Zhangsan with me talk-talk   only/only
      'Zhangsan only [talked a little]$_F$ to me.'

2.5. Prosodic aspects of focus in Chinese

Contrary to a widely held belief, Mandarin Chinese as a lexical tone language does allow for the simultaneous realization of lexical tones and sentence prosody. A growing body of literature converges on this point. I will first provide some background on the tonal system of Mandarin Chinese before describing its interaction with focus prosody.

Except for some functional morphemes, each syllable in Chinese has one of four underlying lexical tones. Since each syllable is, at the same time, also a potential morpheme, there is a direct correspondence between syllables, tone-bearing entities, and potential morphemes. Depending on speech style and the occurrence of the syllable in a complex word or phrasal context, the tone may be neutral/suppressed. Stressed syllables invariably bear their underlying lexical tones, but not all syllables bearing a pronounced tone are stressed. The Mandarin tone system is a mixed register/contour tone system, where register tones have a flat fundamental frequency f_0, and contour tones have an f_0 which varies along the time axis. The tones of Mandarin are analyzed as (i) a high level tone, (ii) a rising contour tone, (iii) a low level tone (or a low tone with a final rise contour; the realization depends on the phonological context, with the rise/high target of the low level tone probably being a superficial phonetic effect), and (iv) a falling contour tone. Cf. Yip (1980) or Zhang and Lai (2010) for representative analyses of the phonology and phonetics of lexical tone in Mandarin.

In a groundbreaking study, Xu (1999) identifies increased word length and f_0 range expansion as the major acoustical correlates of focus in Mandarin. The length parameter affects words, and not so much syllables; what is comparable in terms of (more or less) constant ratios is the duration of focused and neighboring non-focused words, and not the duration of stressed and neighboring non-stressed syllables. The fundamental frequency f_0 is affected in such a way that focused syllables tend to have higher high level tones, lower low level tones, and an expanded frequency range with contour tones. Syllables following focal syllables are deaccented with concurrent lowering of f_0 and compression of the f_0 range. The contrast in prosody between deaccented material and preceding focal material also seems to play a role in the identification of the focus category. Chen and Braun (2006) present evidence to the effect that in replies to constituent questions speakers produce expanded f_0 ranges on focal syllables that target both lower and higher f_0 targets, whereas corrective focus tends to lead to higher maximum f_0 targets only. Chen (2008) presents analogous findings concerning the prosody of contrastive focus in Shanghai Chinese.

3. Topics and related matters

The overview of topic structures and related matters in Mandarin Chinese will be organized along the following dimensions. Following the introduction to this volume, aboutness topics in the sense of Reinhart (1982) are distinguished from frame-setters in the sense of Chafe (1976) by the correspondence of the former to "file cards". File cards are Reinhart's (1982) concept to capture the fact that, in a discourse, information about topical discourse referents is accumulated and kept track of as if it was written on individual file cards for each referent. Frame-setting expressions, by contrast, restrict the domain for which the rest of the utterance is claimed to be true, or relevant. This first distinction is illustrated in (19) and (20).

(19) (aboutness topic)

[*Guānyú zhè-ge wèntí*]$_{abT}$, *wǒ zhíjié   gēn Lǎo Wáng liànxí.*
about   this-CL question I   directly with Old Wang get.in.contact
'[About this problem]$_{abT}$, I'll contact Old Wang directly.'

(20) (frame-setting expression)

[*Wǔ-diǎn zhōng*]$_{Fr}$, *tā   hái méi lái.*
5-o'clock time   (s)he not have come
'[At five o'clock]$_{Fr}$, (s)he still hadn't arrived.'

Unless the discourse in which (20) is embedded is about all the things that happened at five o'clock, this sentence is a clear example of a frame-setting expression. (19), on the other hand, features a clear aboutness topic.

The second dimension along which topics and related matters vary, is their property of indicating alternatives. I will follow Krifka and Musan (this volume) by assuming that frame-setters always indicate alternatives, aboutness topics may or may not do so. Aboutness topics which indicate alternatives are called "contrastive topics"; (21) presents an example of contrastive topic use.

(21) Q: *Zhāngsān fūqī-liǎng   zài zuò shénme?*
     Zhangsan spouses-two ASP do   what
     'What are Zhangsan and his wife doing?'

  A: [*Zhāng tàitai*]$_{CT}$ [*zài shàng bān*]$_F$. [*Zhāngsān*]$_{CT}$ [*zài xiūxī*]$_F$.
     Zhang Mrs.   ASP go.to.work   Zhang Mr.   ASP rest
     '[Mrs. Zhang]$_{CT}$ [is at work]$_F$. [Zhangsan]$_{CT}$ [takes a break]$_F$.'

The distinctions made thus far yield the classification in Table 1.

Table 1. Feature matrix for topics and frame-setters

	description	corresponds to a file card	indicates alternatives
aboutness topic (non-contrastive)	non-contrastive aboutness topic	+	−
contrastive topic	contrastive aboutness topic	+	+
frame-setter	frame-setter (always with a contrastive component)	−	+

The tradition dealing with topics and related matters in Chinese makes frequent reference to two further concepts: dangling topics and multiple, or stacked, topics. A dangling topic is a topic which does not correspond to an argument position in the comment; cf. (22) with a dangling aboutness topic.

(22) [*Zhèi-jiàn shì*]$_{abT}$, *nǐ bù néng guāng máfǎn yi-ge rén.*
  this-CL   matter you not can   only   bother 1-CL person
  '[This matter], you can't bother only one person (with it).'

A standard example of a multiple topic structure is found in (23).

(23) *Zhōngguó*$_{abT3}$, [*dà chéngshì*]$_{abT2}$, *Běijīng*$_{abT1/Subject}$ *zuì yǒu yìsi.*
  China   big city   Beijing   most interesting
  'Among [the big cities of China$_{abT3}$]$_{abT2}$, Beijing$_{abT1}$ is the most interesting one.'

It is assumed here that the two leftmost topics in (23) are (higher-order) aboutness topics, and not frame-setters, but this view may be subject to revision once more studies with a fine-grained information-structural toolkit have been prepared in this empirical domain. Note that multiple topics are always dangling topics (except for the rightmost one).

From among the host of empirical and theoretical issues tied to topics and related matters in Chinese, we will discuss the following five in some more detail here: (i) the purportedly exotic status of dangling topics; (ii) semantic subkinds of multiple topics; (iii) objects as topics; (iv) *bǎ*-marked objects as secondary topics.

3.1. Dangling topics

The availability of dangling topics in Chinese is often taken to be a special feature of this language, or of typologically and/or areally related languages. Some more examples of this type of topic are provided in (24) ((24a) equals (19), except for the omitted preposition in sentence-initial position; (24b/c) are from Li and Thompson 1981: 96, translations are mine; D.H.).

(24) a. [*Zhè-ge wèntí*], *wǒ zhíjié gēn Lǎo Wáng liànxí.*
    this-CL question I   directly with Old Wang get.in.contact
    '[This problem], I'll contact Old Wang (about it) directly.'

b. [*Zhèi-jiàn shì*],   *nǐ   bù   néng   guāng   máfán   yi-ge rén.*
   this-CL   matter you not can   only   bother 1-CL person
   '[This matter], you can't bother only one person (with it).'

c. [*Nèi-chǎng huǒ*], *xiāofángduì   lái-de   kuài.*
   that-CL   fore   fire brigade   come-DE fast
   'That fire, the fire brigade came quickly (to take care of it)'

d. [*Chúfáng*] *rén   hěn   duō.*
   kitchen   people very   many
   'The kitchen, there are many people (in it).'

Gasde (1999) points out that German, for instance, has dangling topics just like Chinese once spoken varieties are taken into account. This observation, which can probably be extended to other languages, greatly reduces the purported exotic status of dangling topics in Chinese. It may be nullified altogether once it is acknowledged that Chinese topic structures as in (24) tend to be colloquial and are avoided in written registers.

3.2. Semantic subtypes of multiple topics

Example (23) was a multiple topic structure with a part-whole relationship holding between the initial and the second topic. The relationship between the second and the rightmost topic was of the kind-instance type. (25) presents some more examples.

(25)   a. [*Xiàng*ₐᵦₜ₂, [*bízi*ₐᵦₜ₁/Subject *cháng*]].   (Li and Thompson 1981: 92)
        elephant   nose   long
        'Elephants have long trunks.'

    b. [*Wǔ-ge píngguǒ*]ₐᵦₜ₂, [*liǎng-ge*]ₐᵦₜ₁/Subject *huài le.*
       5-CL   apple   2-CL   bad   PRT
       'Of the five apples, two are spoiled.'

    c. *Zhāngsān*ₐᵦₜ₂, [*nǚ péngyǒu*]ₐᵦₜ₁/Subject *duō.*
       Zhangsan   girlfriends   many
       'Zhangsan has many girlfriends.'
       (lit.: 'Zhangsan, his girlfriends are numerous.')

    d. *Huā*ₐᵦₜ₂, *méiguī*ₐᵦₜ₁/Subject *zuì   piàoliang.*
       flower   rose   most pretty
       'Roses are the most beautiful flowers.'

(25a–c) can all be subsumed under the notions of part/whole or possession, where (25c) might also be said to instantiate an "aspect-of" relationship, rather than possession (Zhangsan's girlfriends and the matters associated with them may constitute an aspect of Zhangsan's as opposed to a part of his possession). (25d) features a kind-subkind relationship. There may be other relationships underlying multiple topic structures, but the ones discussed here are certainly the most frequent ones.

3.3. Objects as topics

The nominals in (26) are aboutness topics, but their grammatical function has been a matter of debate.

(26) a. [*Nèi-běn shū*]$_{abT}$ *chūbǎn le.*   b. *Yú*$_{abT}$ *chī le.*
     that-CL book   publish PRT   fish eat PRT

    (i) 'That book, (someone)   (i) 'The fish, (someone) has
       published it.'   eaten it.'

    (ii) 'That book has been published.' (ii) 'The fish has been eaten (up).'

                                      (iii) 'The fish has eaten.'

Li and Thompson (1981: 88–89) argue that (26a) is a sentence with a topic, but with no subject nominal (spelled out as reading (i)). A different analysis, favored here at least as a further structural option, would assign the nominal subject status in a passivized structure without overt passive morphology (reading (ii)). The same point is illustrated by the classical example from Chao (1969) in (26b), with the additional complication that the string has a third plausible analysis as an agent-verb sequence (which is of no interest in our context).

3.4. Preposed objects as secondary topics

It has been claimed that Chinese has a secondary topic position between the subject and the VP. Both shifted objects with no specific marking as in (27a) (Shyu 2001, Paul 2005) and *bǎ*-marked nominals as in (27b) (Tsao 1987) have been given analyses along these lines (cf. Li 2001 for a survey of the Chinese *bǎ*-construction, a standard problem of Chinese grammar writing; *bǎ* is a functional element (preposition or light verb) which licenses nominals in pre-verbal position).

(27) a. *Tā   huǒchē méi   gǎnshàng.* b. *Tā   bǎ shū   kàn-wán   le.*
     (s)he train   not.have catch   (s)he BA book read-finish PRT
     '(S)He didn't catch the train.'   '(S)He finished reading the
                                              book.'

(28A) presents two clear cases where the *bǎ*-marked objects are *contrastive* secondary topics.

(28) Q: *Tā   bǎ shū   hé zázhì   dōu kàn-wán   le?*
         (s)he BA book   and magazine all   read-finish PRT
         'Has he finished the book and the magazine?'

     A: *Tā   bǎ [shū]*$_{CT}$ *kàn-wán   le,   [zázhì]*$_{CT}$ *hái méi kàn-wán.*
        (s)he BA book   read-finish PRT magazine still not read-finish
        'The book, he finished; the magazine, he hasn't finished yet.'

3.5. Prosodic aspects of topics in Chinese

Plain aboutness topics have a rather neutral prosody (Chen and Braun 2006). They are neither affected by focal pitch range expansion or longer focal duration, nor by post-focal deaccentuation, nor by compression (cf. §2.5.). Contrastive topics appear to be marked in a similar way as foci in the comment, namely by higher f_0 targets, and by a longer duration than non-focal/non-contrastive segments. Low f_0 targets may be affected less with contrastive topics than with foci in comments. Put differently, contrastive topics seem to involve a mere upper f_0 range expansion while leaving lower f_0 targets unaffected, or even slightly raising them. These generalizations involve some interpretation of my own because the delimitation of information-structural categories like topic or background varies among studies, and sometimes it does not coincide with the one favored in this survey (Chen and Braun 2006, Wang and Xu 2006, Chen 2008).

4. Given vs. new

Major issues pertaining to the given/new dichotomy in Mandarin Chinese include (i) definiteness effects depending on syntactic function/position and (ii) the array of anaphoric expression types in Chinese as well as restrictions on their (non-)use. To appreciate these phenomena in their systematic context, the following characteristics of Chinese nominals must briefly be mentioned. Chinese does not mark number on nouns (the suffix -*men* on nouns denoting humans which is sometimes discussed in this context derives collective denotations). Argument positions may either be occupied by bare nouns or by more complex nominals. Whenever demonstratives or numerical expressions precede the noun, classifiers must be used between these functional elements and the noun. Given these basic properties of Chinese nominals, bare nouns constitute an especially interesting domain of investigation because they contain no functional morphemes indicating their status as *given* or *new*. Despite the lack of definiteness marking, bare nouns display definiteness effects in some syntactic environments. The first such effect concerns subjects vs. objects. Bare nouns in a non-subject (and non-topical) position are typically interpreted as indefinite (unless they denote inherently definite entities), whereas they are invariably definite in the subject position preceding the verb; cf. (29). This contrast is particularly striking with unaccusative verbs of (dis-)appearance, which allow their sole arguments to surface either preverbally or postverbally; cf. (30).

(29) a. *Zhāngsān yùdào-le wàiguórén.*
   Zhangsan meet-PRF foreigner
   'Zhangsan met foreigners/a foreigner.'

 b. *Wàiguórén yùdào-le Zhāngsān.*
   foreigner meet-PRF Zhangsan
   'The foreigner met Zhangsan.'

(30) a. *Lái-le kèrén le.*
   come-ASP guest PRT
   'Guests have/A guest has arrived.'

 b. *Kèrén lái le.*
   guest come PRT
   'The guest(s) has/have arrived.'

In the object position, indefinite nominals with the basic structure *yī* 'one' + classifier + N are frequently used as equivalents of expressions with indefinite articles in English; this allows Chinese speakers to make a choice between (29a) and (31) if they want to describe an event in which Zhangsan met a single discourse-new foreigner. Statistical determinants influencing the choice between either option probably include specificity and whether the foreigner will be topical in the ensuing discourse. Both factors appear to favor the use of the more articulate structure in (31).

(31) *Zhāngsān yùdào-le yī-ge wàiguórén.*
      Zhangsan meet-ASP 1-CL foreigner
      'Zhangsan met a foreigner.'

Indefinite subjects are barred from non-thetic sentences, at least in written registers; cf. (32a). The way to express a translational equivalent of *A foreigner met Zhangsan* is, as in (32b), with presentative *yǒu* 'exist' preceding the indefinite.

(32) a. **Yī-ge wàiguórén yùdào-le Zhāngsān.*
          1-CL   foreigner meet-PRF Zhangsan
          int.: 'A foreigner met Zhangsan.'

      b. *Yǒu yī-ge wàiguórén yùdào-le Zhāngsān.*
          EXS 1-CL foreigner   meet-PRF Zhangsan
          'A foreigner met Zhangsan.'

There is a class of potential counterexamples to the definiteness restriction on subjects in Chinese. Two such examples are provided in (33).

(33) a. *Yī-zhāng chuáng shuì   sān-ge rén.*
          one-CL   bed   sleep 3-CL   people
          'One bed accommodates three people.'

      b. *Wǔ-ge xiǎohái chībuwán   shí-wǎn   fàn.*
          5-CL   children cannot.eat   10-bowl   rice
          'Five children cannot finish ten bowls of rice.'

The peculiar measuring semantics of this type of sentence, and independent syntactic reasons, lead Li (1998) to a treatment of phrases of the type 'numeral + CL + NP' in (33) as NumPs, i.e., as phrases headed by a number head with no empty determiner structure on top. For cases like (31) or (32), however, she assumes a fully projected DP with an empty (in)definite D head. This move, which Li (1998) demonstrates to be independently motivated, allows us to maintain the ban on indefinites in the subject position of non-thetical sentences, where NumPs do not count as indefinite DPs.

Taken together, Chinese is a prime example of a language which renders transparent the close link between the discourse relation of topicality and the grammatical relation of subjecthood. Unlike languages such as English, where subjects just tend to be definite, subject DPs in Chinese must be interpreted as definite.

In §3.4. we discussed the secondary topic position preceding the VP in which the functional element *bǎ* allows preposed objects. A definiteness effect is observed for this secondary topic position, too (cf. (34)).

(34) a. preposed *bǎ* object

    Tā   bǎ shū   kàn-wán-le.
    (s)he BA book read-finished-PRF
    '(S)He finished reading the/*a book(s).'

   b. *in-situ* object

    Tā   kàn-wán-le   shū.
    (s)he read-finish-PRF book
    '(S)He finished reading a book/books/the book.'

We will now turn to the use of pronouns and anaphoric expressions. These expressions have a givenness feature in their lexical specification, and this makes them relevant objects of study in the domain of information structure. This holds true especially against the background of the fact that Mandarin Chinese is a highly discourse-oriented pro-drop language (as opposed to syntax-oriented languages) which allows for a lot of zero anaphora. Li and Thompson (1979) observe that speakers vary in their decisions where to use a pronoun (as opposed to ellipsis) in a given written discourse with anaphoric slots to be filled in. The authors hypothesize that the use of zero anaphora correlates with conjoinability of a given sentence with the preceding discourse. If no topic switch occurs and if no change from foregrounded to backgrounded parts of a narrative (or *vice versa*) occurs in a sentence, then the sentence counts as highly conjoinable, and zero anaphora has a higher probability of occurrence than in sentences that are conjoinable to a lesser degree. In addition to these generalizations, Li and Thompson (1979: 333–334) identify two environments where zero anaphora does not occur: (i) after prepositions as in (35) (there is no preposition stranding in Chinese) and (ii) with so-called pivotal verbs as in (36) (*qǐng* 'invite', *mìngling* 'order', etc.), with ditransitive control verbs, that is, which subcategorize for an addressee nominal and an infinitival clause.

(35) *Wǒ gēn *(tā) xué.*
    I   with (s)he learn
    'I learn from him/her.'

(36) *Wǒ mìngling *(tā) chī fàn.*
    I   order   (s)he eat
    'I order him/her to eat.'

Huang (1984) adopts the general characterization of Chinese as discourse-oriented, but he further assumes the cross-classifying dimension of richness vs. poverty of agreement morphology to distinguish among pro-drop languages with a considerable amount of agreement morphology (most Romance languages, e.g.) and pro-drop languages with less or no agreement morphology (Chinese, Japanese). He combines this classification of Chinese with a more syntax-based view of pronominalization and ellipsis options than previous authors did (cf. the increasingly polemic debate in Xu and Langendoen 1985, Huang 1984, Xu 1986, Huang 1987, cf. also Huang 1999). Huang's (1984) most important generalization for Chinese is that zero anaphora of direct objects in Chinese is more restricted than zero anaphora of subjects, and he relates this observation to analogous asymmetries in Japanese (Kuroda 1965) and topic drop in German (Ross' 1982 "Pronoun Zap"). The contrasts in (37), especially between (37a) and (37b), exemplify the generalization in (38) (Huang 1984: 538; the rather theory-neutral and narrow wording of (38), which does not do justice to the wider consequences of Huang's observation, is mine; D.H.).

(37) a. *Zhāngsān$_i$ xīwàng [$\emptyset_{i/k}$/tā$_{i/k}$ kěyǐ kànjian Lǐsì$_j$].*
          Zhangsan hope $\emptyset$ /(s)he can see   Lisi
          'Zhangsan$_i$ hopes that he$_{i/j}$ can see Lisi.'

      b. *Zhāngsān$_i$ xīwàng [Lǐsì$_j$ kěyǐ kànjian $\emptyset_{*i/*j/k}$].*
          Zhangsan hope   Lisi can see $\emptyset$
          'Zhangsan$_i$ hopes that Lisi can see him$_{*i/j}$.'

      c. *Zhāngsān$_i$ xīwàng [Lǐsì$_j$ kěyǐ kànjian tā$_{i/*j/k}$].*
          Zhangsan hope   Lisi can see   (s)he
          'Zhangsan$_i$ hopes that Lisi can see him$_{i/j}$.'

(38) The antecedent of an elided object in an embedded clause cannot be the matrix subject.

(37a) shows that subjects of embedded clauses, no matter if they are pronominal or elliptical, may refer to the matrix subject, or to a discourse-given topical entity. Things are different in (37b). Here the matrix subject is not a possible antecedent of the elliptical object; only discourse-given topics are. (37c) shows that the pronominal object again has the wider range of interpretive options known from (37a). (The local subject antecedent in (37b/c) is excluded because this configuration would require the reflexive form (*tā-*)*zìjǐ.*) The pattern follows if empty objects, but not empty subjects, always correspond to constituents that were topicalized first, and then deleted (or if they are, more generally, interpreted as variables bound from A-positions; this is Huang's 1985, 1987 generalization). To recapitulate Huang's (1984) implementation of this pattern (cf. also Li's 2007 fresh look at the facts) would lead us too far afield. The point to be brought home is that zero anaphora in Mandarin Chinese is a phenomenon that is not as unconstrained by syntax as it seemed to be at first glance.

Acknowledgements

This chapter is based on work that was conducted with support from the *Deutsche Forschungsgemeinschaft* (i) within the Collaborative Research Center SFB 632 "Information Structure" (Project A5 conducted by Malte Zimmermann) and (ii) in the context of a Heisenberg fellowship grant (Ho 2557/3-1). This support is gratefully acknowledged. I benefitted from discussions with, and written comments prepared by, the editors, Jin Cui (Stuttgart/Cologne) and Jingyang Xue (Göttingen). Mistakes are mine.

References

Alleton, Viviane
    1972   *Les adverbes en chinois moderne*. Den Haag and Paris: Mouton & Co.
Biq, Yung-O
    1984   The semantics and pragmatics of *cai* and *jiu* in Mandarin Chinese. Ph.D. dissertation, Cornell University, Ithaca. [Reprinted 1987. Bloomington: Indiana University Linguistics Club.]
Büring, Daniel and Katharina Hartmann
    2001   The syntax and semantics of focus-sensitive particles in German. *Natural Language and Linguistic Theory* 19: 229–281.
Chafe, William
    1976   Givenness, contrastiveness, definiteness, subjects, topics and point of view. In *Subject and Topic*, Charles N. Li (ed.), 27–55. London / New York: Academic Press.
Chao, Yuen Ren
    1968   *A Grammar of Spoken Chinese*. Berkeley, CA: University of California Press.
Chen, Yiya
    2008   Prosodic marking of information structure in Shanghai Chinese. *Paper presented at The Second International Conference on East Asian Linguistics, Vancouver, British Columbia, Canada, November 7th–9th, 2008.*

Chen, Yiya and Bettina Braun
    2006   Prosodic realization in information structure categories in standard
            Chinese. In *Speech Prosody 2006*, R. Hoffmann and H. Mixdorff
            (eds.). Dresden: TUD Press.
Cheng, Lisa Lai-Shen
    2008   Deconstructing the *shì...de* construction. *Linguistic Review* 25: 235–
            266.
Drubig, Hans Bernhard
    1994   Island constraints and the syntactic nature of focus and associa-
            tion with focus. *Arbeitspapiere des Sonderforschungsbereichs
            340 'Sprachtheoretische Grundlagen der Computerlinguistik' 51.*
            Universität Tübingen.
Ernst, Thomas
    1994   Conditions on Chinese A-not-A questions. *Journal of East Asian
            Linguistics* 3: 241–264.
Gasde, Horst-Dieter
    1999   Are there 'Topic-prominence' and 'Subject-prominence' along the
            lines of Li & Thompson 1976? *Paper presented at the 21st Annual
            Meeting of the Deutsche Gesellschaft für Sprachwissenschaft,
            Universität Konstanz, February 24th–26th, 1999.*
Haiman, John
    1978   Conditionals are topics. *Language* 54: 564–589.
Hole, Daniel
    2004   *Focus and Background Marking in Mandarin Chinese. System and
            theory behind* cái, jiù, dōu *and* yě. London/New York: Routledge
            Curzon.
Hole, Daniel
    2006   Mapping VPs to restrictors: Anti-Diesing effects in Mandarin
            Chinese. In *Where Semantics Meets Pragmatics*, Klaus von
            Heusinger and Ken Turner (eds.), 337–380. Amsterdam: Elsevier.
Hole, Daniel
    2011   The deconstruction of *shì...de* clefts revisited. *Lingua* 121: 1707–1733.
Hole, Daniel and Malte Zimmermann
    to appear Syntactic partitioning in (South) East Asian: A cross-linguistic com-
            parison of clefting in Japanese, Burmese and Chinese. To appear in
            The Structure of Clefts, Andreas Haida, Katharina Hartmann and
            Tonjes Veenstra (eds.). Amsterdam: John Benjamins.
Horn, Lawrence R.
    1989   *A Natural History of Negation.* Chicago, Illinois: University of
            Chicago Press.
Horvath, Julia
    2010   "Discourse features", syntactic displacement and the status of contrast.
            Lingua 120: 1346–1369.

Huang, C.-T. James
    1982   Logical relations in Chinese and the theory of grammar. Ph.D. dissertation, Massachusetts Institute of Technology, Cambridge, MA.
Huang, C.-T. James
    1984   On the distribution and reference of empty pronouns. *Linguistic Inquiry* 15: 531–574.
Huang, C.-T. James
    1987   Remarks on empty categories in Chinese. *Linguistic Inquiry* 18: 321–337.
Huang, Shi-Zhe
    1996   Quantification and predication in Mandarin Chinese: A case study of *dou*. Ph.D. dissertation, University of Pennsylvania.
Huang, Yan
    1999   *Anaphora.* Cambridge: Cambridge University Press.
Jacobs, Joachim
    1983   *Fokus und Skalen. Zur Syntax und Semantik der Gradpartikeln im Deutschen.* Tübingen: Niemeyer.
Krifka, Manfred
    1992   A compositional semantics for multiple focus constructions. In *Informationsstruktur und Grammatik*, Joachim Jacobs (ed.), 17–53. Opladen: Westdeutscher Verlag.
Krifka, Manfred
    2006   Association with focus phrases. In *The Architecture of Focus*, Valéria Molnár and Susanne Winkler (eds.), 105–136. Berlin/New York: Mouton de Gruyter.
Kuroda, Y.
    1965   Generative grammatical studies in the Japanese language. Ph.D. dissertation, Massachusetts Institute of Technology, Cambridge, MA.
Lai, Huei-Ling
    1999   Rejected expectations: The two time-related scalar particles *cai* and *jiu* in Mandarin Chinese. *Linguistics* 37: 625–661.
Lee, Huichi
    2005   On Chinese focus and cleft constrctions. Ph.D. dissertation, National Tsing Hua University, Hsinchu, Taiwan.
Li, Charles N. (ed.)
    1976   *Subject and Topic.* London/New York: Academic Press.
Li, Charles N. and Sandra A. Thompson
    1976   Subject and topic: a new typology of language. In *Subject and Topic*, Charles N. Li (ed.), 457–489. London/New York: Academic Press.
Li, Charles N. and Sandra A. Thompson
    1979   Third-person anaphora and zero-anaphora in Chinese discourse. In *Discourse and Syntax. Syntax and Semantics 12*, Talmy Givón (ed.), 311–335. New York: Academic Press.

Li, Charles N. and Sandra A. Thompson
1981   *Mandarin Chinese. A Functional Reference Grammar.* Berkeley, Los Angeles and London: University of California Press.
Li, Yen-hui Audrey
1998   Argument determiner phrases and number phrases. *Linguistic Inquiry* 29: 693 702.
Li, Yen-hui Audrey
2001   The *ba* construction. Ms., University of Southern California, Los Angeles.
Li, Yen-hui Audrey
2007   Beyond empty categories. *Bulletin of the Chinese Linguistic Society of Japan* 254: 74–106.
Liao, Wei-wen Roger and Yu-yun Iris Wang
2009   Multiple *wh*-construction and its interpretations in Chinese. In *Proceedings of the 38. Meeting of the North Eastern Linguistic Society,* Anisa Schardl, Martin Wakow and Muhammad Abdurrahman (eds.), 63–74. Amherst, Massachusetts: Graduate Linguistic Student Association of the University of Massachusetts.
Lin, Jo-wang
1996   Polarity licensing and wh-phrase quantification in Chinese. Ph.D. dissertation, Amherst, Massachusetts.
Lin, Jo-wang
1998   Distributivity in Chinese and its implications. *Natural Language Semantics* 6: 201–243.
Löbner, Sebastian
1990   *Wahr neben falsch. Duale Operatoren als die Quantoren natürlicher Sprache.* Tübingen: Niemeyer.
Matisoff, James A.
1972   Lahu nominalization, relativization, and genitivization. In *Syntax and Semantics. Vol. 1,* John Kimball (ed.), 237–257. New York: Seminar Press.
Oshima, David
2005   Morphological vs. phonological contrastive topic marking. *Proceedings from the Annual Meeting of the Chicago Linguistics Society* 41: 371–384.
Paris, Marie-Claude
1979   *Nominalization in Mandarin Chinese. The Morpheme 'de' and the 'shi...de' Constructions.* Paris: Université Paris VII.
Paris, Marie-Claude
1981   *Problèmes de syntaxe et de sémantique en linguistique chinoise.* (Mémoires de l'Institut des Hautes Études Chinoise XX.) Paris: Collège de France.

Partee, Barbara H.
    1999   Focus, quantification, and semantics-pragmatics issues. In *Focus: Linguistic, Cognitive, and Computational Perspectives*, Peter Bosch and Rob van der Sandt (eds.), 213–231. Cambridge: Cambridge University Press.

Paul, Waltraud
    2005   Low IP area and left periphery in Mandarin Chinese. *Recherches linguistiques de Vincennes* 33: 111–134.

Paul, Waltraud and John Whitman
    2008   *Shi...de* focus clefts in Mandarin Chinese. *Linguistic Review* 25: 413–451.

Reinhart, Tanya
    1982   *Pragmatics and linguistics: An Analysis of Sentence Topics.* Bloomington, IN: Indiana University Linguistics Club.

Rizzi, Luigi
    1997   The fine structure of the left periphery. In *Elements of Grammar*, Liliane Haegeman (ed.), 281–337. Dordrecht: Kluwer.

Rooth, Mats
    1992   A theory of focus interpretation. *Natural Language Semantics*: 75–116.

Rooth, Mats
    1996   Focus. In *The Handbook of Contemporary Semantic Theory*, Shalom Lappin (ed.), 271–297. Oxford: Blackwell.

Ross, John R.
    1982   Pronoun deleting processes in German. *Paper presented at the Annual Meeting of the Linguistic Society of America, San Diego, California.*

Shyu, Shu-ing
    1995   The syntax of focus and topic in Mandarin Chinese. Ph.D. dissertation, University of Southern California, Los Angeles.

Shyu, Shu-ing
    2001   Remarks on object movement in Mandarin SOV order. *Language and Linguistics* 2: 93–124.

Simpson, Andrew and Zoe Xiu-Zhi Wu
    2002   From D to T – determiner incorporation and the creation of tense. *Journal of East Asian Linguistics* 11: 169–209.

Soh, Hooi Ling
    2006   *Wh*-in-situ in Mandarin Chinese. *Linguistic Inquiry* 36: 143–155.

von Stechow, Arnim
    1982   Structured propositions. *Technical report 59, Sonderforschungsbereich 99.* Universität Konstanz.

Sybesma, Rint
    1996   Review of "The syntax of focus and topic in Mandarin Chinese" by Shyu Shu-ing. *Glot International* 2: 13–14.

Tsao, Feng-fu
    1987   A topic-comment approach to the *ba* construction. *Journal of Chinese Linguistics* 15: 1–53.
Wang, Bei and Yi Xu
    2006   Prosodic encoding of topic and focus in Mandarin. *Paper presented at the 3rd International Conference on Speech Prosody, May 2nd–5th, 2006, University of Technology, Dresden.*
Xu, Liejiong
    1986   Free empty categories. *Linguistic Inquiry* 17: 75–93.
Xu, Liejiong and Terence Langendoen
    1985   Topic structures in Chinese. *Language* 61: 1–27.
Xu, Yi
    1999   Effects of tone and focus on the formation and alignment of f_0 contours. *Journal of Phonetics* 27: 55–105.
Yip, Moria
    1980   The tonal phonology of Chinese. Ph.D. dissertation, Massachusetts Institute of Technology, Cambridge, MA.
Zhang, Jie and Yuwen Lai
    2010   Testing the role of phonetic knowledge in Mandarin tone sandhi. *Phonology* 27: 153–201.
Zhang, Niina Ning
    1997   Syntactic dependencies in Mandarin Chinese. Ph.D. dissertation, University of Toronto.

The information structure of English

Susanne Winkler

The current article describes the linguistic encoding of focus, topic, and givenness in English as dimensions of information structure that regulate the flow of information in the continuous update of the common ground.

Consider example (1). The alternative responses to the question in (1A) show different packaging possibilities of the same constituent due to certain variations with respect to word order, particles, length, or elaboration:

(1) A: *What did Peter buy for his daughter?*
     B1: *Peter bought a [BIcycle].*
     B2: *A [BIcycle].*
     B3: *Peter bought for his daughter a [BIcycle].*
     B4: *A [BIcycle], he bought.*
     B5: *Only a [BIcycle] did he buy for his daughter (not a CAR).*
     B6: *What he bought, was a [BIcycle].*
     B7: *He bought a [BIcycle] for his [DAUGHter] and a [SKATEboard] for his [SON].*

The responses (B1–7) are similar, as each of them serves as a felicitous answer to the same question, which requires the specification of Peter's present for his daughter. The constituent *a bicycle*, which corresponds to the *wh*-phrase in (1A), provides the missing information in the answer and adds it to the common ground. This constituent, which is intonationally highlighted by the main accent and bracketed, is generally referred to in the literature as the *focus* of the sentence. The unbracketed parts of the clauses are not intonationally highlighted and may serve different discourse functions, such as discourse *givenness* or *topichood*. The subject of the answer in (1B1), for example, functions as the *unmarked topic*, since *Peter* is what the discourse is about (cf. Reinhart 1982). It is important to notice that although the different answers to the question in (1A) are felicitous answers since they all provide the same focus constituent *a bicycle*, some answers seem to correspond more optimally to the speaker's request for information than others. Compare, for example, the fragmentary answer in (1B2) to the elaborate answer in (1B7). One could argue that the fragmentary answer is the more appropriate answer to the question, because it is brief, while (1B7) is less appropriate because it actually answers a more complex question, such as *What did Peter buy for whom?* Assuming that specific information packaging strategies in a given discourse context influence working memory and processing load, (1B2) should be preferred over (1B7). The specific differences of the answers with respect to information structure and information structure management in (1B1) to (1B7) will be discussed as we go along.

In Section 1, I will discuss information structural concepts focus, topic, and givenness and describe how they interact. I will pay attention to general tendencies of how information structure is encoded in cases of unmarked SVO word order interacting with intonation in English. In Section 2, I will consider word order variation as it occurs in focus, topic, and givenness marking constructions. I will concentrate on five processes: preposing of a constituent to the left periphery of the clause, postposing to the right periphery, inversion with involvement of pre- and postposing, clefting, and deletion. These constructions divert from unmarked word order and thereby create specific information structural effects.

1.   Core notions of information structure and canonical word order in English

1.1. Focus

Following a long tradition in generative syntax (cf. Jackendoff 1972), focus on a syntactic constituent is taken to be an abstract feature $[\ldots]_F$ that shows its influence in syntactic and phonological form and in semantic interpretation. This feature is assigned in a principally unconstrained fashion in the derivation of the sentence but is ultimately constrained by language specific information packaging and licensing requirements. In English, the overt realization of the focus feature is generally visible as phonological prominence on a specific syllable of a word within a focus constituent, as in (2):

(2)   A: *[MIchael]$_F$ bought a bicycle for his daughter.*
       B: *No, [PEter]$_F$ bought a bicycle for his daughter.*

Semantically, focus indicates the presence of alternatives that are relevant for interpretation (cf. Krifka and Musan (this volume)). In (2A), focus indicates alternatives to the subject referent, which makes this suitable as an answer to the question *Who bought a bicycle for his daughter?* which would have introduced such alternatives as possible answers (Hamblin 1973, Rooth 1992). In (2B), focus again indicates alternatives to the subject referent, and in its context suggests (2A) as an alternative; here we see focus as a correction.

A second effect of focus arises with *focus sensitive operators* (fso) such as *only* or *even*, which take scope over a prosodically highlighted element and associate interpretively with its alternatives (e.g., Jackendoff 1972, König 1991, Krifka 1999, Reich this volume). Focus assignment on the subject or the object is achieved by introducing an fso in the sentence initial position, resulting in subject focus as in (3a), or in preverbal position, resulting in object focus as in (3b).

(3) a. *Only/even [PEter]$_F$ bought a bicycle.*
     b. *Peter only/even bought a [BIcycle]$_F$.*

Negation can associate with focus, as illustrated for subject focus in (4):

(4) a. *[MIchael]$_F$ didn't buy a bicycle, but [PEter]$_F$.*
     b. *Not [MIchael]$_F$ but [PEter]$_F$ bought a bicycle.*
     c. *[PEter]$_F$, not [MIchael]$_F$, bought a bicycle.*

In (3a) the alternatives consist of a set of possible agentive entities who bought a bicycle, in (3b) the set of alternatives is computed over different entities which were bought by Peter. While the set of alternatives in (3) is implicit, the alternatives in (4) are explicitly stated.

The examples show that focus in English can be identified, either as the answer to a *wh*-question or as the accented element associated with a focus sensitive particle or the negation particle. However, the way in which focus is marked by intonational highlighting can be ambiguous. For example, the nuclear pitch accent in (1B1), here repeated in (5), allows for different focus readings. In addition to *What did Peter buy?* or *What did Peter buy for his daughter?* as in (1), (5a) can also be a felicitous answer to the questions *What did Peter do?* and *What happened?*

(5) a. *Peter bought a BIcycle.*
     b. *Peter bought a [BIcycle]$_F$.*

The fact that a single pitch accent realized on *bicycle* allows for different interpretations in relation to specific context questions has been referred to as *focus projection* (cf. Höhle 1982, Rochemont 1986, Selkirk 1984, 1995) or *focus integration* (Jacobs 1993, Drubig 1994). If the pitch accent is realized on a rightmost element in a verb phrase as in (5a), then the noun that carries the accent may be the focus of the object DP as in (5b), or depending on the context, the VP as in (6) or the entire sentence as in (7). The type of focus in (5b) is often referred to as *narrow focus*, and the type of focus in (6) and (7) as *wide focus*. In order to distinguish the focus marked word on which the focus accent is realized from the phrase which is focused, we introduce the term focus phrase (FP) signaled by a subscript as in (6) and (7). The FP is defined as a phrase that necessarily contains a focus (cf. Drubig 1994: 6).

(6)   A: *What did Peter do?*
       B: *Peter [bought a [BIcycle]$_F$]$_{FP}$.*

(7)   A: *What happened?*
       B: *[Peter bought a [BIcycle]$_F$]$_{FP}$.*

Example (5a) shows that prosodic highlighting of the sentence-final noun phrase is potentially ambiguous (cf. Jacobs 1991). The prosodic ambiguity is usually disambiguated by the context in which the utterance occurs, as seen in (6A) and (7A). Cases of object focus contrast with cases of subject focus. A focus on the subject in the answer, as in *PEter did*, is unambiguous, since there is only one felicitous question which it can answer, namely *Who bought a bicycle?*.

    There are two results with respect to the grammatical encoding of focus in English with unmarked SVO word order: On the one hand, the focus tests show that basically any constituent can function as a focus in the appropriate discourse (exceptions being attitude adverbials like *unfortunately* or speech-act adverbials like *frankly*). On the other hand, there is a general tendency in English to assign the focus-related nuclear accent to the most deeply embedded constituent in the sentence. This insight was first captured by Chomsky and Halle (1968: 17), who proposed the nuclear stress rule (NSR), which results in the placement of primary stress on the last stressed vowel of a phrase. On the basis of this approach Cinque (1993) developed a theory in which the effects of the NSR follow from the direction of syntactic embedding. In English, which is a right-branching head-initial language, the nuclear stress is realized on the most deeply embedded constituent to the right of the verb in the VP (as in 8), whereas it is predicted to fall on the most deeply embedded constituent to the left of the verbal head in the VP in German, which is a head-final language, as in (9). In both languages the nuclear accent is realized on the noun *Judea*.[1]

---

[1]   See Musan (2002, 2010) for a comprehensive discussion of the linguistic encoding of information structure in German.

(8)   *[[Jesus] [preached [to the people [of JuDEa]]]]*

(9)   *dass [Jesus [[zu dem Volke [von JuDÄa]] predigte]]*

The question is whether there is a cognitive basis for having both linguistic strategies for encoding focus – the tendency to realize the nuclear accent at the right periphery and the possibility to assign the focus accent in relation to the discourse requirements elsewhere. An initial answer is that if optimal information structure management facilitates processing, the speakers need both options. In the unmarked case, the focus-related nuclear accent in English is realized on the sentence final constituent. One could hypothesize that this tendency has a processing correlate, in the sense that the attention of the interlocutors is geared towards the right edge of the utterance or informational chunk. Free focus assignment, however, is independently necessary to direct the attention of the interlocutors to nondefault readings. Both linguistic encoding strategies constitute a prerequisite for optimal information structural management with maintenance of the SVO word order. A third strategy, based on changes in word order, will be discussed in Section 2.

Returning to example (1), the following question arises: How are these focusing strategies employed in the different question-answer sequences there? Above, we identified (1B1) as the default case with unmarked SVO-word order and focus on the object. B2 provides a fragmentary answer *a bicycle*. The fragment is the focus, and thus is the briefest response to the question in (1A). The answers in B3 to B7 differ from B1 in interesting ways. In short, B3 is an instance of heavy NP shift. B3 repeats the prepositional phrase *for his daughter* and shifts the focused DP *a bicycle* to the right periphery of the clause, thereby changing the word order. In B4 the focused element occurs at the left periphery of the clause, changing the word order to an OSV structure, a method also referred to as topicalization. B5, which is an instance of inversion, is closely related to B4 and also shows an OSV word order. In addition, it occurs with a clause initial focus sensitive operator and an inverted auxiliary which precedes the subject. B6 is a cleft structure and B7 is a structure with multiple contrastive constituents. The specific constructions in B3 to B7 are discussed in Section 2.

1.2. Topic

The topic, which is understood here in terms of aboutness, is that part of the sentence which we are talking about and which anchors the sentence to the common ground (Reinhart 1982). In Reinhart's theory the topic constituent is added onto a file card which has been previously created. This means that the topic constituent identifies the entity or set of entities under which the information expressed in the comment constituent should be stored in the CG content. Example (1A) introduces *Peter* into the discourse, since the question is about him. The answers (1B1) and (1B3) are structured in such a way that *Peter* is assigned topic status, whereas the rest of the utterance constitutes the comment, which is added onto the file card which stores information about *Peter*. Alternatively, the aboutness topic can be pronominalized, as in the answers (1B4) through (1B7).

A newspaper example about the IAAF world championship 2009 illustrates Reinhart's file card approach further. In (10a), the denotation of the entity Usain Bolt is stored on a topic file card. The information which is stored about him on a comment file card is that he ran the fastest 100m in history. (10b) continues with the definite noun phrase *this guy* as part of the topic expression. This epithet is a referential DP which behaves like a pronoun in that it refers to the referent of the topic file card *Usain Bolt*.

(10)   a.   *[Usain Bolt]$_T$ [runs fastest 100m in [HIStory]]$_C$.*
       b.   *[About all this guy can't do]$_T$ [is [FLY]$_F$]$_C$.*
            (Pat Graham, August 17th 2009)

The concept of referential givenness also comprises the notion of *anaphoric topic* used by Kuno (1972) and Lambrecht (1994). A useful test to distinguish topic and focus was noted by Lambrecht (1994: 136). The anaphoric topic *he* in the second conjunct of (11a) can be omitted if the corresponding subject in the antecedent clause is a topic. If it is a focus, as in (11b), the omission of the subject pronoun in the second conjunct results in ungrammaticality.

(11)   a.   A: *What about John?*
            B: *[John]$_T$ married [ROSA]$_F$, but he/[e] didn't really love her.*
       b.   A: *Who married Rosa?*
            B: *[JOHN]$_F$ married Rosa, but he/*[e] didn't really love her.*

A topic can also add a new entity into the universe of discourse, provided that this new entity is linked to a previously established set. Consider example (12):

(12)   A: *Tell me about your two new students in Linguistics 101. Did they turn in their homework on time?*
       B: *[Sandra]$_T$ turned in her homework but [Peter]$_T$ didn't.*

Both *Sandra* and *Peter* are new in the discourse, but the felicitousness of (12) crucially depends on both of them being new members of the set *two new students in Linguistics 101*. In this sense, we consider them to be topics, and we will refer to them as *contrastive topics*. They differ prosodically from regular aboutness topics in being realized by a low-rise accent. Although there is a sense in which *Sandra* and *Peter* are contrastive – they stand in the type of relation that Rooth (1992) calls a symmetric contrast – the relation is distinct from what we call contrastive focus. The difference between contrastive topic and contrastive focus can be seen in (13) and (14):

(13) A: *Tell me about your new male students. Will they turn in their home-work on time?*
      B: *#[Peter]$_T$ won't turn in his homework on time but [Sandra]$_T$ will.*

(14) A: *Tell me about your new male students. Will they turn in their home-work on time?*
      B: *[Peter]$_T$ said he would turn in his homework on time.*
      C: *No, [SANdra]$_F$ said she would.*

The answer in (13B), with unmarked topic intonation, is an infelicitous remark in the given context because *Sandra* is not a member of the set referred to in the question. (14C), with an articulated pitch accent on *Sandra*, is fine as a response to (14B) in the context of (14A). The specific pitch accent on *Sandra* turns this constituent into a contrastive focus, which contradicts the previous assertion *Peter said he would turn in his homework on time* and introduces a referent that does not necessarily belong to the set that constituted the original topic of conversation, *new male students*. Contrastive focus can force an accommodation of the presupposition set, whereas contrastive topic cannot.

Example (1B7) is an interesting example in the context of (1A), repeated in (15):

(15) A: *What did Peter buy for his daughter?*
      B: *He bought [a [BIcycle]$_F$]$_T$ for his [DAUGHter]$_F$ and*
         [a [SKATEboard] $_F$]$_T$ for his [SON]$_F$.

As observed above the aboutness topic of the exchange is *Peter*, which occurs as a pronoun in (15B). The focus is the object, which corresponds to the *wh*-element in the question. However, since (15B) provides more information than asked for, we get a symmetric contrast between the set of presents *a bicycle* versus *a skateboard* and the set of siblings *his daughter* versus *his son*. Thus, (15B) actually answers an implicit multiple *wh*-question *What did Peter buy for whom?* In this case Kuno's (1982) *Sorting Key Hypothesis* in (16) applies.

(16)   Sorting Key Hypothesis:

In a multiple *wh*-word question, the fronted *wh*-word represents the key for sorting relevant pieces of information in the answer.
(Kuno 1982: 141)

Applying (16) to (15B), the first stressed constituent *a bicycle* is the sorting key, in our terminology a contrastive topic, and the second a contrastive focus. From the perspective of information structure management the discourse in (15A, B) is not optimal, because there is an obvious mismatch between the question of (15A) and (15B) in terms of informativeness. This mismatch can be repaired, but requires extra effort.

Two varieties of the core notion of topic have been introduced in this section. The *aboutness topic* and the *contrastive topic*. The discussion confirmed the general tendency that topics precede focus. In the case of normal SVO word order, the aboutness topic coincides with the subject of the clause and generally occurs to the left of the focus. This is also true for contrastive topics. Kuno's sorting key hypothesis suggests that in utterances which answer a multiple *wh*-question, the answer corresponding to the first *wh*-question functions as the sorting key or topic. As seen in (15), the contrastive topics precede the focus in each conjunct.

The question arises of whether the topic-precedes-focus tendency in a given discourse context influences working memory or processing load. Only extensive psycholinguistic testing could provide an adequate answer. However, the tendency that the subject is the aboutness topic and that the VO-sequence provides the comment coincides with the conclusion of the preceding section that focus tends to occur at the right periphery of the clause in a language like English which has a fixed SVO-word order. It would be surprising if the complementarity of the topic-first tendency and the focus-last tendency in SVO sequences in English were completely accidental. Rather the hypothesis is that these two tendencies follow information structure management strategies which guide the default processing of unmarked word order in English.

1.3. Givenness

The term *givenness* describes an essentially pragmatic notion which comprises many different concepts: Halliday's (1967: 206) original definition of *given* describes it as "recoverable information" that "tends to be represented anaphorically, by reference, substitution or ellipsis". He identifies ellipsis as the prototypical case: "Ellipsis involves systemic features having no realization in structure and therefore having no potentiality of association with information focus: what is unsaid cannot be otherwise than taken for granted" (Halliday 1967: 206). Chafe (1976: 30) defines given information from a psychological perspective as "that knowledge which the speaker assumes to be in the consciousness of the addressee at the time of the utterance". Furthermore, he states that "givenness is a status decided on by the speaker" (Chafe 1976: 32) and disagrees with Halliday's notion of recoverability by stating "that it is fundamentally a matter of the speaker's belief that the item is in the addressee's consciousness, not that it is recoverable" (Chafe 1976: 32). Both definitions provide different aspects of the concept of givenness.

Consider the fragmentary answer in (1B2) again, repeated here in (17):

(17)　A: *What did Peter buy for his daughter?*
　　　B: *[A [BIcycle]$_F$]$_{FP}$.*
　　　　given: *[Peter bought for his daughter]$_G$*

Example (17B) provides an illustration for the fact that information that is provided in the question must not be repeated, but can remain silent, indicated here by using strike-through text. The redundant information is *recoverable*, in the sense that it is understood from the question in (17A) without additional processing effort. By choosing the fragmentary answer, the speaker of (17B) provides the missing information corresponding to the *wh*-question in its shortest form. Optionally, however, the speaker can provide more information and repeat parts of the question, as in (1B1) and (1B3). In these answers, the sequence *Peter bought (for his daughter)* is repeated with a low pitch and thereby marked as given.

We assume here that the givenness features of an expression indicate whether its denotation is present in the common ground or not; sometimes we have to differentiate between degrees of givenness (cf. Krifka and Musan (this volume)).

The following discussion will concentrate on the different devices that mark givenness in English. Chafe already notes two different ways in which givenness is expressed in language: "given information is pronounced with lower pitch and weaker stress than new, and it is subject to pronominalization" (Chafe 1976: 31). A third way is the deletion of redundant information, which is discussed in Section 2 together with the other grammatical processes which affect word order and encode information structure in English.

First, let's turn to the givenness marking test based on deaccentuation. Deaccentuation refers to the prosodic reduction or prosodic flattening of the intonational contour. The pitch contour of the deaccented words is flat and does not contain any pitch related accents. This can be nicely observed by the prepositional phrase *for his daughter* following the pitch accent on *a bicycle* in (18). It is pronounced with a flat intonation.

(18)   A: *What did Peter buy for his daughter?*
      B: *Peter bought a[BIcycle]$_F$ for his daughter.*

If a pitch accent were realized on *daughter*, this would be interpreted as a lapse in the communicative process and accommodation processes would have to take place. That givenness is usually signaled by a low flat intonation can be shown by the minimal pair (modeled after Umbach 2005) in (19):

(19)   A: *What did Peter do with the old cottage?*
      B1: *Peter [[SOLD]$_F$ [the shed]$_G$]$_{FP}$.*
      B2: *Peter [sold the [SHED]$_F$]$_{FP}$.*

In (19B1), the response with a flat intonation on *shed* provides the interpretation that Peter sold the old cottage. However, the realization of a pitch accent on *shed* adds a referent to the common ground and triggers the interpretation that the cottage came together with *a shed* which has now been sold.

In general, deaccentuation signals coreference between an unfocused noun phrase and a preceding noun phrase, triggering the interpretation that the entity belongs to the common ground. The same mechanism explains a more complex case of coreference, known as the *weak crossover effect* in the literature. In (20a), the referential expression *John* is deaccented and is therefore interpreted as being coreferent with the preceding pronoun *he*. In (20b), *John* is assigned a pitch accent and therefore does not allow a coreferential interpretation. If the coreferential interpretation is forced in (20b), the sentence is almost impossible to interpret.

(20) a. *The woman* he *loved [[betRAYed]$_F$ [John]$_G$].*
  b. *The woman* he *loved [betrayed [JOHN]$_F$].*

The original observation stems from Chomsky (1976), who showed that deaccentuation of the referential expression *John* in (20a) undoes the *weak crossover violation* which makes (20b) with a coreferent reading ungrammatical. The traditional view explains this violation in terms of the conditions of the syntactic structure and the notion of focus movement. An alternative explanation of the ungrammaticality of (20b) stems from the interrelation of processing and information structure. General discourse processing constraints (e.g., centering) require that if a referent is pronominalized, as in (20a, b), the referent is given and maintains this status throughout the utterance. If, however, the same discourse referent *he* is intonationally highlighted and referred to by a referential expression following the pronoun, as in (20b), a severe processing clash occurs. Looking at information structural relations from the processing perspective solves this longstanding puzzle.

The second test for givenness involves pronominalization. If a noun phrase referent can be pronominalized, that means it is given. An example is provided in (21B) as a response to (19A).

(21) B: *Peter [[SOLD]$_F$ [it]$_G$].*

If, however, the pronominalization test is used in the context of (22A), ungrammaticality results.

(22) A: *What did Peter buy for his daughter?*
  B: **Peter [bought [it]$_G$].*

There are many kinds of anaphoric expressions. They may refer to different constituents within the sentence. In the above examples, the definite NPs and the proforms refer to a nominal referent. In (23), however, we have a verbal proform or "do so" anaphor, which refers to an event.

(23) *When they heard the bear, [PEter] ran away and [so did]$_G$ [MIchael].*

So far, we can observe that there is a general tendency for given constituents, including pronouns, to be deaccented, as stated in the *destress-given* generalization in (24):

(24) Destress-Given:

    A given constituent cannot contain phrasal stress.
    (cf. Féry and Samek-Lodovici 2007)

However, there are some counter-examples, which show that given elements can nevertheless bear an accent in English, as in (25) to (28) (see, e.g., Rochemont 1986, 2009, Schwarzschild 1999, Büring 2008).

(25) A: *I finally went out and bought something today.*
      B: *Oh yeah? What did you BUY?*
      (Rochemont 1986)

(26) A: *Who did John's father vote for?*
      B: *He voted for JOHN.*
      (Rochemont 1986)

(27) A: *Who did John's mother praise?*
      B: *She praised [HIM]$_F$*
      (Schwarzschild 1999)

(28) A1: *What happened?*
      A2: *What did the lawyer do?*
      A3: *Where did the lawyer send the request?*
      B: *The LAWYER sent the REQUEST to their OFFICE.*
      (Büring 2008)

In each of these examples (direct question, answer to a *wh*-question) accent assignment does not conform to (24) for different reasons. Rochemont (2009) concludes that "(i)f these data are reliable, then the conclusion must be that although prominence may be necessary for marking focus, it is not sufficient. English phonology must have a default mechanism of prominence assignment in addition to its focus sensitive mechanisms".

    The initial hypothesis that optimal information structure management reduces processing load also holds true for givenness marking. By deaccenting and pronominalizing given elements the speakers signal that these elements belong to the common ground. Violations of these general packaging requirements as in (25) to (28) above seem to require a specific processing effort. The violations seem to be connected to different reasons. At first sight, all the pitch accents in (25) to (28) seem to fall on the rightmost constituent in each case. However, the intonational contour in (25) is also connected to the specific intonation of *wh*-questions in English, which typically end with a fall on the sentence final constituent. In (26) and (27), the pitch accent assignments on *John* and *him* technically focus a given element in each case, but at the same time the constituents correspond optimally to the *wh*-element of the questions and thereby fulfill the *wh*-test for focus. The pitch accent distribution in (28) is different. It is possible to answer (28A3) by putting a pitch accent on each of the given elements, but this is certainly not the most natural way of answering the question. The overuse of pitch accents comes with an increase in processing effort. For the processor the most economical way to identify the focus is to search for it at the right edge of the clause in instances of unmarked word order. Therefore, the violation of the deaccent given constraint, shown in (24) above, requires the processor to look for a reason for the accent distribution (compare the overuse of accents by English L2 speakers, Gut 2009).

So far, we have discussed linguistic strategies for encoding focus, topic, and givenness in canonical utterances in English. There have been two main results: First, in a rigid SVO language, such as English, the encoding possibilities are reduced to intonation. Second, there is an interaction between the general tendencies of expressing information structure in an SVO language and the specific intonational means which encode the informational status of a constituent in relation to the discourse context. The obvious confinement of linguistic encoding possibilities of information structure is compensated by specific focus, topic, and givenness marking constructions, as discussed in the next section.

2. Noncanonical word order: Focus, topic, and givenness marking constructions

In this section we investigate the interaction between information structure and word order variation in English. The general observation is that the linguistic strategies for encoding information structure in English are extremely limited, since the word order is relatively rigidly SVO. That is, in utterances with unmarked word order, focus and givenness can only be expressed by intonation and through the choice of specific lexical items.

This limitation is counterbalanced by specific focus, topic, and givenness marking constructions, which are characterized by noncanonical word order in English (e.g., Birner and Ward 2004, Rochemont 1986, Rochemont and Culicover 1990, Vallduví 1992, Winkler 2005). Focus constructions and topic constructions typically show word order variation of verb-argument sequences. This type of variation is possible because the specific information structural needs of the interlocutors in building up a coherent discourse cannot be expressed by using the canonical word order. The claim then is that the specific information packaging constructions deviate from the basic SVO order and thereby achieve a particular information structural effect. More specifically, the noncanonical position of one or more constituents is determined by their information status (e.g., topic, focus, new or given). Constructions with noncanonical word order include topicalization at the left periphery of the clause, heavy NP shift and extraposition at the right periphery, inversion involving a reordering of subject and object constituents, clefts highlighting the bracketed constituent, and ellipsis which omits redundant constituents for the purpose of givenness marking or, alternatively, for the purpose of contrast of the remnants. Since the list is not exhaustive, I will concentrate on the core cases and point out some less frequently studied constructions as we go along.

For each information packaging construction, I will pose three questions: i. What is the specific word order variation which the construction employs? ii. What is its specific information structural function? iii. What is the possible cognitive function of the involvement of either the left or the right periphery and how does the expression of information structure interact with processing constraints and the general tendencies of information structure management? Although the third question might be the most interesting, since it focuses on the interaction between the grammatical and the cognitive domain, the answers cannot be more than tentative at this point. Future research will provide further evidence in this interdisciplinary endeavor.

2.1. The left periphery

In English, certain constituents can be preposed to the left periphery, thus changing the regular SVO word order to a noncanonical one, as seen in (29):

(29) a. *[MacaDAmia nuts]$_{DP}$ I like.*
      b   *[Down the RIVer]$_{PP}$ we went.*
      c. *[OUTside]$_{AdvP}$ it was snowing.*
      d. *[Turn his HEAD]$_{VP}$ he could not.*

The examples in (29) are typically referred to as focus fronting, which is often referred to as *topicalization*. The topicalized constituent can be a noun phrase (29a), a prepositional phrase (29b), an adverbial phrase (29c), or a verb phrase, as in (29d). The moved constituent is typically intonationally highlighted with a fall-rise and constitutes a focus with a contrastive interpretation. In (29a), for example, the topicalization indicates that the speaker likes macadamia nuts out of the set of eatables, and not, for example, any other nuts. The focus indicates the presence of alternatives, which are not explicitly stated, here. This corresponds to the definition of focus in Krifka and Musan, this volume. The question arises of whether or not the canonical SVO word order can serve the same function as the noncanonical OSV structure. The answer is straightforward. The canonical SVO word order with a pitch accent on the object, as in *I like MacaDAmia nuts*, is prosodically ambiguous. In addition to providing the contrastive reading on the object, the intonational pattern is also the default pattern, which allows various other interpretations. Thus, topicalization in English is a linguistic encoding strategy by which the violation of the fixed word order is licensed in exactly those cases where the noncanonical word order brings about a special information structural effect, here the contrastive reading of the sentence initial constituent.

Optionally a second accent can be realized on the remaining sequence, as in *MacaDAmia nuts I LIKE*. The intonational contour requires a rise on the topicalized object *MacaDAmia* and a fall on the focused verb. This example is called *topic topicalization* (cf. Gundel 1974: 134–135). It requires an implicit or explicit continuation that spells out the double contrast, such as, for example, *but PEAnuts I HATE*. Also in this case, only the noncanonical word order can unambiguously signal the contrast of two constituents, where the first one functions as a contrastive topic and the second as a focus.

This brief discussion of the two varieties of topicalization constructions shows that intonationally highlighted constituents that are preposed link the statement to the preceding discourse, and those constituents which are marked intonationally at the right periphery tend to be interpreted as foci.

2.2. The right periphery

Another means of highlighting a constituent in English is by postposing it to the right periphery of the sentence and thereby bringing about a specific information structural effect. The canonical word order of $SVO_{direct}O_{indirect}$ in (30a) is changed to a noncanonical object word order by postposing the direct object to the end of the clause as in (30b), traditionally referred to as heavy NP shift (e.g., Rochemont and Culicover 1990).

(30)   a. *She will send [a picture of Harry] [to the [NEWSpaper]$_F$]*
     b. *She will send to the newspaper [a picture of [HARry]$_F$].*

The general tendency to assign nuclear stress to the most deeply embedded constituent causes the prepositional phrase *to the newspaper* to be marked as the focus in (30a). In principle, the same rule applies to (30b), with the difference that now the postposed heavy NP *a picture of Harry* is focused at the right periphery of the clause. The special information structural function of the postposed phrase is that it "necessarily functions as a focus of new information in the sentence" (Rochemont 1986: 27). Note, however, that the definition of focus given in Krifka and Musan (this volume) and the focus-*wh*-test also apply. (30b) but not (30a) could be a felicitous answer to the question *What will she send to the newspaper?* That is, the heavy NP shift construction is employed in those cases where the direct object is focused, but does not occur in a right peripheral position. Note, (1B3) constitutes a further instance of this construction. The focused object *a bicycle* is postposed across the given prepositional phrase.

Another construction in which a constituent is postposed to the right is given in (31). The construction comes about through the rule of extraposition, which relates (31a) to (31b):

(31)   a. *A student [from the lab across the street] [came into the ROOM].*
     b. *[A STUdent] came into the room [from the lab across the STREET].*

In (31b) the prepositional phrase is extraposed from the subject to the right periphery of the clause. The specific information structural effect is that prominence realization on the most deeply embedded constituent marks the focus (cf. Rochemont 1986: chap. 2). Interestingly, also the subject *a student* carries prominence, a fact which has been less frequently noticed in the literature (but see Möck 1994, Göbbel 2007). That is, the linguistic encoding in (31b) differs from (31a) in two ways: First, the prepositional phrase is focused at the right periphery and second, the subject of the construction is also focused. The result of extraposition is a construction which expresses an event.

2.3. Inversion

A further type of information packaging construction changes the canonical word order by inverting the canonical SVX into an XVS word order, where X is a locative prepositional phrase as in (32). Viewed from a descriptive perspective, these constructions provide the impression of postposing the subject and preposing the locative PP, as in (32a) and (32b).

(32)   a.   *[A fierce looking tom-cat] walked [into the [ROOM]$_F$].*
        b.   *[Into the room] walked [a fierce-looking [TOM-cat]$_F$].*

The information packaging construction in (32b) is called *locative inversion* because the prepositional phrase occurs sentence initially and the subject at the right periphery. The function of this construction is two-fold: the initial prepositional phrase sets the scene and the sentence final subject, which is obligatorily focused, constitutes the referent appearing on the scene.

A closely related case of inversion is the so-called *there*-insertion construction in (33).

(33)   a.   *A unicorn is in the garden.*
        b.   *There is [a [UNIcorn]$_F$ in the garden].*

The information packaging function of the *there*-construction is to assign focus to the subject at the right periphery. In contrast to (32b), where the sentence-initial position is filled by a prepositional phrase, the expletive *there* is inserted into the sentence-initial position in (33b). Both constructions are subcases of *stylistic inversion*, which brings about focus on the subject and an eventive reading. Note, a similar information structural effect cannot be achieved by unmarked SVO word order.

A different type of inversion is *comparative inversion*. Example (34a) is an instance of a comparative clause with the subject in its canonical position. (34b) is an instance of comparative inversion.

(34)   *Anna ran much faster*   a.   *than MANNY could have.*
                                             b.   *than could have MANNY.*

(34b) differs from (34a) in two respects. First, the auxiliary cluster precedes the subject *Manny*. Second, the canonical subject position remains syntactically unrealized, which is unusual in present day English. At the same time, the word order violation fulfills a specific goal. Comparative inversion serves to phonologically highlight the subject at the right periphery of the sentence. In contrast to the other types of inversion, the subject in comparative constructions must be interpreted as a contrastive focus. The semantic interpretation of contrast is obligatory in the inverted cases, a feature which distinguishes comparative inversion from both its uninverted counterpart and from stylistic inversion, as seen in (32) and (33).

2.4. Clefts

A well-known information packaging construction is the so-called cleft construction in English. The example in (35a) and (35b) demonstrates clefting:

(35)   a. *John bought a book about SUCculents.*
       b. *It was [JOHN]$_F$ who bought a book about succulents.*

Jespersen (1961: 147–148) noted that "[a] cleaving of a sentence by means of *it is* (often followed by a relative pronoun or connective) serves to single out one particular element of the sentence and very often, by directing attention to it and bringing it, as it were, into focus, to mark a contrast". The general observation is that the canonical SVO word order in English with the tendency to place the focus late in the sentence does not provide an unambiguous means of marking the subject as clearly contrastive. The *it*-cleft construction in (35b), however, provides exactly this possibility by clefting *John*, which in turn is interpreted as contrastive focus (cf. Chafe 1976, È. Kiss 1998, Huber 2002, among many others). Alternative cleft constructions are the so-called *pseudo-cleft* in (36a) and the *wh-cleft* in (36b), which both contrastively focus the constituent at the right edge of the sentence.

(36)   a. *The one who bought a book about succulents was [JOHN]$_F$.*
       b. *What John bought was a book about [SUCculents]$_F$.*

Despite general agreement that clefts bring about a contrastive focus reading of the clefted constituent, Prince (1978) following Erades (1962) observed that there are at least two types of it-*clefts*, the so-called *stressed focus* it-*cleft* as in (35b) and the *informative presupposition* it-*cleft* as in (37):

(37)   a. *It was in 1886 that [...] Lewin published [the first systematic study of the [CACtus]$_F$].*
       b. *It was just about 50 years ago that Henry Ford gave us [the [WEEKend]$_F$].*

In (37) the clefted constituent is not the obvious focus of the sentence, rather the focus of the utterance occurs in the sentence-final position, as in the pseudo-cleft example in (36a).

It is interesting to observe that the information packaging constructions discussed here are not one-dimensional in allowing the bringing about of only one specific information structural function. Rather, it seems as if the constructions depend in their specific interpretation on the interaction of the syntax of the construction and the discourse in which they occur.

2.5. Gaps

Now, I shall discuss an information packaging device which does not visibly reorder the canonical word order of English, but which omits words or phrases and thereby abbreviates sentences and leaves gaps. The result of these deletion processes is called ellipsis. The claim is that there are two kinds of ellipses, which encode two different types of information structural functions: the first type simply marks givenness (cf. 1.3), the second marks contrastive focus by omitting redundant information. The first type marks givenness by leaving an anaphoric constituent unpronounced, as in (38):

(38) a. *The thought came back (...). He tried to stifle it. But the words were forming. He knew he couldn't [stifle it]$_G$.*
          (Hardt 1990)

  b. *One swallow doesn't make a summer, but two [swallows]$_G$ probably do [make a summer]$_G$.*

In (38a), the anaphoric element is the verb phrase *stifle it*, which is the complement of the functional head of the clause, the auxiliary *couldn't*. In (38b), there are two instances of givenness marking by deletion: the noun phrase complement of the functional head *two* and the verb phrase *make a summer* remain unpronounced. The observation is that a constituent can be deleted if it occurs as a complement of a functional head. That is, given or redundant complements can be marked by deaccentuation or phonological deletion if they occur in a mutual entailment relation.

  The second type of ellipsis deletes constituents and thereby isolates parallel contrastive constituents, as in (39) (cf. Konietzko and Winkler 2010, Molnár and Winkler 2010):

(39) A: *Who is liable for violating the national law?*
  B: *[Both the NEW owner and the OLD owner] are liable, but not the [emPLOYee]$_F$.*
      (2009, ELF Labour Law Research)

The utterance of (39B) is a case of *bare argument ellipsis*, also called *stripping*, defined by Hankamer and Sag (1976: 409) as "a rule that deletes

everything in a clause under identity with corresponding parts of the preceding clause, except for one constituent (and sometimes a clause-initial
adverb or negative)". The second conjunct *but not the employee* consists
of one argument and the negation particle *not* and is interpreted as *but the
employee is not liable*. The focus accent on *employee* is interpreted as an
explicit contrast with respect to its correlate, the coordinated noun phrase
the new owner and the old owner. By deleting the redundant information
the highlighted constituent receives a contrastive focus interpretation.

A second case of contrastive ellipsis is brought about by the rule of
gapping, which relates (40a) to (40b):

(40) *Only the asSIStant manager can talk to the MANager*
    a. *and the MANager [~~can talk~~]$_G$ to the GENeral manager.*
    b. *and the MANager to the GENeral manager.*
    (*Penn Treebank*, #...wsj_0037.mrg 805)

The original rule by Hankamer and Sag (1976: 410) states that "[g]apping
(...) applies in coordinate structures to delete all but two major constituents
from the right conjunct under identity with corresponding parts of the left
conjunct". The information structural function of gapping is to contrast the
remaining major constituents with their correlate constituents in the first
conjunct. The information structural observation is that in gapping, the
deleted elements must belong to the background and the remnants must
express a contrastive relation to their correlates. Appying this rule to (40)
provides the following picture: there are parallel foci, and the remnants
(*manager, general manager*) occur in a contrastive relationship to their corresponding parts in the first conjunct (*assistant manager, manager*).

The discussion has shown that the process of deleting a redundant or
contextually given word or constituent can serve two different information
structural functions. It can simply signal that a certain phrase does not need
to be repeated. In this case deletion is an extreme case of deaccentuation.
However, the deletion process of given elements can have a further information structural effect: It can, in addition, extricate the foci in a coordinate
sentence and contrast them with each other.

3. Conclusion

In this chapter, I have discussed the expression of information structure in
English. English is special in that it is a rigid SVO language. At the same

time, English has a set of unusual information packaging constructions which typically violate the canonical word order to bring about special information structural effects.

The idea which has guided the discussion throughout is that there are two fundamentally different ways of expressing information structure in English, which correlate to the type of word order employed. The first set of optimal information structure managing strategies applies for utterances which are canonical SVO structures. These strategies have been discussed in Section 1 with special attention to the informational status of focus, topic, and givenness in relation to intonation. The discussion has shown that there is an interaction between the general tendencies of placing the topic constituent before the focused constituent, which is preferably realized at the right periphery in an SVO language, and specific highlighting and deaccentuation techniques which model the temporal process of the communication in relation to the dynamic changes in the common ground.

The second set of strategies applies if the interlocutors have specific information structural needs which cannot be expressed by SVO word order and intonation alone. In this case, specific focus, topic, and givenness marking constructions are used, as discussed in Section 2. These constructions employ word order variation for the purpose of bringing about specific information structural effects. It has been argued that both strategies, intonation and information packaging constructions, taken together constitute optimal encoding strategies in the cooperative endeavor to communicate effectively and effortlessly.

References

Birner, Betty and Gregory Ward
    2004   Information structure and noncanonical syntax. In *The Handbook of Pragmatics*, Lawrence R. Horn and Gregory Ward (eds.), 153–174. Oxford: Blackwell.
Büring, Daniel
    2008   *What's New (and What's Given) in the Theory of Focus.* Berkeley Linguistic Society.
Chafe, Wallace L.
    1976   Givenness, contrastiveness, definiteness, subjects, topic, and points of view. In *Subject and Topic*, Charles N. Li (ed.), 25–56. London: Academic Press.
Chomsky, Noam
    1976   Conditions on rules of grammar. *Linguistic Analysis* 2: 303–350.

Chomsky, Noam and Morris Halle
    1968   *The Sound Pattern of English*. New York: Harper and Row.
Cinque, Guglielmo
    1993   A null theory of phrase and compound stress. *Linguistic Inquiry* 24: 239–297.
Drubig, Hans Bernhard
    1994   Island Constraints and the Syntactic Nature of Focus and Association with Focus. *Arbeitspapiere des Sonderforschungsbereichs* 340: 51. Heidelberg: Wissenschaftliches Zentrum der IBM Deutschland.
É. Kiss, Katalin
    1998   Identificational focus versus information focus. *Language* 74: 245–273.
Erades, Peter A.
    1962   Points of modern English syntax. *English Studies* 43: 136–141.
Féry, Caroline and Vieri Samek-Lodovici
    2007   Focus projection and prosodic prominence in nested foci. *Language* 82(1): 131–150.
Göbbel, Edward
    2007   Extraposition as PF movement. In *Proceedings of the Thirty-Fourth Western Conference on Linguistics 2006:* 17, Erin Bainbridge and Brian Agbayani (eds.), 132–145. Fresno: California State University, Fresno.
Gundel, Jeanette K.
    1974   The role of topic and comment in linguistic theory. Ph.D. dissertation, University of Texas.
Gut, Ulrike
    2009   *Non-Native Speech. A Corpus-Based Analysis of Phonological and Phonetic Properties of L2 English and German.* Frankfurt: Peter Lang.
Halliday, Michael Alexander Kirkwood
    1967   Notes on transitivity and theme in English, part 2. *Journal of Linguistics* 3: 199–244.
Hamblin, Charles Leonard
    1973   Questions in Montague English. *Foundations of Language* 10: 41–53.
Hankamer, Jorge and Ivan Sag
    1976   Deep and surface anaphora. *Linguistic Inquiry* 7(3): 391–428.
Hardt, Daniel
    1990   A corpus-based survey of VP ellipsis. Ms., University of Pennsylvania.
Höhle, Tilmann N.
    1982   Explikation für 'normale Betonung' und 'normale' Wortstellung. In *Satzglieder im Deutschen. Vorschläge zu ihrer syntaktischen, semantischen und pragmatischen Fundierung,* Werner Abraham (ed.), 75–153. Tübingen: Narr.

Huber, Stefan
  2002   *Es*-Clefts und *det*-Clefts: Zur Syntax, Semantik und Informations-
          struktur von Spaltsätzen im Deutschen und Schwedischen. Ph.D.
          dissertation, University of Lund.
Jackendoff, Ray S.
  1972   *Semantic Interpretation in Generative Grammar. Studies in Linguis-
          tics 2*. Cambridge, MA: Massachusetts Institute of Technology Press.
Jacobs, Joachim
  1991   Focus ambiguities. *Journal of Semantics* 8: 1–36.
Jacobs, Joachim
  1993   Integration. In *Wortstellung und Informationsstruktur*, Marga Reis
          (ed.), 64–116. Tübingen: Niemeyer.
Jespersen, Otto
  1961   *A Modern English Grammar on Historical Principles. Part VII,
          Syntax*. London: Allen and Unwin.
Konietzko, Andreas and Susanne Winkler
  2010   Contrastive ellipsis: Mapping between syntax and information struc-
          ture. *Lingua* 120: 1436–1457.
König, Ekkehart
  1991   *The Meaning of Focus Particles: A Comparative Perspective*.
          London: Routledge.
Krifka, Manfred
  1999   Additive particles under stress. In *Proceedings of Semantics and
          Linguistic Theory 8*, Devon Strolovitch and Aaron Lawson (eds.),
          111–128. Cornell University: Chicago Linguistic Society Publications.
Kuno, Susumu
  1972   Functional sentence perspective. *Linguistic Inquiry* 3: 269–320.
Kuno, Susumu
  1982   The focus of the question and the focus of the answer. In *Papers from
          the Parasession on Nondeclaratives, Chicago Linguistic Society,
          April 17th, 1982*, Robinson Schneider, Kevin Tuite and Robert
          Chametzky (eds.), 134–157. Chicago: Chicago Linguistic Society.
Lambrecht, Knud
  1994   *Information Structure and Sentence Form*. (Cambridge Studies in
          Linguistics 71). Cambridge: Cambridge University Press.
Möck, Juliane
  1994   Extraposition aus der NP im Englischen. *Arbeitspapiere des
          Sonderforschungsbereichs* 340: 1–83.
Molnár, Valeria and Susanne Winkler
  2010   Edges and gaps: Contrast at the interfaces. *Lingua* 120: 1392–1415.
Musan, Renate
  2002   Informationsstrukturelle Dimensionen im Deutschen. *Zeitschrift für
          Germanistische Linguistik* 30: 198–221.

Musan, Renate
    2010   *Informationsstruktur.* Heidelberg: Universitätsverlag Winter.
Prince, Ellen F.
    1978   A comparison of Wh-Clefts and it-Clefts in Discourse. *Language* 54:
              883–906.
Reinhart, Tanya
    1982   *Pragmatics and Linguistics: An Analysis of Sentence Topics.* Bloom-
              ington, Indiana: Indiana University Linguistics Club.
Rochemont, Michael S.
    1986   *Focus in Generative Grammar. Studies in Generative Linguistic
              Analysis 4.* Amsterdam: John Benjamins.
Rochemont, Michael S.
    2009   Out of the blue – discourse new and contrastive focus. Paper given
              at the Syntactic Constructions, Focus and Meaning Workshop at the
              University of Tübingen, July 24th, 2009.
Rochemont, Michael S. and Peter W. Culicover
    1990   *English Focus Constructions and the Theory of Grammar.* Cam-
              bridge, MA: Cambridge University Press.
Rooth, Mats E.
    1992   A theory of focus interpretation. *Natural Language Semantics* 1:
              75–116.
Schwarzschild, Roger
    1999   GIVENness, avoidF and other constraints on the placement of accent.
              Natural Language Semantics 7: 141–177.
Selkirk, Elisabeth O.
    1984   *Phonology and Syntax. Current Studies in Linguistics 10.* Cam-
              bridge, MA: Massachusetts Institute of Technology Press.
Selkirk, Elisabeth O.
    1995   Sentence prosody: Intonation, stress, and phrasing. In *The Hand-
              book of Phonological Theory*, John A. Goldsmith (ed.), 550–569.
              Cambridge, MA: Blackwell.
Umbach, Carla
    2005   Contrast and information structure: A focus-based analysis of *but.*
              Linguistics 43: 207–232.
Vallduví, Enrique
    1992   *The Informational Component.* New York: Garland.
Winkler, Susanne
    2005   *Ellipsis and Focus in Generative Grammar.* (Studies in *Generative
              Grammar 81*). Berlin/New York: Mouton de Gruyter.

The information structure of French[1]

Wolfgang Klein

La violence, si tu te tais, elle te tue.[2]
Metro sign

1. Introduction

French, the native language of about 80 million speakers and a medium of daily communication for another 200 million speakers, belongs with Portuguese, Spanish and Italian to the Western group of Romance languages. Three centuries of erudite research on its grammatical and lexical rules, a rigid educational policy which does not appreciate deviations from these rules, and a limited tolerance on the part of those who have managed to master them towards those who are less fortunate in that regard have made it one of the most extensively studied and best-codified languages of the world. In spite of that fact, it is not easy to outline the principles of French information structure for at least three reasons:

(a) Like that well-known small village of indomitable Gauls which once held out against the rigid Roman rule, a growing number of people on the street have managed to escape the rigid rules of grammarians and speak versions of French that are not found in the books. As a result, there are now at least two major versions of French, for which no generally accepted labels exist; some simply call them "French" and "bad French"; the most common terms, however, are "Français standard" and "Français parlé". Français standard is what is taught in school – to French kids as well as to foreigners learning French as a second language. It is the language of literature, newspapers, and scholarly works – basically of whatever is written. But it is not just a written language – it is also the spoken language of the educated in formal contexts. So, the opposing term "Français parlé (spoken French)" is a misnomer: It is the kind of French that people on the street

---

[1] I wish to thank Christine Dimroth, Renate Musan, Daniel Véronique and Jürgen Weissenborn for most helpful comments. As this might not be apparent in the text, since my views are somewhat different, I should also point out here how much I owe to the work of Lambrecht (1994) and de Cat (2007)

[2] Violence kills you, if you remain silent, lit: the violence, if you you be-silent, it you kills.

speak in informal contexts, not spoken French in general. The precise conditions of use are difficult to determine and not relevant here. As for the structural differences, they are difficult to determine, too, partly because there is still little systematic work on the properties of "Français parlé"[3], and partly because "Français parlé" is not so much a stable and uniform linguistic system as it is a group of varieties with a number of typical features. In what follows, I shall sum up these variants of French under the label "français avancé (FA)" (literally: advanced French) and contrast it to "français traditionel (FT)" (traditional French) – the French you learn in the classroom, read in books, and hear in formal contexts. These terms are not meant to express an evaluation – they just relate to the historical development, may it be seen as decay or as progress.

(b) The established analysis of FT is strongly based on the model of Latin, the language from which it evolved. Considerable weight is given to the inflection of irregular verbs in their written form or to the idiosyncratic conditions under which the subjunctive is used in subordinate clauses. But there is, for example, hardly anything on the way in which information structure is marked by word order or intonation. In the authoritative grammar of Grevisse (15th ed.), just four out of about 1600 pages are devoted to this issue under the label "la mise en relief" (highlighting).

(c) While the description of FT is based on the model of Latin, the description of FA in turn is usually based on the model of FT. Thus, FA is more or less perceived as a deviation from good French, rather than as something with its own inherent systematicities. Such a perspective, while perfectly understandable for historical reasons, is not favorable to a real understanding of how, for example, the flow of information is organized in everyday interaction.

In view of these problems, on the one hand, and the notorious conceptual problems with information structure that make it very difficult to integrate the findings and accounts of different researchers, on the other, any attempt at giving a consistent picture of French information structure would be presumptuous. In the following, I will therefore not try to be comprehensive but rather concentrate on a few central findings and observations and ignore many details and exceptions. This also applies to what is said about French grammar in general, which, as mentioned above, lies in the shadows

---

[3]   See, for example, Gadet (1989), Andersen and Hansen (2000), Blanche-Benveniste (2005), Detey et al. (2009). The University of Leuven hosts a large corpus of spoken French (http://bach.arts.kuleuven.be/elicop).

of a long, impressive, but also biased and thus misguiding tradition. Here, I will not simply recapitulate the received picture, but try to look at French as it might be represented in the head of an intelligent six-year old, who has not yet been under the influence of the written language as taught in the classroom.

2. Some characteristic features of French grammar

Among all Romance languages, French is probably the one that is most remote from their common ancestor Latin, a language with a sumptuous inflectional morphology and a very free word order. This distance is largely due to massive sound changes, and the very different phonological shape of the words resulting from them. But there have also been substantial developments in morphosyntax, some of which will be illustrated now.

2.1. Inflection

In Latin, nouns, adjectives and verbs are abundantly inflected for case, number, gender, tense, mood, and person. In French, inflectional morphology is radically reduced. The amount of this reduction is often hidden by the conservative orthography of French, which preserves many traits of older developmental stages. We will briefly illustrate this for the regular forms of verbs, nouns and adjectives in written French and spoken French[4]:

'I love'	*amo*	*j(e)'aime*	[ʒ ɛm]
'you love'	*amas*	*tu aimes*	[ty ɛm]
'he loves'	*amat*	*il aime*	[il ɛm]
'we love'	*amamus*	*nous aimons*	[nuz ɛmõ] (FA: [òn ɛm])
'you love'	*amatis*	*vous aimez*	[vuz ɛme]
'they love'	*amant*	*ils aiment*	[ilz ɛm]

Whereas in English, all forms except for the third person singular are identical, spoken French uses the same forms except for the second person plural in FA and the first and second person plural in spoken FT. In other

---

4   About 90 % of French verbs, including all new ones, follow the pattern of *aimer*, as illustrated above. There is a second class (type *saisir*), which is also considered to be regular, but it is much more limited and no longer productive, and there are about 500 irregular verbs.

verb paradigms, this reduction is somewhat less strong, but still much stronger than in Spanish, Portuguese, or Italian. We note a similar reduction in the nominal paradigms, here illustrated for the word 'father":

NOM.SG.	*pater*	*le père*	[lə pɛr]
GEN.SG.	*patris*	*du père*	[dy pɛr]
DAT.SG.	*patri*	*au père*	[o pɛr]
ACC.SG.	*patrem*	*le père*	[lə pɛr]
NOM.PL.	*patres*	*les pères*	[le pɛr]
GEN.PL.	*patrum*	*des pères*	[de pɛr]
DAT.PL.	*patribus*	*aux pères*	[o pɛr]
ACC.PL.	*patres*	*les pères*	[le pɛr]

Turning finally to adjectives, the only category which is regularly marked by inflection is number, and this only in the written language: *rouge – rouges* ('red'). There are, however, a number of irregular adjectives which preserve gender marking in the written as well as in the spoken form: *grand – grande* ('big').

In other words, there is hardly any inflectional case marking nor – a few exceptions aside – inflectional number or gender marking in spoken French; the orthography, though, preserves remnants of this marking. This reduction is balanced by another development, also visible in the examples above.

2.2. Phrase-initial grammatical elements

In French, grammatical functions tend to be marked at the beginning of a phrase. Latin has neither obligatory subject pronouns nor obligatory determiners. French has developed them and uses them very systematically. One might even argue that elements such as *je, tu, il, on, le, les,* etc are not really pronouns but a sort of word-initial or phrase-initial prefixes. This view may be an exaggeration (see de Cat 2007: 9–26, for a useful discussion of the arguments in the verbal domain), but the development has clearly been moving in this direction. We may sum this up in a simple maxim:

(1)   French is moving from head-final to phrase-initial marking of gram-
       matical functions.

This development is neither complete nor exceptionless; but it goes much beyond what traditional orthography suggests.

2.3. Word order

Latin is generally known for its relatively free word order; moreover, grammatical relations are often non-local: Adjectives, genitive attributes or several parts of verb complexes can easily be detached from the elements to which they belong. Aside from the complex inflection of Latin, it is these two features which we hated so much in school. French is generally assumed to have a much more rigid word order, and non-local relations are avoided – two core ingredients of what is referred to as 'la clarté de la langue française' (the clarity of the French language). If you have learned French in school, and you want to say that Jean likes apples, and you remember that the generic use is often expressed with a definite article in French, then you would probably say (here and in what follows, I tried to make the glosses as simple as possible; for reasons of space, they are sometimes placed after rather than under the French sentence):

(2)   *Jean aime les pommes.*   'John likes (the) apples.'

But as Trévise (1986: 187/188) puts it: "this canonical ordering is in fact rarely found in everyday spoken French (and indeed looks like an example made up by a linguist)." Instead, people would use one of the following constructions (adapted from Trévise):

(3)   *Jean il aime les pommes.*   'John he likes (the) apples.'
(4)   *Il aime les pommes Jean.*   'He likes (the) apples John.'
(5)   *Jean il les aime les pommes.*   'John he them likes (the) apples.'
(6)   *Jean les pommes il les aime.*   'John (the) apples he them likes.'
(7)   *Jean les pommes il aime.*   'John (the) apples he likes.'
(8)   *Jean les pommes il aime ça.*   'John (the) apples he likes that.'
(9)   *Jean il aime ça les pommes.*   'John he likes that (the) apples.'
(10)   *Il les aime les pommes Jean.*   'He them likes (the) apples John.'
(11)   *Il aime ça les pommes Jean.*   'He likes that (the) apples John.'
(12)   *Il aime ça Jean les pommes.*   'He likes that John (the) apples.'
(13)   *Il les aime Jean les pommes.*   'He them likes John (the) apples.'
(14)   *Les pommes il les aime Jean.*   '(The) apples he them likes John.'
(15)   *Les pommes il aime ça Jean.*   '(The) apples he likes that John.'
(16)   *Les pommes il aime ça Jean*   '(The apples) he likes that John
       les pommes.   the apples.'
(17)   *Les pommes ça il aime Jean.*   '(The) apples that he likes John.'
(18)   *Les pommes il aime ça les*   '(The) apples he likes that the
       pommes Jean.   apples John.'

(19) *Les pommes il les aime Jean les pommes.*	'(The) apples he them likes John the apples.'
(20) *Les pommes Jean il aime ça.*	'(The) apples John he likes that.'
(21) *Les pommes Jean il les aime.*	'(The) apples John he them likes.'
(22) *Les pommes ça Jean il aime.*	'(The apples) that John he likes.'
(23) *Les pommes ça Jean il les aime.*	'(The) apples that John he them likes.'
(24) *Les pommes Jean il aime.*	'(The) apples John he likes.'
(25) *Ya Jean il aime les pommes.*	'There-is John he likes (the) apples.'
(26) *Ya Jean il les aime les pommes.*	'There-is John he them likes (the) apples.'
(27) *Ya Jean les pommes il les aime.*	'There-is John (the) apples he likes them.'
(28) *Ya Jean il aime ça les pommes.*	'There-is John he likes that (the) apples.'
(29) *Ya Jean les pommes ça il aime.*	'There-is John (the apples) that he likes.'
(30) *Ya Jean les pommes il aime ça.*	'There-is John (the) apples he likes that.'

And so on. Out of context, some of these constructions sound odd at first. None of them but (2) would be tolerated in FT. But all of them – except perhaps (2) – are regularly found in everyday interaction at the market or in the métro – and not in the sense of a repair or a correction. In other words, an unbiased look at FA suggests a very different picture of how sentences are structured in French.

This variability of word order does not seem to apply to FT. But note that even in FT, it is not clear whether the 'basic word order' is Subject-Verb-Object or Subject-Object-Verb. This depends on whether the direct object is a lexical noun (including names) or a personal pronoun:

(31)   a. *Jean aime ses enfants.* 'John loves his children'.
       b. *Jean les aime.* 'John them loves'.

This remarkable flexibility and its interaction with a few other devices is crucial to the way in which the flow of information is organized in French.

3.   Means to mark information structure

The marking of information structure is usually based on a complex interplay of a few devices, four of which are of particular importance and found in many languages; French is no exception.

3.1. Choice of NP type

In French, as in all languages, one and the same entity can be described by different types of noun phrases, such as *une femme – la femme – Marie – celle-ci – elle – 0* 'a woman – the woman – Marie – that one – she – 0'. The choice between these NP types is often connected to the distinction between 'given' (or 'maintained') vs. 'new' information. This is not false but it misses a crucial point: in the first place, these items differ in the amount of descriptive information which they carry.[5] Thus, they provide the speaker with different possibilities to adapt the utterance to the context. If some entity is available in the context and is salient, not much descriptive information is needed to make it identifiable. French is quite similar to English in this regard, with two noteworthy exceptions:

(a) There is a systematic difference between 'weak' and 'strong' personal pronouns: *je – moi*, 'I', *il – lui* 'he', etc. Only the latter allow for a contrastive usage and can be stressed.
(b) There are differences in the marking of definite and indefinite NPs. With the exception of names, it is normally not possible to use a bare NP in French: **(La) vie est dure – Life is hard, On a mange *(des) pommes de terre – we had potatoes.*

This latter difference is a repercussion of Maxim (1) stated above: French shows a preference for phrase-initial grammatical marking.

3.2. Word order

As was already shown in Section 2.3, word order in FT has always been considered to be relatively fixed, whereas we find substantial variation in word order in FA. This discussion shall not be repeated here, but I will simply add one important point. The relative freedom of word order in FA does not include 'weak elements', in particular personal pronouns and a few particles, such as *y, en, ne*, which must be placed in front of the verb, and this in a fixed order. This will be crucial for the analysis suggested in Sections 6 and 7 below.

---

[5] Note that this is also true for proper names: the descriptive content of *Marie* is the property to be called *Marie*.

3.3. Constructions

Many languages use special constructions in order to indicate a particular information status. Such constructions are very frequent in FA and, albeit to a lesser extent, also in FT. The main types are (for additional possibilities, see examples (2)–(30)):

(a) Left and right dislocations, such as

(32)	a.	*La pomme, elle est rouge.*	'The apple, it is red.'
	b.	*La pomme, je l'ai mangée.*	'The apple, I it have eaten.'

(33)	a.	*Elle est rouge, la pomme.*	'It is red, the apple.'
	b.	*Je l'ai mangée, la pomme.*	'I it have eaten, the apple.'

(b) Cleft constructions, such as:

(34)	a.	*C'est la pomme qui est rouge.*	'It is the apple that is red.'
	b.	*C'est la pomme que j'ai mangée.*	'It is the apple that I have eaten.'

(c) Presentationals, which come in two variants – with *il y a* or with *avoir*:

(35)	a.	*Il y a une jeune fille qui m'a téléfoné.*	'A GIRL called me.'
	b.	*J'ai ma voiture qui est en panne.*	'My CAR is broken'.

In FA, the first of these often shows up in a form, in which the historical *il y a* is reduced to a sort of particle *ya* and the original relative pronoun *qui* (or *que*) does not appear any more (cf. (25) – (30) in Section 2).

3.4. Intonation

In many languages, intonation is the main tool to indicate a particular information structure – as long as this language is spoken.[6] As Hermann Paul first illustrated (cf. the introduction to this volume), the answers to the following four questions differ saliently in their intonation, whereas the segmental structure is the same:

---

[6] It is a non-trivial question whether one should also assume that written utterances carry intonation. Surely, it is normally not noted down, except occasionally by bold type or similar means. But this does not preclude that the reader mentally reconstructs an intonational pattern, just as a reader is able to reconstruct vowels in a writing system which does not note vowels (see also Müller et al. 2006).

(36) a. *Wer fährt morgen nach Berlin? – PETER fährt morgen nach Berlin.*
       'Who goes tomorrow to Berlin? – Peter goes tomorrow to Berlin.'

   b. *Wann fährt Peter nach Berlin? – Peter fährt MORGEN nach Berlin.*
      'When goes Peter to Berlin?   – Peter goes tomorrow to Berlin.'

   c. *Wohin fährt Peter morgen?   – Peter fährt morgen nach BERLIN.*
      'Where goes Peter tomorrow?   – Peter goes tomorrow to Berlin.'

   d. *Was macht Peter morgen?   – Peter FÄHRT MORGEN NACH BERLIN.*
      'What does Peter tomorrow?   – Peter goes tomorrow to Berlin.'

Roughly speaking, elements which are already found in the question are de-stressed, and elements which correspond to the wh-word are felt to be highlighted (roughly indicated by capital letters). In actual fact, the situation is much more complicated; it is arguable, for example, whether the word *morgen* in (36d) is de-stressed or, as indicated above, highlighted). But the general idea is clear: the element which corresponds to the wh-element forms the 'focus' of the answer and is marked by a pitch-accent.

In French, opinions are at variance as to whether there is such a pitch-accent that would suffice to mark focus status. Lambrecht (1994: 22, see also 230), for example, states: 'In spoken French, a canonical sentence such as *Ma voiture est en panne*, with the accented NP in preverbal position, would be unacceptable, because [it is] prosodically ill-formed.' The relevant constituent may well be highlighted, but this does not suffice: Another construction must be used in addition, typically a cleft:

(37) a. *Qui va a Berlin demain? – ?Jean va a Berlin demain.*
   b. *Qui va a Berlin demain? – C'est Jean qui va a Berlin demain.*

On the other hand, Fery (2004) showed in a set of experiments, that in simple question-answer settings, French speakers indeed use intonational highlighting to indicate the 'focused' constituent; this is not done by using bare pitch accents, however, but by using a combination of various prosodic parameters. It is also beyond doubt that the question in (37) could be answered with the NP *Jean* alone; but it does not make much sense to say that an isolated constituent bears a pitch accent. There has not been much comparable work on this issue thus far, so, it remains unsettled.[7] Most

---

[7] It is interesting, though, that French does not seem to have a "verum focus", i.e., intonational highlighting of the carrier of finiteness, as in English *John HAS arrived* or German *Hans IST angekommen*. In order to highlight the assertive

research on the role of prosody for information structure in French does not explicitly address this issue but rather investigates the prosodic properties of particular constructions, for example dislocations or clefts. In what follows, the intonation shall therefore not be examined in isolation but it is embedded within the discussion of these constructions.

We shall now have a closer look at these four types of devices, taking two salient constructions as a starting point – dislocations, which are considered to be the main device that indicates topic status, and cleft constructions, which are considered to be the main device that indicates focus status.[8]

4. Dislocations

Dislocations are constructions which occur at the left or at the right periphery of a clause and which are somehow felt to be detached from its core part. In spoken FA, they are very common. Examples were already given in (2)–(30) above; here are a few others which illustrate the range (examples are given in standard orthography; the comma is used to indicate the detachment):

(38) a. *Jean, il est malade.*
  'Jean, he is ill.'

  b. *Il est malade, Jean.*
  'He is ill, Jean.'

(39) a. *Paul, je le déteste.*
  'Paul, I him hate.'

  b. *Je le déteste, Paul.*
  'I him hate, Paul.'

(40) a. *A Paul, je lui ai donné le livre.*
  'To Paul, I him have given the book.'

  b. *Je lui ai donné le livre, a Paul.*
  'I to-him have given the boom, to Paul.'

(41) a. *Marie, Jean, elle l'aime.*
  'Marie, Jean, she him loves.'

  b. *Elle l'aime, Marie, Jean.*
  'She him loves, Marie, Jean.'

---

function, encoded by this element, French would have to use other means, for example a particle such as *Jean est bien arrivé*, with an accent on that particle (see Turco et al. (submitted), for a careful investigation).

[8] Much to my regret, presentationals, like (25–30 or 35a,b) – which are actually quite frequent in FA – had to be sacrificed for reasons of space. See, for example, Giacomi and Véronique (1982), Morel (1992), Lambrecht (1994: 143–146), Gast and Haas (2011) offer a comparative analysis, which also includes FT.

(42) a. *A Aix, j'y était tres heureux.*   b. *J'y étais tres heureux, a Aix.*
'At Aix, I there was very happy.'   'I there was very happy, at Aix.'

(43) a. *De sa divorce, il en parle.*   b. *Il en parle souvent, de sa*
souvent   *divorce.*
'Of his divorce, he of-it speaks   'He of-it speaks, often, of his
often.'   divorce.'

(44) a. *Boire, c'est pas la bonne*   b. *C'est pas la bonne solution,*
solution.   *boire.*
'To drink, that is not the right   'That is not the right solution,
solution.'   to drink.'

In FT, these constructions are exceptions. In FA, they abound. This may be due to the fact that FA has developed further structurally or to the fact that FT is normally investigated in its written form, and that the information flow is different in spoken interaction. I am not aware of any systematic work on the grammatical peculiarities of spoken FT, in contrast to written FT, which would allow us to decide on this. In the following, the main formal and functional properties of dislocations will be outlined.

Formal properties

(a) Dislocations are syntactically optional: when omitted, the remainder – the 'core' of the clause, as I shall call it – is still a grammatical sentence. So, their use reflects a free decision on the part of the speaker as to how much information is provided about the NP referent or whatever else is described by the dislocation.

(b) A dislocation is matched by a weak element in its core; this may be a clitic pronoun such as *je, il, le*, a clitic demonstrative, *ce* or *ça*, or a clitic particle such as *y* ('there, at-it') or *en* ('of it, from it, from there'). Such a weak element provides no or only minimal descriptive content and relates to the same entity as does the matching dislocation.

(c) They are perceived to be 'detached' in some way from the core. This need not be due to a pause; normally, intonation marks a break, a point to which I will come below.

(d) Various types of constituents can be used as dislocations. In the most common cases, these are lexical noun phrases, names, prepositional phrases, or stressed personal pronouns. As shown in (44a), other constituents – here an infinitive – are also possible; in these cases, the matching clitic is normally the demonstrative *ce* or *ça*.

(e) A dislocation must be definite, if the clitic is definite. Thus, (45a) is not possible, whereas (45b) is:

(45) a. **Un homme, il était dans la chambre.* 'A man, he was in the room.'
      b. *Des pommes, j'en prends.*   'Apples, I take some.'

Note, however, that 'generic indefinites' can be dislocated, as in examples such as *Les pommes, Jean les aime* or *Jean les aime, les pommes*. In fact, it is arguable whether these are definite or indefinite, because what is meant here is 'the class of apples'.

So far, no difference has been made between left dislocations and right dislocations. These differ when it comes to intonation.

(f) Left as well as right dislocations have a salient intonational pattern. There are several studies (Rossi 1999, Beyssade et al. 2004, de Cat 2007, Meertens 2008), which diverge in their underlying frame of analysis, but largely converge on the facts which they have uncovered.

Left dislocations show a salient pitch rise towards the end of the constituent. As a rule, the peak of this rise has the highest pitch of the entire sentence. The core then begins low; it is probably this onset which is primarily responsible for the impression of detachment which comes with the dislocation.

Right dislocations show a much less salient intonational pattern. Normally, they echo the last part of the core, i.e., they show a weak rise if the whole sentence happens to be a question (with an intonational rise on the core), or a diminished fall, if the sentence is an assertion. Often, the contour as a whole is almost completely flat. It is much less clear what creates the impression of detachment in right dislocations. Sometimes, there is a pause, but this need not be the case.

Functional properties

Authors agree that dislocated constituents have topic status. This sounds clear, but there are two problems. The first problem is the notion of topic itself. Views on what constitutes a topic vary considerably (c.f. the discussion in the introductory chapter of this book), and therefore, analyses are less uniform than they may appear to be. As for French in particular, there are essentially two – not necessarily incompatible – theoretical lines of analysis. In his ground-breaking work on the information structure of spoken French, Knud Lambrecht (1981, 1986, 1994) adopts an 'aboutness definition' of topic-hood.[9] He carefully distinguishes between the pragmatic category 'topic' and the grammatical category 'topic expression', which are defined as follows (Lambrecht 1994: 131):

> Topic: A referent is interpreted as the topic of a proposition if in a given situation the proposition is construed as being about this referent, i.e., as expressing information which is relevant to and which increases the addressee's knowledge of this referent.

> Topic expression: A constituent is a topic expression if the proposition expressed by the clause with which it is associated is pragmatically construed as being about the referent of this constituent.

More recent analyses, in particular de Cat (2007) and Delais-Roussarie et al. (2004) have been conducted in the spirit of alternative semantics (see introductory chapter of this book). Under this approach, the topical parts of a clause provide background information, which identifies, or helps to identify, a number of alternatives, one of which is then specified by the focal part of the sentence.

Here, I will essentially follow this second view, because all aboutness analyses, while intuitively very appealing, run into an elementary problem. Consider the following the sentences:

(46) a. *Cain slew Abel.*
      b. *Abel was slain by Cain.*

There is wide agreement that in (46a), Cain is the topic, whereas in (46b), Abel is the topic. But in both cases, the proposition also provides information that is about the other referent and that increases the addressee's knowledge of this referent. So, aboutness applies to 'topical referents' as well as to 'non-topical referents'. I do not think, incidentally, that an aboutness definition of topic-hood is meaningless; but it is very difficult to make it so precise that it discriminates between what one feels is the topic and between other elements of a sentence.

---

[9] Note that in Lambrecht's approach, "topic" does not form a pair with "focus" or "comment". The notion of comment plays no role in his framework. Focus is defined as follows: "The semantic component of a pragmatically structured proposition whereby the assertion differs from the presupposition." (Lambrecht 1994: 213, see also 51–56). It is that part which leads to an update in the addressee's knowledge or convictions.

The second problem is the fact that there are many similarities between left dislocations and right dislocations, but also some salient differences. We already noted different intonation patterns. These are not accidental but coincide with differences in functional potential. Thus, left dislocations can be used contrastively:

(47)　*Jean, il est parti de bonne heure,*　　*et MaRIE, elle est restée.*
　　　'Jean, he has left early,　　　　　　and Marie, she has stayed.'

Right dislocations usually do not allow such a contrastive usage; (48) is distinctly odd:

(48)　*Il est parti de bonne heure, Jean,*　**et elle est restée, MaRIE.*
　　　'He has left early, Jean,　　　　　　and she has stayed, Marie.'

Right dislocations rather give the impression that something is already established, and that for one reason or the other, a bit more information about it is being added. They do not serve to introduce something as a topic, be it in contrast to some other topic or without such a contrast.

A correlate to this difference is the fact that left dislocations can be paraphrased by a *quant à*-construction ('*as for*-construction'), whereas this is not possible for right dislocations:

(49)　a.　*Quant à Jean, il est parti de bonne heure.*
　　　b.　**Il est parti de bonne heure, quant à Jean.*

Like *as for* in English, *quant à* is often used in FT to introduce a topic; such topics always have a contrastive flavor, although this contrast need not be as immediate as in (47), where the two opposing topics are in adjacent sentences.

So, assigning topic status to left dislocations as well as to right dislocations is perhaps not false; but this topic status is not the same in both cases. In a way, right dislocations give the impression that they go beyond notions such as topic, focus and the like. They do not mark anything as topic, nor do they mark anything as focus: they just provide additional information about something that has already been said – information that the speaker feels to be useful for the listener and for communicative success. I will come back to this important point in Section 6.2.

5. *C'est ... qui/que* constructions

In contrast to dislocations, constructions of this sort are regularly found in all varieties of French. Historically, they were derived from relative clauses (see Dufter 2008 for a careful study of their historical development):

(50) *C'est mon oncle qui a perdu le match.*
       'This-is my uncle who has lost the match.'.

Note that this structure can still function as a sentence with a normal relative clause. Thus, (50) has two readings, indicated by slightly different intonations, which can be paraphrased as follows:

(50)' a. *The person/entity that has lost the match is my uncle.*
      b. *This person/entity is my uncle that has lost the match.*

In the second reading, the weak element *c'* (= *ce*) picks up some entity that is contextually given, either because it was explicitly mentioned, or because it is somehow salient for other reasons. In the first reading, it is much less clear what *c'* refers to. In fact, one wonders whether a speaker of French, who is not influenced by the orthographical tradition, would decompose *c'est* into two separate parts at all. An intelligent six-year old, who has normally mastered this construction perfectly well, may well interpret it as a particle [sɛ], which is matched by another particle [ki] or [kə].

   Let us now take a closer look at the formal and functional properties of this construction.

Formal properties

(a) The general form is *c'est X qui/que Y*, where
–   X is an NP, a PP (including strong pronouns), an adverb, or even a full subordinate clause
–   X can be definite or indefinite
–   X can be an argument of the verb in the following clause (this is the most common case) or an adjunct of that clause
–   *qui/que Y is* a subordinate clause, where *qui* is used if it is the subject of this clause, and *que* otherwise.
–   Y is a clause of which X is an argument or an adjunct.

(b) Unlike in the case of dislocations, there is no matching element for X in the following clause, unless *qui/que* is considered as such. Note that this element does not always behave like a relative pronoun:

(51) a. *C'est vers midi qu'on est parti.*   'That-is around noon that we left.'
     b. *C'est à toi qu'on veut donner*   'That-is to you that we want to give
       le prix.   the award.'

(c) Although *est* ('is') is historically a finite verb, it is normally neither inflected for number nor for tense. In FT, there are occasional remnants of inflection:

(52) *C'était le Sire de Coussy qui a dit ça.*
     'That-was the Sire de Coussy who has said that.'

This gives some substance to the idea that an intelligent six-year old might just see *c'est* as a sort of particle which can precede an NP or a PP in initial position, before a very conventional writing system makes him believe that it is a construction with a finite verb.

(d) Unlike left dislocations, the *c'est...que/qui* construction does not have a defined intonational pattern. But there are some typical prosodic features which it exhibits: There is a rise, followed by a fall within the cleft, if the whole sentence is an assertion; the subordinate clause is more or less flat. If the entire sentence is a question, then there is no such fall in the cleft; the pitch remains more or less high until the end. Note, however, that there are many variants of this pattern (see Delais-Roussarie et al. 2004, Rossi 1999):

(53) *Jean est bien difficile, sans doute. Mais c'est à lui que je dois mon job.*
     'Jean is quite difficult, surely. But it is he to whom I owe my job'

Here, there may be a fall (after rise) in *à lui* with the remainder being flat. Otherwise, this assertive fall is only in *mon job*. This has different functional consequences, to which we will turn in a moment.

Functional properties

(a) Traditionally, *c'est X qui/que* is seen as a highlighting device ('mise-en-relief'). It indicates that something holds for X, in contrast to the possibility that it holds for something else. Thus, it seems to mark X as the focus of the utterance, in the sense of alternative semantics. This is in line with the fact that, when used in an answer to a wh-question, it corresponds to the wh-part:

(54) *Qui a obtenu le Prix Goncourt en 1913.* *– C'est Proust qui l'a obtenu en 1913.*

'Who got the Prix Goncourt in 1913.' – 'Marcel Proust got it in 1913.'

(55) *Qu'est ce que Proust a obtenu en 1913.* *– C'est le Prix Goncourt qu'il a obtenu en 1913.*

'What did Proust get in 1913.' – 'He got the Prix Goncourt in 1913.'

(56) *Quand a Proust obtenu le Prix Goncourt?* *– C'est en 1913 qu'il l'a obtenu.*

'When did Proust get the Prix Goncourt?' – 'He got it in 1913.'

In all of these cases, English, too, would allow a cleft construction ('It was Proust who ...'); but it would somehow sound marked; in French, the situation is rather the opposite – the cleft construction is quite normal, if not the unmarked case. Note, furthermore, that in all of these cases, the subordinate clause can be entirely omitted.

The idea that *c'est X qui/que* serves to isolate a constituent and to mark it as a focus is not without problems, though. I will come back to this in a moment, but let us first have a look at a different though related functional property.

(b) *C'est X qui/que* indicates that the entity, or entities, referred to by X is the only one which – within a given context – has the property assigned to it by the subordinate clause: X has this property, and no (contextually relevant) alternative to X has it. This is compatible with, but not required by, the notion of focus in alternative semantics: one element is selected from a set of alternatives, but this does not necessarily exclude the possibility that other elements from this set have the same property. The utterance *I want a beer* in answer to the question *Who wants a beer?* does not preclude that other people want a beer, as well (whereas the answer *It is me who wants a beer.* seems to suggest this). So, the *c'est X qui/que* construction does not just indicate focus but a 'contrastive focus' – the relevant property applies to X and to nothing else (within a given context).

Note, however, that in many languages, including French, there are at least two other devices which indicate uniqueness. These are restrictive focus particles like *only*, on the one hand, and definiteness marking, (at least under a uniqueness analysis of definiteness, such as Russell's), on the other. For ease of exposition, I use English examples; French is the same in that regard:

(57) a. *The queen came in.*
      b. *Only the queen came in.*
      c. *It was the queen who came in.*

Whereas (57a) does not really compete, since the uniqueness condition is within the NP (the only entity which, in this context, has the property of being a queen), both (57b) and (57c) are unique with respect to the NP-external property, i.e., the property of coming in on that occasion. Hence, double uniqueness should be redundant. But the addition of *only* is perfectly functional, for example in order to correct an earlier assumption according to which the queen and her beloved spouse came in:

(58) *It was only the queen who came in.*

Note, moreover, that if the relevant property is such that only one entity can have it, we get a clear contrast:

(59) a. *It was the queen who died first.*
      b. **Only the queen died first.*
      c. **It was only the queen who died first.*

If *c'est X qui/que Y* indeed meant 'X, and nothing else but X, has property Y', as is assumed in the literature, then (59a) should be as odd as (59b) and (59c); but it is not. So, if there is a uniqueness effect beyond the bare focus function, it must be of a different sort. There has been no satisfactory analysis of this problem so far.

Let us now come to a problem which is not related to uniqueness but to the focus status of the *c'est X qui/que* construction. It occurs with the varying prosodic patterns in sentences like (53), repeated here:

(53) *Jean est bien difficile, sans doute.   Mais c'est à lui que je dois mon job.*
      'Jean is quite difficult, surely.   But it is to him that I owe my job.'

As was said above, there can be a fall (after an initial rise) at the end of the cleft, with the remainder being more or less flat, or this fall can be deferred to the end of the entire sentence, i.e., in *mon job*. In both cases, the focus should be *à lui*. But how should one then analyze the remainder – does it provide mere background? This may be tenable with the first intonational pattern, in which *que je dois mon job* is low and flat. But note that even with this pattern, it need not express background information: The addressee might not know at all that the speaker has a job. And this analysis is completely implausible for the second intonational pattern, in which the final fall is in *mon job*; this looks suspiciously like typical focus marking with a pitch accent, whereas the rise in or towards *à lui* rather seems to indicate a contrastive topic marking. If this is true, the entire idea of *c'est X qui/que* being a focus marker completely breaks down. So, one must either give up that idea, or one must give up the usual mapping between the intonational marking of contrastive topic and intonational marking of (contrastive or non-contrastive) focus. I do not see how this problem can be solved within current frameworks of information structure.

This concludes our survey of the most characteristic information structural constructions in French and their main properties. In the next section, an attempt is made to integrate these observations into an incipient picture of French information structure. I shall also include the speaker's options to encode varying amounts of descriptive information by choosing a particular type of NP.

6. A tentative synthesis

The following picture deviates in some respects from the received way of looking at French grammar. I will first sketch what I believe to be the 'core version' of a French clause, and then look at various elaborations, which reflect different ways of how the flow of information is organized.[10]

6.1. The structural core

In general, a full sentence requires that the argument slots provided by the lexical verb (or the verb cluster) must be filled appropriately. In French, as in most languages, it is also necessary that the verb be made finite; this aspect will not be examined here.[11] French – unlike Latin, for instance – does not

---

[10] The distinction between a structural core and various lexical expansions, as made in the following, is a barely structural one; it is not meant to reflect the time course of language production (let alone language comprehension). I am not aware of any psycholinguistic work in that respect.

[11] As I have argued elsewhere (Klein 2006, 2010), I believe that finiteness is not just an inflectional category of the verb but in many ways fundamental to the syntactic and the semantic organization of sentences; but a discussion of these aspects would lead us too far away here.

like phonologically empty arguments in finite clauses. Hence, the minimal pattern of a structurally complete French sentence is something like this[12]:

(60) a. *J'y travaille.*
          'I here work.'

      b. *Tu les as aimées.*
          'You them have loved.'

      c. *Elle le lui a donné.*
          'She it to-him/her has given.'

      d. *J'en parle.*
          'I about-it speak.'

      e. *Ça me plaît.*
          'That to-me pleases.'

In other words, a minimal sentence in French consists of

(a) A string of weak elements; these are elements which carry minimal descriptive content and which cannot be used contrastively (two points which, incidentally, are closely related)[13]; the order of these elements is rigidly fixed.
(b) A finite verb. The finite and lexical components of the verb can be split (as in *a donné*), in which case the finite element comes first. In this case, too, the lexical component belongs to the core, because it is that component which defines the argument slots.

The string of weak elements precedes the finite part of the verb (there are some exceptions, if the non-finite part is compound, again not to be discussed here).

Such a sequence of weak elements and the finite verb will be called here a 'core sentence' or briefly a 'core'. It contains everything that is structurally necessary; but its descriptive information is highly restricted;

---

[12] In the interest of clarity, a number of minor complications are ignored in the following. I also do not discuss the possibility of phonologically empty material, in particular ellipsis, which allows further reduction of what is made explicit in a sentence.

[13] In general, expressions can only be intonationally contrasted if they express some content that can be related to some other content (except in metalinguistic usage, where everything can be contrasted and in which, as it were, the form is the content).

essentially, only the verb carries more than bare grammatical information. The core can be now enriched in various ways:

A. The verb can be expanded into a more complex verb cluster, an aspect which is not considered here.
B. Non-clitic NPs or PPs can be used, thus providing more descriptive content.
C. Adverbials and various particles can be added. In FT, one of these, the negation particle *ne*, can intrude into the weak string; it is quite characteristic of the overall structural development of French that this has been given up in its 'advanced' versions.[14]

Since the information flow in discourse is systematically based on the interplay of information which comes from the context, on the one hand, and information which is explicitly expressed by the sentence, on the other, these possibilities to enrich the structural core by adding more lexical information are crucial to information structure. So, if we want to understand how French works in that regard, two questions must be addressed:

– What is the information structure of the core?
– How do elements with more descriptive information go beyond this structure?

These questions will now be discussed in turn.

6.2. The information structure of the core

This issue has never been investigated, so, we must be a bit speculative here. Two things are clear in a core such as, for example, (60c):

(a) It makes an assertion, and
(b) The situation about which something is asserted must be clear from the context.

---

[14] In FT, the usual negation of (60b) is: *Je ne les ai pas aimées*. Thus, the finite part of the verb is "framed" by two negative elements. In FA, only the second of these survived. In other word, the "weak string" is now completely opaque for other elements. It is still possible to insert elements into the core; these, however, cannot precede the finite element. So, the weak string and the finiteness marking form a unit that is structurally locked.

The first point is indicated by the form of the sentence. The second point is less obvious; but it becomes immediately clear if one is supposed to say whether *Elle le lui a donné*, uttered by someone here and now, is true or false. This question cannot be answered unless one knows *what situation the claim is about*. This information is often provided by the (verbal or non-verbal) context, as in (61):

(61) *Est-ce que Marie a donné l'ordinateur a son père? – Elle le lui a donné.*
'Is-it that Marie has given the computer to her father? – She it to-him has given.'

What is the topic and what is the focus in *Elle le lui a donné*? To my mind, there is no single constituent which could figure as a topic, in the sense that the sentence is specifically 'about this entity', or that this, and only this, constituent provides background information. What the sentence is about, is equally described by *elle, le,* and *lui*: It is about a situation which involves three arguments of this sort in the roles of subject, direct object and indirect object, respectively; it is also said by the temporal marking on the verb that this situation, and thus the time talked about ('the topic time'), is in the past. The only open issue is whether this situation has the property described by *donner* or rather the property described by *pas donner*.[15] And the answer asserts that it is the former – the situation specified by the question has the property *prêter* in relation to the various arguments in the weak string. Hence, the information structure of the core has two components:

(62)   a. It picks up a situation with a particular configuration between the referents of the 'weak string'.
       b. It asserts that the property specified by the verb applies to this situation.

This is, so to speak, the root of French information structure: There is a component which picks up the situation talked about, and there is a component which adds a descriptive property to the already identified situation. The first of these components deviates from established notions of 'topic'. It does not provide background information, nor does it relate to a

---

[15] The lexical content of the compound expression *pas donner* is very general – it is the property "being different from *donner*". Note that one could vary (61) to: *Est-ce Marie a donné ou est-ce qu'elle a prêté l'ordinateur a son père?* ("Has Marie given or has she lent the computer to her father?"). In this case, a more restricted alternative to *donner* is specified as to be settled by the answer.

distinguished referent, for example the grammatical subject; rather, it helps to identify the situation talked about – the 'topic situation', as one may call it.[16] The second component, on the other hand, does indeed come very close to the notion of focus in alternative semantics, but also comes close to the notion of focus in the sense in which Lambrecht uses it: it reflects a choice between various alternatives which are up for decision, and it corresponds to the part of the sentence which is relevant for the update of the address-ee's knowledge.

6.3. Expanding the core

The core is structurally complete, and often, it suffices for communicative purposes. But it requires a rich context, in which the situation talked about and the protagonists which play a role in it are sufficiently clear. Often, however, the speaker feels the need to provide more lexical information. This then leads to what has traditionally been seen as a 'typical' sentence – a sentence with full lexical NPs and perhaps other elements with descriptive content. Such expansions beyond structural necessity raise two questions:

(63) a. What are the reasons for going beyond what is structurally neces-sary?
      b. How are the expansions integrated into the core – are they added at the beginning, at the end, or within (thus somehow breaking up the core), and does such an expansion affect the core elements themselves, for example by modifying or replacing them?

As for the possible reasons why speakers choose to expand the core, there are at least four, which will be considered in turn.

   A. The speaker believes that in a given context, the sparse informa-tion of the core is not enough for the listener to understand which entity is intended as a subject, an object, a place, etc. So, if the communication is to be successful, he or she must provide more explicit information.

   B. The speaker wants to give an additional description of the same entity, although this entity is already identifiable by the listener. This, I believe, is the source of many right dislocations, as in (64):

---

[16] The situation talked about can also be compound of several subsitutions, for example in answer to questions like *Who met whom on which occasion?* These complications are not discussed here.

(64) a. *Il l'a fait, cet idiot.*
          'He it has done, this idiot.'

      b. *J'en parle souvent, de mon enfance.*
          'I of-it speak often, of my childhood.'

In (64a), the relevant entity must be given in the preceding context, it is then picked up by *l[e]* and by *en* in the role of subject and prepositional object, respectively, without providing more descriptive information. The additional description in the right dislocation provides more information, which was initially not felt to be necessary for the identification of the entity. This additional information may reflect the speaker's view about the referent, as in (64a), or it may reflect some change in the speaker's opinion about whether the referent is indeed identifiable for the listener ('afterthought'), as in (64b). In this case, the additional description may even be contrastive – which is at odds with the common view on right dislocations (see Section 3):

(65) *Tu dois la prendre, celle à DROITE.*
      'You must it take, the-one to the RIGHT.'

Such a subsidiary description can, of course, also be used when the first description in the sentence is already a lexical NP rather than a weak element:

(66) a. *Jean, il l'a fait, cet idiot.*
          'Jean, he it has done, this idiot.'

      b. *Marie, elle a épousé Jean, son premier ami.*
          'Marie, she has married Jean, her first friend.'

All of this explains the somewhat ambivalent nature of certain right dislocations, as discussed in Section 3 (see examples (47) – (49)). They do not serve to identify the situation talked about, nor do they select an alternative; in this sense, they are neither topic nor focus. But they may enrich the addressee's knowledge about one of the referents.

   C. An expansion allows the speaker to set the relevant entity off against other entities that one might consider in the given context. Weak elements, such as *il, le, y, en, lui* (as indirect object) do not allow this, since they are practically void of lexical content: they only indicate a grammatical function. One might argue that, for example, a particle like *y* indeed carries some descriptive content – it relates to a location. But the only lexical contrast would be between 'location – no location', not between a location in contrast to some other location, making this a contrast which hardly ever makes sense. Similarly, *je* only specifies that the speaker is the referent, so, it is rather a role difference than a difference between various people that could be referred to by *je*. If such a contrast is to be made, other pronominal elements must be used; in these cases, however, additional contextual information must be available to render identification possible.

D. An expansion may contribute to identify the situation talked about, for example by saying: the situation involves my uncle as an agent, or: it is a situation which is situated in London. Note that this is not the same function which an expansion has when it serves to identify an entity itself: the issue is not to identify my uncle or London, but to indicate that these entities characterize the situation about which something is said; the latter function presupposes the former.

Function D may therefore go together with Reasons A or C, but not with Function B. With a type D expansion, the speaker indicates: I am going to make a claim about (or ask a question about) a situation which involves Jean as a subject[17], perhaps in contrast to a situation which involves Pierre as a subject. In such a case, the speaker also says something 'about Peter' – but this is not crucial; the speaker also says something about the other referents in the same sentence. What is crucial is rather that the speaker says something about Jean as an agent in the topic situation. Consider (67):

(67) *Hier, Jean a tué son chien.*
      'Yesterday, Jean has killed his dog.'

In such a sentence, something is said 'about Jean', but something is said 'about the dog', as well (in fact, the addressee probably learns more about the dog than about Jean by hearing the sentence). The true 'topic' is, however, the situation talked about, which is situated in time by *hier* and characterized as a 'Jean-be-agent situation.' One might say here that the temporal characterization is something external to the situation, a sort of 'frame', whereas the characterization 'Jean-be-agent' is a sort of internal property. Indeed, some authors make a distinction between an 'individual topic and a 'stage topic' (see, for example, Lahousse 2011). But this is just due to the nature of these properties, times versus agents; in terms of what they do for information structure, they serve the same function.

---

[17] I shall leave open here whether this role should be seen as a grammatical role (such as subject), a semantical role (such as agent), or a combination of both. This is not a trivial issue, and it would require considerable discussion.

This concludes our discussion of why a speaker may want or feel the need to go beyond the bare structural core. Let us turn now to the question of how this additional material can be integrated into the core. Essentially, there are three possibilities, depending on whether the weak element is preserved or not and on where the expansion is placed:

A. *Addition*: The weak element is preserved, which automatically means that the expansion must be in a different position that the weak element.
B. *Replacement, type A*: The weak element disappears, the expansion takes its position.
C. *Replacement, type B*: The weak element disappears, the expansion shows up in a different position.

Languages may have different preferences here. In French, one notes a considerable variation between FT and FA. I will now briefly illustrate some possibilities, with *Elle le lui a donné* (= 60c) as a core.

(68) a. *Marie, elle le lui a donné.*
  b. *Le livre, elle le lui a donné.*
  c. *Marie, le livre, elle le lui a donné.*

All three expansions are additions before the core. If there is more than one such addition, as in (68c), the order of the corresponding weak elements is matched. These additions are 'situation-identifying'; they say, for example, that the situation talked about is a situation with Marie as a subject/agent, or that it is a situation with Marie as a subject/agent and the book as a direct object/theme. In all three cases, the situation talked about involves a third person, only identifiable by contextual information, as an indirect object.

(69) a. *Elle le lui a donné, Marie.*
  b. *Elle le lui a donné, le livre.*

Here, we have additions at the right periphery; they do not contribute to the identification of the situation talked about but just provide descriptive material about one of the arguments involved in that situation.

In the following expansions, the weak element is replaced rather than maintained, but the position of the replacement varies (remember, the core is *Elle le lui a donné*):

(70) a. *Marie le lui a donné.*
  b. *Elle lui a donné le livre.*
  c. *Marie lui a donné le livre.*

These sentences correspond to what children and second language learners normally are taught in school, that is, to FT. But in FA, sentences (70a) and (70c) are quite unusual. In other words, FA prefers additions over replacements: It tends to maintain the grammatical core as an intact unit.

A case of replacements that is found in FT as well as in FA is that of clefts:

(71) a. *C'est Marie qui le lui a donné.*
      b. *C'est à son oncle qu'elle l'a donné.*
      c. *C'est un livre qu'elle lui a donné.*

They replace one, and only one, weak element[18], and they are always in initial position; if the first element of the weak string is replaced, the position is maintained, and it is not maintained otherwise. The new lexical material is only provided by X, the constituent that is framed by *c'est ... qui/que*. This frame indicates that this constituent is not situation-identifying but belongs to the updating part of the sentence. Compare the following four sentences:

(72) a. *Il est venu.*
      b. *Jean, il est venu.*
      c. *C'est Jean qui est venu.*
      d. *C'est un de mes amis qui est venu.*

(72a) is the bare core. In order to decide whether or not it is true, when uttered on some occasion, it must be clear what the situation talked about is; the bare core only expresses that this situation involves some (male) person as a subject/agent (and that it is in the past, a point not examined here). The addressee may still be able to decide whether it is true or not, if there is sufficient information from the context. But the speaker may also be so kind as to provide additional information about whom this subject/agent is, if there is reason to assume that the listener does not know this yet. This is what happens in (72b). In FT, this would lead to a replacement of the weak element; in FA, an addition is used instead. This is the traditional 'topic status' of left dislocations.

If the additional lexical material is framed by *c'est ... qui/que*, then the framed constituent, which provides this material, is meant to identify the

---

18 Alternatively, one might say that they are added, and the weak element is replaced by *qui/que*. I see no major difference in these two way to look at it, except that the latter is a bit more in the spirit of a traditional analysis, in which the lexical NP is picked up by a relative pronoun.

situation talked about: This situation is assumed to be entirely given in the context, and to be about this situation; it is then assigned the property of having X as – in this example – a subject/agent. It is also indicated that X is the only entity which has this function in this situation (but see the discussion of (57) – (59)). There is no reason to assume that X was already mentioned in that context at all, nor is it excluded that other issues are to be decided with respect to that situation. This entirely depends on how rich the contextual information is. Thus, after a question like *Qui est venu?*, the only issue to be decided is who indeed takes the subject-role in that situation. After a question like *Qui est venu et qui est parti?* 'Who did what?', the situation about which something has to be said in the answer is only weakly specified, apart from more general contextual knowledge: It must be a compound situation in the past, which involves two subsituations, each of which with a person as an agent. The answer then decides on who these two persons are. In both cases, (72c) or (72d) would be appropriate; but they would differ in intonation: In the first case, the assertive fall (after the initial rise) is already in the cleft, whereas this fall is deferred to *venu* in the second case.

8. Summing up

Que pensez-vous de l'amour? –
L'amour? Je le fais souvent,
mais je n'en parle jamais.[19]
Marcel Proust (1954: 178)

As was argued in Section 1, a clear and consistent outline of information structure in French is at present out of reach. In what precedes, I first outlined some essential observations, and then tried to integrate them into a coherent view. In both respects, the picture is painted with a broad brush. Many facts are disputable, there are numerous exceptions, numerous riddles, and the synthesis can only give an incipient picture. As any attempt to give such a picture, this one has to fight with the notorious unclarity of even the most elementary notions in information structure. I tried to avoid theoretical deliberations in that direction and to adopt, wherever possible, the frameworks used in the literature on French information structure. But as was shown in Sections 3 and 4, neither an account in which the 'topic' provides background information, nor an account in which it is the referent

---

[19] "What think-you of the love? – The love? I it make often, but I not about-it never talk."

'about' which something is said do justice to the observations. So, I made some use of two slightly different ideas, each of which is very simple.

The first of these two ideas concerns the 'topic status'. It is assumed that the 'topic', about which something is said is the whole situation relative to which the proposition expressed by the sentence is true or false (in more complex cases, it can also be a compound situation, comprised of several subsituations, a case only marginally mentioned here). This situation has somehow to be identifiable; otherwise, one cannot judge whether an assertion is true or not. This can be done by contextual information, for example by a preceding question. But it is also possible to use material from the crucial sentence itself in order to identify the 'topic situation'. Other material in the sentence serves to say that the situation thus identified has a certain property, about which a decision is taken. And it might also be that the speaker adds material which does not serve any such function.

The second idea that was exploited here concerns the varying richness of descriptive information which a certain expression provides. There are elements which are very poor in that regard and, in a way, only give a bit of structural information, such as clitic elements. And there are expressions which are very rich in that regard. An economical speaker tries to work as much as possible with the former – he or she would operate with a bare structural core. This is possible, when the context is rich enough. If not, the speaker has to add descriptive information, and this leads to various kinds of elaborate structures and thus to a different information flow.

From its Latin origin, French grammar differs by a very reduced inflection, by the tendency to mark grammatical relations at the beginning of a phrase, and the increasing preference for a quite rigid structural sentence core. This core consists of a string of weak elements which correspond primarily to the argument slots provided by the lexical verb, on the one hand, and of this verb, on the other. The order of these elements is fixed. But the need and the possibility to expand the core by all sorts of lexically richer material leads to rich variety of syntactic patterns. The structural difference between traditional French and advanced French is much less in these three developments but in the way in which the core is expanded. The citation from Proust at the beginning of this section illustrates the classical language, examples such as (2)–(30) in Section 1 illustrate the advanced way. In fact, all three developmental trends are observed in traditional French, be in its written or in its spoken form, as well as in advanced French, which, as a rule, is only spoken. But since the traditional grammatical analysis of French in all forms, including spoken French, is mostly based on written material, and this in a most conservative orthography, the amount of these developments is often underrated. This blurs the picture of French grammar. Only if we overcame this tradition, we may proceed to a correct idea which role information structure plays in this grammar.

References

Ambrose, Jeanne
 1996 *Bibliographie des études sur le français parlé*. Paris: Didier.
Andersen, Hanne Leth and Anita Berit Hansen (eds.)
 2000 *Le français parlé. Corpus et résultats*. Copenhagen: Museum Tusculanum.
Beyssade, Claire, Elisabeth Delais-Roussarie, Jenny Doetjes, Jean-Marie Marandin and Annie Rialland
 2004 Prosodic, syntactic and pragmatic aspects of information structure – an introduction. In *Handbook of French Semantics*, Francis Corblin and Henriëtte de Swart (eds.), 455–475. Stanford: CSLI Publications.
Beyssade, Claire, Elisabeth Delais-Roussarie, Jenny Doetjes Jean-Marie Marandin and Annie Rialland
 2004 Prosody and information in French. In *Handbook of French Semantics*, Francis Corblin and Henriëtte de Swart (eds.), 477–499. Stanford: CSLI Publications.
Blanche-Benveniste, Claire
 1990 *Le Français parlé. Études grammaticales*. Paris: Éditions CNRS.
de Cat, Cécile
 2007 *French Dislocation. Syntax, Interpretation, Acquisition*. Oxford: Oxford University Press.
Delais-Roussarie, Elisabeth, Jenny Doetjes and Petra Sleeman
 2004 Dislocation. In *Handbook of French Semantics*, Francis Corblin and Henriëtte de Swart (eds.), 501–528. Stanford: CSLI Publications.
Corblin, Francis and Henriëtte de Swart (eds.)
 2004 *Handbook of French Semantics*. Stanford: CSLI Publications.
Detey, Sylvain, Jacques Durand, Bernard Laks and Chantal Lyche (eds.)
 2011 *Les variétés du français parlé dans l'espace francophone: ressources pour l'enseignement*. Paris: Ophrys.
Doetjes, Jenny, Georges Rebuschi and Annie Rialland
 2004 Cleft sentences. In *Handbook of French Semantics*, Francis Corblin and Henriëtte de Swart (eds.), 529-552. Stanford: CSLI Publications.
Dufter, Andreas
 2008 On explaining the rise of *c'est*-clefts in French. In *The Paradox of Grammatical Change: Perspectives from Romance*, Ulrich Detges and Richard Waltereit (eds.), 31–56. Amsterdam: Benjamins.

Féry, Caroline
    2001   Focus and phrasing in French. In *Audiatur Vox Sapientiae. A Fest-schrift for Arnim von Stechow*, Caroline Féry and Wolfgang Sternefeld (eds.), 153–181. Berlin: Akademie Verlag.
Gadet, Françoise
    1989   *Le français ordinaire*. Paris: Armand Colin.
Gast, Volker and Florian Haas
    2011   On the distribution of subject properties in formulaic presentationals of Germanic and Romance: A diachronic-typological approach. In *Impersonal Constructions: A cross-linguistic perspective*, Andrej Malchukov and Anna Siewierska (eds.), 127–166. Amsterdam: Benjamins.
Giacomi, Alain and Daniel Véronique
    1982   A propos de "il y a…"/"il y en a…". *Le français moderne* 3: 237–242.
Grevisse, Maurice
    2011   *Le bon usage*. Bruxelles: Duculot. (15th edition).
Klein, Wolfgang
    2006   On finiteness. In *Semantics in Acquisition*, Veerle van Geenhoven (ed.), 245–272. Dordrecht: Springer.
Klein, Wolfgang
    2010   On times and arguments. *Linguistics* 48: 1221–1253.
Lambrecht, Knud
    1981   *Topic, antitopic, and verb agreement in non-standard French*. Amsterdam: John Benjamins.
Lambrecht, Knud
    1986   The grammar of spoken French. Ph.D. dissertation, Austin: University of Texas.
Lambrecht, Knud
    1994   *Information Structure and Sentence Form*. Cambridge: Cambridge University Press.
Lahousse, Karen
    2011   *Quand passent les cigognes. Le sujet nominal postverbal en français moderne*. Paris: Presses Universitaires de Vincennes.
Mertens, Piet
    2008   Syntaxe, prosodie et structure informationnelle: une approche prédictive pour l'analyse de l'intonation dans le discours. *Travaux de Linguistique* 56: 87–124.
Morel, Mary-Annick
    1992   Les présentatifs en français. In *La deixis*, Mary-Annick Morel and Laurent Danon-Boileau (eds.), 507–516. Paris: Presses Universitaires de France.

Müller, Anja, Barbara Höhle, Michaela Schmitz and Jürgen Weissenborn
    2006   Focus-to-stress alignment in 4 to 5-year-old German-learning chil-
                dren. In *Language Acquisition and Development*, Adriana Belletti,
                Cristiano Chesi and Elisa Di Domenico (eds.), 379–392. Cambridge:
                Cambrige University Press.
Proust, Marcel
    1954   *A la recherche du temps perdu*, Vol. II. Paris: Gallimard.
Rossi, Mario
    1999   *L'intonation. Le systeme du français*. Paris: Ophrys.
Turco, Giusy, Christine Dimroth and Bettina Braun
    to appear   Focusing on function words: intonational means to mark Verum
                Focus in German and in French. *Language and Speech.*
Trévise, Anne
    1986   Topicalisation, is it transferable? In *Crosslinguistic Influence in
                Second Language Acquisition*, Mike Sharwood Smith and Eric
                Kellerman (eds.), 186–206. Oxford: Pergamon Press.
Weil, Henri
    1844   *De l'ordre des mots dans les langues anciennes comparées aux
                langues modernes*. Paris: Vieweg.

The information structure of Georgian

Rusudan Asatiani and Stavros Skopeteas

1. Introduction[1]

Georgian is a Kartvelian language, spoken by about 4 million people, mostly in Georgia. Georgian has its own alphabetic writing system and a long literary tradition. In typological perspective, Georgian grammar displays several properties that are of particular interest for the study of information structure. At the phonological level, the crucial property of this language is that lexical stress is only weekly implemented. This property is relevant for the intonational reflexes of information structure, since the stressed syllable is the host of pitch accents (in languages like English and German). At the morphological level, the most interesting property is the availability of rich inflectional marking of syntactic relations comprising case suffixes as well as person affixes for subjects, objects, and indirect objects on the verb. Hence, syntactic relations are completely disambiguated through inflectional morphology, which goes hand in hand with an enormous flexibility in word order and optional realization of argument constituents (i.e., subject and object drop). A very particular research question in this language relates to the potential interaction of case marking with discourse concepts. Case marking in Georgian displays a threefold split (nominative pattern, ergative pattern, inverse pattern) determined by the inflectional properties of the verb. There are several assumptions in the literature about the effects of this split on the prominence of the verbal arguments; the crucial question for our purposes is to what extent this notion of prominence relates to discourse phenomena. Constructional means that affect the linearization of propositional content and – in several languages – interact with information structure, such as passivization and clefting, play a less important role in Georgian and occur less frequently in spontaneous discourse. A less

[1] We are grateful to Renate Musan and Manfred Krifka for their substantial contribution to this article. The major part of the generalizations in this article are the product of our joint work with Gisbert Fanselow and Caroline Féry within the collaborative research center 632 *Information Structure* at the University of Potsdam and the Humboldt University Berlin, funded by the German Research Foundation (DFG).

understood domain of grammar is the role of several classes of particles, whose placement is sensitive to information structural categories, possibly mediated through their relation to the prosodic domains of the utterance.

The challenge of studying information structure in Georgian lies in understanding the role of these grammatical properties, in particular, the possibilities provided by the flexible word order, the restrictions of the intonational possibilities due to the lack of hosts for pitch accents, and the role of case marking patterns. The following sketch summarizes the findings in the current research on Georgian information structure and offers a synthesis of the insights gained at the different layers of grammar. We first introduce the properties of the canonical word order and the neutral prosodic structure (see Section 2). The sections 3 and 4 deal with the phenomena related to focus and topic, respectively. Section 5 outlines some remaining issues that involve an interaction with information structural concepts in this language and Section 6 presents our conclusions.

2.   Canonical configurations

Georgian is a language with flexible word order. It is clear that the subject precedes the verb phrase in the basic order, but the order within the verb phrase displays considerable variation. Crucially, both head-final and head-initial verb phrases appear in all-new contexts, see Section 2.1. The prosodic structure of Georgian declaratives contains a sequence of rising pitch excursions that determine prosodic phrases, see Section 2.2.

2.1. Canonical word order

Georgian has been described as a *flexible word order* language, which refers to the fact that all six permutations of the order of the three major constituents, S, O, and V, are grammatical and occur with considerable frequency in corpora (cf. Shanidze 1948, Pochkhua 1962, Asatiani 1982, Apridonidze 1986, Kvachadze 1996, and others). There is a consensus in the available literature that the subject precedes the predicate in the basic order, i.e., all deviations from the subject-first orders require a contextual trigger. However, SOV and SVO orders can occur out of the blue, i.e., there is no evidence that any of these orders is contextually restricted by the presence of a contextual trigger, see illustration in (1a)–(1b). Quantitative studies in larger corpora show that both orders occur very frequently with a slight preference for SOV in the conservative registers (written styles) and for SVO in the colloquial registers (see Apridonidze 1986: 136–143, Vogt 1971: 222).

(1)   a. *nino-m   c'ign-i   a-i-γ-o.*
         Nino-ERG   book-NOM PV-SV-take-AOR.S.3.SG
         'Nino took the book.'

       b. *nino-m   a-i-γ-o   c'ign-i.*
          Nino-ERG   PV-SV-take-AOR.S.3.SG book-NOM
          'Nino took the book.'

The straightforward implication of the observation that both SOV and SVO may appear out of the blue is that *both orders are basic* (see Anderson 1984: 186, Harris 1981: 22). However, there is a series of asymmetries between the V-final and V-initial orders in Georgian that suggest that the head-final configuration is the basic one. A first piece of evidence comes from idiomatic VPs (see Skopeteas and Fanselow 2010). The relevance of this data comes from the assumption that an idiomatic string has non-compositional meaning. Since discourse features such as focus and topic apply to pieces of information, i.e., semantic objects, it is not possible to assign such a feature to a part of the idiomatic string since it does not have an independent semantic representation in the construction at issue. This view predicts that syntactic operations that are driven by discourse features cannot apply to parts of idiomatic strings. The observation in the Georgian data is that idiomatic VPs are consistently V-final: the VP in (2a) has – next to the literal meaning – an array of idiomatic meanings such as 'giving up' or 'acting as a ruthless person'. The crucial observation is that idiomatic meanings are only available in the OV order. Native speakers either reject the VO order in (2b) or interpret it compositionally. This view does not imply that the order of idiomatic strings is invariable. Word order variation is possible with idiomatic VPs if a syntactic operation is licensed by a discourse feature applying outside the idiom. For instance, the SVO order in (2b) is possible with the idiomatic meaning if the subject is in focus (preverbal focus has to be adjacent to the verb, see Section 3.1). This data shows that the order of idiomatic strings is not 'frozen', but it lacks the variation that is licensed by the assignment of discourse features to their parts.

(2)   a. *nino-m   xel-i   a-i-γ-o.*
Nino-ERG hand-NOM PV-SV-take-AOR.S.3.SG
'Nino took a hand.' / 'Nino gave up.'

   b. *nino-m   a-i-γ-o   xel-i.*
Nino-ERG V-SV-take-AOR.S.3.SG hand-NOM
'Nino took a hand.'/ 'Nino gave up.' (only possible if subject in focus)

The intuitions reported in (2) account for the frequencies found in the corpus. The prediction is that the proportion of non-V-final orders with compositional VPs will be significantly greater than the corresponding proportion with idiomatic VPs. This expectation is borne out, as shown in Table 1, which displays the frequencies and proportions of the OV and VO orders of the constructions illustrated in (1) and (2). The counts of idiomatic strings are the frequencies of the idiomatic VP *xel-i a-i-γ-o* 'hand-NOM PV-SV-take-AOR.S.3.SG' in (2). The counts of the compositional string are the sums of the occurrences of four nouns (*c'ign-i* 'book-NOM', *pul-i* 'money-NOM', *švebuleba* 'vacation(NOM)', *xelpas-i* 'salary-NOM') with the same verb form *a-i-γ-o* 'PV-SV-take-AOR.S.3.SG'. The obtained data shows that V-final sentences are significantly more frequent with idiomatic VPs (86.5%) than with compositional VPs (64.1%), as justified by the chi-square test ($\chi^2 = 258$, $p < .001$).

Table 1. OV vs. VO orders in idiomatic and compositional VPs[2]

	idiomatic	*n*	%	compositional	*n*	%
OV		3,410	86.5		593	64.1
VO		530	13.5		332	35.9
total		3,940	100.0		925	100.0

In addition to the evidence from idiomatic VPs, Georgian patterns with V-final languages in an array of constructions that correlate with the head directionality of the verbal projections. Non-finite verbs canonically precede finite verbs as expected for OV languages (see Greenberg 1963), see (3a). Georgian allows for right-node raising (see 3b): This construction is reported for V-final languages such as Japanese, while languages with head-initial VPs have gapping, i.e., elision of the V in the second conjunct, see for instance the English translation of (3b) (see Ross 1970).

---

2   Data retrieved from Google, 27.03.2009.

(3)   a. Relative order of finite and non-finite verbs
      nino-s   c'ign-is   a-γ-eb-a
      Nino-DAT book-GEN PV-take-TM-INF(NOM)
      u-nd-a.
      (SINV.3).CV-want-OINV.3(SINV.3.SG)
      'Nino wants to take a book.'

      b. Right node raising
      Nino-m   švebuleba,   Gogi-m   k'i   xelpas-i
      Nino-ERG vacation(NOM) Gogi-ERG and/but salary-NOM
      a-i-γ-o.
      PV-SV-take-AOR.S.3.SG
      'Nino took vacation and Gogi took salary.'

If we take into account that non-V-final orders are less likely in non-compositional VPs and that Georgian patterns with V-final languages in a number of constructions, then we have an empirical asymmetry between the two orders indicating that the V is final in the basic configuration (see Skopeteas and Fanselow 2010). The assumption that the basic order is V-final leads to the question of how a VO order is derived from an OV basis. There are two logical possibilities: Either the O is right-dislocated beyond the clausal domain or the V is fronted to a position preceding the O. Both options are possible in Georgian: Right dislocation accounts for cases of rightwards heavy shift (see 4a), in which speakers prefer the option with a fronted verb. Right dislocation involves adjunction of the dislocated constituent to the higher clausal level (see Frascarelli 2004, Samek-Lodovici 2006). This operation is generally expected to be triggered by some factor (such as weight) that leads a constituent outside the core layer of the clause. However, it is not plausible to assume that right-dislocation occurs out of the blue and underlies SVO sentences in which the O is part of the broad focus domain as in (1b). These cases can be accounted for through a semantically vacuous head-movement operation that fronts the V to a position above the object constituent (see argumentation in Skopeteas and Fanselow 2010). The question is whether there are empirical arguments for this operation beyond the conceptual basis that it generally fits to the discourse properties of the resulting linearization. There are indeed some constructions in Georgian that strongly favor an analysis in terms of V-fronting, namely constructions that involve the fronting of the finite V alone as for instance (4b). This construction can be straightforwardly accounted for, if we assume that the finite V is fronted to a higher position within the thematic layer of the clause.

(4)   a.   *nino-m   a-i-γ-o   ʒvirpas-i*
            Nino-ERG PV-SV-take-AOR.S.3.SG expensive-NOM
            saint'ereso   c'ign-i   k'avk'asi-is   šesaxeb.
            interesting.NOM book-NOM Caucasus-GEN about
            'Nino took an expensive, interesting book about the Caucasus.'

       b.   *nino-s   u-nd-a   c'ign-is*
            Nino-DAT (SINV.3)CV-want-OINV.3(SINV.3.SG) book-GEN
            a-γ-eb-a.
            PV-take-TM-INF.NOM
            'Nino wants to take the book.'

The crucial generalization for the study of information structure is that the alternation between OV and VO orders in Georgian does not depend on a semantic or pragmatic trigger. Structural evidence suggests that the VO order is a derived option, however the crucial point is that apart from some cases in which a trigger is available (e.g., instances of heavy shift) VO and OV alternate in free variation. Furthermore, the freedom in the head-directionality of verb projections is reflected in the focus options of this language, as we will show in Section 3.1. A closer inspection of the interaction of narrow focus with word order shows that the mixed OV/VO properties result in a long array of focus possibilities that correspond to the possibilities known for OV and the possibilities known for VO languages.

2.2. Unmarked prosodic pattern

There is a long tradition of study in the field of Georgian prosody, which differs markedly from prosody in languages like Russian or Turkish (cf. Alkhazishvili 1959, Tevdoradze 1978, Zhghenti 1963). An autosegmental account of Georgian prosody is developed in Bush (1999), Jun, Vicenik and Lofstedt 2007, and Skopeteas, Féry and Asatiani (2009). Experiments on Georgian intonation with special emphasis on information structure are reported in Skopeteas, Féry and Asatiani (2009), and Skopeteas and Féry (2010).

The basic prosodic pattern of Georgian declarative sentences is a sequence of rising contours as illustrated in (5) by means of an idealized F_0 excursion (see Jun, Vicenik and Lofstedt 2007: 43, and Skopeteas, Féry and Asatiani 2009 for examples and further discussion). These rising contours correspond to prosodic phrases that are determined by two tonal targets: a low target L at the left edge of the prosodic phrase and a high target H at the right edge of the phrase. The subsequent H targets are normally down-stepped, as illustrated in (5). The final prosodic phrase ends with a low target L, which corresponds to the final lowering of a declarative utterance.[3]

(5)   Idealized intonational contour of a declarative sentence

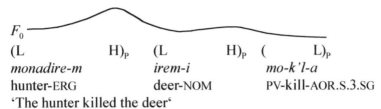

(L	H)$_P$	(L	H)$_P$	(	L)$_P$
monadire-m		*irem-i*		*mo-k'l-a*	
hunter-ERG		deer-NOM		PV-kill-AOR.S.3.SG	

'The hunter killed the deer'

Jun, Vicenik and Lofstedt (2007) show that prosodic phrases correspond to syntactic constituents, e.g., complex constituents such as complex noun phrases or relative clauses are mapped on single prosodic phrases at the phonological level. Furthermore, Skopeteas and Féry (2010) observed that 25% of the all-new utterances have a prosodic structure in which the pre-verbal material is integrated in a single prosodic constituent with an early high tonal target in its left side and a further tonal target at the right edge, as illustrated in (6) (see examples and measurements in Skopeteas and Féry 2010).

(6)   Idealized intonational contour of a declarative sentence

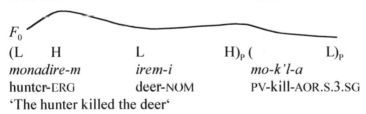

(L	H	L	H)$_P$ (	L)$_P$
monadire-m		*irem-i*		*mo-k'l-a*
hunter-ERG		deer-NOM		PV-kill-AOR.S.3.SG

'The hunter killed the deer'

3. Focus

As introduced in Section 2.1, the particular property of Georgian syntax is the flexibility of the verb projections. Section 3.1 shows that this flexibility

---

3   The phonological analyses of the prosodic structure in this article are based on the results of our common work with Caroline Féry. Details are reported in Skopeteas, Féry, and Asatiani 2009, Skopeteas and Féry (2010).

explains the rich narrow focus options found in this language. The prosodic realization of foci does not involve a strict association with a particular pitch accent, as in the familiar European languages. The major prosodic effects of focus are found in the prosodic phrasing, i.e., in a preference to create a prosodic boundary that separates the focus from the phonological material on its left side, see Section 3.2.

3.1. Syntactic properties

As introduced in Section 2.1, there are two word order configurations that are possible in wide focus contexts, SOV and SVO. A special instance of a wide-focus context is found in discourse-initial utterances. Interestingly for a V-final language, Georgian allows for V-initial utterances at the beginning of narratives, as already observed in corpus studies (see Apridonidze 1986: 86–91). Example (7) illustrates a typical form for the beginning of fairy tails.

(7) *i-q'-o*   da ara *i-q'-o*   *ra,*
     CV-be.PST-AOR.S.3.SG and not CV-be.PST-AOR.S.3.SG what(NOM)
     i-q'-o   *ert-i*   *xelmc'ipe.*
     CV-be.PST-AOR.S.3.SG one-NOM king(NOM)
     'Once upon a time there was a king.'

The observation of V-initial orders in discourse-initial contexts raises a question about the discourse properties of these contexts. Is this context a pragmatically neutral configuration, i.e., a configuration without a pragmatic feature that could trigger a syntactic operation? In this context the common ground between the interlocutors is empty, i.e., all parts of the utterance are a novel contribution to the discourse. However, the subset of discourse-initial utterances that appear in the V-initial order has an additional property. These utterances involve a particular type of verbs such as the copula *q'opna* 'be' in example (7) or unaccusative verbs such as *i-sm-eb-a* 'drink-THM-3.SG (it is drinkable)' and *čn-d-eb-a* 'appear-PASS-THM-S.3.SG' (see further examples and detailed discussion in Tuite 1998: 42). These verbs are part of the wide focus domain that encompasses the entire utterance, but the weight of their contribution to the propositional content is limited. A V-initial configuration with a verb having a substantial contribution to the propositional content, as illustrated in (8), is not an appropriate way to start a fairy tale in which the individuals are not already introduced in the context. Hence, the type of utterance illustrated in

(7) is a particular type of all-new configuration that involves an asymmetry between the verb and its argument(s) relating to the fact that the contribution of these utterances to the common ground is to introduce the referents that are denoted by the argument constituent(s).

(8)   *#mo-k'l-a*   *monadire-m irem-i*   *da*
      PV-kill-AOR.S.3.SG hunter-ERG   deer-NOM and
      c'a-vid-a   *saxl-ši.*
      PV-go.PST-AOR.S.3.SG house[DAT]-in
      'The hunter killed the deer and went home.'

The question with regard to the structure is whether the V-initial configuration in this context is an instance of V-fronting of the type discussed in Section 2.1. The data presented so far suggest that the landing site of the head-fronting operation is not the same. The instances of V-fronting presented in Section 2.1 lead the verb to a position below the subject, while the operation illustrated in (7) leads the verb to the leftmost position in the utterance, presumably the specifier of the highest clausal projection (spec-CP).

Narrow focused constituents are found in two realizations in Georgian word order. The first option is typical for V-final languages: The focused constituent occurs left-adjacent to the V (see Armenian in Comrie 1984, Basque in Arregi 2003: 173, Sinhala in Herring and Paolillo 1995, Turkish in Kılıçaslan 2004: 722, etc.). Preverbal focus in Georgian is illustrated by the examples in (9). The SOV order in (9a) is congruent with a question licensing narrow focus on the object and the OSV order in (9b) is congruent with a question licensing narrow focus on the subject. The generalization is that preverbal focus *must* be adjacent to the finite verb. This fact is a very robust effect of Georgian word order already reported in studies with singular intuition data (see Alkhazishvili 1959, Nash 1995, McGinnis 1995) as well as in experimental studies (see Skopeteas, Féry and Asatiani 2009: 104, Skopeteas and Fanselow 2010: 1374). This property is not shared by all SOV languages: in some languages such as Turkish, Sinhala, and Armenian (see sources cited above), but not Basque, adjacency is not obligatory in the canonical word order, which would render (9a) felicitous in all narrow focus options.

(9)   a. #'Who bought tomatoes?'
         'What did Nino buy?'

         nino-m   *p'amidor-i*   *i-q'id-a.*
         Nino-ERG   tomato-NOM SV-buy-AOR.S.3.SG
         'Nino bought tomatoes.'

b. 'Who bought tomatoes?'
#'What did Nino buy?'

p'amidor-i   nino-m   i-q'id-a.
tomato-NOM Nino-ERG SV-buy-AOR.S.3.SG
'Nino bought tomatoes.'

The syntactic phenomenon in (9) can be replicated for further constituents, as illustrated in the examples under (10). Example (10a) illustrates that the adjacency of the focus and the verb also holds for adjunct constituents. Examples (10b–c) show that the same phenomenon even applies for subconstituents, which results in at least superficially discontinuous constituents, as illustrated by a focused modifier in (10b) and by a focus noun phrase head in (10c).[4]

(10) a. *dye-s   i-q'id-a   nino-m   p'amidor-i.*
         day-DAT SV-buy-AOR.S.3.SG Nino-ERG tomato-NOM
         'TODAY Nino bought tomatoes.'

      b. *c'itel-i   v-i-q'id-e   pexsacmel-i.*
         red-NOM S.1-SV-buy-AOR(S.1.SG) shoe-NOM
         'I bought RED shoes.'

      c. *pexsacmel-i v-i-q'id-e   kal-is-i.*
         shoe-NOM   S.1-SV-buy-AOR(S.1.SG) woman-GEN-NOM
         'I bought the SHOES of the woman.'

There is only one element that may intervene between the focus and the finite verb, namely the negation particle, as illustrated in (11) (see Harris 1981: 14, Hewitt 2005: 17).

(11) *sc'ored K'AC-S   ar   a-xur-av-s*
      exactly man-DAT not (SINV.3)CV-cover-THM-PRS.OINV.3(SINV.3.SG)
      kud-i.
      hat-NOM
      'Exactly the man does not have a hat on.'

Adjacency to the finite verb also applies for *wh*-elements (see (12)), indefinite and negative pronouns, as well as *only*-phrases (see Harris, 1981: 14,

---

4 Note the double case of the possessor noun phrase in (10c), which would not appear in the corresponding continuous noun phrase, suggesting that the two noun phrases are free heads.

1993: 1385; Kvačadze, 1996: 250; McGinnis 1997, Skopeteas and Fanselow 2010: 1384, 1388).

(12) a. *vin   i-q'id-a   p'amidor-i?*
      who(ERG) SV-buy-AOR.S.3.SG tomato-NOM
      'Who bought tomatoes?'

  b. **vin p'amidor-i i-q'id-a?*

The question is which syntactic operation underlies this construction. The first possibility is to assume that the focused constituent α moves to the specifier position of a functional projection (= FP) hosting focused material and that the head F′ of this projection attracts the verb (see Skopeteas and Fanselow 2010 on Georgian, É. Kiss 1998 on Hungarian), as shown in (13).

(13) Discourse Configurational Account
  a. A constituent bearing the feature [foc] moves to spec,FP where this feature is checked.
  b. If a constituent occupies spec,FP, the head of this projection attracts the finite V.
  c. The product of these rules is the following syntactic configuration:
     $[_{FP} \, \alpha_i^{\text{foc}} \, [_{F'} \, V_j \, [_{vP} \, t_i \, t_j]]]$

The second account would be to assume that the non-focused material that intervenes between the focus and the V vacates the thematic layer of the clause and lands in a peripheral position, as shown in (14) (see Arregi 2003: 199 for Basque and Kılıçaslan 2004: 719 for Turkish). The crucial point is that the non-focused constituent β is in an adjoined position outside the core clause. It can be realized in either periphery, i.e., either to the left or to the right of the thematic layer of the clause. The condition in (14a) postulates a linearization property that results from the application of the nuclear stress rule (or from a principle of alignment with the left edge of a p-phrase, see Féry 2011). Hence, the stipulation of a rule requiring 'left adjacency of the focus to the verb' can be reduced by the assumption of two rules that hold independently: (a) The focus is realized in a prosodically prominent position and (b) the nuclear stress of the utterance is assigned to the position to the left of the verb in a V-final language. However, we refrain from making strong claims about nuclear stress in Georgian at this point and we will discuss the effects of prosodic prominence on linearization in Section 3.2.

(14)   Interface Condition Account

    a. Foc-to-V adjacency condition
The output linearization of the syntactic rules has to meet the condition:

$$<\ldots, \alpha^{\text{foc}}, V, \ldots>$$

    b. Whenever non-focused material intervenes between focus and V, this material has to leave the VP.

    c. The product of this rule is the following syntactic configuration:

$$[_{\text{CP}} \, \beta_i \quad [_{\text{vP}} \, \alpha^{\text{foc}} \, t_i \, V \,]\,]$$

These analyses make different predictions about the focus set of the $<\alpha, V>$ part of the utterance (see also Section 3.1 for the consequences of these accounts of the properties of topics). The account in (13) predicts that this operation will be licensed only if the constituent α bears a focus feature, which targets spec-FP, while the account in (14) predicts that the same linearization will appear in all cases in which the constituent α is part of a focus domain and the constituent β is not (see Arregi 2003: 199). This difference can be empirically tested with respect to the OSV order. According to the former account, this order will surface in contexts that license a narrow focused S, while according to the latter account this order will surface whenever the O is out of focus. Hence, both accounts correctly predict the data pattern in (9b) but only the latter account predicts that the same order will appear in SV focus domains. An SV string is not a constituent, but it is a possible focus domain that occurs in contexts in which the object constituent is part of the presupposed information. Indeed, OSV utterances occur in this context as exemplified in (15) that was elicited in a speech production study (see Skopeteas and Fanselow 2009: 310).

(15)   'There is a box on the table…'
    … q'ut-s   k'ac-i   a-gd-eb-s.
    … box-DAT man-NOM NV-throw-THM-PRS.S.3.SG
    '…a man is throwing the box.' (Skopeteas and Fanselow 2009: 310)

The utterance in (15) is evidence that the configuration in (14) is possible in Georgian. This fact does not exclude the possibility of the structural operation in (13), but shows that the operation of extracting non-focused information out of the VP independently exists in this language.

    In a V-final language such as Turkish or Basque, postverbal material cannot be focused, which reflects the fact that postverbal material is right dislocated in these languages. However, as shown in Section 2.1, Georgian has mixed OV/VO properties. Crucially, the verb can be fronted to a higher position without a contextual trigger and this operation results to a configuration with postverbal material within the thematic layer of the clause. As it is the case for many VO languages (e.g., English, Russian, Greek, etc.), postverbal material can be narrow focused, and this is the case in Georgian as well, as illustrated in (16). Postverbal focus is free, i.e., both the object *p'amidor-i* 'tomato-NOM' and the adjunct *dye-s* 'day-DAT' can be focused in (16a). The observation that focus can be postverbal implies that the Interface Condition in (14a) only restricts the possible linearizations of preverbal constituents. The possibilities of immediately preverbal and postverbal focus imply a rich array of focus options, as illustrated in (16b–c). An SVO and an OVS sentence are felicitous both in subject focus as well as in object focus contexts. The only restriction in Georgian is that if the focus is preverbal, then it has to be adjacent to the finite verb, see (9a–b).

(16)   a.   *nino-m   i-q'id-a   p'amidor-i   dye-s.*
             Nino-ERG   SV-buy-AOR.S.3.SG   tomato-NOM   day-DAT
             'Nino bought tomatoes today.'

       b.   'Who bought tomatoes?'
             'What did Nino buy?'
             nino-m   i-q'id-a   p'amidor-i.
             Nino-ERG   SV-buy-AOR.S.3.SG   tomato-NOM
             'Nino bought tomatoes.'

       c.   'Who bought tomatoes?'
             'What did Nino buy?'
             p'amidor-i   i-q'id-a   nino-m.
             tomato-NOM   SV-buy-AOR.S.3.SG   Nino-ERG
             'Nino bought tomatoes.'

The next issue is the structural representation of postverbal focus. Since postverbal focus is free, i.e., it does not necessarily immediately follow the verb and it is not necessarily clause-final, we cannot assume a unique landing site of the focused constituent in all of these cases. The straightforward generalization is that any postverbal constituent can be assigned focus in situ. The question is what triggers V-fronting in these examples. Presumably, the fronting of the verbal head in these examples has the same trigger as in the out-of-the-blue sentences. The intuition is that Georgian has an optional syntactic operation that fronts the finite verb to an early position within the thematic layer of the clause (let's assume as a landing site the lexical projection of the head of the inflectional phrase I°). This operation is an instance of head movement that is not triggered by a discourse feature and has the effect of giving Georgian mixed OV/VO properties. The postverbal focus option is a consequence of exactly these mixed properties. The difference between a head-final language such as Turkish that consistently does not allow for postverbal focus and a head-final language such as Georgian, is that the latter but not the former has an optional operation of V-fronting with the following effects: (a) VO order may appear in all focus contexts; (b) *in situ* focus surfaces as postverbal whenever the verb is fronted. The intuition behind this syntactic operation is that to the extent that the V is fronted without a discrete trigger, Georgian behaves like a head-initial language. The consequence of optional V-fronting is the possibility of postverbal focus which is available in head-initial languages such as Russian or English. This is the crucial difference from a consistently head-final language: In an OV language without V-fronting postverbal focus is not possible (which is the case for OV languages like Turkish).

The presented data shows that narrow focus either appears immediately preverbal or within the postverbal domain. This opens an array of alternative options of expressing focus; the only option that is excluded is a preverbal focus that is not adjacent to the verb. It is reasonable to ask whether these possibilities correspond to different types of focus. For instance, in Hungarian preverbal focus is reserved for identificational foci, while postverbal focus is used for new information focus (see É. Kiss 1998: 249). However, it is not possible to establish a similar distinction in the Georgian data. The distributional properties of focus particles as well as several exhaustivity tests show that preverbal and postverbal foci do not have interpretational differences (see detailed discussion in Skopeteas and Fanselow 2010: 1385–1389). Example (17) illustrates that the focused constituent is not necessarily exhaustively identified – either in the preverbal position, see (17a), or in the postverbal domain, see (17b). The adjunct *sxv-eb-tan ert-ad* 'among others' (lit. together with others) takes scope over the focus constituent. There are several scopal interpretations of the sentences in (17) depending on the intonational nucleus. The crucial point for our considerations is that this adjunct can take scope over the preverbal and the postverbal focus, which shows that the focus constructions at issue do not necessarily involve an exhaustive identification of the focused element.

(17) a. *Maria-m   sxv-eb-tan   ert-ad   Soso-c*
Maria-ERG other-PL-[DAT]at with.one-ADV Soso-also

da-pat'iž-a.
PV-invite-AOR.S.3.SG

'Maria also invited Soso among others.'

b. *Maria-m   sxv-eb-tan   ert-ad   da-pat'iž-a*
Maria-ERG other-PL-[DAT]at with.one-ADV PV-invite-AOR.S.3.SG

Soso-c.
Soso-also

'Maria also invited Soso among else.'

Frequencies of focus types in production data show that contrastive focus is significantly more frequent in the preverbal position – though possible in both configurations (see Skopeteas and Fanselow 2010: 1374). However, since this preference in the behavioral data cannot be replicated by a discrete difference in the interpretation, there is not enough evidence to assume that [+contrast] is a morphosyntactic feature that triggers a syntactic operation in this language. Thus, according to the available evidence about Georgian word order, we cannot conclude that the two alternative focus realizations are associated with two different types of focus.

3.2. Prosodic properties

There are two different accounts on the effects of focus on prosody. Jun, Vicenik and Lofstedt (2007) identify in their corpus instances of a high pitch accent (H* or L+H*) associated with the stressed syllable of narrow focused constituents, as illustrated in (18). The rising pitch excursion (L+H) reaches the F_0-maximum in the stressed syllable of the constituent in narrow focus. The focus is followed by a falling contour and the postfocal domain is deaccented, i.e., the pitch accents are deleted.

(18) Idealized intonational contour: initial focus

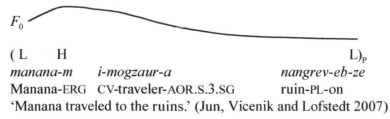

(L   H   L)$_P$
manana-m   i-mogzaur-a   nangrev-eb-ze
Manana-ERG   CV-traveler-AOR.S.3.SG   ruin-PL-on
'Manana traveled to the ruins.' (Jun, Vicenik and Lofstedt 2007)

Skopeteas and Féry (2010) present a different view on Georgian focus. In their experimental data, there is no evidence for a pitch accent, i.e. for a tonal event that is associated with the stressed syllable of the focused constituent. We have shown in Section 2.2 that there are two prosodic realizations that occur in all-new contexts, see (5) and (6). When the preverbal constituent is in focus, speakers produce utterances of the type in (5) more frequently, i.e., they prefer to phrase the focused constituent in a separate prosodic phrase than to integrate it into a larger prosodic unit, see (19). This observation implies that object-focus utterances have the same prosodic structure with a subset of the all-new utterances, compare (5) and (19). Skopeteas and Féry (2010) report a phonetic difference in the pitch expansion of the tonal event at the left edge of the focus phrase: The pitch difference between the phrase-final H of the subject constituent and the phrase-initial L of the object constituent is larger when the second constituent is in narrow focus. This quantitative difference is a further reflex of the general preference to separate the focus phrase with a prosodic boundary at its left edge.

(19) Idealized intonational contour: preverbal focus

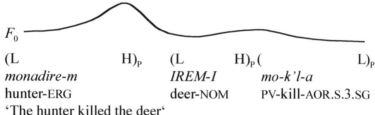

(L	H)$_P$	(L	H)$_P$ (	L)$_P$
monadire-m		*IREM-I*	*mo-k'l-a*	
hunter-ERG		deer-NOM	PV-kill-AOR.S.3.SG	
'The hunter killed the deer'				

Postverbal focus is realized with a different contour. The domain that precedes the nuclear stress is integrated within a single prosodic constituent wrapping the subject and the verb, see (20). A H tone at the right edge of the verb creates a prosodic boundary between the prefocal domain and the focus phrase. Sentence-final focus is frequently realized with a particular tonal pattern, namely a flat contour that differs markedly from the usual declination in the Georgian final prosodic phrases. This tonal pattern is analyzed as a sequence of two L targets and is termed 'super-low' in Skopeteas and Féry (2010). This is also the only phenomenon that cannot be interpreted without reference to a notion of pitch accents. Otherwise, the focus-related phenomena can be captured by the generalization that focus is intonationally separated through a tonal boundary at its left edge.

(20) Idealized intonational contour: postverbal focus

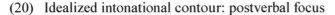

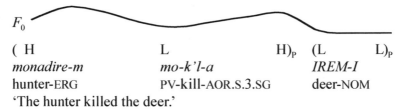

(H	L	H)ₚ	(L	L)ₚ
monadire-m	*mo-k'l-a*		*IREM-I*	
hunter-ERG	PV-kill-AOR.S.3.SG		deer-NOM	

'The hunter killed the deer.'

4. Topic

Topic phrases precede the focus. Interestingly, the two alternative accounts on foci introduced in Section 3.1 make different predictions about the discourse properties of the pre-focal constituents. These predictions, together with the further properties of topic constructions in Georgian, will be examined in Section 4.1. Topics are wrapped within the boundaries of a prosodic phrase that distinguishes the topic from its comment, see Section 4.2.

4.1. Syntactic properties

Non-focused material can either precede or follow the focus. For instance, when the subject of a transitive verb is part of the presupposed information, it can surface either before the focus (SOV order), see (21a), or after the verb (OVS order), see (21b) (as shown in Section 3.1, a focused object is adjacent to the finite V).

(21) 'What did Nino buy?'

    a. *nino-m   p'amidor-i   i-q'id-a.*
        Nino-ERG tomato-NOM SV-buy-AOR.S.3.SG
        'Nino bought tomatoes.'

    b. *p'amidor-i   i-q'id-a   nino-m.*
        tomato-NOM SV-buy-AOR.S.3.SG Nino-ERG
        'Nino bought tomatoes.'

The difference between the two alternative realizations of presupposed information (preceding or following the focus) is subtle. These two options correspond to the difference between a topic-comment and a focus-background articulation that are known from many other languages. Preposing the presupposed information establishes an aboutness relation to the comment of the utterance; however it is not rare to find contexts that license only one of these options – to the exclusion of the other one.

The question is whether the alternative syntactic accounts introduced in Section 3.1 have consequences concerning the interpretation of the material preceding the focus. The Interface Condition Account implies that a syntactic operation is only triggered if there is material intervening between the focus and the finite verb. Taken together with the basic SOV order in the language, this account implies a subject/object asymmetry: While the prefocal subject is in its basic position, the prefocal object has undergone a syntactic operation in order to vacate the thematic layer of the clause, removing the non-focal material intervening between focus and verb, as indicated in (22).

(22)   Interface Condition Account[5]

    a. $[_{vP}$ Sbj $[_{VP}$ Obj^{foc} V $]$ $]$
    b. $[_{CP}$ Obj$_i$ $[_{vP}$ Sbj^{foc} t_i V $]$ $]$

The consequences of the Discourse Configurational Account are presented in (23). The basic assumption is that the FP is higher than the subject position, which implies that the landing site of the prefocal subject and object is in both cases the specifier of a projection that is higher than the FP, presumably the spec-CP.[6] The straightforward implication of this assumption is that the trigger of the syntactic operation that leads the subject to the spec-CP should be the same as the trigger that leads the object to this position (see Arregi 2003).

(23)   Discourse Configurational Account

    a. $[_{CP}$ Obj$_k$ $[_{FP}$ Sbj$_i$^{foc} $[_{F'}$ V$_j$ $[_{vP}$ t_i t_k $t_j$$]$ $]$
    b. $[_{CP}$ Sbj$_k$ $[_{FP}$ Obj$_i$^{foc} $[_{F'}$ V$_j$ $[_{vP}$ t_k t_i $t_j$$]$ $]$

The crucial empirical question is whether prefocal subjects and objects have the same discourse properties. Indeed, the data which have been reported

---

[5] We ignore the question whether the subject is fronted to a higher position for case checking purposes, since this problem introduces further questions that are independent of the matter at issue.

[6] See further discussion and argumentation in Skopeteas and Fanselow (2010: 1380).

for Georgian suggest a large subject/object asymmetry in the material preceding the focus. In utterances that involve (either contrastive or non-contrastive) object focus, the SOV order is more frequent than the OVS order, hence the background subject is preferably realized before the focus. In utterances that involve (either contrastive or non-contrastive) subject focus, we observe the opposite tendency: the SVO order is more frequent than the OSV order; i.e., the non-focused object is more frequently realized after the verb (see counts in Skopeteas and Fanselow 2010: 1373). We assume that the differences in frequency reflect different degrees of markedness that correspond to the derivational costs of the compared constructions. According to the Interface Condition Account, the SOV order with object focus is just the canonical order, while the OVS order involves an operation that leads the S to a peripheral position. This asymmetry accounts for the preference for SOV in object focus contexts. The fact that the OSV order is less frequent in subject focus contexts shows that the difference at issue cannot be reduced to a general preference for V-final configurations. According to the Interface Condition Account, both OSV and SVO satisfy the Interface Condition by means of an operation that leads the presupposed object to a (left or right) peripheral position. I.e., the Interface Condition alone does not predict any difference between OSV and SVO, which accounts for a part of our data. The fact that the SVO option is indeed more frequent than the OSV option is related to the fact that SVO is a kind of second neutral order in Georgian, i.e., an order that may appear out-of-the-blue as a result of a semantically vacuous head-fronting operation (see Section 2.1). Thus, the frequencies of linearizations in different information structural conditions result from the cumulation of the Interface Condition with the general word order preferences in this language. Theoretically, this is the kind of data pattern that we expect to see for a condition that is at work at the interfaces, while a feature-movement rule in the core grammar ideally corresponds to an empirical situation, in which the presence of a morphosyntactic feature for focus is a sufficient trigger for the constituent at issue to land at the designated position for checking purposes.

Hence, the frequencies in the occurrence of presupposed information before the preverbal focus suggest a subject/object asymmetry. This finding in the behavioral data goes hand in hand with an asymmetry in the acceptability of quantified noun phrases in the same configuration. Example (24a) shows a construction in which the auxiliary verb precedes the non-finite verb form, hence the element preceding negation is the stressed element that receives a focus interpretation. While it is possible to use a polarity item as a subject in the SOV order, see (24a), speakers have the intuition that the

utterance in (24b) with a quantified object in OSV is generally not acceptable – apart from a particular context in which the negative pronoun *araper-i*
'nothing-NOM' is linked to a previous mention of the same element in the
pretext, e.g. 'Do you know if somebody said nothing?'.[7] The requirement of
a mention of the very same element suggests that the discourse relation that
we observe in these contexts is stronger than the availability of a referent in
the common ground (which cannot apply for negative quantifiers). In the
contexts in which (24b) is licit, it should be interpreted as a citation of the
pretext, i.e., it is not a negative quantifier anymore.

(24) a. *aravi-s   araper-i   (ar)*
          nobody-DAT nothing-NOM NEG
          a-kv-s   še-nišn-ul-i.
          (SINV.3)CV-have-OINV.3(SINV.3.SG) PV-note-PTCP-NOM
          'Nobody has noted nothing.'

      b. **araper-i   aravi-s   (ar)*
          nothing-NOM nobody-DAT NEG
          a-kv-s   še-nišn-ul-i.
          (SINV.3)CV-have-OINV.3(SINV.3.SG) PV-note-PTCP-NOM
          'Nobody has noted nothing.'

The subject/object asymmetry in (24) shows that the information structural
properties of prefocal subjects are not identical with the corresponding
properties of the prefocal objects, which supports the view that these two
configurations correspond to different constituent structures as predicted
by the Interface Condition Account in (22).

There is evidence that Georgian also displays a higher position that may
host topic phrases, as illustrated by the examples in (25a–c). The common
denominator of these examples is that they involve a left dislocated phrase
that precedes the subject constituent. The point is that the properties of this
configuration are not uniform and this is illustrated by the variety of syntactic relations and discourse functions in these examples. Example (25a)
illustrates a sentence initial adjunct that introduces the property to which
the question applies. Example (25b) involves a topic phrase that corresponds
to the head of the quantifier in situ and delimits the set of entities for which

---

[7] Crucially, this asymmetry does not hold for the SVO/OVS orders, i.e., the phe-
     nomenon cannot be reduced to a general preference for subjects to precede non-
     subjects.

the quantified expression applies. The notion of delimitation cannot apply in example (25c), since the left dislocated first person pronoun is the subject of the last clause, i.e., the truth conditions of the expression with the topic phrase are identical to the truth conditions of the corresponding expression without the topic phrase. This configuration can be licensed by particular discourse conditions, for instance it may occur in order to introduce a new topic in the discourse flow. The diversity of these examples shows that Georgian has a configuration of left dislocation that may be used for a variety of communicative purposes.

(25) a. *k'arg-ad,   ɣmert-o   čem-o,   aba   vin   ari-s?*
         good-ADV God-VOC my-VOC indeed who(NOM) be.PRS-S.3.SG
         'As for being well, my God, who is that?'

      b. *c'inadadeba   ma-s   bevr-i*
         sentence(NOM) 3.SG-DAT many-NOM
         a-kv-s   ga-rče-ul-i.
         (SINV.3)CV-have-OINV.3(SINV.3.SG) PV-analyze-PTCP-NOM
         'As for sentences, he has analyzed a lot.'

      c. *Me,   did-i   xan-i=a,   ak*
         I-NOM big-NOM period-NOM=be.PRS.S.3.SG here
         v-cxovr-ob.
         S.1-live-THM(S1.SG)
         'As for me, I live here for a long time.'
         (lit. as for me, there is a long time (that) I live here.)

In constructions with parallel conjuncts that involve a contrastive topic and a contrastive focus, Georgian speakers show a robust preference for a linear order in which the contrastive topic precedes the verb and the contrastive focus follows it. This preference can be observed in utterances involving lists of pairs (see Skopeteas and Féry 2007). In answers to multiple constituent questions, speakers order a list of pairs by the highest constituent as in (26), producing a set of utterances with subjects as contrastive topics and objects as contrastive foci. The crucial issue is that speakers strongly prefer the V-medial order instead of the basic V-final option.

(26) 'Who is throwing what?'

gogona   *i-svr-i-s*   *burt-s,*   *bič'una*
little.girl(NOM) CV-throw-PRS-S.3.SG ball-DAT little.boy(NOM)
i-svr-i-s   *rgol-s.*
CV-throw-PRS-S.3.SG circle-DAT
'A/he little girl throws a/the ball and a/the little boy throws a/the
circle.' (Skopeteas and Féry 2007: 334)

The same pattern holds if the contrasted alternative is not explicit. Example
(27) is a paraphrase of Büring's (1997: 56) examples on partial topics. The
answer of B is a partial answer to A, which would be realized in English
with a "topic accent" (in Büring's terms). The crucial point is that Georgian
speakers have a preference for the V-medial order in this context.

(27) A: There is a male singer and a female singer. What do the singers wear?
      B: *momyeral*   *k'ac-s*   *a-kv-s*
         singer[DAT] man-DAT (SINV.3)CV-have-OINV.3(SINV.3.S)
         c'itel-i   *pexsacmel-eb-i.*
         red-NOM shoe-PL-NOM
         'The male singer has red shoes.'

The last examples are striking, in particular because they are not compatible with our conclusion in Section 3.1 that contrastive and exhaustive
foci can be equally realized either in the preverbal slot or in the postverbal
domain. We may hypothesize that we are discovering a language in which
contrastive topics behave like foci, i.e., they compete with foci for one and
the same position (which could be an instantiation of the assumption that
contrastive topics are topics containing a focus, see Krifka and Musan (this
volume)).

However, the adjacency of the topic to the verb is epiphenomenal, as the
examples in (28) clearly show (see the corresponding examples in English
in the introduction to this volume). Both examples involve a non-focused
subject constituent that intervenes between the contrastive focus and the
verb. Hence, contrastive topics do not seek adjacency to the finite verb and
this means that the preference of the contrastive foci to surface postverbally
is independent from the position of the contrastive topics (i.e., it does not
result from the fact that they compete with contrastive topics for the same
position).

(28) a. 'How is business going for Daimler-Chrysler?'

> *germania-ši mat-i   biznes-i*
> Germany-in they-NOM business-NOM
>
> *vitar-d-eb-a   karg-ad,   amerik'a-ši*
> develop-PASS-THM-PRS.PASS.S.3.SG good-ADV America-in
>
> *k'i   da-k'arg-es   pul-i.*
> and/but PV-loss-AOR.S.3.PL money-NOM
>
> 'In Germany, their business is going well, but in America they are losing money.'

> b. *žanmrtelob-is mxriv, is*
> heath-GEN   as.for 3.SG.NOM
>
> *gamo-i-q'ur-eb-a   mšvenivr-ad*
> PV-CV-look-THM-PRS.PASS.S.3.SG beautiful-ADV
>
> 'Healthwise he is fine.'

It has to be underlined that the tendency towards final contrastive foci in (26)–(28) is a preference, i.e., V-final orders are also possible in all these examples. Hence, we are reluctant to assume that this phenomenon is the result of a syntactic operation involving movement triggered by a morphosyntactic feature (i.e., a [contrast] feature needs to be checked in a ContrastP). It is more plausible to assume that speakers select a rhythmical/ accentual pattern, in which the topic is clearly separated from the rest by a prosodic boundary and the focus appears in the opposite edge of the utterance in which it is accented.

4.2. Prosodic properties

As shown in Section 3.2, see (19), topic constituents are realized in a separate prosodic phrase that is enclosed by a high boundary tone associated with the right edge. As already established in prosodic phonology, the correlation of topic phrases with a particular tonal pattern should not be interpreted as an intonational means of encoding topicalization (see Féry 2008). The rising pitch excursion of a topic constituent is just the consequence of the height boundary tone of any non-final prosodic phrase. Skopeteas and Féry (2007: 341) show that answers containing lists of pairs – as with the examples in (26) – have a consistent prosodic structure which is independent of the context (multiple constituent question or multiple subject question). The reported data, schematically illustrated in (29), suggest that there is a preference to realize the preverbal constituent in a separate prosodic phrase in the first conjunct and to integrate the preverbal constituent and the verb in a single prosodic phrase in the second conjunct.

(29) Idealized intonational contour: pair lists

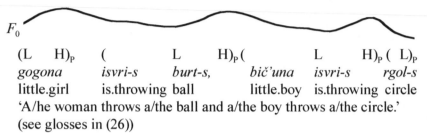

(L H)$_P$	(	L	H)$_P$(	L	H)$_P$ (L)$_P$
gogona	*isvri-s*	*burt-s,*		*bič'una*	*isvri-s* *rgol-s*
little.girl	is.throwing	ball		little.boy	is.throwing circle

'A/he woman throws a/the ball and a/the boy throws a/the circle.'
(see glosses in (26))

5.   Residual issues

5.1. Further syntactic constructions: passives and clefts

Already in earlier studies on information structure was pointed out that passive voice is an alternative strategy to achieve a linearization of the propositional content that is felicitous in particular contexts. Hence, Mathesius (1975: 156ff.) observed that passivization in English occurs in the same contexts with object-first orders in Czech. Georgian has an inflectional passive, hence a patient topic could be either expressed through O-fronting as in (30a) or though passivization as in (30b). However, experimental data show that Georgian speakers consistently select marked word orders instead of passivization in contexts that license a patient-first linearization (see Skopeteas and Fanselow 2009: 311). Indeed the use of passive voice for the expression of information structure is restricted by the fact that the inflectional passive in Georgian has rich semantic effects, e.g., epistemic modality, change of the aspectual properties, as well as many lexically determined deviations from the meaning of the corresponding active verb (see Asatiani 2009). Ivanishvili and Soselia (1999) report that only 2% of the occurrences of passive voice in a literary text corpus represent cases of diathesis which arguably were triggered by information-structural purposes.

(30) 'What about the deer?'

    a. *irem-i   monadire-m   mo-k'l-a.*
       deer-NOM   hunter-ERG   PV-kill-AOR.S.3
       'The hunter killed the deer.'

    b. *irem-i   monadir-is mier mo-i-k'l-a.*
       deer-NOM   hunter-GEN by   PV-PASS-kill-AOR.S
       'The deer was killed by the hunter.'

A further syntactic construction that is selected for the expression of information structure is the cleft construction. A characteristic instance of the use of clefts in English or French is a context that licenses focus on the clefted constituent (see Rochemont 1986: 127ff., Hedberg 2000: 907–912, Lambrecht 2001). Cleft constructions are available in Georgian too, as illustrated in (31). The clitic copula *=a* is the verb of the matrix clause, while the relative clause is introduced by a relative pronoun. However, cleft constructions occur less frequently than in English and French and bear additional discourse properties. A sentence such as (31) may occur in a context in which the focus has to be particularly emphasized, e.g., as a correction of a previous utterance in discourse.

(31) *es   bič'-i=a   vi-s-a-c   kal-i*
     this(NOM) boy-NOM=be.3.SG who-DAT-∅-also woman-NOM
     u-rt'q'-am-s.
     (IO.3)OV-hit-THM-S.3.SG
     'It's this boy whom the woman is hitting.'

In conclusion, syntactic constructions such as passives and clefts, that are sensitive to information structure, are available in Georgian. However, the main structural device for the formation of a contextually optimal linearization is the reordering of the basic constituents, as discussed in the sections 3.1 and 4.1.

5.2. Case marking

Probably the most salient property of Georgian syntax is the alternation between different case marking patterns depending on the inflectional properties (inflectional class and tense) of the verb. There are three case marking patterns of transitive verbs: the highest thematic role (agent) is marked (a) with a nominative case in the present/future tense of the inflectional classes 1 and 3 and in all tenses of the inflectional class 2, (b) with a dative case in the perfect tenses of the inflectional classes 1 and 3 and in all tenses of the inflectional class 4, or (c) with an ergative case in the aorist of the inflectional classes 1 and 3 (see details in Tschenkéli 1958, Harris 1981, Hewitt 1995 among others). A recurrent question in Georgian grammar is whether the case marking patterns reflect discourse-related asymmetries. For instance, the dative marking of agents in the perfect tense correlates with the fact that the Georgian perfect has epistemic properties, which motivates the idea that the dative subject reflects the fact that agents are less prominent than patients in the epistemic modality (see Asatiani 2007, Harris 1985: 295–300). A similar hypothesis has been examined for the ergative case. Enukidze (1981: 109) has shown that ergative agent ellipsis (aorist tense) is more frequent than nominative agent ellipsis (present/future tense and class 2 verbs). This finding indicates that there is a correlation between the perfective aspect and the discourse status of the agent.

However, empirical studies using corpora (see Tuite 1998: 41 f., based on the counts of Apridonidze 1986) show that case marking patterns do not interact with word order, which is the primary indicator of information structure in Georgian. Intuition data show that case marking does not affect the intuition of felicity in several contexts (see Skopeteas, Féry and Asatiani 2009: 123). Hence, it may be the case that the correlations of aspect and mood with the prominence of particular arguments account for the evolution of the complex case marking pattern that we can observe in several Kartvelian languages (compare also similar arguments for the evolution of split ergative systems in Chafe 1971). However, the synchronic facts show that speakers do not select case in order to express particular information structural concepts, which makes sense, since the case marking pattern depends on the inflectional properties of the verb.

5.3. Particles

Georgian has a long array of particles that interact with information structure. First, there are various focus-sensitive particles that take scope over the focused constituent: *mxolod* 'only', *sc'ored* 'just, exactly', *-c* 'also', *arc* 'not also', etc. An element that is directly associated with a discourse function is the particle *ai*. This particle frequently occurs in early stages of language acquisition as a demonstrative, e.g., *ai deda* 'that's a mother' or *ai c'igni* 'that's a book' (cf. Tsereteli 2007). In examples such as (32), this particle evokes a set of excluded alternatives.

(32) A: 'Who is smoking?'

  B: *ai   MONADIRE   ar   e-c'ev-a.*
  PRT   hunter(NOM)   not   CV-smoke-PRS.PASS.S.3.SG
  'The hunter doesn't smoke.'

The question is whether the *ai*-phrase is a contrastive topic or a contrastive focus. In case of a contrastive focus we expect the inference that all alternatives are excluded, i.e., the 'hunter' should be interpreted as the only member of the set of relevant alternatives for which the background of the answer holds true. A contrastive topic evokes a set of alternatives that is above the set of alternatives of the focus within the predication (see Büring 2003, Krifka and Musan, this volume), implying that there is at least a member of the set of alternative topics for which a further member of the set of alternative foci may hold true. Hence, the critical test is, what speakers infer from (32B) in a context containing further relevant alternatives, e.g., {hunter, fisher, teacher}. Native speakers have the intuition that the utterance implies that either the 'fisher' and/or the 'teacher' smokes or that there is no evidence whether these members of the set smoke. I.e., the utterance in (32B) is a partial answer to the question (see Büring 1997: 56) that restricts the truth of the proposition to the instantiation of the subject by the *ai*-phrase without implying anything about further alternatives. From these facts, we conclude that the *ai*-phrase is a contrastive topic.

6. Summary

This article has outlined the means of signaling information structure in Georgian. Beyond some constructional (passive, clefts) and morphological (discourse particles) means that interact with information structure, the major effects of focus and topic are found in syntax and prosody. At the syntactic level, there are two possible realizations of foci that do not correspond to different focus types. The first option is to realize the focus in a position that is left adjacent to the finite verb, while the second option is to realize the focus in the postverbal domain. Topic phrases precede the focus. The crucial issue with respect to topics is that there is evidence for a syntactic position that is higher than the subject constituent and that this position hosts topics.

  The effects on word order are accompanied by effects on the prosodic realization of the utterance. The major influences of information structure are found in prosodic phrasing. Preverbal foci are accompanied by a prosodic boundary on their left edge separating the focus from preceding non-focused material. The preverbal focus and the verb are integrated in a single prosodic phrase. Postverbal foci are also separated from the preceding material by a prosodic boundary, resulting in a prosodic structure in which the focus and the verb are realized in different prosodic phrases.

From a typological perspective, Georgian represents a language with mixed OV/VO properties. We have seen that the flexibility within the VP constituent has important consequences for the realization of information structure. The first peculiarity is that both OV and VO clauses may occur out of the blue. The second property is the array of possibilities for the expression of narrow focus: Georgian shares with V-final languages the preverbal position but is different from typical V-final languages in that it allows focusing on the postverbal material.

Glosses

∅: zero, 1: 1st person, 3: 3rd person, ADV: adverbializer, AOR: aorist, CV: characteristic vowel, DAT: dative, ERG: ergative, GEN: genitive, IO: indirect object, NEG: negation, NOM: nominative, NV: neutral version, OINV: inverted object, OV: objective version, PASS: passive, PL: plural, PV: preverb, PRS: present, PRT: particle, PST: past, PTCP: participle, S: subject, SG: singular, SINV: inverted subject, SV: subjective version, THM: thematic suffix, VOC: vocative.

References

Alkhazishvili, A.
    1959   porjadok slov i intonacija v prostom povestvovateljnom predlojenii
            gruzinskogo jazyka [Word order and intonation in simple affirmative sentences of the Georgian Language]. *Phonetics* (Moscow) 1: 367–414.
Anderson, Stephen R.
    1984   On representations in morphology: case, agreement, and inversion in Georgian. *Natural Language and Linguistic Theory* 2: 157–218.
Apridonidze, Shukia
    1986   *sit'q'vatganlageba axal kartulši* (XIX–XX sauk'unis p'rozis mixedvit. mart'ivi c'inadadeba) [Word order in Modern Georgian (according to the prose of the XIX–XX centuries. Simple sentence)]. Tbilisi: mecniereba.

Arregi, Carlos
    2003   Focus on Basque movements. Ph.D. dissertation, MIT.
Asatiani, Rusudan
    1982   mart'ivi c'inadadebis t'ip'ologiuri analizi (tanamedrove kartuli
                salit'erat'uro enis masalaze [The typological analysis of a simple
                sentence (on the data of modern literary Georgian)]. Tbilisi: mecnie-
                reba.
Asatiani, Rusudan
    2007   The main devices of foregrounding in the information structure of
                Georgian sentences. In *Proceedings of the Tbilisi Symposium on
                Language, Logic and Computation 2005*, Balder David ten Cate and
                Henk Zeevat (eds.), 21–30. Amsterdam: Springer.
Asatiani, Rusudan
    2009   *c'inadadebis sainpormacio st'rukt'ura: vnebiti gvaris pormata
                semant'ik'ur-k'ognit'iuri int'erp'ret'acia kartulši* [Information
                structure of a sentence: A cognitive-semantic interpretation of pas-
                sive verb forms in Georgian]. In *Kartvelological Library, dedicated
                to Guram Kartozia*, Iza Chantladze and Maia Lomia (eds.), 81–93.
                Tbilisi: sezani.
Bush, Ryan
    1999   Georgian yes-no question intonation. *Phonology at Santa Cruz* 6,
                1–11. Santa Cruz, CA: UC Santa Cruz.
Büring, Daniel
    1997   *The Meaning of Topic and Focus: the 59th Street Bridge Accent.*
                London and New York: Routledge.
Büring, Daniel
    2003   On D-trees, beans, and B-accents. *Linguistics and Philosophy* 26:
                511–545.
Comrie, Bernard
    1984   Some formal properties of focus in Modern Eastern Armenian.
                Annual of Armenian Linguistics 5: 1–21.
Chafe, Wallace L.
    1971   *Meaning and the Structure of Language.* Chicago, London: Chicago
                University Press.
É. Kiss, Katalin
    1998   Identificational vs. information focus. *Language* 74: 245–273.
Enukidze, Leila
    1981   c'inadadebis akt'ualuri danac'evreba da misi mimarteba sint'aksuri
                da semant'ik'uri analizis tanamedrove metodebtan [Actualization
                of a sentence and its relation to the contemporary methods of syn-
                tactic and semantic analysis]. *Tanamedrove zogadi enatmecnierebis
                sak'itxebi. Vol. VI,* 96–110. Tbilisi: LI Press.
Féry, Caroline
    2008   The fallacy of invariant phonological correlates of information
                structural notions. *Acta Linguistica Hungarica* 55: 347–360.

Féry, Caroline
2011   Focus realization as prosodic alignment. Ms., University of Frankfurt.
Frascarelli, Mara
2004   Dislocation, clitic resumption and minimality. A comparative anal-
            ysis of left and right topic constructions in Italian. In: Reineke Bok-
            Bennema, Bart Hollebrandse, Brigitte Kampers-Manhe and Petra
            Sleeman (eds.), *Romance Languages and Linguistic Theory 2002*,
            99–118. Amsterdam/Philadelphia: Benjamins.
Greenberg, Joseph H.
1963   Some universals of grammar with particular reference to the order of
            meaningful elements. In *Universals of Language* Joseph H. Green-
            berg (ed.), 73–75. London: MIT Press.
Harris, Alice
1981   *Georgian Syntax: A Study in Relational Grammar.* Cambridge: Cam-
            bridge University Press.
Harris, Alice
1985   *Diachronic Syntax: The Kartvelian Case.* New York: Academic Press.
Harris, Alice
1993   Georgian. In *Syntax: An International Handbook of Contemporary
            Research*, Joachim Jacobs, Arnim von Stechow, Wolfgang Sternefeld
            and Theo Vennemann (eds.), 1377–1397. Berlin/New York: Mouton
            de Gruyter.
Hedberg, Nancy
2000   The referential status of clefts. *Language* 76: 891–920.
Hewitt, George
1995   *Georgian: A Structural Reference Grammar.* Amsterdam: Benjamins.
Hewitt, George
2005   *Georgian: a Learner's Grammar* (first edition, 1995). London/New
            York: Routledge.
Herring, Susan C. and Paolillo, John C.
1995   Focus position in SOV languages. In *Word Order in Discourse*,
            Pamela Downing and Michael Noonan (eds.), 163–198. Amsterdam/
            Philadelphia: Benjamins.
Kılıçaslan, Yılmaz
2004   Syntax of information structure in Turkish. *Linguistics* 42: 717–765.
Kvachadze, Levan
1996   *Tanamedrove kartuli enis sint'aksi* [Syntax of the contemporary
            Georgian language]. (the fourth revised edition). Tbilisi: rubikoni.
Ivanishvili, Marine and Ether Soselia
1999   A morphological structure and semantics of the Georgian so-called
            passive form. *Proceedings of the 3rd and 4th International Symposium
            on Language, Logic and Computation.* Amsterdam: Institute for Logic,
            Language and Computation.

Jun, Sun-Ah, Chad Vicenik and Ingvar Lofstedt
  2007   Intonational phonology of Georgian. *UCLA Working Papers in Linguistics* 106: 41–57.
Lambrecht, Knud
  2001   A framework for the analysis of cleft constructions. *Linguistics* 39: 463–516.
Mathesius, Vilém
  1975   *A Functional Analysis of Present Day English on a General Linguistic Basis* [ed. by J. Vachek]. The Hague, Paris: Mouton.
McGinnis, Martha
  1995   Projection and position: Evidence from Georgian. In *Proceedings of Console IV, HIL*, Leiden. J. Costa, R. Goedemans, R. van der Vijver (eds.), 203–220.
McGinnis, Martha
  1997   Case and locality in L-syntax: Evidence from Georgian. In *MITWPL 32: The UPenn/MIT Roundtable on Argument Structure and Aspect*, Heidi Harley (ed.).
Nash, Lea
  1995   Portée argumentale at marquage casuel dans les langues SOV et dans les langues ergatives: l'exemple du géorgien. Ph.D. dissertation. Université de Paris VIII.
Pochkhua, B.
  1962   sit'q'vata rigi kartulshi [Word order in Georgian]. *Ibero-Caucasian Linguistics*. Vol. XIII, 109–125. Tbilisi: Georgian Academic Press.
Rochemont, Michael S.
  1986   *Focus in Generative Grammar*. Amsterdam: Benjamins.
Ross, John Robert
  1970   Gapping and the order of constituents. In *Progress in Linguistics*, Manfred Bierwisch and Karl Heidolph (eds.). The Hague: Mouton.
Samek-Lodovici, Vieri
  2006   When right dislocation meets the left-periphery. *Lingua* 116: 836–873.
Shanidze, Akaki
  1948   *Kartuli enis gramat'ik'a. II. sint'aksi* [Grammar of the Georgian language. II. Syntax]. Tbilisi: TSU Press.
Skopeteas Stavros and Gisbert Fanselow
  2009   Effects of givenness and constraints on free word order. In *Information Structure. Theoretical, Typological and Experimental Perspectives*, Malte Zimmermann and Caroline Féry (eds), 307–331. Oxford: Oxford University Press.
Skopeteas, Stavros and Gisbert Fanselow
  2010   Focus in Georgian and the expression of contrast. *Lingua* 120 (6): 1370–1391.

Skopeteas, Stavros and Caroline Féry
2007   Contrastive topics in pairing answers: A cross-linguistic produc-
        tion study. In *Linguistic Evidence 2006*, Samuel Featherston and
        Wolfgang Sternefeld (eds.), 327–347. Berlin/New York: Mouton de
        Gruyter.
Stavros Skopeteas and Caroline Féry
2010   Effect of narrow focus on tonal realization in Georgian. *Speech
        Prosody 2010*, 100237: 1–4.
Skopeteas Stavros, Caroline Féry and Rusudan Asatiani
2009   Word order and intonation in Georgian. *Lingua* 119: 102–127.
Tschenkéli, Kita
1958   *Einführung in die georgische Sprache, Bd. I–II.* Zürich: Amirani
        Verlag.
Tevdoradze, Izabella
1978   *Kartuli enis p'rosodiis sak'itxebi* [Issues of prosody of the Georgian
        language]. Tbilisi: TSU Press.
Tsereteli, Nutsa
2007   *c'inadadebis sainpormacio st'rukt'ura: implik'aciuri t'op'ik'i kartulši*
        [Information structure of the sentence: Implicational topic in
        Georgian]. Tbilisi: TSU Press (Issues of Linguistics).
Tuite, Kevin
1998   *Kartvelian morphosyntax: Number agreement and morphosyntactic
        orientation in the South Caucasian Languages.* Munich: Lincom
        Europa.
Vogt, Hans
1971   *Grammaire de la langue géorgienne.* Oslo: Universitetsforlaget.
Zhghenti, Sergi
1963   *Kartuli enis rit'mik'ul-melodik'uri st'ruk't'ura* [Rhythmic and
        melodic structure of the Georgian language]. Tbilisi: codna.

The information structure of Hungarian

Beáta Gyuris

1. Introduction

This contribution is an attempt to give a summary of how the most important categories of information structuring, particularly, focus, topic, and givenness/newness are expressed in Hungarian. Since this is a theme that has prominently figured in discussions during the last 30 years, we cannot even begin to do justice to the many important proposals found in the literature. What we intend to do here is to take the definitions of the relevant concepts of information structuring provided by Krifka and Musan (this volume) as our starting point, and look at how they are expressed in Hungarian sentences that occur in well-defined contexts, instead of only investigating isolated sentences.

In order to be able to follow the discussion below, it is important to know the following facts about Hungarian. Hungarian is a pro-drop language, in which agreement is present in several areas of the grammar. Particularly, the verb agrees with its subject and marks the definiteness of its object. Hungarian is a nominative-accusative language with 18 cases, which are lexically selected, encoded by morphosyntactic means, and not connected to particular sentence positions. This is one of the reasons why the major structural positions of the sentence are available for encoding certain logical and information structural functions. The relevant positions include (from left to right) the so-called *topic position(s)* ([Spec,TopP] in É. Kiss 2002), the position(s) for distributive quantifiers ([Spec,DistP]),[1] and the *focus position* ([Spec,FP]). The Hungarian sentence has been postulated, from É. Kiss (1981) onwards, to display a basic underlying division in a *topic* and a *comment* or *predicate part*, the latter of which constitutes all material following the topic(s),[2] and bears the only obligatory major stress of the

---

[1] According to current assumptions about the syntactic structure of Hungarian, both the TopP and the DistP projections are iterable (cf. É. Kiss 2002 for detailed discussion).

[2] The first proposal about there being such a basic division within the Hungarian sentence was put forth by Brassai (1860, 1863–65), whose views are summarized in É. Kiss (2008).

sentence on its left periphery.[3] As will be evident from the discussion to follow, placement of a constituent into a particular position is neither necessary nor sufficient for it to acquire the corresponding information structural status, and the names of the positions listed above are best viewed as convenient mnemonics reflecting the information structural status of their prototypical occupants.

2.   The expression of focus

2.1. Pragmatic uses of focus

The *wh*-phrases in constituent questions and the foci in their answers are normally situated in an immediately preverbal position in the Hungarian sentence, which has traditionally been referred to as the *focus position* (first proposed in É. Kiss 1981, claimed to be identical to the specifier of the functional projection FP by Brody 1990, 1995). A constituent in the focus position, as opposed to those in the *topic position(s)* (discussed in Section 3 below), forces verbal modifiers, situated as a default immediately in front of the verb in all-new sentences, to appear behind the verb.

As discussed by Komlósy (1994), verbal modifiers are constituents that form a complex predicate with the verb. The class includes verbal prefixes, predicate nominals and adjectives, various kinds of adverbials, arguments of the predicate lacking a determiner (objects, oblique complements expressing a goal, and non-agentive subjects), as well as bare infinitives (cf. also Komlósy and Ackermann 1983, Komlósy 1986, É. Kiss 2002). Verbal prefixes (also called *preverbs*) are "detachable pieces of lexical entries [which] they constitute together with a verbal root", which could be viewed historically as "incorporated verbal modifiers of various sorts" (Komlósy 1994: 101–102). Their contribution to the meaning of the sentence ranges from encoding a directional or locational meaning that can be added productively to the meaning of various verbs, through encoding various *Aktionsart* properties, or contributing to an idiosyncratic interpretation of the prefix+verb complex that cannot be derived from the interpretations of the components, to encoding the perfectivity of the verb.[4]

---

[3] According to Varga (2002: 5), major-stressed syllables have an extra intensity and are pitch-accented.

[4] Many of the constituent types in the verbal modifier category can also serve as foci. Tests for finding out whether a particular constituent in particular sentence

(1)–(3) show that there is no distinction between subjects, objects or adverbials as to whether they can occupy the focus position. As a default, constituents in this position must bear major stress (cf. Varga 2002), which will be marked by capitalization in what follows.[5]

In the full answers shown in (1B)–(3B), the constituents not marked with the 'F' subscript are destressed, due to the obligatory destressing of the verb following a preverbal focus (cf. Kálmán and Nádasdy 1994, Varga 1983, 2002) and to the destressing of given constituents. In most natural discourses, constituents of the latter type are normally elided, as the brackets indicate (cf. Section 4 for further discussion).

(1) A: *Ki   főzte   meg tegnap   a   vacsorát?*   (Subject)
       who cooked PFX yesterday the dinner.ACC
       'Who cooked dinner yesterday?'

    B: *[JÁnos]_F (főzte   meg tegnap   a   vacsorát).*
       John   cooked PFX yesterday the dinner.ACC
       '[John]_F (cooked dinner yesterday).'

(2) A: *Mit   főzött   meg tegnap   János?*   (Object)
       what.ACC cooked PFX yesterday John
       'What did John cook yesterday?'

    B: *[A VAcsorát]_F (főzte   meg tegnap   János).*
       the dinner.ACC cooked PFX yesterday John
       '(John cooked) [dinner]_F (yesterday).'

(3) A: *Mikor főzte   meg János a   vacsorát?*   (Adverb)
       when cooked PFX John   the dinner.ACC
       'When did John cook dinner?'

---

is to be classified as a preverbal focus or a verbal modifier include checking whether it can be negated (which only applies to foci) and whether the sentence encodes VP- or sentence-focus (see (11)–(12) below for the relevant criteria and (13)–(14) for qualifications on their applicability). To account for the adjacency between the constituent in focus position and the V, as well as for the apparent complementary distribution of the verbal prefix and the former, Brody (1990, 1995) assumes V-to-F movement. É. Kiss (2002) proposes, however, that verbal modifiers are situated in the specifier of AspP, which is not projected simultaneously with an FP.

[5] Note that lexical stress always falls on the first syllable of the word in Hungarian.

B: *[TEGnap]$_F$ (főzte   meg János a   vacsorát).*
yesterday cooked PFX John   the dinner.ACC
'(John cooked dinner) [yesterday]$_F$.'

As the following mini-dialogue shows, the focus is also situated in the immediately preverbal focus position in answers to 'mention-some' questions (cf. Section 2.2 for discussion of the significance of the latter fact):

(4)   A: *Hol   vehetem   meg a   mai   újságot?*
where buy.poss.1SG PFX the today's newspaper.ACC
'Where can I buy today's newspaper?'

B: *Például   [az ÁLlomáson]$_F$ (veheted   meg).*
example.for the railway.station.on buy.poss.2SG PFX
'(You can buy it) [at the station]$_F$, for example.'

The contrast between the grammaticality of (5B) versus (5B′) as potential answers to question (5A) shows that a constituent smaller than a phrase can only be moved to the focus position if the rest of the phrase is also pied piped there. The acceptable answer in (5B″) indicates that the given part of the NP in focus position can also be elided, provided that the case marking suffix is cliticized on the overt subconstituent:

(5)   A: *Milyen   vacsorát   főzött   János?*
what.kind dinner.ACC cooked John
'What kind of dinner did John cook?'

B: *[FInom]$_F$ vacsorát   (főzött János).*
tasty   dinner.ACC cooked John
'(John cooked) a [tasty]$_F$ dinner.'

B′: **[FInom]$_F$ (főzött János vacsorát).*
tasty   cooked John dinner.ACC
Intended: '(John cooked) a [tasty]$_F$ dinner/one.'

B″: *[FInomat]$_F$.*
tasty.ACC
'A [tasty]$_F$ one.'

As shown in (6B), the same strategy, that is, placement into the focus position, is used for marking corrective focus as well.

(6)   A: *MAri MEGfőzte   TEGnap   a   VAcsorát.*
Mary PFX.cooked yesterday the dinner.ACC
'[Mary cooked dinner yesterday.]$_F$'

B: *Nem, [JÁnos]*_F *főzte   meg (tegnap   a   vacsorát).*
no John   cooked PFX yesterday the dinner.ACC
'No, [John]_F cooked dinner/it (yesterday).'

There are two notable exceptions to the generalizations described above about the placement of *wh*-words and foci in answers. First, as shown in (7), as opposed to the rest of the *wh*-constituents, *miért* 'why' can also occur in front of a constituent situated in the focus position (cf. É. Kiss 2002 for discussion):

(7) *MIért JÁnos főzte   meg tegnap   a   vacsorát?*
      why   John cooked PFX yesterday the dinner.ACC
      'Why did (exactly) [John]_F cook dinner yesterday?'

Second, universal DPs or adverbial phrases cannot appear in the preverbal focus position if their determiner or quantificational adverb is focused, cf. (8B) vs. (8B'), but they do turn up there if (a subconstituent of) the rest of the phrase constitutes the focus of an answer or a corrective focus, as (9B) shows. The universal noun phrase in (8B) and (9A) is situated in the quantifier position of the sentence, which hosts distributive quantifiers (cf. É. Kiss 1991, 1994, Szabolcsi 1997 for discussion), and which precedes the immediately preverbal position, where the verbal modifier is situated:

(8) A: *Hány   diák   jött   el   az előadásra?*
        how.many student came PFX the talk.onto
        'How many students came to the talk?'

     B: *[MInden]*_F *diák   eljött   az előadásra.*
        every   student PFX.came the talk.onto
        '[Every]_F student came to the talk.'

     B': **[MInden]*_F *diák   jött   el   az előadásra.*
         every   student came PFX the talk.onto
         Intended: '[Every]_F student came to the talk.'

(9) A: *Minden tanár   eljött   az előadásra.*
        every   teacher PFX.came the talk.onto
        'Every teacher came to the talk.'

     B: *Minden [DIák]*_F *jött   el   az előadásra.*
        every   student came PFX the talk.onto
        'Every [student]_F came to the talk.'

As shown in (10B–B'), whenever the quantifier position contains a focused universal determiner, the simultaneous filling of the focus position is allowed as well. The latter is occupied by the proper name *János* in the example, which plays the role of a so-called second occurrence focus (cf. Krifka 1999). (10B') illustrates an alternative prosodic realization of (10B), which shows that the constituent in the focus position is optionally deaccented if it is preceded by a constituent in the quantifier position, which must bear major stress (cf. Kenesei 1989):

(10)   A: *[JÁnos]$_F$ olvasta el   a   Háború és   békét.*
         John   read   PFX the war   and peace.ACC
         '(It was) [John]$_F$ (who) read *War and Peace.*'

       B: *[MINden könyvet]$_F$ JÁnos olvasott el.*
         every   book.ACC John   read   PFX
         'It was John who read [every]$_F$ book.'

       B': *[MINden könyvet]$_F$ János olvasott el.*
         every   book.ACC John   read   PFX
         'It was John who read [every]$_F$ book.'[6]

We turn now to cases of VP- and sentence-focus. As the examples in (11)–(12) illustrate, VP- or sentence focus normally does not involve movement to the focus position. In these sentences, both the verb and the postverbal constituents normally bear stress (cf. Kálmán et al. 1986, Kálmán C. et al. 1989 for sentence focus, and Kenesei 1986, 1989, 1998 for VP-focus). The sentence-initial subject noun phrases in (11B) and (12B) are assumed to be in the topic position (cf. Section 3 for a discussion about their topic status).

(11)   A: *Mit   csinált János?*
         what.ACC did   John
         'What did John do?'

       B: *János [MEGfőzte a   VAcsorát]$_F$.*
         John PFX.cooked the dinner.ACC
         '[John]$_T$ [cooked dinner]$_F$.'

---

[6]   Cf. 2.2 for an explanation of why the preferred English translations of (10 A,B,B') contain the cleft construction.

(12) A: *Mi   történt?*
      what happened
      'What happened?'

   B: *[JÁnos MEGfőzte   a   VAcsorát]_F.*
      John PFX.cooked the dinner.ACC
      '[John cooked dinner]_F.'

   B': *[MEGfőzte JÁnos a VAcsorát]_F.*
      '[John cooked dinner]_F.'

However, it is not impossible for arguments of the verb (as opposed to adjuncts) to appear in the focus position in sentences containing a VP-focus (cf. É. Kiss 1987–88, Kenesei 1998, Varga 1983). (13) shows an example of this phenomenon:

(13) *PÉter a   [HAMletet   olvasta fel   MArinak]_F,   míg   JÁnos*
      Peter the Hamlet.ACC read   PFX Mary.DAT while John
      az [Autót   szedte APró DArabokra]_F.
      the car.ACC took   small pieces.onto
      'Peter [was reading Hamlet to Mary]_F while John [was taking the car into small pieces]_F.'   (Kenesei 1998: 74, notation amended)

An important condition (not mentioned by the above authors) for the above configuration to be realized seems to be, on the one hand, that the verbal prefix or other verbal modifier, if present, should appear behind the verb for independent reasons (e.g., to indicate the lack of perfectivity of the verb, cf. Piñón 1995), and that the property expressed by the rest of the sentence should not apply for any relevant alternatives of the constituent in the focus position. (For (13), it is the property of being read by Peter to Mary. Cf. Section 2.2 for more detailed discussion of the second condition.)[7]

---

[7] In the language of the news one often finds text-initial sentences (thus encoding sentence-focus) with a constituent in focus position and a verbal modifier situated behind the verb, as illustrated in i):

   i) *[KÉT gyalogost   ütött el   egy TAxisofőr BUdán.]_F*
      two pedestrian.ACC hit   PFX one taxi-driver Buda.on
      'A taxi-driver hit two pedestrians in Buda.'

   Although the above uses of sentences like i) have not been systematically analyzed in the literature, it appears that they are used for the special prosodic effect that the stressing of the constituent in focus position and the simultaneous destressing of the following verb results in.

There are a range of constituents including downward monotonic and non-monotonic quantifiers, negative adverbs of frequency, degree, and manner (like *ritkán* 'seldom', *alig* 'barely', *csúnyán* 'in an ugly manner', *rosszul* 'badly'), as well as bare plural noun phrases, which must occupy the focus position as a default in sentences with VP or sentence-focus[8]. This phenomenon is illustrated in (14a–c), which are all appropriate answers to the question *What happened?*:

(14) a. *[KEvés diák   bukott meg a   VIzsgán.]*$_F$
          few   student failed PFX the exam.on
          'Few students failed the exam.'

      b. *[JÁnos CSÚnyán   írta   meg a   LECkét.]*$_F$
          John   in.an.ugly.way wrote PFX the homework.ACC
          'John wrote the homework in an ugly way.'

      c. *[FÁkat   csavart ki   a   SZÉL.]*$_F$
          trees.ACC turned   PFX the wind
          'The wind turned trees out.'

The surface constituent order of sentences expressing verum focus is similar to those expressing VP- or sentence focus, cf. (11) and (12) above, as illustrated in (15), but without the option of moving a constituent to the focus position. The prosody of the two kinds of structures is different, however: In sentences expressing verum focus, only the verbal modifier situated in preverbal position bears stress, or the verb in the case of the latter's absence; the rest of the constituents get destressed, normally even elided.

(15) A: *János nem főzte   meg vacsorát.*
          John   not cooked PFX dinner.ACC
          'John did not cook dinner.'

      B: *De, (János) [MEGfőzte]*$_{Verum}$ *(vacsorát).*[9]
          no   John   PFX.cooked   dinner.ACC
          'No, John/he [did]$_{Verum}$ (cook dinner).'[10]

---

[8] É. Kiss (1998) attributes this fact to an inherent [+focus] feature of the types of constituents listed.

[9] This sentence has the same surface constituent order and prosody as its counterpart with the verb focused, which would be an appropriate answer to the following question, for example: *What did John do with the dinner?*

[10] *De* is response particle in Hungarian marking a positive answer to a negative *yes-no* question, thus having an analogous interpretation as the German response particle *doch*, for example.

There is, however, a class of verbs referred to by Komlósy (1989) as *stress-avoiding* ones, which can only bear stress under exceptional circumstances. In the presence of stress-avoiding verbs, VP- and sentence focus, as well as verum focus are expressed by placing one particular argument in the focus position, causing the verb to become destressed, as illustrated in (16B)–(18B), respectively.

(16) A: *Mit   csinált János?*
      what.ACC did   John
      'What did John do?'

   B: *János [PÉternél felejtette a   FÜzetét]_F.*
      John Peter.at forgot   the exercise.book.his.ACC
      'John [left his exercise-book at Peter's]_F.'   (Komlósy 1989: 174)

(17) A: *Mi   történt?*
      what happened
      'What happened?'

   B: *[JÁnos PÉternél felejtette a   FÜzetét]_F.*
      John Peter.at forgot   the exercise.book.his.ACC
      '[John left his exercise-book at Peter's]_F.'

(18) A: *János nem felejtette Péternél a   füzetét.*
      John not forgot   Peter.at the exercise-book.his.ACC
      'John did not leave his exercise-book at Peter's.'

   B: *De, János [PÉternél felejtette]_{Verum} (a   füzetét).*
      No, John   Peter.at forgot   the exercise.book.his.ACC
      'No, John [did]_{Verum} leave his exercise-book/it at Peter's.'

Although the majority of stress-avoiding verbs are prefixless, there are some with a prefix as well, like the one illustrated below:

(19) A: *János nem néz ki   betegnek.*
      John not look PFX ill.DAT
      'John does not look ill.'

   B: *De, (János) [BEtegnek néz ki]_{Verum}.*
      No, John   ill.DAT   look PFX
      'No, John/he [does]_{Verum} look ill.'

Multiple constituent questions come in two sorts in Hungarian. The first one, which expects a pair-list answer, is formed by placing all the *wh*-expressions preverbally. In the conjuncts of the corresponding list answer, the constituents providing an answer to the last of the *wh*-expressions, which is in turn situated in the focus position of the question, occupy the focus positions in the answer (if allowed to appear there for independent reasons), whereas the constituents providing answers to the other interrogative expressions are situated preferably in front of the latter (in the topic position, cf. Section 3) or postverbally. (As discussed by É. Kiss 1993, the first among two interrogative expressions in the multiple constituent question type illustrated above must be *specific*, a property referred to as D-linked by Comorovski 1996.)

(20) A: *Ki   mit   vett   meg?*
      who what.ACC bought PFX
      'Who bought what?'

    B: *MAri*[11] *[egy ÚJságot]$_F$ (vett   meg),*
      Mary a   newspaper.ACC bought PFX
      JÁnos [egy KÖNYvet]$_F$ (vett   meg).
      John a   book.ACC   bought PFX
      'Mary bought [a newspaper]$_F$ and John (bought) [a book]$_F$.'

The second kind of multiple constituent question, which asks for a single pair answer, is formed by placing one *wh*-expression into the focus position and the rest of them after the verb:

(21) A: *Ki   látogatott   meg   kit?*
      who   visited PFX   who.ACC
      'Who visited whom?'

    B: *[MAri]$_F$ látogatta meg [JÁnost]$_F$, (nem [JÁnos]$_F$ [MArit]$_F$).*
      Mary   visited PFX John.ACC not John   Mary.ACC
      '[Mary]$_F$ visited [John]$_F$, (not [John]$_F$ [Mary]$_F$).'

---

[11] The initial constituents in the two conjuncts would, on the one hand, satisfy the definition of focus, because they answer *wh*-questions. On the other hand, they are situated in the topic positions of their sentences, therefore, as discussed in Section 3, they also satisfy the information structural properties of topics. It appears, therefore, that they are best classified as *contrastive topics* (cf. Section 3.2) when appearing in the question-answer sequence (20).

As noted by É. Kiss (1993), the latter type of multiple constituent question is only possible if the domains of the two *wh*-expressions are identical.[12]

2.2. Semantic uses of focus

The property most often discussed in the literature in connection with the Hungarian focus position is that placement of a constituent in that position seems to have an effect on the truth conditions of the sentence, in addition to indicating certain information structural properties of the relevant constituent. In particular, the constituents occupying the focus position are traditionally associated with an exhaustive (or identificational) interpretation, which means, modulo some qualifications discussed below, that the constituent is interpreted as if it were associated with the exclusive particle *only*. (The above property of the preverbal focus was first noted by Szabolcsi 1980, 1981a, 1981b, and Hunyadi 1981, for detailed discussion consider, for example, Szabolcsi 1994, Kenesei 1986, 1989, É. Kiss 1998, Van Leusen and Kálmán 1993, Horvath 1986, 2000, 2006.) Due to the latter interpretational feature of the Hungarian preverbal focus, isolated sentences are normally translated into English in the literature with the help of the cleft or the pseudo-cleft construction, which is normally attributed the same kind of exhaustive/identificational interpretation (cf. É Kiss 1998 for detailed discussion). From now on, we will also indicate the availability of the latter strategy in the translations of the Hungarian examples. The fact that the preverbal focus makes the contribution discussed above to the truth conditions of the sentence is usually demonstrated by the invalidity of certain inferences that would have to be valid if placement in the focus position only had an effect on information structuring. First, as noted by Szabolcsi (1981a, b), (22a) does not entail (22b), and the truth of (22b) excludes the truth of the proposition that John cooked dinner and lunch (cf. É. Kiss 1998 for further discussion). Second, according to the observation attributed to

---

[12] For example, the interrogative sentence in i) can only have an interpretation of an echo-question, which is also indicated by the fact that it can only be uttered with a final rise-fall tone with the peak on the penultimate syllable (an intonation pattern characteristic of echo-questions):

i) *Ki   vásárolt mit?*
   who bought   what.acc
   'Who bought what?'

Donka Farkas by É. Kiss (1998), among (22c) and (22d) only the latter can be uttered as a reaction to (22b).[13]

(22) a. *János [a   VAcsorát   és   az   Ebédet]$_F$ főzte   meg.*
       John   the dinner.ACC and the lunch.ACC cooked PFX.
       '(What) John cooked (was) [dinner and lunch]$_F$.'

   b. *János [a   VAcsorát]$_F$ főzte   meg.*
      John   the dinner.ACC cooked PFX
      '(What) John cooked (was) [dinner]$_F$.'

   c. *Igen, és   János az   Ebédet   is   megfőzte.*
      yes   and John   the lunch.ACC too PFX.cooked
      'Yes, and John also cooked [lunch]$_F$.'

   d. *Nem, János az   Ebédet   is   megfőzte.*
      no   John   the lunch.ACC too PFX.cooked
      'No, John also cooked [lunch]$_F$.'

Third, as observed by Van Leusen and Kálmán (1993), (23B), as opposed to (23B'), is anomalous, no matter whether it be uttered in the context of (23A) or in isolation, due to the fact that the conjuncts individually would entail that John did not cook anything else, other than dinner and that he did not cook anything else, other than lunch, respectively:

(23) A: *Mit   főzött   meg János?*
        what.ACC cooked PFX John
        'What did John cook?'

   B: #*János [a   VAcsorát]$_F$ főzte   meg és   [az Ebédet]$_F$ (főzte meg).*
      John   the dinner.ACC cooked PFX and the lunch.ACC cooked PFX
      '(What) John cooked (was) [dinner]$_F$ and (what) he cooked (was) [lunch]$_F$.'

---

[13] The exhaustive interpretation of the constituents in the focus position of the Hungarian sentence can also be demonstrated by the following data. In a school setting, an answer to the question *What are the properties of the number 12?*, shown in i) (where the sentence-final participle is assumed to follow a covert copula, which is immediately preceded by the suffixed number word in focus position), does not simply count as incomplete but as false (since it entails that 12 does not have any other divisors than 2):

i) *A   tizenkettő [KETtővel]$_F$ osztható.*
   the twelve   two.with   divisible
   '(What) twelve is divisible by (is) [two]$_F$.'

B': *János [a VAcsorát és az Ebédet]ᵣ főzte meg.*
John the dinner.ACC and the lunch.ACC cooked PFX
'(What) John cooked (was) [dinner and lunch]ₚ.'

The contribution of constituents situated in the preverbal focus position and those (additionally) associated with the Hungarian focus sensitive exclusive particle *csak* 'only' to the interpretation of sentences, however, is not completely identical. As pointed out by Szabolcsi (1994), (22b) and its counterpart with the exclusive particle, shown in (24), differ as to where the division between presupposed and asserted components lies: Roughly, (22b) presupposes that there is a unique maximal entity that John cooked, and asserts that it is equivalent to the dinner, whereas (24) presupposes (in accordance with Horn's 1972 proposal on the interpretation of *only*) that John cooked dinner and asserts that it is the only thing that John cooked.

(24) *János csak [a VAcsorát]ᵣ főzte meg.*
John only the dinner.ACC cooked PFX
'John only cooked [dinner]ₚ.'

Comparison of the negated versions of (22b) and (24), shown in (25a–b), makes the difference more visible: Whereas (25a) does not entail that John cooked dinner, (25b) does.

(25) a. *János NEM [a vacsorát]ᵣ főzte meg.*
     John not the dinner.ACC cooked PFX
     'What John cooked was not [dinner]ₚ.'

  b. *János NEMcsak [a vacsorát]ᵣ főzte meg.*
     John not.only the dinner.ACC cooked PFX
     'John not only cooked [dinner]ₚ.'

The contrast between the well-formed (26a) and the ill-formed (26b) illustrates the same difference:

(26) a. *[MAri]ᵣ érkezett meg elsőnek.*
     Mary arrived PFX first.DAT
     '(It was) [Mary]ₚ (who) arrived first.'

  b. **Csak [MAri]ᵣ érkezett meg elsőnek.*
     only Mary arrived PFX first.DAT
     *'Only [Mary]ₚ arrived first.'
     (variant of É. Kiss 1998: 267, ex. (66b))

The claim that the constituents occupying the preverbal focus position in Hungarian receive an exhaustive reading is challenged by examples like (4A–B), discussed above. Additionally, there are several focus-sensitive expressions with an inherently non-exhaustive meaning like *jórészt* 'for the most part' or *többek között* 'among others', which can associate with the constituent in the focus position (cf. Wedgwood, Pethő and Cann 2006 for examples and discussion):

(27)   *Mari többek között [JÁnost]$_F$ léptette   elő.*
       Mari others among John.ACC promoted PFX
       'Mary promoted [John]$_F$, among others.'

Let us now consider the range of syntactic positions *csak* 'only' can occupy in the sentence. In addition to immediately preceding the preverbal focus, illustrated in (24), the exclusive particle can also occupy postverbal positions while maintaining its association with the preverbal focus, provided that it bears a major stress, and is separated from other postverbal constituents with a pause, as illustrated in (28a, b) (cf. É. Kiss 2002 for discussion):

(28)   a. *[A VAcsorát]$_F$ főzte   meg CSAK | János.*
          the dinner.ACC cooked PFX only   John
          'John only cooked [dinner]$_F$.'

       b. *[A VAcsorát]$_F$ főzte   meg János | CSAK.*
          the dinner.ACC cooked PFX John   only
          'John only cooked [dinner]$_F$.'

If and only if another constituent occupies the preverbal focus position, can *csak* also be associated with a postverbal (second occurrence) focus, from which it is not separated by a pause, as illustrated in (29a, b).

(29)   a. *[JÁnos]$_F$ főzte   meg csak [a vacsorát]$_F$.*
          John   cooked PFX only the dinner.ACC
          '(It was) [John]$_F$ (who) only cooked [dinner]$_F$.'

       b. *[JÁnos]$_F$ főzte   meg [a vacsorát]$_F$ csak.*
          John   cooked PFX the dinner.ACC only
          '(It was) [John]$_F$ (who) only cooked [dinner]$_F$.'

As shown in (30), it is possible to have more than one occurrence of the exclusive particle in a Hungarian sentence; these are then associated with different foci:

(30) *Csak [MAri]$_F$ olvasta el   csak [a cikket]$_F$.*
      only Mary   read   PFX only the paper.ACC
      'Only [Mary]$_F$ read only [the paper]$_F$.'

Although the default interpretation of sentences like (30) is the one where the postverbal *csak* is associated with a second occurrence focus, it is also possible for both *csak*-phrases to be corrective foci, which would be the case if (30) were uttered as a reaction to a sentence like *John and Mari both read the paper and the book* (with major stress on the postverbal focus as well).

   Csak 'only' can also be associated with the verb or the VP, as the following examples indicate:

(31) *János csak [DÚdolta]$_F$ a dalt,   mert   nem tudta a   szövegét.*
      John only hummed   the song.ACC because not   knew the text.its.ACC
      'John only [hummed]$_F$ the song because he did not know its text.'
      (É. Kiss 1998: 265)

(32) *János szinte semmit   sem csinált egész nap, csak [LEvitte*
      John almost nothing.ACC not did   whole day only PFX.took
      a   KUtyát SÉtálni]$_F$.
      the dog.ACC walk.INF
      'John did almost nothing the whole day, he only [took the dog for a walk]$_F$.'   (É. Kiss 1998: 265)

The Hungarian equivalents of the focus-sensitive particles *also* and *even*, *is* and *még...is*, respectively, must be associated with a constituent outside the focus position, as shown in (33a, b) and (34a, b), respectively. (33c) and (34c) illustrate ill-formed examples where the constituent associated with the above particles is situated in the preverbal focus position. (The ungrammaticality of the latter examples is attributed by É. Kiss 1998 to the fact that the exclusion-by-identification meaning of the preverbal focus position focus is incompatible with the basic meaning of these particles.)

(33) a. *[A VAcsorát]$_F$ is   megfőzte   János.*
          the dinner.ACC also PFX.cooked John
          'John also cooked [dinner]$_F$.'

      b. *János megfőzte   [a   VAcsorát]$_F$ is.*
          John PFX.cooked the dinner.ACC also
          'John also cooked [dinner]$_F$.'

c. *[A   VAcsorát]$_F$ is   főzte   meg János.
   the dinner.ACC also cooked PFX John
   Intended: 'John also cooked [dinner]$_F$.'

(34) a. *Még [a   VAcsorát]$_F$ is   megfőzte   János.*
        even the dinner.ACC also PFX.cooked John
        'John even cooked [dinner]$_F$.'

    b. *János megfőzte   még [a   VAcsorát]$_F$ is.*
       John PFX.cooked even the dinner.ACC also
       'John even cooked [dinner]$_F$.'

    c. **Még [a   VAcsorát]$_F$ is   főzte   meg János.*
       even the dinner.ACC also cooked PFX John
       Intended: 'John even cooked [dinner]$_F$.'

In Hungarian, it is possible for focus to occur in a syntactic island with respect to the exclusive particle, both in the preverbal focus position and postverbally (in the presence of a preverbal focus):

(35) a. *János csak a   [PIros]$_F$ inget   veszi fel.*
        John only the red   shirt.ACC takes PFX
        'John only wears the [red]$_F$ shirt.'

    b. *[János]$_F$ veszi fel   csak a   [piros]$_F$ inget.*
       John   takes PFX only the red   shirt.ACC
       '(It is) [John]$_F$ (who) wears only the [red]$_F$ shirt.'

This ends our description of how focus is expressed in Hungarian. In the next section we turn to another syntactically encoded category, that of topics.

3. The expression of topics

3.1. Expression of aboutness topics

Aboutness topics are expressed in Hungarian by putting the relevant constituent into one of the topic positions, which are situated on the left periphery of the sentence, and which will be referred to together as the *topic field* (cf. É. Kiss 1981 for a first discussion). According to É. Kiss (2002), topics occupy the specifier position of an iterable TopP projection. As mentioned in the introduction and as illustrated in (36B) and (37B), the topic field precedes both the focus and the (distributive) quantifier positions in the preverbal domain of Hungarian (cf. É. Kiss 2002). Continuing topics are always deaccented, and preferably even deleted, as is given material following the focus, as indicated by the brackets in (36B) (see Section 4 for further discussion).

(36) A: *Hová   ment el   János?*
      where.to went PFX John
      'Where did John go?'

   B: *([János]$_T$) [BRAzíliába]$_F$ (ment el).*
      John   Brazil.into   went PFX
      '[John]$_T$ went to [Brazil]$_F$.'

(37) A: *Mi   van Jánossal?*
      what is   John.with
      'What about John?'

   B: *([János]$_T$) [MINdenkit   MEGsértett]$_F$.*
      John   everybody.ACC PFX.offended
      '[John]$_T$ [offended everybody]$_F$.'

É. Kiss (1987, 1994, 2002, etc.) offers two tests for determining whether a particular constituent is situated in the topic field or not. First, whereas a verb following a preverbal focus is obligatorily destressed, as discussed above,[14] one following a constituent in topic position is not. Second, whereas sentence-adverbials are allowed to occur in front of, among, and immediately after the constituents in the topic positions, they cannot appear after the constituent in focus position. These tests show that the sentence-initial proper name in the second sentence of the discourse in (38A–B) is also situated in topic position, even if its status as a topic is not obvious from the context. Although the preceding question, (38A), does not ask about the referent of *János*, (38B) is a legitimate answer to it, but as it stands, it must be interpreted as being about John. The sentence-initial proper name in (38B), due to its referent being *new*, has to bear a major stress in addition (Varga 1983):

(38) A: *Mi   történt?*
      what happened
      'What happened?'

---

[14] Cf. Kálmán and Nádasdy (1994), who propose that preverbal focus bears an 'eradicating stress'.

B: *[[JÁnos]ₜ sajnos   ELment   BRAzíliába]ꜰ.*
John   unfortunately PFX.went Brazil.into
'[[John]ₜ unfortunately went to Brazil]ꜰ.'

According to the tests listed above, (39a), in contrast to (39b), has two constituents within the topic field:

(39) a. *(Szerencsére) [JÁnos]ₜ (szerencsére) [MArit]ₜ   (szerencsére)*
          luckily   John   luckily   Mary.ACC luckily
          MEGlátta a   BUliban.
          PFX.saw   the party.in
          '(Luckily,) [John]ₜ saw [Mary]ₜ at the party.'

      b. *(Szerencsére) [JÁnos]ₜ (szerencsére) [MArit]ꜰ   (*szerencsére)*
          luckily   John   luckily   Mary.ACC luckily
          látta meg a   buliban.
          saw PFX the party.in
          '(Luckily,) [John]ₜ saw [Mary]ꜰ at the party.'

If placement of a constituent in a topic position were always a sign of the topical status of that constituent, (39a) would have to mean, according to standard assumptions (cf. Krifka and Musan, this volume) that the sentence is to be interpreted as being about the pair constituted by the referents of these expressions. Empirical evidence does not seem to confirm this assumption, however, since (39a) is not an appropriate answer to a question like *What did you hear about John and Mary?*, only to a question like *What happened?* As the following dialogue shows, a natural answer to the former question can only be formulated with both the proper names *John* and *Mary* within the topic field if they are coordinated and thus form one constituent, as seen in (40B). When the two proper names assume different grammatical roles in an answer to the same question, only one of them can be placed in topic position, the other one should be left in a postverbal position, as shown in (40B'):

(40) A: *What did you hear about John and Mary?*

      B: *[János és   Mari]ₜ TAlálkoztak a   BUliban.*
         John and Mary met   the party.in
         '[John and Mary]ₜ met at the party.'

      B': *[János]ₜ MEGlátta [Marit]ₜ a   BUliban.*
          John PFX.saw Mary.ACC the party.in
          '[John]ₜ saw [Mary]ₜ at the party.'

As discussed at length by É. Kiss (1987, 1994, 2002, etc.), the topic position of the Hungarian sentence can only be filled by referring expressions with a specific or generic reading. Thus, the sentence-initial indefinite noun phrase in (41a) can only refer to an element of a familiar set of cars, which the sentence is taken to be about. There is no corresponding requirement for an indefinite noun phrase in the quantifier position, as in (41b), which can thus be given a nonspecific reading as well:

(41) a. *[Egy Autó]$_T$ (szerencsére) MEGállt   a   HÁZ   Előtt.*
       one car   luckily   PFX.stopped the house in.front.of
       '(Luckily,) [a car]$_T$ stopped in front of the house.'

   b. *(Szerencsére,) egy Autó MEGállt   a   HÁZ   Előtt.*
       luckily   one car PFX.stopped the house in.front.of
       '(Luckily,) there was a car stopping in front of the house.'

This ends the discussion of how aboutness topics are expressed in Hungarian. Next, we turn to contrastive topics.

3.2. Expression of contrastive topics and delimitators

As the following dialogue shows, contrastive topics, as a default, are placed within the topic field in Hungarian, just as ordinary aboutness topics are:

(42) A: *Mit   csinálnak a   testvéreid?*
       what.ACC do.3PL   the siblings.your
       'What do your siblings do?'

   B: *[[Az Öcsém]$_F$]$_T$ (sajnos)   [JOgot tanul]$_F$*
       the younger.brother.my unfortunately law.ACC studies
       [[a BÁtyám]$_F$]$_T$ (szerencsére) [DOLgozik]$_F$.
       the older.brother.my luckily   works
       '[[My younger brother]$_F$]$_T$ [studies law]$_F$, (unfortunately), [[my older brother]$_F$]$_T$ is [working]$_F$, (luckily).'

In spite of their identical positions, contrastive topics and ordinary aboutness topics are easy to distinguish even in isolated sentences, due to the special intonation contour of the former, which has traditionally been described as consisting of a rise followed by a marked pause (Szabolcsi 1981a) or as consisting of a fall-rise (É. Kiss 2002). Based on experimental evidence, Gyuris and Mády (2010) show that the observed differences between the prosody of ordinary vs. contrastive topics in topic position do not lie in the type of their pitch accent, but between the intonation contour of the stretch between the accented syllables of the topic vs. contrastive topic constituents and the accented syllable of the focus following them: for contrastive topics, a rising contour was found more frequently than a falling one,[15] whereas for ordinary topics the number of rises superseded that of the falls.[16]

Whenever an expression in the topic position is intended to have a contrastive interpretation, it allows the insertion of a resumptive element into the sentence without a change of meaning, the (inflected form of the) distal demonstrative element *az* 'that', intended to be coreferential with the sentence-initial constituent, as in (43B),[17] or of the particles *pedig, bizony, ugyan* 'however' (observed by Szabolcsi 1980), as well as of *bezzeg, azért* 'however', as in (43B'):[18]

(43)   A: *Meghívták   Marit?*
           PFX.invited.3PL Mary.ACC
           'Was Mary invited?'

       B: *[[Marit]$_F$]$_T$, azt   MEGhívták.*
           Mari.ACC   that.ACC PFX.invited.3PL
           '(As for) [[Mary]$_F$]$_T$, she was invited.'

       B': *[[Marit]$_F$]$_T$ bizony   MEGhívták.*
           Mari.ACC however PFX.invited.3PL
           '(As for) [[Mary]$_F$]$_T$, she was invited, however.'

---

[15] É. Kiss (1987) does mention the final rise as a characteristic feature of the intonation of contrastive topics, which she assumes to be base-generated in left-dislocated position under an E(xpression) node.

[16] Cf. Rosenthall (1992) for the observation that the focus peak is significantly lower than the peak of aboutness topics in Hungarian.

[17] The fact that contrastive topics license resumptive pronouns as illustrated in (43B) supports É. Kiss' (1987, 1994) proposal about them being generated in left-dislocated position. This assumption, however, is contradicted by the data discussed in (42).

[18] These sentences are used preferably in contexts where the sentence-initial topic refers to the entity asked about in the question, but the speaker wishes to convey that the same property cannot be attributed to an alternative of the topic denotation (cf. Krifka and Musan's example (45B)).

Although it is possible for several topics and contrastive topics to appear in the topic field of the Hungarian sentence at the same time, their order is not completely free: Two contrastive topics cannot be separated from each other by an ordinary aboutness topic, the former have to be situated within one block.[19]

It was noticed by Szabolcsi (1980, 1981a, 1981b), that constituent types otherwise excluded from the topic position can legitimately appear there if pronounced with the intonation contour characteristic of contrastive topics. It is illustrated below that adjectives, as in (44a, b), bare nominals, as in (44c, d), and infinitivals, as in (44e, f), are all allowed in the topic position when pronounced with the rising contour, indicated with a '/' after the constituent. The relevant expressions seem to satisfy Krifka and Musan's (this volume) definition of delimitators, therefore, they are subscripted accordingly.

(44)   a. *[SZÉP/]*$_{Delimitator}$ *NEM vagyok.*
           beautiful   not   be.1SG
           'As for beauty, I am [not]$_F$ beautiful.'

       b. *[SZÉPnek/]*$_{Delimitator}$ *NEM vagyok szép.*
           beautiful.DAT   not   be.1SG beautiful
           'As for beauty, I am [not]$_F$ beautiful.'

       c. *[SZAkács/]*$_{Delimitator}$ *VOLtam.*
           cook   was.1SG
           'As for being a cook, I [was]$_F$ a cook.'

       d. *[SZAkácsnak/]*$_{Delimitator}$ *SZAkács voltam.*
           cook.DAT   cook   was.1SG
           'As for being a cook, I [was]$_F$ a cook.'

       e. *[ENni/]*$_{Delimitator}$ *SZAbad a buszon.*
           eat.INF   allowed the bus.ON
           'As for eating, [it is allowed]$_F$ on the bus.'

       f. *[ENni/]*$_{Delimitator}$ *ETtem.*
           eat.INF   ate.1SG
           'As for eating, I [did]$_F$ eat.'

Quantificational noun phrases otherwise excluded from the topic position can also appear there if pronounced with the contrastive intonation, with an additional truth-conditional effect: they obligatorily take narrow scope with

---

[19] This fact could be best accounted for in É. Kiss's (2002) framework by assuming a separate projection hosting contrastive topics, e.g., a Delimitator Phrase.

respect to the preverbal operators following them in the sentence, as in (45a,b) (first described by Szabolcsi 1981b and Hunyadi 1981). The obligatoriness of the narrow scope reading makes it impossible to account for the Hungarian data along purely pragmatic principles, as proposed by Büring (1997, 2003) for German and English (see Gyuris 2009a, b for further discussion).

(45) a. *[ÖTnél   több   almát/]*$_{Delimitator}$ *NEM ettem   meg*
           five.than more apple.ACC   not   ate.1SG PFX
           'As for more than five apples, I did [not]$_F$ eat that many.'

      b. *[MINden könyvet/]*$_{Delimitator}$ *JÁnos olvasott el.*
           every   book.ACC   John read   PFX
           'As for every book, [John]$_F$ read them/that many.'

Frame-setting expressions display the same properties concerning syntactic position and prosody as do the delimitators discussed so far: They normally occur within the topic field and are pronounced with a rising tone. (46) provides an illustration:

(46) A: *Hogy van János?*
           how   is   John
           'How is John?'

      B: *{Egészségileg / Ami az egészségét illeti}   (János) rendben van.*
           healthwise   what the health.his concerns John   order.in is
           '{Healthwise /As for his health}, he is fine.'

This ends the discussion of the expression of contrastive topics and delimitators in Hungarian. We turn now to the question of how givenness and newness are expressed in this language.

4. Expression of givenness and newness

In Hungarian, the given/new status of expressions is marked with the help of the definite and indefinite articles (according to essentially the same principles as in English), (de)accentuation, the use of personal pronouns and demonstratives, and deletion.

As already mentioned, other things being equal, given material in the Hungarian sentence is at least deaccented. At the same time, each sentence has to contain at least one major stress, which falls on the first constituent of the predicate part, which is the constituent in the first quantifier position, if any constituents are present in this position, as in (8B), otherwise the stress falls on the constituent in focus position, cf. (1B), (2B), (3B), (4B), (5B), (6B). If the latter is also missing, the stress falls on the verbal modifier, if present, as in (11B), (18B), and (19B), or on the verb itself, as in (15B), even if the latter count as given. (Cf. É. Kiss 1987–88, 2002, Kálmán and Nádasdy 1994, Kenesei 1989, Varga 1983, 2002 for discussion.) In addition to this compulsory major stress, new material is accented in Hungarian, as illustrated in (13), with the exception of the verb following a preverbal focus or verbal modifier, as already discussed in Section 2.[20] Within the constituent in focus position, the place of the major stress is again determined by the given/new status of subexpressions, as illustrated in the three possible ways of correcting (47A), shown in (47B–B″):

(47) A: *MAri [PIros SZOKnyát]$_F$ vett fel.*
        Mary red   skirt.ACC   put PFX
        'Mary put on a [red skirt]$_F$.'

     B: *Nem, [KÉK szoknyát]$_F$ vett fel / [KÉKet]$_F$.*
        no blue skirt.ACC put PFX blue.ACC
        'No, she put on a [blue]$_F$ one.'

     B′: *Nem, [piros NADrágot]$_F$ vett fel.*
        no red   trousers.ACC put PFX
        'No, she put on red [trousers]$_F$.'

     B″: *Nem, [KÉK NADrágot]$_F$ vett fel.*
        no blue trousers.ACC put PFX
        'No, he put on [blue]$_F$ [trousers]$_F$.'

In the case of complex constituents in focus position that count as new as a whole, but are not contrasted pairwise with alternatives, or as given as a whole, special rules determine the position of major stress (cf. Kálmán and Nádasdy 1994, Varga 2002).[21]

---

[20] Cf. Szendrői (2003) for an approach that aims to account for the syntactic properties of the preverbal focus position in Hungarian by claiming that it is the position where the neutral, main stress rule assigns stress, and therefore movement from a position that otherwise would not get stress to this one is to satisfy Reinhart's (2005) Stress-focus Correspondence Principle.

[21] Generally, phrasal stress is normally situated on the initial element of the phrase, cf. Vogel and Kenesei (1987), É. Kiss (1987–88, 1994), which makes É. Kiss assume that in Hungarian the mirror image version of the canonical Nuclear Stress Rule operates.

As already noted, in most natural discourses, deletion of given constituents is the option preferred to deaccenting. In answers to constituent questions, all given expressions in topic position and all postverbal given expressions can be deleted, and, simultaneously with the deletion of the latter, the verb can also be elided, provided that it is unaccented and is not preceded by an accented verbal modifier, as shown in (1B)–(5B). As illustrated in (5B″) above, even the given subexpressions of the expression in focus position can be deleted, provided that relevant morphological information does not get lost this way. In case the preverbal focus is to express confirmation or correction, the verb can only be deleted if the constituent to be corrected was also situated in the focus position in the sentence to be corrected or confirmed, as the contrast between (48A–B) and (49A–B) shows:

(48) A: *[JÁnos]$_T$ [MEGfőzte   a   VAcsorát]$_F$.*
        John   PFX.cooked the dinner.ACC
        '[John]$_T$ [cooked dinner]$_F$.'

      B: *Igen, [JÁnos]$_F$ főzte   meg (a   vacsorát).*
        yes   John   cooked PFX the dinner.ACC
        'Yes, [John]$_F$ cooked dinner.'

(49) A: *[JÁnos]$_F$ [főzte   meg a   VAcsorát]$_F$.*
        John   cooked PFX the dinner.ACC
        '[John]$_F$ cooked dinner.'

      B: *Igen, [JÁnos]$_F$ (főzte   meg a   vacsorát).*
        yes   John   cooked PFX the dinner.ACC
        'Yes, [John]$_F$ (cooked dinner).'

(48B) and (49B) also provide a good illustration of the fact that the focus status of a constituent, more precisely, its placement in the preverbal focus position, is independent of its given/new status. A corresponding illustration for postverbal foci is provided in (21B) above.

Since, as we have seen, deletion of given noun phrases is usually possible in cases where they do not bear a major accent, their substitution by personal or demonstrative pronouns is a preferred option only in cases where the noun phrase would have to be accented due to the fact that it marks focus. A relevant example is (50) below, which would be equally acceptable as a reaction to (48A) as to (49A):

(50) *Igen, [Ő]$_F$ (főzte   meg a   vacsorát).*
       yes   he/she cooked PFX the dinner.ACC
       'Yes, (it was) [he]$_F$ (who cooked dinner).'

References

Brassai, Sámuel
  1860   A magyar mondat [The Hungarian sentence]. *Magyar Akadémiai Értesítő. A Nyelv- és Széptudományi Osztály Közlönye* 1: 279–399.
Brassai, Sámuel
  1863–65   A magyar mondat [The Hungarian sentence]. *Magyar Akadémiai Értesítő. A Nyelv- és Széptudományi Osztály Közlönye* 3: 3–128, 173–409.
Brody, Michael
  1990   Some remarks on the focus field in Hungarian. *University College London. Working Papers in Linguistics* 2: 201–225.
Brody, Michael
  1995   Focus and checking theory. In *Approaches to Hungarian 5: Levels and Structures*, István Kenesei (ed.), 29–44. Szeged: JATE.
Büring, Daniel
  1997   *The Meaning of Topic and Focus. The 59th Street Bridge Accent.* London / New York: Routledge.
Büring, Daniel
  2003   On D-trees, beans, and B-accents. *Linguistics and Philosophy* 26: 511–545.
Comorovski, Ileana
  1996   *Interrogative Phrases and the Syntax-Semantics Interface.* Dordrecht: Kluwer.
É. Kiss, Katalin
  1981   Structural relations in Hungarian, a free word order language. *Linguistic Inquiry* 12: 185–213.
É. Kiss, Katalin
  1987   *Configurationality in Hungarian.* The Hague: Mouton.
É. Kiss, Katalin
  1987–88   Még egyszer a magyar mondat intonációjáról és hangsúlyozásáról. [Once more on the intonation and stressing of the Hungarian sentence.] *Nyelvtudományi Közlemények* 89: 1–52.
É. Kiss Katalin
  1991   Logical structure in syntactic structure: The case of Hungarian. In *Logical Structure and Syntactic Structure*, James Huang and Robert May (eds.), 111–148. Dordrecht: Reidel.
É. Kiss, Katalin
  1993   Wh-movement and specificity. *Natural Language and Linguistic Theory* 11: 85–120.
É. Kiss, Katalin
  1994   Sentence structure and word order. In *The Syntactic Structure of Hungarian*, Ferenc Kiefer and Katalin É. Kiss (eds.), 1–90. San Diego / London: Academic Press.

É. Kiss, Katalin
1998   Identificational focus versus information focus. *Language* 74: 245–273.
É. Kiss, Katalin
2002   *The Syntax of Hungarian*. Cambridge: Cambridge University Press.
É. Kiss, Katalin
2008   A pioneering theory of information structure. *Acta Linguistica Hungarica* 55: 23–41.
Gyuris, Beáta
2009a   *The Semantics and Pragmatics of the Contrastive Topic in Hungarian*. Budapest: The Library of the Hungarian Academy of Sciences and Lexica Ltd.
Gyuris, Beáta
2009b   Quantificational contrastive topics with verum/falsum focus. *Lingua* 119: 625–649.
Gyuris, Beáta and Katalin Mády
2010   Contrastive topics between syntax and pragmatics in Hungarian: an experimental analysis. Paper presented at the annual meeting of the Chicago Linguistic Society 46, April 8th–10th, 2010, Chicago.
Horn, Laurence
1972   On the semantic properties of logical operators in English. Doctoral dissertation, University of California Los Angeles. Distributed by Indiana University Linguistics Club (1976).
Horvath, Julia
1986   *FOCUS in the Theory of Grammar and the Syntax of Hungarian*. Dordrecht: Foris.
Horvath, Julia
2000   Interfaces vs. the computational system in the syntax of focus. In *Interface Strategies*, Hans Bennis and Martin Everaert (eds.). Amsterdam: HAG.
Horvath, Julia
2007   Separating "focus movement" from focus. In *Phrasal and Clausal Architecture*, S. Karimi, V. Samiian and W. Wilkins (eds.), 108–145. Amsterdam: John Benjamins.
Hunyadi, László
1981   Remarks on the syntax and semantics of topic and focus in Hungarian. *Acta Linguistica Academiae Scientiarum Hungaricae* 31: 107–136.
Kálmán, László, Gábor Prószéky, Ádám Nádasdy and György Kálmán C.
1986   Hocus, focus, and verb types in Hungarian infinitive constructions. In *Topic, Focus, and Configurationality*, Werner Abraham and Sjaak de Meij (eds.), 129–142. Amsterdam/Philadelphia: John Benjamins.
Kálmán, László and Ádám Nádasdy
1994   A hangsúly. [Stress.] In *Strukturális magyar nyelvtan 2. Fonológia. [A structural grammar of Hungarian. 2. Phonology.]*, Ferenc Kiefer (ed.), 393–467. Budapest: Akadémiai Kiadó.

Kálmán, György C., László Kálmán, Ádám Nádasdy and Gábor Prószéky
1989   A magyar segédigék rendszere. [The system of Hungarian auxiliaries.] *Általános Nyelvészeti Tanulmányok* XVII: 49–103.
Kenesei, István
1986   On the logic of word order in Hungarian. In *Topic, Focus and Configurationality*, Werner Abraham and Sjak de Mey (eds.), 143–159. Amsterdam: John Benjamins.
Kenesei, István
1989   Logikus-e a magyar szórend? [Is Hungarian word order logical?] *Általános nyelvészeti tanulmányok* XVII: 105–152.
Kenesei, István
1998   Adjuncts and arguments in VP-focus in Hungarian. *Acta Linguistica Hungarica* 45: 61–88.
Komlósy, András
1986   Focussing on focus in Hungarian. In *Topic, Focus, and Configurationality*, Werner Abraham and Sjaak de Meij (eds.), 215–226. Amsterdam / Philadelphia: John Benjamins.
Komlósy, András
1989   Fókuszban az igék. [Verbs in focus.] *Általános Nyelvészeti Tanulmányok* XVII: 171–182.
Komlósy, András
1994   Complements and adjuncts. In *The Syntactic Structure of Hungarian*, Ferenc Kiefer and Katalin É. Kiss (eds.), 91–178. San Diego: Academic Press.
Komlósy, András and Farrell Ackermann
1983   Néhány lépés a magyar szórend megértése felé. [Some steps towards understanding Hungarian word order.] Talk given at Janus Pannonius University, Pécs, Hungary.
Krifka, Manfred
1999   Additive particles under stress. *Proceedings of Semantics and Linguistic Theory* 8, 111–128. Cornell, CLC Publications.
Piñón, Christopher
1995   Around the progressive in Hungarian. In *Approaches to Hungarian 5: Levels and Structures*, István Kenesei (ed.), 153–189. Szeged: JATE.
Reinhart, Tanya
1995   *Interface Strategies.* OTS Working Papers in Theoretical Linguistics 1995 (002), Utrecht: Institute of Linguistics, Utrecht University.
Rosenthall, Sam
1992   The Intonation of simple sentences in Hungarian. *Proceedings of the Formal Linguistics Society of Midamerica* 3, 297–310.
Szabolcsi, Anna
1980   Az aktuális mondattagolás szemantikájához. [On the semantics of functional sentence perspective.] *Nyelvtudományi Közlemények* 82: 59–83.

Szabolcsi, Anna
1981a   Compositionality in focus. *Folia Linguistica* 15: 141–161.
Szabolcsi, Anna
1981b   The semantics of topic-focus articulation. In *Formal Methods in the Study of Language, Part 1*, Jeroen Groenendijk, Theo Janssen and Martin Stokhof (eds.), 1–28. (Mathematical Centre Tracts 135.) Amsterdam.
Szabolcsi, Anna
1983   Focussing properties, or the trap of first order. *Theoretical Linguistics* 10: 125–145.
Szabolcsi, Anna
1994   All quantifiers are not equal: The case of focus. *Acta Linguistica Hungarica* 42: 171–187.
Szabolcsi, Anna
1997   Strategies for scope taking. In *Ways of Scope Taking*, Anna Szabolcsi (ed.), 109–154. Dordrecht: Kluwer.
Szendrői, Kriszta
2003   A stress-based approach to the syntax of Hungarian focus. *The Linguistic Review* 20: 37–78.
Van Leusen, Noor and László Kálmán
1993   *The Interpretation of Free Focus.* Institute for Logic, Language and Computation Prepublication Series CL-93-01. Institute for Logic, Language and Computation, University of Amsterdam.
Varga, László
1983   Hungarian sentence prosody: an outline. *Folia Linguistica* 17: 117–51
Varga, László
2002   *Intonation and Stress: Evidence from Hungarian.* Basingstoke / New York: Palgrave Macmillan.
Vogel, Irene and István Kenesei
1987   The interface between phonology and other components of grammar: The case of Hungarian. *Phonology Yearbook* 4: 243–263.
Wedgwood, Daniel, Gergely Pethő and Ronnie Cann
2006   Hungarian 'focus position' and English *it*-clefts: the semantic under-specification of 'focus' readings. Ms. University of Edinburgh.

The information structure of Japanese

Reiko Vermeulen

This chapter describes various means in Japanese of expressing information-structural functions. Japanese is interesting in several respects: it is a head-final language with case marking, which allows for relatively "free" word order – that is, the ordering of constituents partly reflects information-structural properties. Most famously, it has a morphological marker for topichood, *wa*, which has figured prominently in the theoretical discussion of information structure. Moreover, it has no articles, so givenness is expressed by other means. Many of these properties can also be seen in Korean, a structurally similar language, although they are not always realized under the same circumstances. In this article, we will consider focus, topic and givenness, as defined in the introduction to this volume, in this order.

1. Focus

1.1. Constituent questions

In Japanese constituent questions, both the *wh*-phrase and the constituent that answers the *wh*-part of the question are typically realized in-situ: [1]

(1) A: *dare-ga   wain-o   nonda no?* (Subject)
       who-NOM wine-ACC drank Q
       'Who drank wine?'

     B: *[Taro-ga]$_F$ wain-o   nonda.*
       Taro-NOM   wine-ACC drank
       'Taro drank wine.'

---

[1] The examples in (1)–(4) are based on an example in Ishihara (2004:80). Abbreviations: ACC = accusative, COP = copula, GER = gerund, NMZ = nominalizer, NOM = nominative, PASS = passive, Q= question particle, SFP = sentence final particle.

(2)   A: *Taro-wa   nani-o   nonda no?* (Object)
           Taro-WA   what-ACC   drank   *Q*
           'What did Taro drink?'

      B: *Taro-wa   [wain-o]$_F$ nonda.*
           Taro-WA   wine-ACC   drank

(3)   A: *Taro-wa   nani-o   sita no?* (VP)
           Taro-WA·   what-ACC   did   *Q*
           'What did Taro do?'

      B: *Taro-wa   [wain-o   nonda]$_F$.*
           Taro-WA   wine-ACC   drank

(4)   A: *nani-ga   atta   no?* (Sentence)
           what-NOM   happened   *Q*
           'What happened?'

      B: *[Taro-ga   wain-o   nonda (no)]$_F$.*
           Taro-NOM   wine-ACC   drank   SFP

The answers are given as full sentences above, but as will be discussed in Section 4, given items are preferably unpronounced. Thus, the above answers are actually rather awkward. It is more natural to simply pronounce the relevant constituent plus a copula, or the verb, as illustrated for subject below:

(5)   a.   *[Taro]$_F$ desu.*[2]   b.   *[Taro-ga]$_F$ nonda.*
           Taro   COP   Taro-NOM   drank
           'It's Taro.'   'Taro drank (it).'

Prosodically, *wh*-phrases are expressed obligatorily with an emphatic stress, that is, a sharply raised F_0-peak of the first high tone of the *wh*-phrase, followed by compression of F_0-movement of the following material (Nagahara 1994, Deguchi and Kitagawa 2002, Ishihara 2002, 2004, 2007).[3] This point is illustrated below. CAPITALS indicate the position of the sharply raised F_0-peak, and <u>underlining</u> indicates the post-focal pitch compression.[4]

---

[2] Nominals before a copula cannot have a case marker, while a postposition is usually retained (Fukaya and Hoji 1999).

[3] See also Chen (this volume).

[4] The post-focal compression is variously known as 'deaccenting', 'dephrasing', and 'eradication' in the literature. I will indicate it by underlining only where relevant to make the point. There is a clause-final rising intonation for questions here, hence the question particle is not underlined.

(6) *Naoya-wa NAni-o nomiya-de nonda no?*   (Ishihara 2004: 80)
Naoya-WA what-ACC bar-at   drank *Q*
'What did Naoya drink at the bar?'

A constituent that answers the *wh*-part of a preceding question is not necessarily marked with a sharp rise of the F_0-peak like *wh*-phrases. Rather, it typically bears only a slight rise in the F_0-peak (Deguchi and Kitagawa 2002, Ishihara 2004, 2007). The contour associated with *wh*-phrases is observed with contrastive focus, which is discussed below.

Scrambling – optional movement of constituents into non-canonical positions – can affect the focus structure of a sentence in various ways. First, scrambling may target the focus constituent itself, in which case the scrambled item bears an emphatic stress of the type borne by *wh*-phrases. Some speakers are able to scramble the answer constituent in (2B), for instance, even long-distance, but they report that it necessarily leads to a contrastive interpretation:

(7) A: 'What did Taro drink?'

  B: *[WAin-o$_i$]$_F$ Taro-wa t$_i$ nonda.*
    wine-ACC Taro-WA drank
    'Taro drank wine (and not beer).'

Second, it has been argued that an immediately pre-verbal item in Japanese receives the default main stress of the sentence. Scrambling can manipulate this default stress position for focus purposes (Neeleman and Reinhart 1998, Ishihara 2000). It can remove an item from the default stress position so that a focused item ends up in that position. Thus, one way of answering (8A) is to scramble the object. The adverbial is now in the pre-verbal position, receiving the main stress of the sentence, allowing for a focus interpretation.[5] (The default stress is marked with an acúte accent here):

---

5 This option is also available for focusing the subject (Ishihara 2000), but additional factors are involved, which are not yet well understood. The reply in (i-B) is felicitous only if in the preceding question in (i-A), the object is scrambled so that the subject *wh*-phrase is already in the preverbal position. B's utterance is infelicitous as an answer to a question with the canonical word order, such as (1A). There is no comparable restriction on the preceding question when the object scrambles over a focused adverbial, as in (8), or a focused indirect object.

  (i) A: *wain-o$_i$ DAre-ga t$_i$ nonda no?*   B: *wain-o$_i$ Táro-ga t$_i$ nonda.*
      wine-ACC who-NOM drank Q   wine-ACC Taro-NOM drank
      'Who drank (the) wine?'   'Taro drank (the) wine.'

(8)   A: 'Where did Taro drink wine?'

　　　B: *Taro-wa   wain-o_i   [nomíya-de]_F   t_i   nonda.*
　　　　 Taro-WA   wine-ACC   bar-at   drank
　　　　 'Taro drank wine at a bar.'

An item bearing a default main stress, as in the example above, can project the focus to a larger domain. Thus, in (3B) and (4B) the pre-verbal object bears the default main stress, projecting focus to VP and the sentence. The example in (8B) can have a different focus, such as [adverbial + verb].

　　Wh-phrases may also undergo scrambling, short- or long-distance. The same intonational pattern is obtained in such cases: the fronted *wh*-phrase has a sharp F_0-rise and the following material shows a significant downtrend. Miyagawa (2006) claims that scrambled *wh*-phrases are interpreted as D(iscourse)-linked, that is, there is a presupposed, contextually given set which contains the answer to the *wh*-phrase. Thus, the following example means 'among the things in a presupposed set, the speaker wants to know which of them Taro drank.'

(9)   *NAni-o_i   Taro-wa t_i nondano?*
　　　 what-ACC   Taro-WA   drank Q
　　　 'What did Taro drink?'

1.2. Multiple *wh*-questions

A question sentence may contain multiple *wh*-phrases. They may appear in-situ, as in (10a), or one may undergo scrambling across the other, as in (10b), without yielding a superiority effect. Prosodically, all the *wh*-phrases in multiple *wh*-questions must have sharply raised F_0-peaks, but the post-focal F_0-compression takes place only after the last *wh*-phrase (Ishihara 2000, 2002).

This shifts the issue to the question of which discourse contexts allow an object to scramble over a focused or *wh*-subject. The discourse effects of short object scrambling of the above sort have not received much attention and currently, there does not appear to be any consensus (Aoyagi and Kato 2008, Miyagawa 2010).

(10) a. *DAre-ga   NAni-o   kinoo-no   paatii-ni motte-kita   no?*
         who-NOM what-ACC yesterday-GEN party-to bring-came   Q

   b. *NAni-o$_i$ DAre-ga   kinoo-no   paatii-ni t$_i$ motte-kita   no?*
      what-ACC   who-NOM   yesterday-GEN party-to   bring-came   Q
      'Who brought what to yesterday's party?'

Multiple wh-questions can be answered by sentences containing multiple
foci. There is a preference to keep the order of arguments the same as in the
preceding question: (11a) sounds most natural for the question in (10a) and
(11b) for (10b).

(11) a. *[TAro-ga]$_F$ [WAin-o]$_F$ motte-kita.*
         Taro-NOM   wine-ACC   bring-came

   b. *[WAin-o$_i$]$_F$ [TAro-ga]$_F$ t$_i$ motte-kita.*
      wine-ACC   Taro-NOM   bring-came
      'Taro brought wine.'

Multiple *wh*-questions like (10) can be answered with one of the questioned
items bearing the particle *wa*, a marker that is also used for contrastive
topics, as we will see below, and the other with a case marker. This pattern
is observed cross-linguistically. As is well known, in English and German,
for example, one of the questioned items can be marked with a rising tone,
a tone associated with contrastive topics, and the other with a falling tone,
a tone associated with focus (Jackendoff 1972, Büring 1997). The XP-*WA*
YP-case$_{FOCUS}$ pattern is particularly natural if the answer lists several pairs
(see Hara and van Rooij 2007 on this use of *wa*):

(12) a. *[TAro-wa]$_{CT}$ [WAin-o]$_F$ motte-kite,   [HAnako-wa]$_{CT}$*
         Taro-WA   wine-ACC   bring-come.GER Hanako-WA

      [ZYUusu-o]$_F$ motte-kita.   Sosite...
      juice-ACC   bring-came   and...

   b. *[WAin-wa$_i$]$_{CT}$ [TAro-ga]$_F$ t$_i$ motte-kite,   [ZYUusu-wa$_j$]$_{CT}$*
      wine-WA   Taro-NOM   bring-come.GER juice-WA

      [HAnako-ga]$_F$ t$_j$ motte-kita.   Sosite...
      Hanako-NOM   bring-came   and...

1.3. Contrastive focus

Contrastive focus, found in cases of correction and confirmation, can appear
in-situ or fronted. Contrastively focused items show the same intonation as

wh-phrases: a sharply raised F_0-peak on the contrastive focus followed by compression of F_0-movement (Beckman and Pierrehumbert 1988, Selkirk and Tateishi 1991, Nagahara 1994, Ishihara 2000, 2007, Deguchi and Kitagawa 2002, Sugahara 2003, among others). It is worth noting that while an emphatic stress necessarily indicates a contrastive interpretation, a contrastive interpretation may arise from the context and does not necessitate an emphatic stress (Kuroda 2005: Appendix II).

In both cases of correction and confirmation, the relevant focus constituent may stay in-situ, may undergo scrambling, or a cleft construction may be used. The following examples demonstrate the possibilities of scrambling, (13B-i), and a cleft construction, (13B-ii), for an object in an instance of correction. Other arguments and adverbials display the same pattern (Hoji 1987, Kizu 2005, Takano 2002, Hiraiwa and Ishiara 2002, among others).

(13) A: *Hanako-ga   kukkii-o   nusunda.*
         Hanko-NOM cookie-ACC stole
         'Hanako stole cookies.'

    B: i. *tigai-masu.   [oSEnbee-o$_i$]$_F$ <u>Hanako-wa t$_i$ nusunda no</u> desu.*
          incorrect-COP rice.cracker-ACC Hanako-WA   stole   NMZ COP
          'That's not true. Hanako stole ricecrackers.'

      ii. *tigai-masu.   [Hanako-ga e$_i$ nusunda no]-wa   [oSEnbee$_i$]$_F$ desu.*
          incorrect-COP Hanako-NOM stole   NMZ-WA rice.cracker COP
          'That's not true. It is ricecrackers that Hanako stole.'

A contrastive focus can undergo long-distance scrambling. Long-distance scrambling is most typically accompanied by an emphatic stress, followed by a pause (Saito 1989). Consequently, a contrastive interpretation is obligatory (Miyagawa 2006). Some speakers allow only corrective or confirmative kinds of focus to undergo long-distance scrambling, while others allow an item that merely answers the *wh*-part of a preceding question to do so, but report that they have supplemented it with a contrastive interpretation.[6] These speakers are interpreting the exchange in a particular discourse context, accommodating a contrastive interpretation.

---

[6] Subjects in Japanese cannot undergo scrambling (Saito 1985), thus long-distance scrambling is not an option for subjects. Ko (2005) argues that theoretically, subjects in Japanese and Korean can scramble. But, Saito's descriptive observation that an embedded subject cannot scramble over a matrix argument remains correct and is relevant here.

Furthermore, it is interesting to note that when the focused constituent is a case-marked nominal or a PP, there are two potential positions in which the sharp F_0-rise may be observed within the focused item, namely on the position of the lexical accent of the nominal, or on the case marker or the postposition. Thus, instead of the emphatic stress placement depicted above, i.e., *oSEnbee-o* and *KUkkii-o*, the case marker can bear the emphatic stress, i.e., *osenbee-O* and *kukkii-O*. This option is available only if the nominal is lexically accented.[7] In cases of unaccented nominals, the sharp F_0-rise is possible on the case marker or the postposition only. The same optionality is found with focal particles discussed in Section 1.5 and the contrastive use of *wa*.

I shall mention here a further instance of what appears to be focus undergoing scrambling, which has not yet received much attention in the literature.[8] It involves scrambling within a focused constituent, as shown below. This kind of scrambling is associated with a particular intonation. Within the fronted object, only the nominal can bear the sharp F_0-rise; the case marker cannot. Moreover, native speakers do not perceive the following material to have compressed F_0-movements.

(14)   [Hearing some noise in a different room.] 'What happened?'
[kaGAmi-o$_i$ / #kagami-O$_i$ Hanako-ga   t$_i$ kowasite-simatta   no]$_F$.
mirror-ACC   mirror-ACC   Hanako-NOM   break-ended.up   SFP
'Hanako broke a mirror.'

In terms of interpretation, speakers report a sense of 'surprise' at the fact that it was a mirror that was broken, as opposed to other things. This kind scrambling differs syntactically from contrastive focus in that it cannot undergo long-distance movement:

(15)   'What happened?'
#kaGAmi-o$_i$ Taroo-ga [$_{CP}$ Hanako-ga   t$_i$ kowasite-simatta to]   itta.
mirror-ACC Taro-NOM   Hanako-NOM   break-ended.up   that said
'Taro said that Hanako broke a mirror.'

Fanselow and Lenertová (2011) discuss a similar kind of movement in a variety of languages, but not in Japanese.

---

[7]   Not all words are lexically accented in Japanese. See Haraguchi (1999) for general discussion on this issue.

[8]   Thanks to Naoyuki Yamato for discussion on this phenomenon.

1.4. Verum focus

Japanese *yes/no* questions do not allow answers in the form of *do*-support as in English. As with constituent questions, it is possible, but rather awkward, to answer with full sentences. A more natural answer consists simply of the fully inflected verb with an emphatic stress. These properties are demonstrated for affirmative answers below. Japanese finite verbs are morphologically complex, with, minimally, the tense morpheme attaching to the verbal root, and these two morphemes forming a phonological word. It is not clear where the sharp F_0-rise is located. The whole verbal complex is therefore in CAPITALS here (Ishihara to app.). An emphatic stress on the verb in the question is optional.[9]

(16) A: 'Did Taro buy that book?'

   B: i.   *un, si-ta   (yo).
            yes, do-PAST SFP

      ii. un, Taro-wa ano hon-o   KATTA (yo).
           yes, Taro-WA that book-ACC bought SFP

      iii. un, KATTA   (yo).
           yes, bought SFP
           'Yes, Taro bought that book.'

Exactly the same means as shown in the example above can be used for instances in which the polarity of a statement is confirmed or corrected. Thus, the utterances in (16B-ii) and (16B-iii) may be used in affirming the statement *Taro-wa ano hon-o katta* 'Taro bought that book.'

1.5. Focus sensitive particles

The focus sensitive particles *dake* 'only', *mo* 'also', and *sae* 'even', and the negative polarity item (NPI) *sika* 'only' are widely reported to display similar properties. First, they can appear on nominals, (17)/(19), PPs, (18), and

---

[9] The sentence final particle *yo* is often described as a marker of new information, or assertion. It is optional in the examples in the main text, though the examples are much more natural with it. The emphatic stress on the verb can remain on the verb in the presence of *yo*, but it seems to me that it is also possible to shift the emphatic stress to the particle without difference in meaning, thus the choice is *KATTA yo* or *katta YO* for (16B-ii) and (16B-iii).

verbs, (20), and in the last case *do*-support is required. When attaching to a nominal, the case marker is omitted. Examples with *sika* are not provided here, but see Futagi (2006).

(17) *Taro-dake/mo/sae   ano mise-de nihongo-no   syoosetu-o katta.*
      Taro-only/also/even that shop-at Japanese-GEN novel-ACC bought
      'Only/Also/Even Taro bought Japanese novels at that shop.'

(18) *Taro-ga   ano mise-de-dake/mo/sae nihongo-no   syoosetu-o katta.*
      Taro-NOM that shop-at-only/also/even Japanese-GEN novel-ACC bought
      'Taro bought Japanese novels only/also/even at that shop.'

(19) *Taro-ga   ano mise-de nihongo-no   syoosetu-dake/mo/sae katta.*
      Taro-NOM that shop-at Japanese-GEN novel-only/also/even   bought
      'Taro bought only/also/even Japanese novels at that shop.'

(20) *Taro-ga   ano mise-de nihongo-no   syoosetu-o kai-dake/mo/sae   sita.*
      Taro-NOM that shop-at Japanese-GEN novel-ACC buy-only/also/even did
      'Taro only/also/even bought Japanese novels at that shop.'

The target of the focus sensitive particles is not limited to the lexical item that they are attached to. Thus, for instance, the target in (19) may be the object *nihongo-no syoosetu* 'Japanese novels', as well as its subparts, *syoosetu* 'novel' and *nihongo-no* 'Japanese'. In (20), the target of the particle can be the verb *kai-* 'buy', the object *nihongo-no syoosetu* 'Japanese novels', *syoosetu* 'novel', *nihongo-no* 'Japanese', the VP, as well as the locative *ano mise-de* 'at that shop'. Association with the subject in (18)–(20) is not possible (Kuroda 1979, 2005, Futagi 2005, Kishimoto 2009). The following paraphrases with added contextual material describe readings available for the various potential associations with *dake* 'only' in (20).

(21) a. *kai-*'buy': 'Taro only bought Japanese novels at that shop, but he didn't read them.'
      b. *nihongo-no syoosetu* 'Japanese novels': 'Taro bought only Japanese novels at that shop, but not any other reading material, Japanese or not.'
      c. *syoosetu* 'novel': 'Taro bought only Japanese novels at that shop, but not Japanese non-fiction, Japanese poetry, etc.'
      d. *nihongo-no* 'Japanese': 'Taro bought only Japanese novels at that shop, but not English, French, etc. novels.'

    e. *nihongo-no syoosetu-o kai-* 'buy Japanese novels': 'The only thing
       Taro did was to buy Japanese novels at that shop. He didn't go and
       see a film at the cinema.'

    f. *ano mise-de* 'that shop-at': 'The only place that Taro bought
       Japanese novels is that shop.'

Association with a lexical item across an island is also possible. In (22), the
focus sensitive particles are attached to the relative head noun and they can
associate with it, but they may also associate with an item inside the relative clause. Thus, for *dake* 'only', it has the reading 'Taro bought only the
book that Hanako recommended' as well as 'Taro bought the book that
only Hanako recommended'. The target of the focus preferably bears an
emphatic stress.

(22) *Taro-wa [$_{CP}$ Hanako-ga e$_i$ suisensita]   hon$_i$-dake/mo/sae   katta.*
     Taro-WA   Hanako-NOM   recommended book-only/also/even bought

The particle *dake* 'only' shows further properties that are strikingly distinct
from the other focus sensitive particles, which are discussed extensively in
Futagi (2004) and Kishimoto (2009).

1.6. Focus and nominative case marker

I note here two further peculiarities of Japanese regarding focus. First,
Japanese shows an asymmetry in the default reading between nominative
subjects and non-subjects marked with canonical case markers or postpositions. Specifically, a nominative subject of an individual-level predicate
must be interpreted as exhaustive, as in (23a), while if the predicate is
stage-level, either the subject is interpreted as exhaustive or the sentence is
interpreted as all focus, ("exhaustive listing reading" and "neutral description" in Kuno's (1973) terminology), as in (23b) (Kuroda 1965, 1972, Kuno
1973, Diesing 1988, Heycock 1993a, Tomioka 2001, 2007a,b).

(23) a. *Taro-ga   gakusee desu.*   b. *Taro-ga   hasitta.*
        Taro-NOM student COP   Taro-NOM ran
        'It is Taro who is a student.'   'It is Taro who ran.' or 'Taro ran.'

The exhaustive reading appears to be an implicature rather than entailment,
as it may be cancelled easily. Thus, (23a) can be followed felicitously by
sosite Hanako-mo gakusee desu 'and Hanako too is a student'. If the subject

is not to be interpreted as exhaustive or part of focus, it is marked with *wa*.[10] These obligatory focus-related readings for nominative subjects are limited to matrix clauses, and do not arise in subordinate clauses (Kuroda 1988). In fact, it is often not possible to mark a given subject with *wa* in subordinate clauses, without an additional contrastive interpretation. Non-subjects need not receive an exhaustive or part-of-focus reading when they appear with their canonical case markers or postpositions in any kind of clause.

A second peculiarity of Japanese regarding focus concerns the so-called multiple nominative construction, where more than one nominative phrase appears in the left periphery of the clause. The additional nominative phrases may be a possessor or modifier of the following nominative phrase, as in (24), or a sentential adverbial, as in (25). In these sentences, the first nominative phrase receives an exhaustive reading, which again is an implicature rather than entailment.[11] (Kuno 1973, Saito 1985, Heycock 1993b, 2008, Tateishi 1994, Vermeulen 2005, Akiyama 2006)

(24) *zoo-ga   hana-ga   nagai.*
     elephant-NOM   trunk-NOM   long
     'It's the elephants that have long trunks.'

(25) *Tokyo-ga   ziko-ga   ooi.*
     Tokyo-NOM   accident-NOM   many
     'It's in Tokyo that there are many accidents.'

There is a vast amount of work on the two default focus-associated readings of nominative subjects and the multiple nominative construction. I will not pursue these topics here. Heycock (2008) has an extensive overview, where she also considers the question of whether the nominative case marker in these constructions should be considered a focus marker.

---

[10] This statement is too strong in some respects. There are instances of given, non-focused subjects in matrix clauses being *ga*-marked, but this is associated with some rhetorical effects (see Hinds et al. 1987)

[11] The multiple nominative construction is not always judged as perfect by speakers. It appears that a variety of factors are involved here, such as the type of the main predicate and the kind of relation between the additional nominative and the rest of the clause (Ishizuka 2009).

2. Topic

Topics in Japanese have received an overwhelming amount of attention in the literature from both formal and functional perspectives due to the presence of a topic marking device, the particle *wa*. Japanese has figured prominently in the theoretical discussion of topichood, for example in the treatment of "categorical" vs. "thetic" sentences – or sentences with or without a topic – in Kuroda (1972), cf. also Sasse (1987). Here, I will discuss some basic facts about Japanese topics, but will focus on highlighting some aspects that have received relatively little attention. The reader is referred to Heycock (2008) for a comprehensive overview of the literature.

Before we proceed, a remark is in order regarding the treatment of the particle *wa*. While there is general agreement that topics are marked by *wa* in Japanese, it is not clear whether all *wa*-marked items are topics. There are contexts where a *wa*-marked item is not necessarily interpreted as what the sentence is about, for example, when it functions as a frame-setter or delimitator, or is interpreted contrastively. In other words, the interpretive properties of a *wa*-marked item are not uniform and therefore, whether the particle *wa* should be considered a 'topic marker' depends to a great extent on the definition of 'topic'.[12] Here, I will generally follow the notion of topic in Reinhart (1982), as discussed in the introduction to this volume, but I will also point out cases where the topic status of a *wa*-marked item is not so obvious.

Ever since the seminal works of Kuroda (1965) and Kuno (1973), two uses of *wa* have been widely recognized: 'thematic' and 'contrastive' (in Kuno's terminology). Items marked with *wa* in its thematic use roughly correspond to 'sentence topics' in the sense of Reinhart (1982), while items marked with *wa* in its contrastive use roughly correspond to contrastive topics in the sense discussed in the introduction to this volume. Following Heycock's (2008) practice, I will refer to the former as 'non-contrastive' topics, to be more theory-neutral.[13]

---

[12] For this reason, I gloss the particle *wa* as 'WA' throughout.

[13] It is a valid question to ask whether there is one lexical item *wa* or two. At an observational level, the particle shows different syntactic, semantic and phonological behavior in the two uses. Thus, for the present purposes, I will treat them separately (see Kuroda (2005: Appendix II) for discussion on this point).

2.1. Non-contrastive topics

Non-contrastive topics typically appear in sentence initial position. Thus, in an answer to the request *tell me about X*, which is a standard test for identifying *X* as the topic in the response, *X* is *wa*-marked and most naturally occupies sentence-initial position:

(26) A: *Taro-nituite nanika   osiete-kudasai.*
          Taro-about   something tell-give
          'Tell me something about Taro.'

    B: i.   *[Taro-wa]$_T$ kinoo   ano boosi-o katta.*
              Taro-WA   yesterday that hat-ACC bought

        ii. *#ano boosi-o$_i$ [Taro-wa]$_T$ kinoo   t$_i$ katta.*
              that hat-ACC Taro-WA   yesterday bought
              'Taro bought that hat yesterday.'

(27) A: *ano boosi-nituite nanika   osiete-kudasai.*
          that hat-about   something tell-give
          'Tell me something about that hat.'

    B: i.   *[ano boosi-wa$_i$]$_T$ Taro-ga   kinoo   e$_i$ katta.*[14]
              that hat-WA   Taro-NOM yesterday bought

        ii. *#Taro-ga [ano boosi-wa]$_T$ kinoo   katta.*
              Taro-NOM that hat-WA   yesterday bought
              'Taro bought that hat yesterday.'

Argument topics are insensitive to islands (Kuno 1973, Hoji 1985, Saito 1985). In other words, an argument topic can appear in a non-thematic, left-peripheral position, and be construed as an argument inside an island, such as a relative clause, as illustrated below (Hoji 1985: 152). The topic *ano boosi-wa* 'that hat-WA' is interpreted as the object inside the relative clause and can be resumed by a pronominal *sore-o* 'it-ACC'.

---

[14] *e* here indicates an empty pronominal, which can be overtly realised, as discussed immediately below. For reasons most likely to do with prosody, a *wa*-phrase prefers not to surface adjacent to the verb (a non-contrastive *wa*-phrase typically has a prosodic boundary following it (Nakanishi 2001, 2003), while a verb prefers to form a prosodic unit with the preceding item (Nagahara 1994)). Adverbials are inserted to circumvent this effect. Obj-Adv-V is assumed here to be base-generated, following Neeleman and Reinhart (1998), but nothing hinges on this assumption.

(28) *ano boosi_j-wa John-ga   [_{NP} [_{TP} e_i (sore_j-o) kabutteita]   hito-o*
that hat-WA   John-NOM   it-ACC   wearing.was person-ACC
yoku sitteiru.
well know
'Speaking of that hat, John knows well the person who was wearing it.'

Non-arguments, including extra nominative phrases in the multiple nominative construction mentioned above, can be topics. Each sentence below can
be an answer to the request of the form *tell me something about X*, where *X*
is the *wa*-marked item in the response.

(29) a. *[zoo-wa]_T   hana-ga   nagai.*
elephant-WA trunk-NOM long
'An elephant has a long trunk.'

b. *[Tokyo-wa]_T ziko-ga   ooii.*
Tokyo-WA   accident-NOM many
'There are many accidents in Tokyo.'

c. *[ano kooen(-de)-wa]_T kodomotati-ga yoku asobu.*
that park-at-WA   children-NOM often play
'Children often play in that park.'

Frame-setters are also *wa*-marked and they generally occupy sentence initial
position. Examples are given below. The *wa*-marked adverbials in (30) and
(32), sometimes called 'pure topics' and 'conditional topics', respectively,
are not interpreted as what the sentence is about in a most obvious way
(Kuroda 1986a,b, Tateishi 1994).

(30) *kyoo-wa Taro-ga   tosyokan-e iku.*
today-WA Taro-NOM library-to go
'Today, Taro is going to the library.'

(31) *hannin-wa   Jiroo-ga   ayasii.*
perpetrator-WA Jiro-NOM suspicious
Lit.: 'As for the perpetrator, Jiro is suspicious.'
(slightly modified from Tateishi 1994: 31)

(32) *[_{NP}[_{CP} e_i sinbun-o   yomi-tai] hito_i]-wa   koko-ni arimasu.*
newspaper-ACC read-want person-WA here-at exist
'If you want to read newspapers (they) are here.'   (Kuroda 1992: 283)

It is not the case that non-contrastive *wa*-marked items can never appear elsewhere. Moreover, we observe an asymmetry between subjects and non-subjects in such cases: subject *wa*-phrases have a freer distribution (Kuroda 1988, Watanabe 2003). This point is illustrated in two instances below. First, a sentential adverbial may precede the topic in the responses to the requests in (26) and (27). Both of the following are less preferred to those in (26B-i) and (27B-i), but (33a), where the subject topic is preceded by an adverbial, is not as dispreferred with respect to (26B-i), as (33b), where the object topic is preceded by an adverbial, is dispreferred with respect to (27B-i).

(33) a. *kinoo*   *[Taro-wa]$_T$ ano boosi-o katta.*
          yesterday Taro-WA   that hat-ACC bought

      b. *kinoo*   *[ano boosi-wa$_i$]$_T$ Taro-ga e$_i$ katta.*
          yesterday that hat-WA   Taro-NOM bought
          'Yesterday, Taro bought that hat.'

Second, as discussed above, some speakers allow a focus constituent answering the *wh*-part of a preceding question to undergo scrambling. For such speakers, an object focus can be scrambled across a subject *wa*-phrase, as in (34B-ii). So, the subject *wa*-phrase can be preceded by an object focus. By contrast, an object *wa*-phrase cannot be preceded by a subject focus, as demonstrated by (35). It is widely reported that an object *wa*-phrase in-situ must be interpreted contrastively (Saito 1985, Hoji 1985). Thus, (35B-ii) states that Taro bought a hat but also implicates that there is something else that he did not buy, an infelicitous implicature in the given context.

(34) A: *Taro-wa nani-o   katta   no?*
          Taro-WA what-ACC bought Q
          'What did Taro buy?'

      B: i. *Taro-wa kinoo   ano boosi-o katta.*
              Taro-WA yesterday that hat-ACC bought

          ii. *ano boosi-o$_i$ Taro-wa kinoo t$_i$ katta.*
              that hat-ACC Taro-WA yesterday bought
              'Taro bought that hat yesterday.'

(35) A: *ano boosi-wa dare-ga   katta   no?*
          that hat-wa   who-nom bought Q
          'Speaking of that hat, who bought it?'

B: i. *ano boosi-wa$_i$ Taro-ga   kinoo e$_i$ katta.*
      that hat-WA   Taro-NOM yesterday bought

ii. *#Taro-ga   ano boosi-wa kinoo   katta.*
    Taro-NOM that hat-WA   yesterday bought
    'Taro bought that hat yesterday.'

Recall that we saw in (26) that the word order in (34B-ii) is infelicitous as a response to the request *tell me about Taro*. One relevant difference between the two contexts appears to be the status of *X* in the requests. In (34), the question introduces *Taro* as the topic, which is suggested by the fact that *Taro* is marked by *wa*, and the question is interpreted as being about *Taro*. Consequently, *Taro* in the response is a continuing topic in the sense of Givón (1983). On the other hand, *tell me about Taro* is an explicit instruction to the hearer to introduce *Taro* as the topic. Thus, *Taro* in the response introduces the topic and is not a continuing topic. The latter point is supported by the fact that the request can be less specific such as *tell me about someone in your class*, for which the utterance in (26B-i)/(34B-i) can still be used. (See Reinhart 1982, Givón 1983, Lambrecht 1994, Vallduví and Engdahl 1996, among others, for discussion on this distinction)

A clause may have multiple non-contrastive *wa*-phrases. At typical examples involves a frame-setter and a subject (Kuroda 1988). The adverbial may appear without *wa*, but the difference in the interpretation is not very clear.

(36) *Paris-de-wa Masao-wa [$_{NP}$ Eiffel-too-to   Notre Dame-no*
     Paris-in-WA Masao-WA   Eiffel-tower-and Notre Dame-GEN

     too]-ni nobotta.
     tower-in climbed

     'In Paris, Masao climbed up the Eiffel tower and the tower of Notre Dame.'

Non-contrastive *wa*-phrases are root phenomena and are excluded from most subordinate clauses such as conditionals, relative clauses, adverbial clauses, complement clauses of nouns and factive predicates (Maki et al. 1999). These clauses normally do not allow a topic-comment structure of their own. However, non-contrastive *wa*-phrases do occur in argument clauses headed by verbs like *sinziteiru* 'believe', as in (37), and others that arguably subcategorize for speech acts, such as embedded interrogative clauses, as in (38). The examples are modified from Maki et al. (1999: 8–9) (cf. also Kuroda 2005, Hara 2006).

(37) *John-wa [kono hon-wa Mary-ga   yonda to]   siziteiru.*
John-WA this book-WA Mary-NOM read   that believe
'John believes that this book, Mary read.'

(38) *John-wa [kono hon-wa   Mary-ga   yonda kadooka] siritagatteiru.*
John-WA this book-WA Mary-NOM read   whether   want.to.know
'John wants to know whether this book, Mary read.'

In terms of prosody, not as much attention has been paid to *wa*-marked phrases as to contrastive focus and *wh*-phrases. It has been claimed on occasion that a non-contrastive *wa*-phrase forms a separate intermediate phrase (Nagahara 1994), and Nakanishi (2001, 2003) provide some suggestive evidence from an experimental study bearing out the claim.

Finally, there are a few other particles that may indicate topichood, such as *-nara* (Munakata 2006) and *-to ieba*. Such particles are comparable to the English phrases *as for...* and *speaking of...*

2.2. Contrastive topics

Contrastive topics are also marked by the particle *wa*. They typically display the prosody associated with contrastive focus and *wh*-phrases, discussed above: a sharp F_0-rise followed by F_0-compression (Nakanishi 2001, 2003, Tomioka 2010).

The standard description in the literature is that contrastive topics may remain in-situ.[15] We saw such an example in (35B-ii). Nevertheless, when contrastive *wa*-phrases are set in discourse contexts requiring contrastive topics, they obligatorily appear in clause-initial position (Vermeulen to appear). In the following examples, an explicit contrast is made to an alternative, and the leading utterances in B's responses ensure the topic status of the intended contrastive topics 'Bill' and 'beans' (Vermeulen to appear: Ex. (15)–(18)).

---

[15] More specifically, the generalization is that a *wa*-marked object in-situ must be interpreted contrastively. However, this generalization seems to hold only if the preceding subject is marked with the nominative case marker (Kuroda 1965, Vermeulen to appear). If the preceding subject is marked with *wa*, then it is possible for the object *wa*-phrase in-situ to be interpreted without contrast.

(39) A: 'What did John eat at the party yesterday?'

B: *hmm, John-wa doo-ka   sir-anai   kedo,*
well, John-WA how-whether know-not but
'Well, I don't know about John, but…'

   i. *[BIll-wa]$_{CT}$ 8-zi-goro   [maME-o]$_F$ tabeteita (yo).*
      Bill-WA   8 o'clock-around beans-ACC eating.was SFP

   ii. #*[maME-o$_i$]$_F$ [BIll-wa]$_{CT}$ 8-zi-goro t$_i$ tabeteita (yo).*
      beans-ACC Bill-WA   8 o'clock-around eating.was SFP
      'as for Bill, he was eating beans around 8 o'clock.'

(40) A: 'Who ate the pasta at the party yesterday?'

B: *hmm, pasuta-wa doo-ka   sir-anai   kedo,*
well, pasta-WA   how-whether know-not but
'Well, I don't know about the pasta, but…'

   i. #*[BIll-ga]$_F$ [maME-wa]$_{CT}$ 8-zi-goro   tabeteita (yo).*
      Bill-NOM beans-WA   8 o'clock-around eating.was SFP

   ii. *[maME-wa$_i$]$_{CT}$ [BIll-ga]$_F$ 8-zi-goro t$_i$ tabeteita   (yo).*
      beans-WA   Bill-NOM 8 o'clock-around eating.was SFP
      'as for the beans, Bill was eating them around 8 o'clock.'

Unlike non-contrastive topics, contrastive topics are sensitive to island conditions. This is illustrated below (slightly modified from Hoji 1985: 161):

(41) ?*(*Susan-zyanakute*) *[MAry$_j$-wa]$_{CT}$ John-ga [$_{NP}$[$_{TP}$ e$_i$ (kanozyo$_j$-o) butta]*
     (Susan-not.but)   Mary-WA   John-NOM   she-ACC   hit

hito$_i$-o   sagasiteiru.
person-ACC looking.for
Lit.: '(Not Susan, but) Mary, John is looking for a person who hit (her).'

Different kinds of contexts are required for contrastively *wa*-marked items to appear elsewhere felicitously. Such contexts include partial answers, (42), and cases where they are part of a larger focus, (43). Interestingly, in the latter case, the contrastive implicature of contrastive *wa* can percolate to a larger constituent, like focus. Thus, in (43), 'rain' and 'umbrella' are not contrasted with each other, but rather the two events described by the clauses, that 'it was raining' and that 'John did not take an umbrella with him', are. Furthermore, *wa* may attach directly to verbs, contrasting them explicitly, in which case *do*-support is required, (44). Whether these *wa*-phrases should be analyzed as contrastive 'topics' depends on one's definition of 'contrastive topic'. In particular, the relevant sentences do not appear to be 'about' the *wa*-marked items nor are they specific, both of which are characteristics of 'topics'.

(42) A: 'Did John buy the sweets?'

B: *John-wa oSEnbee-wa   katta   (kedo, KUkkii-wa kaw-anakatta).*
John-WA rice.cracker-WA bought but   cookies-WA buy-not.PAST
'John bought rice crackers, but (he) didn't buy cookies.'

(43) *[$_{TP}$ Ame-wa hutteita-ga] [$_{TP}$ John-ga KAsa-wa   motte-ik-anakatta].*
rain-WA falling.was-but John-NOM umbrella-WA bring-go-not.PAST
'It was raining, but John did not take an umbrella with him.'

(44) *John-wa ano hon-o   kaI-wa sita-ga, mada yoMI-wa site-inai.*
John-WA that book-ACC buy-WA did-but still   read-WA do-not
'John bought that book, but he hasn't read it yet.'

The distribution of *wa* in (42)–(44) is reminiscent of the focus sensitive particles *mo, sae,* and *sika,* discussed in Section 1.5: it may attach to DPs in-situ and to verbs. Indeed, its syntactic, semantic, and prosodic properties have been likened to those of contrastive focus or focus sensitive particles on some occasions (Kuroda 1969, 2005, Nagahara 1994, Hara 2006, Oshima 2008). Like the other focal particles, contrastive *wa* can associate with an item at a distance, even across an island (slightly modified from Hara 2006: 74).

(45) *Itsumo [$_{NP}$ [$_{CP}$ CHOmsky-ga e$_i$ kai-ta] hon$_i$]-wa*
always   Chomsky-NOM wrote book-WA
shuppan-sa-re-ru.
publish- do-PASS-NON.PAST
'As for books that Chomsky wrote, they are always published.'
(Implicature: 'but books that other people wrote are not always published.')

Contrastive *wa*-phrases are permitted in a wider range of environments than non-contrastive *wa*-phrases (Hara 2006). For instance, they may appear in *because*-clauses, as shown below. The example is slightly modified from Hara (2006: 91).

(46) *itsumo [uti-ni   John-wa kuru node]   oyatsu-o   youi-suru.*
always house-to John-WA come because sweets-ACC prepare-do
'Because at least John comes to our house, I always prepare some sweets.'

However, their distribution is still limited compared to that of other focus sensitive particles. Although varying judgements have been reported for some subordinate clauses,[16] the judgement is robust and shared by most speakers with respect to relative clauses (Maki et al. 1999, Kuroda 2005, Hara 2006): A contrastive *wa*-phrase cannot appear inside a relative clause (Hara 2006: 73). Other focus sensitive particles can appear inside relative clauses, however.

(47) **Itsumo $[_{NP} [_{CP}$ CHOmsky-wa e_i kaita] $hon_i]$-ga*
always   Chomsky-WA   wrote book-NOM
shuppan-sa-re-ru.
publish-do-PASS-NON.PAST
'A book which at least Chomsky wrote is always published.'

(48) *Taro-wa $[_{NP} [_{CP}$ Hanako-mo e_i suisensita] $hon_i]$-o   katta.*
Taro-WA   Hanako-also   recommended book-ACC bought
'Taro bought the book that Hanako too recommended.'

A final instance of sentence-medial contrastive *wa*-marked phrases to be mentioned is so-called 'mini-topics' (Kuroda 1990, 1992), which have not received much attention. Two examples are given below (slightly modified from Kuroda 1990: 13).

(49) *Tanaka-ga   (ano kaigi-ni)   huransu-zin-wa   (ano kaigi-ni)*
Tanaka-NOM that meeting-to France-person-WA that meeting-to
gengogakusya-oyonda
linguist-ACC   invited
'Tanaka invited linguists, so far as the French are concerned, to that meeting.'

---

[16] For instance, Kuroda (2005) reports that a contrastive *wa*-phrase is permitted inside a conditional clause, while Hara (2006) reports that this is disallowed.

(50) *Tanaka-ga (kyonen) wain-o   Amerika-kara-wa (kyonen)*
Tanak-NOM last.year wine-ACC America-from-WA last.year
Karihorunia-kara yunyuu-sita.
California-from   imported
'Tanaka imported wine from California last year, so far as America is concerned.'

An interesting feature of mini-topics is that they seem to have a part-whole or set-subset relation with the following object or adverbial and have the same semantic relation to the verb. The latter point can be seen from the fact that in (50) the *wa*-phrase bears the postposition *kara* 'from'. This is not visible in (49), as case markers are generally omitted in the presence of *wa*. Syntactically, they are separate from the associated object or adverbial at the clausal level, as a sentential adverbial may intervene between them, as indicated above. In terms of interpretation, Kuroda claims that a contrast with alternatives is implicated. For instance, the speaker may follow (49) with 'but as far as the Koreans are concerned, Tanaka invited psychologists'. Furthermore, the following object or adverbial receives a focus interpretation. (49) implies that Tanaka invited French linguists and not French psychologists, for example, and (50) implies that the wine was from California and not from New York. Mini-topics are not interpreted as what the rest of the sentence is about, rather, their function seems akin to frame-setters, limiting the domain in which the focus should be interpreted.

3. Givenness

There are several ways of expressing the given status of an item. First of all, given items, including continuing topics, are often not realized by overt expressions. The antecedent may be in the previous sentence, as in the case of (5b), as an answer to (1A), and in example (16); it may be within the same sentence, as in (51); or it may only be given contextually, as in (52). See Takahashi (2008) for an overview of the syntactic literature on zero expressions. (51) and (52) are slightly modified from Takahashi (2008: 394, 416) and *e* indicates a zero expression here.

(51) *Taro$_i$-ga   Hanako$_j$-ni [$_{CP}$ e$_i$ e$_j$ kekkon-suru to] yakusoku-sita.*
Taro-NOM Hanako-DAT   marry   that promised
'Taro promised Hanako that he would marry her.'

(52) [Observing a student smoking in the classroom]

    a. *e haigan-de   sinu kamosirenai.*
       lung.cancer-of die   may
       'He may die of lung cancer.'

    b. *sensee-ga   e sikaru daroo*
       teacher-NOM   scold will
       'The teacher will scold him.'

On the other hand, an item introducing a new topic, contrastive or not, cannot be a zero expression, even if the relevant lexical item is mentioned previously, thus in (26) and (27), the non-contrastive topic cannot be absent, and in (53), the contrastive topic must be overt.

(53) A: 'What did Taro and Jiro eat?'

    B: *Hmm, Taro-wa doo-ka   sir-anai   kedo, [Jiro-wa/ #e]$_{CT}$*
       well, Taro-WA how-whether know-not but   Jiro-WA
       pasuta-o   tabeta.
       pasta-ACC ate
       'Well, I don't know about Taro, but Jiro ate pasta.'

Second, an intermediate level of givenness may be indicated by case-marker drop. An object adjacent to the verb allows this more easily than a subject, but the latter is in principle possible, as shown below. Case-marker drop on the subject requires a higher level of informality and a sentence-final particle (Tsutsui 1984, Masunaga 1987, 1988, Fukuda 1993, Lee 2002).

(54) *ame(-ga) hutteiru yo.*
    rain-NOM falling SFP
    'Oh, it's raining.'

The particle *wa* may be dropped from a topic, although this also requires informality and a high level of saliency of the host item (Tsutsui 1984).

    A third way of expressing givenness is by compression of F_0-movement. This option is available only to post-focal or post-*wh* material (Sugahara 2003, Hwang 2008, Hara and Kawahara 2008, Féry and Ishihara 2009).

    Finally, given material can right-dislocate, that is, appear to the right of the verb, with or without a case marker, a postposition or *wa* (Kuno 1978, Endo 1996, Tanaka 2001), and more than one argument/adverbial may do so simultaneously. In (55), the subject and the object are right-dislocated. See

Shimojo (2005) for the different levels of givenness associated with some of the strategies mentioned here.

(55) *yonda yo, John(-ga/wa)   sono hon(-o/wa)*
      read   SFP John-NOM/WA this book-ACC/WA
      'John read this book.'/Lit.: '(he) read (it), John, this book.'

A given item may be (part of) a focus. In such instances the given item cannot generally be a zero expression, as shown in the following examples. They are best realized as full DPs.

(56) A: [Hearing some noise in Taro's room] 'What happened in Taro's room?'
      B: *[$_{TP}$ Taro-ga / $^?$kare-ga / #e kabin-o   kowasite-simatta]$_F$.*
         Taro-NOM   he-NOM   vase-ACC break-ended.up
         'Taro has broken a vase.'

(57) A: 'What did Taro's mother do?'
      B: *kanozyo-wa / Ø [$_{VP}$ Taro-o / $^?$kare-o / #e hometa]$_F$.*
         she-WA   Taro-ACC he-ACC   praised
         'She praised Taro.'

The situation does not seem so clear-cut, however. For instance, the examples in (52) demonstrate an instance of zero expressions inside focus. Also, some speakers report that a zero expression in the subject position is fine in (56B), if it refers to the speaker.

Finally, a remark is in order regarding two cross-linguistically common ways of realizing givenness that do not seem prevalent in Japanese. First, pronominals can be used to refer to given items and they are possible in the above examples in principle. Nonetheless, Japanese pronominals have particular social connotations, such as intimacy or formality (Shibatani 1990), and their use is a much less preferred option, compared to full DPs.[17] Second, in many languages that allow scrambling, the operation is employed to mark givenness, so that given items precede new items. However, as mentioned in footnote 5, discourse effects of scrambling, espe-

---

[17] See Clancy (1980) for a comparative study in the use of pronouns between Japanese and English. She reports that in recounting stories, Japanese speakers used a full DP twice before resorting to zero expressions referring to the same entity, while English speakers used a full DP once before employing a pronominal.

cially when the scrambled item is not focused, are still unclear in Japanese. Thus, at this stage, it is difficult to say to what extent givenness bears on the apparent optional nature of scrambling in this language.

References

Akiyama, Masahiro
  2005   On the general tendency to minimize moved elements: The multiple
          nominative construction in Japanese and its theoretical implications.
          The Linguistic Review 22: 1–68.
Aoyagi, Hiroshi and Sachiko Kato
  2007   On information packaging of topicalized and scrambled sentences
          in Japanese. *Current Issues in Unity and Diversity of Languages:
          Collection of Papers Selected from CIL (International Congress of
          Linguists) 18, Held at Korean University in Seoul.* Published by The
          Linguistic Society of Korea. 276–294.
Beckman, Mary and Janet B. Pierrehumbert
  1988   *Japanese Tone Structure.* Cambridge: Massachusetts Institute of
          Technology Press
Clancy, Patricia M.
  1980   Referential choice in English and Japanese narrative discourse. In
          *The Pear Stories: Cognitive, Cultural, and Linguistic Aspects of
          Narrative Production*, Wallace L. Chafe (ed.), 127–202. Norwood:
          Ablex.
Büring, Daniel
  1997   *The Meaning of Topic and Focus.* London: Routledge.
Deguchi, Masanori and Yoshihisa Kitagawa
  2002   Prosody and wh-questions. *North East Linguistic Society 32*: 73–92.
Diesing, Molly
  1988   Bare plural subjects and the stage/individual contrast. In *Genericity
          in Natural Language: Proceedings of the 1988 Tübingen Conference*,
          Manfred Krifka (ed.).
Endo, Yoshio
  1996   Right dislocation. *Formal Approaches to Japanese Linguistics 2:
          Massachusetts Institute of Technology Working Papers in Linguistics*
          29: 1–20.
Fanselow, Gisbert and Denisa Lenertová
  2011   Left peripheral focus: Mismatches between syntax and information
          structure. *Natural Language and Linguistic Theory* 29: 169–209.
Féry, Caroline and Shinichiro Ishihara
  2009   How focus and givenness shape prosody. In *Information Structure
          from Different Perspectives*, Malte Zimmermann and Carolin Féry
          (eds.), 36–68. Oxford: Oxford University Press.

Fukuda, Minoru
   1993   Head government and case marker drop in Japanese. *Linguistic Inquiry* 24: 168–172.
Fukaya, Teruhiko and Hajime Hoji
   1999   Stripping and sluicing in Japanese and some implications. *West Coast Conference on Formal Linguistics* 18.
Futagi, Yoko
   2005   Japanese focus particles at the syntax-semantics interface. Ph.D. dissertation, Rutgers University.
Givón, Talmy
   1983   *Topic Continuity in Discourse: A Quantitative Cross-Language Study.* Amsterdam: John Benjamins.
Hara, Yurie
   2006   Grammar of knowledge representation: Japanese discourse items at interfaces. Ph.D. dissertation. University of Delaware.
Hara, Yurie and Shigeto Kawahara
   2008   De-accenting, MAXIMIZE PRESUPPOSITION and evidential scales. In *Proceedings of the Speech Prosody 2008 Conference*, 509–512.
Hara, Yurie and Robert van Rooij
   2007   Contrastive topics revisited: a simpler set of topic-alternatives. Talk presented at *North East Linguistic Society* 38, University of Ottawa, Canada.
Haraguchi, Shosuke
   1999   Accent. In *The Handbook of Japanese Linguistics*, N. Tsujimura (ed.), 1–30. Oxford: Blackwell.
Heycock, Caroline
   1993a   Focus projection in Japanese. *Proceedings of North East Linguistic Society* 24: 157–171.
Heycock, Caroline
   1993b   Syntactic predication in Japanese. *Journal of East Asian Linguistics* 2: 167–211.
Heycock, Caroline
   2008   Japanese -*wa*, -*ga*, and information structure. In *The Oxford Handbook of Japanese Linguistics* Mamoru Saito and Shigeru Miyagawa (eds.), 54–83. Oxford: Oxford University Press.
Hinds, John, Senko Maynard and Shoichi Iwasaki
   1987   *Perspectives on Topicalization: the Case of Japanese WA.* Amsterdam: John Benjamins.
Hiraiwa, Ken and Shinichiro Ishihara
   2002   Missing links: cleft, sluicing, and "no da" construction in Japanese. *Massachusetts Institute of Technology Working Papers in Linguistics* 43: 35–54.
Hoji, Hajime
   1985   Logical form constraints and configurational structures in Japanese. Ph.D. dissertation, University of Washington.

Hoji, Hajime
    1987   Japanese clefts and reconstruction/chain binding effects. Handout
            of talk presented at West Coast Conference on Formal Linguistics 6,
            University of Arizona.
Hwang, Hyun Kyung
    2008   Wh-intonation and information structure in South Kyeongsang
            Korean, Fukuoka Japanese and Tokyo Japanese. Talk presented at
            Workshop on Interface-based Approaches to Information Structure.
            University College London.
Ishihara, Shinichiro
    2000   Stress, focus, and scrambling in Japanese. *Massachusetts Institute of
            Technology Working Papers in Linguistics 39: A Few from Building
            E39.* 142–175.
Ishihara, Shinichiro
    2002   Invisible but audible wh-scope marking: Wh-constructions and
            deaccenting in Japanese. *Proceedings of West Coast Conference on
            Formal Linguistics* 21: 180–193.
Ishihara, Shinichiro
    2004   Prosody by phase: evidence from focus intonation – *wh*-scope cor-
            respondence in Japanese. *Interdisciplinary Studies on Information
            Structure* 1: 77–119.
Ishihara, Shinichiro
    2007   Major phrase, focus intonation, multiple spell-out. *The Linguistic
            Review* 24: 137–167.
Ishihara, Shinichiro
    to appear Intonation of *wh*- and *yes/no*-question in Tokyo Japanese. In *Con-
            trastiveness and Scalar Implicature*, Ferenc Kiefer, Manfred Krifka
            and Chungmin Lee (eds.).
Ishizuka, Tomoko
    2010   Alienable-Inalienable Asymmetry in Japanese and Korean Possession.
            UPenn Working Papers in Linguistics 16.
Jackendoff, Ray
    1972   *Semantic Interpretation in Generative Grammar.* Cambridge: Massa-
            chusetts Institute of Technology Press.
Kim, Soowon
    1999   Sloppy/strict identity, empty objects, and NP ellipsis. *Journal of East
            Asian Linguistics* 8: 255–284.
Kishimoto, Hideki
    2009   Topic prominency in Japanese. *The Linguistic Review* 26: 465–513.
Kizu, Mika
    2005   *Cleft Constructions in Japanese Syntax.* New York: Palgrave Mac-
            millan.
Ko, Heejeong
    2005   Syntactic edges and linearization. Ph.D. dissertation, Massachusetts
            Institute of Technology.

Kuno, Susumu
    1973   *The Structure of the Japanese Language*. Cambridge, Massachusetts: Massachusetts Institute of Technology Press.

Kuno, Susumu
    1978   *Danwa-no bunpoo* [Grammar of discourse]. Tokyo: Taishuukan-shoten.

Kuroda, Sige-Yuki
    1965   Generative grammatical studies in the Japanese language. Ph.D. dissertation, Massachusetts Institute of Technology. Reproduced by Garland, New York 1979.

Kuroda, Sige-Yuki
    1969   Remarks on the notion of subject with reference to words like *also*, *even*, and *only*. Part 2. *Annual Bulletin* 4: 127–152. Research Institute of Logopedics and Phoniatrics, University of Tokyo.

Kuroda, Sige-Yuki
    1972   The categorical and the thetic judgment: evidence from Japanese syntax. *Foundations of Language* 9: 153–185.

Kuroda, Sige-Yuki
    1986a   Movement of noun phrases in Japanese. Reprinted in Sige-Yuki Kuroda 1992.

Kuroda, Sige-Yuki
    1986b   What happened after the movement of noun phrase in La Jolla. Reprinted in Sige-Yuki Kuroda 1992.

Kuroda, Sige-Yuki
    1988   Whether we agree or not: A comparative syntax of English and Japanese. *Linguisticae Investigationes* 12: 1–47.

Kuroda, Sige-Yuki
    1990   Cognitive and syntactic bases of topicalized and non-topicalized sentences in Japanese. In *Japanese/Korean Linguistics*, Hajime Hoji (ed.), 1–26. Stanford: Center for the Study of Language and Information.

Kuroda, Sige-Yuki
    1992   *Japanese Syntax and Semantics: Collected Papers*. Dordrecht: Kluwer.

Kuroda, Sige-Yuki
    2005   Focusing on the matter of topic: A study of *wa* and *ga* in Japanese. *Journal of East Asian Linguistics* 14: 1–58.

Lambrecht, Knud
    1994   *Information Structure and Sentence Form*. Cambridge: Cambridge University Press.

Lee, Kiri
    2002   Nominative case-marker deletion in spoken Japanese: an analysis from the perspective of information structure. *Journal of Pragmatics* 34: 683–709.

Maki, Hideki, Lizanne Kaiser and Masao Ochi
1999   Embedded topicalization in English and Japanese. *Lingua* 109: 1–14.
Masunaga, Kiyoko
1987   Non-thematic positions and discourse anaphora. Ph.D. dissertation,
           Harvard University.
Masunaga, Kiyoko
1988   Case deletion and discourse context. In *Papers from the Second
           International Workshop on Japanese Syntax*, William J. Poser (ed.),
           145–156. Stanford: Center for the Study of Language and Information.
McCready, Eric
2006   On the meaning of Japanese *yo*. *Lecture Notes in Computer Science*.
           141–148.
Miyagawa, Shigeru
2006   On the "undoing" property of scrambling: A response to Bošković.
           Linguistic Inquiry 37: 607–624.
Munakata, Takashi
2006   Japanese topic-constructions in the minimalist view of the syntax
           semantics interface. In *Minimalist Essays*, Cedric Boeckx (ed.), 115–
           159. Amsterdam: John Benjamin.
Nagahara, Hiroyuki
1994   Phonological phrasing in Japanese. Ph.D. dissertation, University of
           California Los Angeles.
Nakanishi, Kimiko
2001   Prosody and information structure in Japanese: A case study of topic
           marker *wa*. *Japanese/Korean Linguistics* 10: 434–447.
Nakanishi, Kimiko
2003   Prosody and scope interpretations of the topic marker *wa* in Japanese.
           In *Topic and Focus: Cross-linguistic Perspectives on Meaning and
           Intonation*, Chungmin Lee, Matthew Gordon and Daniel Büring
           (eds.), 177–193. Dordrecht: Springer.
Neeleman, Ad and Tanya Reinhart
1998   Scrambling and the PF interface. In *The Projection of Arguments*,
           Miriam Butt and Wilhelm Geuder (eds.), 309–353. Stanford: Center
           for the Study of Language and Information.
Oshima, David Y.
2008   Morphological vs. phonological contrastive topic marking. *Proceedings
           of Chicago Linguistic Society* 41: 371–384.
Saito, Mamoru
1985   Some Asymmetries in Japanese and their theoretical implications.
           Ph.D. thesis, Massachusetts Institute of Technology.
Saito, Mamoru
1989   Scrambling as semantically vacuous A'-movement. In *Alternative
           Conceptions of Phrase Structure*, Mark Baltin and Anthony Kroch
           (eds.), 182–200. Chicago: University of Chicago Press.

Sasse, Hans-Jürgen
  1987   The thetic/categorical distinction revisited. *Linguistics* 25: 511–580.
Selkirk, Elisabeth and Koichi Tateishi
  1991   Syntax and downstep in Japanese. In *Interdisciplinary Approaches to Language: Essays in Honor of S.-Y. Kuroda*, Carol Georgopoulous and Roberta Ishihara (eds.), 519–43. Dordrecht: Kluwer.
Shibatani, Masayoshi
  1990   *The Languages of Japan.* Cambridge: Cambridge University Press.
Shimojo, Mitsuaki
  2005   *Argument Encoding In Japanese Conversation.* New York: Palgrave Macmillan.
Sugahara, Mariko
  2003   Downtrends and post-focus intonation in Tokyo Japanese. Ph.D. dissertation, University of Massachusetts.
Takahashi, Daiko
  2008   Noun phrase ellipsis. In *The Oxford Handbook of Japanese Linguistics*, Mamoru Saito and Shigeru Miyagawa (eds.), 395–423. Oxford: Oxford University Press.
Takano, Yuji
  2002   Surprising constituents. *Journal of East Asian Linguistics* 11: 243–301.
Tanaka, Hidekazu
  2001   Right-dislocation as scrambling. *Journal of Linguistics* 37: 551–579.
Tateishi, Koichi
  1994   *The Syntax of Subjects.* Stanford: Center for the Study of Language and Information.
Tomioka, Satoshi
  2001   Information structure and disambiguation in Japanese. *West Coast Conference on Formal Linguistics* 20: 552–564.
Tomioka, Satoshi
  2007a   Pragmatics of LF intervention effects: Japanese and Korean *wh*-interrogatives. *Journal of Pragmatics* 39: 1570–1590.
Tomioka, Satoshi
  2007b   The Japanese existential possession: A case study of pragmatic disambiguation. *Lingua* 117: 881–902.
Tomioka, Satoshi
  2010   Contrastive topics operate on speech acts. In *Information Structure: Theoretical, Typological, and Experimental Perspectives* Malte Zimmermann and Carolin Féry (eds.). Oxford: Oxford University Press.
Tsutsui, Michio
  1984   Particle ellipses in Japanese. Ph.D. dissertation, University of Illinois.
Vallduví, Enric and Elisabet Engdahl
  1996   The linguistic realization of information packaging. *Linguistics* 34: 459–519.

Vermeulen, Reiko
    2005   Possessive and adjunct multiple nominative constructions in Japanese. *Lingua* 115: 1329–1363.
Vermeulen, Reiko
    2010   Non-topical *wa*-phrases in Japanese. In *Interfaces in Linguistics: New Research Perspectives*, Raffaella Folli and Christiane Ulbrich (eds.), 135–148. Oxford: Oxford University Press.
Vermeulen, Reiko
    to appear   On the position of topics in Japanese. To appear in *The Linguistic Review* 30.
Watanabe, Akira
    2003   Wh and operator constructions in Japanese. *Lingua* 113: 519–558.

The empirical investigation of information structure

Stavros Skopeteas

1. Preliminaries[1]

The underdetermination of theory by empirical data is an inherent property of scientific research, also beyond the study of language. For instance, it was widely held at the time of Copernicus that his theory and Ptolemaic theory do not necessarily make different predictions concerning the available astronomical data at that time (see Newton-Smith 2000: 532). Nevertheless, it is virtually impossible to carry out a scientific investigation that is free from theoretical considerations. First, even if empirical data exist independently of theories, their relevance for the scientific knowledge can only be judged in the light of a particular theory (see Feyerabend 1983: §3). Second, it is not possible to report on observations without reference to background assumptions that are derived by inductive procedures and are necessarily theory-specific. Hence, an astronomer adopting a geocentric theory such as Ptolemy and an astronomer adopting a heliocentric theory such as Copernicus may observe the same empirical phenomenon, i.e., the perceived position of the sun, but keep track of different observations.

The challenge of the present article is to report on the methods of investigating information structure abstracting away from the theoretical possibilities that are used in order to interpret the empirical data. The empirical question is: What are the linguistic forms and the information-structural concepts that constitute the building blocks of a research paradigm? For example, accent as a formal property was presumably only established by Paul (1880), and it seems that Dretske (1972) was first in claiming a specific category of contrastive focus. Given a set of linguistic forms and a set of information-structural properties, we can address the question of whether

---

[1] The line of thought presented in this article is influenced by a long number of discussions with Gisbert Fanselow, Caroline Féry, and Malte Zimmermann about the concepts of information structure and their empirical manifestation. I am particularly grateful to Manfred Krifka and Renate Musan for their comments on the final manuscript. This article is part of my work for the research institute 632 *Information Structure* (sponsored by the German Research Foundation).

there is a correlation between *form* and *function*, such as 'movement to the preverbal position' ~ 'focus' or 'left dislocation' ~ 'topic'. The observation of such a correlation only allows for weak statements concerning the form-function correspondence. Such a correlation raises the next empirical question: Is the functional concept a necessary and/or sufficient condition for the occurrence of the form at issue? The respective kind of evidence is required in order to qualify statements about the association between form and function.

Empirical statements concerning the association between form and function are supported by different types of linguistic evidence. There are principally two types of observations that lead to the conclusion that particular formal properties of the utterance depend on contextual properties. They are presented in (1) and (2), whereby E_i is a generalization over linguistic expressions and C_j is a generalization over contexts.

(1)   A property E_i of linguistic expressions *occurs* if a contextual condition C_j holds true.

For instance, it has been observed that passive voice in English more frequently occurs when the patient constituent is part of the given information (see Mathesius 1975: 156). Statements of this type result from observational research on corpora (see Section 2) and can be experimentally tested in studies on language production (see Section 3).

(2)   A property E_i of linguistic expressions *triggers the intuition of felicity* if a contextual condition C_j holds true.

For instance, it has been observed that an utterance with a narrow focus domain on the subject constituent (manifested through the nuclear stress on this constituent) is felicitous in the context of constituent questions on the subject (see Krifka 2002: 295). Statements of this type prove the congruence of particular formal properties of the utterance with particular contexts and are based either on the intuition of an (ideal) native speaker or on rating experiments carried out by a representative sample of native speakers (see Section 4).

The types of data talked about in (1) and (2) require several paradigms of empirical investigation. These range from qualitative and quantitative observational studies on naturalistic data to experimental studies on language production or perception. Current debates on linguistic methodology led some researchers to the exclusion of particular types of evidence from the scope of grammatical studies. For instance, Newmeyer (2003) argues that corpus-frequencies are irrelevant for grammatical models, while Sampson (2007) claims that the intuition of grammaticality is a delusion. However, contemporary linguistic research has arrived at the consensus that different methodological approaches are rather complementary in that they shed light on different aspects of the research object, a view that is clearly reflected in the contributions of a recent forum hosted by the *Zeitschrift für Sprachwissenschaft*, Issue 28 (see especially Featherston 2009, Haspelmath 2009). The present article supports this line of thought in showing that the generalizations on information structure that are obtained by means of a particular data-gathering method can only partially be replicated through a different method. A significant correlation between properties of linguistic expressions and information structural concepts in any type of data reveals an empirical phenomenon, which is a challenge for any theoretical attempt on this issue. By consequence, exclusion of a data type is equivalent to narrowing down the scope of descriptive adequacy of a linguistic theory.

Main emphasis is given to phenomena on the morphological and syntactic levels (e.g., word order, passivization, clitic doubling, etc.); the reader is referred to Chen (this volume) for the empirical study of prosodic issues. The present article discusses straightforward reflexes of the context on the form of the utterance, as manifested in observational research on corpora or experimental research on native speakers' production or intuition. Studies that explore the processing mechanism of the same range of phenomena (such as experiments on reading times or neurophysiological studies) are not included in the present summary; the reader is referred to Cowles (this volume) for further discussion.

In the following summary of empirical research, no sharp distinction is drawn between qualitative and quantitative data, since the majority of hypotheses can be examined in both types of evidence. Relying on qualitative data implies the assumption that singular observations are not affected by the variation that is involved in linguistic phenomena. Hence, the crucial difference lies on the reliability of these types of linguistic evidence, since generalizations out of singular observations are very likely to be biased – especially if they are obtained by native speakers that have been initiated into the targets of the investigation.

2.   Occurrence in context: Naturalistic evidence

This section deals with observational research on naturalistic data, i.e., corpora of spoken or written discourse. The range of observable phenomena in naturalistic discourse contains those information structural concepts that can be identified in a text corpus by means of operational definitions applying to observational data. As it is argued below, not every informational structural concept can be identified in observational data.

2.1. Overview

The most frequently used information structural concepts in corpus studies relate to the discourse status of the referents (given, new, and related distinctions). For instance, Prince (1981: 243) supports her taxonomy of new, inferable, and evoked referents (as well as subtypes thereof) with quantitative evidence from the frequency of occurrence of these concepts in oral and written text. Birner (1994: 244) distinguishes between given/new in the discourse and given/new from the hearer's perspective in order to find out the licensing factors of word order inversion in English. Weber and Müller (2004) use a binary distinction of givenness: referents are coded as given if they are mentioned within the last two sentences, otherwise they are coded as new. In a study of dative alternation in English, Bresnan and Hay (2007) classify the referents as 'evoked' (mentioned within the previous 10 lines of discourse), 'situationally-evoked' (first or second person), and 'non-given'.

A paradigm of empirical investigations of the influence of contextual factors on the choice of order and voice evolved within the framework of Givón (1994), based on previous ideas of Cooreman (1987). In this framework, discourse status is conceived as a scalar notion (i.e., anaphoric distance to the antecedent in the pretext, counted in n of sentences) and is combined with a cataphoric measure, which captures the persistence of the discourse referent in the subsequent text (counted in n of occurrences in the 10 subsequent clauses). This quantitative framework has been used in order to identify the contextual conditions that license voice alternations, e.g., active/direct vs. passive vs. inverse in Kutenai (see Dryer 1994) and particular word order configurations such as clitic left dislocation in Modern Greek (see Roland 1994). Furthermore, the role of anaphoric relations in combination with their structural properties is also a central part of the empirical studies that have been conducted within the framework of Centering Theory (see Grosz and Sidner 1986, Walker, Joshi and Prince

1998, Beaver 2004, Poesio et al. 2004, and Stede, this volume). In this framework, any utterance establishes a set of referents that are hierarchically ordered on the basis of structural properties (argument hierarchy). The choice of the discourse prominent referent among the members of this set depends on several strategies for the maintenance of discourse coherence.

A number of corpus studies examine focus-related properties. Herring and Polillo (1995) investigate the question of whether focus is expressed in the preverbal position in V-final languages (based on corpus data from Sinhala and Tamil). Their observations on the placement of focused referents are based on the criterion of 'new mentions', i.e., they capture instances of new information focus. A further concept that can be effectively identified in corpora is the concept of contrast. Brunetti (2009a) presents a qualitative corpus study on focus fronting in Italian and Spanish. The analysis of the contexts in which these utterances occur shows that only a subset of the fronted foci relates to an antecedent in discourse that is contrasted or corrected by the focused referent. A further focus-related concept is exhaustivity, which is used by Wedgwood, Pethő and Cann (2003) in the analysis of Hungarian corpus data. An occurrence of focus-fronting is classified as 'non-exhaustive' if it contains an expression implying that the fronted referent is not the only member of the set of relevant referents for which the presupposition holds true, e.g., 'primarily', 'for the most part' or 'least of all'. Another property related to focus is the occurrence of focus-sensitive particles, such as 'only', 'also', and 'even'. Matić (2003) observes the occurrence of focus-sensitive particles in focus-fronted constituents in Albanian, Greek, and Serbo-Croatian and Brunetti (2009a) makes similar observations in Italian and Spanish corpora.

Apart from the studies that examine the impact of givenness on topicalization, some empirical studies consider the concept of delimitation as found in contrastive topics and frame-setters (see Krifka and Musan, this volume, Section 5.2). Speyer (2007: 104–110) describes the types of elements in the German prefield that violate the expectations of topic continuity as postulated within the theorems of Centering Theory. In these utterances, he identifies instances of contrastive topicalization and frame setting (among other things). Brunetti (2009b: 283f.) reports that contrastive topicalization is among the factors that may induce non-canonical orders with non-subject topics in Italian and Spanish texts.

The overview of corpus studies presented in this section reveals an asymmetry with respect to the use of information structural concepts in observational studies. We may observe that an overwhelming number of studies examine givenness as a contextual factor, while there are no empirical studies based on the notion of aboutness. This asymmetry relates to inherent limitations of the observational data and these limitations reflect essential differences in the nature of information structural concepts.

The first difference relates to the fact that some information-structural concepts relate to properties of the common ground, while others relate to properties of the target utterance. Hence, categories relating to givenness distinctions are observable in the corpus: Given referents can be identified by the previous mentionings in the context, and inferable referents can be deduced on the basis of assumptions about bridging inferences (see Clark 1977, Prince 1981). On the other hand, the exhaustive interpretation of particular structural configurations is an interpretational property of the utterance and not a contextual property, hence there are no contexts that require an exhaustive expression. Hence, the identification of exhaustive expressions does not relate to the examination of the context. Rather, it relates to selectional restrictions of the construction at issue (e.g., combination with adverbials such as 'primarily'), i.e., to the potential of the constructions at issue to host information that is explicitly not exhaustively identified. In contrast to studies on givenness, there is no paradigm of investigations collecting the contexts that induce an exhaustive expression and reporting the range of linguistic expressions that are attested in these contexts.The second difference lies in the availability of observable properties that can be operationalized for the identification of an information structural concept. The givenness of a referent can be quite straightforwardly identified in the corpus by means of an operational definition: E.g., a referent is decoded as given if it is mentioned in the last two sentences as in Weber and Müller (2004), or in the last ten lines of discourse as in Bresnan and Hay (2007), etc. A similar operationalization is not possible for the concept of aboutness: This concept reflects an intuition about the relation between the topic constituent and its comment; hence, it does not refer to a contextual property that can be observed in corpus data.

2.2. Empirical statements

The choice of the appropriate data from naturalistic discourse depends on the empirical statement at issue. A type of statement that is usually tested in corpora is that some properties of linguistic expressions, e.g., particular word orders, depend on certain contextual conditions. A basic approach is to collect tokens of a particular type of linguistic expression in a text corpus and to identify the range of contexts in which the target expression occurs.

The findings of such corpus studies verify *existential hypotheses*, i.e., they examine the possibility of a particular expression to occur under certain contextual conditions, as given in (3).

(3) A property E_i of linguistic expressions may occur, if a contextual condition C_j holds true.

For instance, Herring (1994: 121) collects utterances with postverbal material in written and spoken Tamil narratives and identifies three contextual conditions in which this structural configuration can occur: (a) afterthoughts, (b) background material, and (c) focused material. In a similar vein, Brunetti (2009b) collects utterances with non-canonical orders in the corpus, i.e., utterances whose word order cannot be accounted for by the structural configuration or the semantic properties of the referents (e.g., non-canonical orders of the arguments of experiencer verbs) and identifies the information structural properties of the fronted constituents: contrastive/corrective focus, contrastive topic, topic shift.

   The observation of the possibility of a linguistic expression to occur in a particular context can refute *universal negative hypotheses*, i.e., hypotheses of the type presented in (4).

(4) A property E_k of linguistic expressions does not occur when a contextual condition C_l holds true.

For instance, a number of accounts conclude that movement to the preverbal position is associated with an exhaustive operator (see Szabolcsi 1981, Horvath 1986, Kiss 1998). Empirically, this statement implies that every instance of movement to the preverbal position requires an exhaustive interpretation. This is a falsifiable universal hypothesis that has been tested in the Hungarian national corpus by Wedgwood, Pethő and Cann (2003). In order to refute the hypothesis of exhaustive interpretation, the authors extracted a number of sentences (approx. 1000) involving a constituent in the preverbal position from the corpus and examined their contextual properties. The critical sentences for the refutation of the universal hypothesis of an exhaustive operator are those that involve a non-exhaustively identified referent, in particular sentences that involve the expressions 'for the most part', 'least of all', 'primarily', etc. in the preverbal position. The occurrence of non-exhaustively identified referents in the preverbal position, as exemplified in (5), is evidence against the universal hypothesis at issue. Hence, the authors conclude that this construction in Hungarian is not parallel to the English it-cleft construction. This conclusion opens a new empirical challenge, namely to look for occurrences of similar expressions in a corpus of English: indeed, cleft sentences containing an expression such as 'among else' within the clefted constituent occur very frequent in English as can be shown by a simple query in a search engine, which is evidence against the hypothesis that English and Hungarian are different in this respect (Anna Szabolcsi, p.c.).

(5)   *A   küldöttségben Chris Patten, az   unió   külügyi*
       the delegation-in Chris Patten the union foreign
       biztosa   mellet helyet kap Javier Solana,
       commissioner-POSS.3SG beside place gets Javier Solana
       akiket útjukra <u>*többek között Anna Lindh svéd   külügyminiszter*</u>
       whom way-on others among Anna Lindh Swedish foreign-minister
       <u>*kisér   majd el.*</u>
       accompany FUT   VM
       'In the delegation, Javier Solana will be included in addition to Chris Patten, the foreign commissioner of the EU, and they will also be accompanied by among others the Swedish foreign minister Anna Lindh.'
       (see Wedgwood, Pethő and Cann 2003: 14)

In a similar vein, Brunetti (2009a) rejects the universal hypothesis that fronted foci in Italian and Spanish are associated with the concept of contrastive focus in presenting tokens of the target construction without a contrasted or corrected antecedent. The methodological approach in the studies of Wedgwood, Pethő and Cann (2003) and Brunetti (2009a) is similar: Since the aim was to refute a universal hypothesis concerning the functional properties of focus fronting, the authors extracted tokens of the target construction from the corpus and investigated the range of contexts in which this construction occurs.

   Universal negative hypotheses can even be refuted by a single (positive) counterexample in naturalistic discourse. For instance, Davison (1984: 814) claims that only specific indefinites can be topicalized, which amounts to the universal negative hypothesis that non-specific indefinites cannot be topicalized. Interestingly, Gundel (1974: 187) makes exactly the opposite claim: Only non-specific indefinites can be topicalized, which implies that specific indefinites cannot. Ward and Prince (1991) reject both hypotheses by presenting single counterexamples from naturalistic discourse. Example (a) presents a topicalized non-specific indefinite, which is evidence against

Davison's hypothesis, and Example (b) a topicalized specific indefinite, which is evidence against Gundel's hypothesis. (But note that there are accentual differences between the sentences, which means that the underlying concept of "topicalization" is presumably not a uniform one).

(6) a. *Brains you're born with. A great body you have to work at.*
     [Brooke Shields, in health club commercial]
     (Ward and Prince 1991: 170)

     b. *Several of these questions I will try to answer – but, let me emphasize, from a personal rather than a general viewpoint.*
     [Nixon 1962: xiii] (Ward and Prince 1991: 171)

Another case, in which a universal hypothesis is refuted, can be found in Gundel, Hedberg and Zacharski (2005), who examined third person personal pronouns that do not have an explicit antecedent in discourse. They extracted a sample of 2.046 third person personal pronouns from the Santa Barbara Corpus of Spoken American English, showing that in some tokens the personal pronoun does not refer to an explicit antecedent, as exemplified in (7). In this example, the third personal pronoun in the answer of B refers to the couple (Trish and her husband) that is inferable from the introduction of the referent Trish in the common ground.

(7) A: *Was it Trish who told me she was pregnant?*
     B: *She looked really good. Where are they going to church?*
     [13.221] (Gundel, Hedberg and Zacharski 2005)

Beyond citing single counterexamples, the authors report the frequency of pronouns without an explicit antecedent in the data set (330 tokens classified in several types, i.e., 16.3% of the examined tokens of third person pronouns). However, the observation of a single counterexample would have been sufficient evidence to reject the universal hypothesis that every personal pronoun has an explicit antecedent in discourse.[2] Reporting counts is informative in order to reject the intuition that a single counterexample may be accidental. However, in the absence of a baseline that indicates the

---

[2] The aim of the authors is not to reject the universal hypothesis, but to describe the types of reference resolution of third person pronouns and their frequency in spontaneous discourse. Hence, the discussion about the relevance of the quantitative study for the refutation of the universal hypothesis is independent from the aims of this article.

amount of accidental occurrences, there is no principled way to prove that the reported frequency is sufficient, i.e., it corresponds to a probability of occurrence that is beyond the chance level.

So far we discussed deterministic hypotheses concerning the correlation of properties of linguistic expressions with contextual conditions. We have exemplified empirical situations that confirm the truth of existential hypotheses or reject the truth of universal hypotheses. The question is whether the opposite claims can be justified by observational data, i.e., whether it is possible to refute an existential statement as in (3) or to justify a universal hypothesis as in (4) if the expression-context pair does not occur in the data (see also Krifka 2010: §2.1, for a discussion of this problem in semantic research). For instance, Birner (1994) reports that in a data set of 703 tokens of inversion in English, 533 tokens (75.8%) involve a discourse-old initial constituent and discourse-new final constituent, 141 tokens (20.1%) involve two discourse-new constituents, 29 tokens (4.1%) involve two discourse-old constituents, and no utterance involves a discourse-new initial constituent and a discourse-old final constituent. On the basis of this empirical finding she induces a pragmatic constraint: "the preposed element in an inversion must not be newer in the discourse than the postposed element" (Birner 1994: 245).

This conclusion is confronted with Hume's problem of induction, i.e., with the problem that we are not justified in inferring a universal statement out of singular ones. In the words of Karl Popper "no matter how many instances of white swans we may have observed, this does not justify the conclusion that *all* swans are white" (Popper 1934: ch. I, §1). In a strict empiricist viewpoint, universal hypotheses can be never justified, which is equivalent to saying that existential hypotheses can be never refuted. However, this problem concerns the validity of the inference and not the relevance of the empirical statement per se. Hence, the fact that no exceptions to a universal hypothesis (or no justifying instances of an existential hypothesis) are attested is a relevant empirical statement as such. The inference of a universal generalization out of such observations is an unnecessary risk (see Kuhn 1970: 18). However, the evidential basis of linguistic generalizations is particular in that it may be complemented by intuition data, which allow universal generalizations to be confirmed, as argued in Section 4 below.

The corpus studies mentioned so far were based on samples of the target expression only. This approach is effective in order to identify the range of contexts in which the target construction does or does not occur. An inherent limitation of these empirical studies comes from the fact that they only observe a subset of the data that is determined by properties of the dependent variable. The interpretation of the findings involves the assumption that the range of encountered contexts deviates from the range of possible contexts that appears in discourse independently of the target expression. For instance, Birner's (1994: 245) observation that the occurrences of inversion in English do no involve utterances with a discourse-new initial constituent and a discourse-old postverbal constituent could also be accounted for through the hypothesis that lower constituents (i.e., the initial ones in inversion) always outrank higher constituents (i.e., the postverbal ones in inversion) in discourse-givenness. The belief that this conflicting hypothesis is false is reasonable and may be supported through reference to empirical studies that show that the opposite holds, but the reported data does not allow to discriminate between these theoretical options.

In order to empirically prove that a particular property of an expression depends on context, we not only need to know the range of contexts in which the target property occurs but also whether this range significantly differs from the range of contexts in which the target property does not occur. There are fundamentally two ways to formulate a differential hypothesis of this kind. A straightforward formulation of the functional distinction between two alternative expressions is based on the conditional probability of particular contextual properties to occur, as in (8).

(8)   The conditional probability of a context C_i given a property of expression E_k is greater than the conditional probability of the same context C_i given a property of expression E_l, i.e., $prob(C_i | E_k) > prob(C_i | E_l)$.

The aim of the corpus study of Weber and Müller (2004) was to identify the impact of definiteness, givenness, and pronominalization on the choice between the SVO and the OVS order in German (based on the NEGRA newspaper corpus). In order to obtain comparable frequencies, the authors extracted the exhaustive set of tokens of the less frequent option (OVS sentences) in the corpus ($n=625$) and an equal random sample of tokens of the more frequent option (625 SVO sentences out of total 2773). In order to observe the effects of givenness, subject, and object constituents were coded as given (i.e., mentioned in the two last sentences) or non-given. The reported counts allowed for generalizations with respect to the likelihood of the four possible permutations of ±given subjects and ±given objects to apply, when German speakers use SVO or OVS utterances. The empirical findings show that the OVS order is more likely to occur than the SVO order when the object of a sentence is given and the subject new.

The reverse empirical question is how likely it is for a set of properties of linguistic expressions to occur when particular contextual conditions hold true.

(9)   The conditional probability of a property of expression E_i given a context C'_k is greater than the conditional probability of the same property E_i given a context C_l, i.e., $prob(E_i | C_k) > prob(E_i | C_l)$.

The hypothesis in (9) cannot be tested in the data set of Weber and Müller (2004) since the sample only includes a subset of the SVO sentences in the corpus. I.e., the likelihood for the restricted order (OVS) to occur in a particular contextual condition cannot be estimated since a subset of the occurrences of the unrestricted option (SVO) are excluded from the sample. This type of hypothesis can be examined in the empirical study on dative alternation by Bresnan and Hay (2007), which reports the frequencies of two word order options (*give* NP NP; *give* NP PP) in all occurrences of the verb *give* in the 'Origins of New Zealand English' corpus: A non-given recipient is approximately four times more likely than a given recipient to be expressed in the prepositional dative.

3. Occurrence in context: Experimental evidence

This section discusses semi-naturalistic data, i.e., data that are induced by production experiments on information structure (for further experimental approaches see also Cowles, this volume). Similarly to the naturalistic data, data from experimental speech production allows for generalizations concerning the dependence of particular aspects of linguistic expressions on contextual properties.

There are several reasons why experimental data are used to complement or substitute the observations in naturalistic discourse. First, corpora allowing for large-scale quantitative studies are only available for certain well-studied languages. Second, many structural phenomena do not depend on a single factor but rather on the interplay of a large number of factors. Take for instance the studies on German word order: Structural asymmetries (subject > object), semantic asymmetries such as animacy (animate > inanimate), asymmetries relating to information structure such as definiteness (definite > indefinite), and pure formal asymmetries such as weight (short > long constituent) have an impact on the choice of word order in discourse (see empirical findings in Bader and Häussler 2010). I.e., even in a large corpus, the selection of minimal pairs in order to observe the exact effect of each factor in isolation results in a substantial reduction of data set. Furthermore, naturalistic data involve further sources of variation from random factors such as different speakers, different genres, different discourse situations, etc.[3] The methodological contribution of experimental studies is exactly this: The interaction of information structural factors with further relevant factors as well as the influence of random factors can be controlled in the experimental design.

3.1. Overview

An overwhelming number of studies on language production examine the preference for given information to precede new information. A straight-forward implementation of the givenness asymmetries is to elicit semi-spontaneous narratives by means of non-verbal stimuli (pictures or videos) that induce repeated mentioning of the (intended) given referent. Such a manipulation is reported in Skopeteas and Fanselow (2009).[4] The speaker is presented a series of two pictures and is instructed to describe the pictures one after the other. The first scene introduces the relevant context; the second scene induces the target utterance in which the effects of givenness may be observed. The contextual manipulation that induces utterances with a given agent and a new patient is exemplified in (10) with illustrative data produced by a native speaker of American English.

(10)   Contextual condition "given agent"
       Stimulus: {Pict. 1: A man. Pict. 2: The man is attacking a woman.}
       Speaker's reaction:
       There's a man walking. Now the man is attacking a woman.
       (see Skopeteas and Fanselow 2009: 324)

---

[3]   The diversity of sources of variation in the naturalistic data is not a fatal problem: statistical models based on logistic regression can be used in order to calculate the effect of the involved factors (see Bresnan et al. 2007, Bader and Häussler 2010).

[4]   The experimental procedure used in this study is part of QUIS (= Questionnaire on information structure) that is a collection of production experiments for the study of information structure developed within the research institute 632 *Information Structure* at the University of Potsdam and the Humboldt University Berlin (see documentation of the experiments in Skopeteas et al. 2006).

The contextual manipulation that induces utterances with a given patient and a new agent is illustrated in (11), again with data from American English. The effect of givenness may be observed in the choice of a linearization in which the patient constituent precedes the agent constituent. This is achieved by a passive clause in languages such as American English, Canadian French, Dutch, Yucatec Maya, and German. Speakers of other languages such as Georgian, Czech, Hungarian, Konkani (Indo-European), Prinmi (Tibeto-Burman), and Teribe (Chibchan) produce utterances with a non-canonical word order such that the patient precedes the agent constituent (see discussion of the data in Skopeteas and Fanselow 2009).

(11)   Contextual condition "given patient"
       Stimulus: {Pict. 1: A woman. Pict. 2: The man is attacking a woman.}
       Speaker's reaction:
       There's a woman who's walking. Now she's attacked by a man from behind. (see Skopeteas and Fanselow 2009: 324)

There are numerous experimental studies that manipulate givenness by means of stimuli inducing repeated mentionings of the given referent. Prentice (1967) was among the first to mention that in a picture description task entities introduced in an immediately preceding picture were more likely to appear early in the sentence. MacWhinney and Bates (1978) present an experimental study on English, Italian, and Hungarian based on the repeated mentioning of referents or actions and examine hypotheses relating to ellipsis, pronominalization, definiteness, and word order. Prat-Sala (1997) examines the interaction between animacy and information structure in the choice of word order in English, Spanish, Catalan, and Brazilian Portuguese and makes use of a contextual manipulation that reveals the impact of discourse saliency on the choice of linearization (see also Prat-Sala and Branigan 2000 on English and Spanish). Hörnig and Féry (2009) present a production study on spatial configurations manipulated through the presentation of toy animals and discuss the effects of givenness on role choice, word order, definiteness, and prosodic structure of locative expressions in German. Herbert Clark also conducted a number of production studies examining the effects of the repeated mentioning of the referents in discourse (see Clark and Brennan 1991, see Isaacs and Clark 1987 for a picture-based experiment, and Clark and Wilkes-Gibbs 1986 for an experiment on descriptions of tangram figures). These studies show that during the progress of the conversation, speakers establish the discourse referents in the common ground to the effect that the reference to these discourse entities is simplified proportionally to their salience, from complex descriptions to descriptions with a full NP, to descriptions with pronominal expressions and finally ellipsis.

Some production studies manipulate the focal attention of the speaker at the moment of the utterance. Tomlin (1995, 1997) elicited descriptions of a film presenting a series of scenes with two fish with the same shape and different colors. In the film, the two fish enter the screen from opposite directions and meet at the center of the screen, at which point one of them eats the other. In each scene, an arrow accompanies one of the two fish, and the test subject is instructed to keep his/her eyes on the character which the arrow is pointing at. The data produced in this study are exemplified in Examples (12)–(13) from Bahasa Indonesia. When the speaker keeps his eyes on the agent constituent, (s)he produces active sentences, as exemplified in (12).

(12)   Contextual condition "agent=primed"

Stimulus: {A pink fish pointed at by the arrow eats a white fish.}
Speaker's reaction:

ikan merah muda ber-temu   dengan ikan putih.
fish red   light INTR-meet with   fish white

Dan me-makan ikan putih.
and ACT-meet fish white

'The pink fish meets the white fish. And it eats the white fish.'
(see Tomlin 1995: 535)

When the speaker's attention is directed towards the patient constituent, (s)he produces passive sentences, as exemplified in (13). Similar results are obtained in English, Burmese, and Mandarin (see Tomlin 1995: 531–537).

(13)   Contextual condition "patient=primed"

Stimulus: {A white fish eats a pink fish pointed at by the arrow.}
Speaker's reaction:

ikan merah muda ber-temu   dengan ikan putih.
fish red   light INTR-meet with   fish white

Dan di-makan   oleh ikan putih.
and PASS-meet by   fish white

'The pink fish meets the white fish. And it is eaten by the white fish.'
(see Tomlin 1995: 535)

Experiments concerning the attention of the speaker are reported in several studies (see Myachykov 2005: 353–358 for an overview). Forrest (1997) observed similar effects by manipulating the speaker's attention to particular parts of the presented scene. Furthermore, a speaker's attention can be manipulated through asymmetries in the salience of the presented entities (see Johnson-Laird 1968). Manipulations of a speaker's attention or asymmetries in the salience of the presented entities are not information structural concepts but rather perceptual properties of the stimulus. The question is how these manipulations relate to information structure. The related concept is the concept of aboutness: Speakers tend to produce expressions about the entity that is at the center of their attention at the critical time of producing the utterance at issue. The expectation that the center of attention is likely to be realized as an aboutness topic is in line with the observation in these studies that the referent at issue tends to appear early in the utterance.

A further experimental technique that is used for the study of information structure is the elicitation of semi-spontaneous answers to questions. Christianson and Ferreira (2005) present an empirical study on the voice and order alternation in Odawa (a dialect of Ojibwa, Algonquian). Verb forms in this language show a tripartite alternation between active/direct, inverse, and passive voice. In the production study, the speaker was presented a picture and was instructed to answer a question relative to it. The types of questions used in this study are exemplified in (14). The semi-spontaneously elicited answers show that the frequency of occurrence of inverse/passive clauses increases depending on the question type: agent question < general question < patient question (see results and discussion in Christianson and Ferreira 2005: 121–132).

(14) Stimulus: {a boy is pinching a girl}

    a. General question: "What is happening here?"
    b. Agent question: "What is the boy doing?"
    c. Patient question: "What is happening to the girl?"

Answers to questions have been used for a wide range of information structural concepts: see Arnold et al. (2000), who investigate the interaction of givenness with constituent weight in the choice between a theme-goal and a goal-theme linearization in postverbal orders in English; see Skopeteas and Fanselow (2010) on the elicitation of contrastive/non-contrastive types of narrow focus, and Skopeteas and Féry (2007) on the elicitation of contrastive topicalization through multiple constituent questions.

Apart from the experimental paradigms illustrated in this section, several further types of controlled speech production have been used in the investigation of information structure, such as recall techniques (see, e.g., Bock 1977, Bock and Irwin 1980 on givenness effects in several English constructions, Ferreira and Yoshita 2003 on givenness effects in Japanese scrambling), forced-choice experiments (see Vion and Colas 1995 on French clefts), and sentence completion tasks (see, e.g., Kaiser 2006 on the effects of focus and clefting on discourse prominence, Weskott et al. 2006 on the influence of discourse status on the choice between OVS and SVO order in German, Onea and Heusinger 2009 on the contextual conditions that license clitic pronouns in Romanian; Quesada and Skopeteas 2010 on incremental properties of the choice of voice in Teribe).

3.2. Empirical statements

A frequently stated problem of hypothesis-driven investigations is that they draw generalizations out of a small number of data points. Experimental studies have to obey several technical limitations relating to the proportion of targets and fillers, the number of repeated observations per participant, and the reasonable size of an experimental session. These limitations have the effect that the information resulting from experimental findings is restricted to the differences between a few categories. However, linguistic theories often require a large amount of empirical data especially when dealing with multifactorial problems, such as the occurrence of particular properties of linguistic expressions in discourse (see Fanselow 2009: 134–135).

The selection of hypotheses out of a set of potentially relevant factors necessarily implies an inductive step. These empirical studies face a classical problem of the inductive relation between hypotheses and data, which is illustrated by Nelson Goodman's (1954) riddle. Assume that we examine the truth of the statement "all emeralds are green" and after a (sufficient) number of verifications we conclude that this statement is confirmed. Assume now a predicate 'grue' that applies to the observed 'green' entities and also to not yet observed 'blue' entities. The problem is exactly that the statement "all emeralds are grue" is also confirmed by the range of data that we considered so far, i.e., that the empirical data is underspecified for the hypotheses it potentially verifies. One might argue that 'grue' is an unnatural concept, but the problem of the naturalness of the concepts is independent from the problem of induction (see discussion in Sloman and

Lagnado 2005: 97). The following example illustrates how this inductive problem applies on "entrenched" concepts (in Goodman's terms), i.e., concepts that have a past history of use in scientific research.

We observed in Section 3.1 that in contexts in which the agent constituent is part of the given information English speakers tend to produce utterances with agent subjects as in (10), while in contexts in which the patient constituent is part of the given information the same speakers tend to produce utterances with patient subjects. On the basis of this observation, we may conclude that givenness has an impact on hierarchical syntax, such that given referents are encoded in higher syntactic roles (as Bock and Warren 1985 argue for conceptually accessible referents). The data presented so far can be accounted for by the hypothesis "Given information is more likely to be realized in a higher syntactic constituent". However, English is a subject-initial language, and the same range of data can be also accounted for by the hypothesis "Given information is more likely to be realized early in the utterance" (see Clark and Haviland 1977). Both hypotheses are verified through the data, which implies that the empirical data is underspecified for these theoretical options.

In order to discriminate between these two theoretical possibilities we need to consider the critical conditions that test conflicting predictions of the alternative hypotheses. Hence, Bock and Warren (1985) report that the accessible-first principle does not influence the order of coordinated conjuncts, which supports the view that the observed phenomenon relates to hierarchical structure. However, several studies on the influence of discourse factors on word order show that the choice of passive is cross-linguistically in complementary distribution with word order operations. Given-first effects affect syntactic relations only in constructions/languages in which two alternative syntactic realizations of the same propositional content such as passive/active are available. Otherwise, the impact of givenness is observed in the choice of word order, as is observed in languages with flexible word order (see Prat-Sala 1997, Tomlin 1997, Skopeteas and Fanselow 2009). The cross-linguistic complementarity between passive and marked word order indicates that passivization is a member of a set of syntactic operations that create a linearization in which the given information occurs early in the utterance.

The conclusion is that the inductive problem is a necessary concomitant of hypothesis-driven investigations. The only way to overcome this shortcoming is to enlarge the data base, i.e., to carry out further empirical studies that disentangle the possible effects of further relevant theoretical concepts.

4. Speakers' intuitions of contextual felicity

We have seen in Section 2.2 that an inherent limitation of observational data is that they cannot empirically justify universal hypotheses. The observation that a linguistic expression does not occur under certain contextual conditions in our data set does not allow us to infer that this generalization holds for the totality of occurrences of this linguistic expression in the universe of discourse.

The study of language is particular in that it involves another type of evidence that allows us to justify universal statements. This is the role of intuition data. Linguistic intuition involves a number of different things: Knowledge of grammatically correct forms that are based on more or less general productive rules, but also knowledge of how forms are used in particular contexts. To the extent that speaker's intuition is reliable, a negative judgment confirms the truth of a universal negative hypothesis. The background assumption is that the psychological phenomenon of judging a context-expression pair as infelicitous is a generalization over the infinite number of potential context-expression pairs in discourse. Hence, speakers' intuition is a very particular type of meta-linguistic evidence that allows for proving deterministic hypotheses in overcoming the problem of induction in the observational data.

4.1. Overview

The basic phenomenon is the intuition that different grammatically well-formed structures are either felicitous or not felicitous in particular contexts. The concept of 'contextual felicity' refers to the intuition of the speaker whether the target utterance fits to the expectations created through the context. This intuition reflects the extent to which the target utterance presupposes the propositional content that is introduced through the context and presents an assertion that falls within the range of possible contributions to the discourse that are expected in the context.[5] For instance, Lambrecht (2001) observes that the well-formed target utterances in (15) differ with respect to their felicity in the presented context. He claims that the second target is not felicitous because it evokes a presupposition of exhaustivity that is not licensed by the context.

---

5   See Matthewson (2004) on empirical issues on the elicitation of contextual felicity and Rooth (1992: 84–85) and Krifka (2002, 2007) on the felicity of question-answer pairs.

(15) Context: *District attorney to potential juror in the trial of a black man:*
                Do you think you might have any bias that would prevent you
                from reaching a finding of not guilty, given that the defen-
                dant is a black man?

      Target 1: *Why no. I have my NEIGHBOR (who's black).*
      Target 2: *Why no. #It's my NEIGHBOR who's black.*
                 (Lambrecht 2001: 505–506)

Kiss (1998) presents a test of exhaustive identification (with reference to Donka Farkas) that is based on the felicity of an utterance that follows the target utterance, see (16)–(17). The basic assumption is that the felicity of the latter utterance depends on whether it is among the logical consequences of the former one. In cases in which the target utterance involves an exhaustive interpretation of the focused constituent, as is the case with the preverbal focus in Hungarian in (16), the negation of a statement rejecting the presupposition of exhaustivity is felicitous.

(16) Target 1: *Mari <u>egy kalapot</u> nézett ki   magának.*
                 Mary a   hat.ACC picked out herself.DAT
                 'It was a hat that Mary picked for herself.'

      Context: *Nem, egy kabátot is   ki   nézett.*
                 no   a   coat   too out picked
                 'No, she picked a coat, too.'
                 (É. Kiss 1998: 251)

If the target utterance does not evoke an exhaustive interpretation, as is the case with the postverbal focus in Hungarian in (17), the negation of a statement that rejects the exhaustive interpretation is not felicitous.

(17) Target 1: *Mari ki nézett magának   EGY KALAPOT.*
                 Mary out picked herself.DAT a   hat.ACC
                 'It was a hat that Mary picked for herself.'

      Context: *#Nem, egy kabátot is   ki   nézett.*
                 no   a   coat   too out picked
                 'No, she picked a coat, too.'
                 (É. Kiss 1998: 251)

Judgments of contextual felicity are certainly a very widely used type of evidence in the investigation of information structure (see also Krifka 2010:

§2.8). In the last years, a paradigm of experimental studies evolved that is based on repeated observations of the intuition of contextual felicity in speakers' samples. Native speakers are presented pairs of context and target utterances and are instructed to judge whether the target utterance fits the context. Judgments can be either categorical (the target utterance fits or does not fit the context) or scalar, either using a numerical scale, e.g., from '1 = utterance does not fit the context at all' to '7 = utterance fits the context very well' or using magnitude estimation (Bard et al. 1996), in which case the participant is asked to assign a numerical value to a stimulus that serves as a reference point and then to express his/her intuition of acceptability in numerical values relative to that reference point (see Weskott and Fanselow 2009 for a discussion of the alternatives in measuring acceptability intuitions).

Keller and Alexopoulou (2001) report on two experimental studies on the interaction of word order, clitic doubling, and intonation in Greek. Combinations of these factors were tested in several contextual conditions, i.e., absence of context, all-focus context, subject-focus context, object-focus context, and verb-focus context. The intended contextual conditions were established by means of questions, as exemplified in (18)–(19) for object questions. The background assumption is that in the context of an object question only those answers will be judged as felicitous that involve operations licensed by object focus. The examples (18)–(19) illustrate the effects of clitic doubling on the intuition of contextual felicity. Literature on Greek shows that clitic doubling, i.e., the resumption of a case complement of the verb by a coreferential pronoun, is felicitous when the complement is part of the given information (see Alexopoulou 1999: 46 and references therein). Both examples illustrate an SVO' answer with accent (') on the object in the context of an object question. Example (18) does not involve clitic doubling, hence it is expected to be felicitous in this context.

(18) Context: *ti   θa   δiavási   o   tásos?*
            what FUT read.3SG DEF.NOM Tasos.NOM
            'What will Tasos read?'

      Target: o   tásos   θa   δiavási   *tin   EFIMERIDA.*
            DEF.NOM Tasos.NOM FUT read.3SG DEF.ACC newspaper.ACC
            'Tasos will read the newspaper.'
            (Keller and Alexopoulou 2001)

Example (19) illustrates a target utterance with clitic doubling presented in the same context, i.e., as answer to an object focus question. The effect of clitic doubling on the intuition of contextual felicity is reflected in the average judgments reported in Keller and Alexopoulou (2001): SVO′ answers (without clitic doubling) obtained the value 0.54 (S.E. = 0.05) in the normalized log-transformed data, while SclVO′ answers (with clitic doubling) obtained the value 0.12 (S.E. = 0.08).

(19) Context: *ti θa διavási o tásos?*

     Target: *o*   *tásos*   *θa* *tin*   *διavási*
               DEF.NOM Tasos.NOM FUT 3SG.ACC read.3SG
               tin   *EFIMERIDA.*
               DEF.ACC newspaper.ACC
               'Tasos will read the newspaper.'
               (Keller and Alexopoulou 2001)

Quantitative studies on contextual felicity have been carried out on several issues relating to the interaction of particular properties of the utterance with the context. For instance, Birch and Clifton (1995) present experimental judgments on the appropriateness of several prosodic patterns in the context of different question types in English; Arnold (1998) examines the effects of English clefts on establishing discourse topics by observing the accept-ability of pronominal and lexical mentioning of referents; Keller (2000) reports the findings of a rating experiment on the interaction of word order and pronominalization in several contexts in German subordinate clauses; Skopeteas, Féry and Asatiani (2009) study the influence of the context on the felicity of several word orders, prosodic patterns and morphological properties (case inversion) in Georgian.

4.2. Empirical statements

A crucial issue with respect to the empirical findings of quantitative studies is the observation that contextual felicity involves gradience. For instance, we have seen in Section 4.1 that SVO′ answers are judged to be more felici-tous than SclVO′ answers in the context of object questions in Greek. The mean values reported in 4.1 are obtained when accentual prominence is realized on the constituent in question. When the prosodic structure is non-congruent with the context, e.g., when accentual prominence is realized on the subject, then a cumulative negative effect is observed in the values that are assigned by the native speakers (average judgments for S′VO obtained the value 0.2 and judgments for S′clVO obtained the value 0.08, see Keller and Alexopoulou 2001). These findings indicate that the empirical phenomenon of contextual felicity is not categorical (±felicitous) but scalar. The degree of felicity observed in these results may be accounted for by the fact that they reflect the influence of two factors (clitic doubling and accentuation) that have a cumulative effect on the intuition of felicity (see also Sorace and Keller 2003).

The observation that the intuition of felicity is a scalar psychological phenomenon does not imply that the licensing of particular operations for the expression of particular information structural concepts is a gradient notion. Assuming that random sources of variation are outbalanced in the experimental design (e.g., different speaker, different lexicalizations of a construction, etc. see Schütze 1996), the observed gradience in speakers' intuitions may result from the fact that speakers perceive multiple violations of the licensing conditions as reducing the likelihood that the presented stimulus will occur in the context at issue (see Schütze 1996: §3.3.1, Vogel 2005, Weskott and Fanselow 2009 for further discussion concerning the difference between acceptability and grammaticality). Moreover, further sources of variation contribute to the gradience of experimental results. For instance, people differ in their willingness to invent larger contexts than the one actually given, which may boost the acceptance of a linguistic form.

Several recent studies have pointed out that the gradience obtained through speakers' intuition is not directly mapped on to the observational data that we can obtain from corpora (see Featherston 2005, Kempen and Harbush 2005, 2006). The text counts do not show a frequency distribution that corresponds closely to the felicity degree observable in scalar judgments. Text counts rather lead to categorical results, in which the optimal construction is frequently attested and the further alternatives either display very few tokens or are not attested at all. This discrepancy is expected, since in speech production speakers tend to select the optimal candidate, such that suboptimal alternatives have very few chances to occur (see Featherston 2005).

5. Conclusions

This article presented the main paradigms of empirical studies that are used for the investigation of information structure. The particular issue in the methods used for this linguistic domain is that the main evidence for the assumption of information structural concepts comes from the context. Section 2 presented several types of empirical studies that are based on the observation of naturalistic data. Section 3 discussed data from language production experiments. Section 4 discussed evidence from the intuition of contextual felicity – either based on singular observations or on experimental studies.

The two former paradigms of empirical methods, corpus studies and production experiments, constitute alternative approaches to the same phenomenon, namely the speaker's choice of particular properties of linguistic expressions depending on the context. Corpus studies provide evidence from naturalistic data, hence allowing for observation of the context-expression dependencies in real communication. Experimental studies in speech production have the advantage that they allow for controlling the sources of variation and comparing the exact effect of discourse factors that may influence the form of the utterance.

Production data differ from data obtained through speakers' judgments. In this case, we are not dealing with alternative methodological approaches but with different phenomena. Rating experiments deal with the intuition of contextual felicity which is a phenomenon independent of corpus frequencies (see Section 4.2). Since utterances are complex configurations that may involve choices at several layers (e.g., prosodic structure, syntax, morphological phenomena, etc.), contextual felicity comes up as a gradient phenomenon reflecting the felicity of several properties of a single expression. The gradience observed in intuition data cannot be directly mapped on the frequency distributions that result from the corpus data, since the latter show a predominance of the most felicitous option in each context.

Intuition data are complementary to production data in two respects. First, they allow us to justify universal negative hypotheses (or to reject existential positive hypotheses), which is not possible through production data due to the inherent limitations of the problem of induction. Second, intuition data reveal the gradience of the interacting factors that cannot always be observed in the production data, since speakers' production is necessarily based on the choice of the single optimal linguistic expression for a given propositional content.

References

Alexopoulou, Theodora
    1999   The syntax of discourse-functions in Greek. A non-configurational approach. Ph.D. dissertation, University of Edinburgh.
Arnold, Jennifer E.
    1998   Reference form and discourse patterns. Ph.D. dissertation, Stanford University.

Arnold, Jennifer, Thomas Wasow, Anthony Losongco and Ryan Ginstrom
  2000   Heaviness vs. newness: The effects of structural complexity and dis-
            course status on constituent ordering. *Language* 76: 28–55.
Bader, Markus and Jana Häussler
  2010   Word Order in German: A corpus study. *Lingua* 120: 717–762.
Bard, Ellen Gurman, Dan Robertson and Antonella Sorace
  1996   Magnitude estimation of linguistic acceptability. *Language* 72:
            32–68.
Beaver, David
  2004   The optimization of discourse anaphora. *Linguistics and Philosophy*
            27: 1–53.
Birch, Stacy and Charles Clifton Jr.
  1995   Focus, accent, and argument structure: Effects on language compre-
            hension. *Language and Speech* 38: 365–391.
Birner, Betty J.
  1994   Information status and word order: An analysis of English inversion.
            Language 70: 233–259.
Bock, J. Kathryn
  1977   The effect of a pragmatic presupposition on syntactic structure in
            question answering. *Journal of Verbal Learning and Verbal Behavior*
            16: 723–734.
Bock, J. Kathryn and David E. Irwin
  1980   Syntactic effects of information availability in sentence production.
            Journal of Verbal Learning and Verbal Behavior 19: 467–484.
Bock, J. Kathryn and Richard K. Warren
  1985   Conceptual accessibility and syntactic structure in sentence formu-
            lation. *Cognition* 21: 47–67.
Bresnan, Joan, Anna Cueni, Tatiana Nikitina and R. Harald Baayen
  2007   Predicting the dative alternation. In *Cognitive Foundations of Inter-
            pretation*, Gerlof Bouma, Irene Kraemer and Joost Zwarts (eds.),
            69–94. Amsterdam: Royal Netherlands Academy of Science.
Bresnan, Joan and Jennifer Hay
  2007   Gradient grammar: An effect of animacy on the syntax of *give* in
            New Zealand and American English. *Lingua* 118: 245–259.
Brunetti, Lisa
  2009a   Discourse functions of fronted foci in Italian and Spanish. In *Focus
            and Background in Romance Languages*, Andreas Dufter and Daniel
            Jacob (eds.), 43–82. Amsterdam: Benjamins.
Brunetti, Lisa
  2009b   On the semantic and contextual factors that determine topic selection
            in Italian and Spanish. *The Linguistic Review* 26: 261–289.
Christianson, Keil and Fernanda Ferreira
  2005   Conceptual accessibility and sentence production in a free word
            order language (Odawa). *Cognition* 98: 105–135.

Clark, Herbert
    1977   Bridging. In *Thinking: Readings in Cognitive Science*, Philip N.
                Johnson-Laird and Peter C. Wason (eds.), 411–420. London: Cam-
                bridge University Press.
Clark, Herbert H. and Susan E. Brennan
    1991   Grounding in communication. In *Perspectives on Socially Shared
                Cognition*, Lauren B. Resnick, John M. Levine and Stephanie D. Teasley
                (eds.), 127–149. Washington: American Psychological Association.
Clark, Herbert H. and Susan Haviland
    1977   Comprehension and the given-new contrast. In *Discourse Production
                and Comprehension*, Roy O. Freedle (ed.), 1–40. Hillsdale, New Jersey:
                Lawrence Erlbaum Associates.
Clark, Herbert H. and Deanna Wilkes-Gibbs
    1986   Referring as a collaborative process. *Cognition* 22: 1–39.
Cooreman, Ann
    1987   *Transitivity and Discourse Continuity in Chamorro Narratives.* Berlin/
                New York: Mouton de Gruyter.
Davison, Alice
    1984   Syntactic markedness and the definition of sentence topic. *Language*
                60: 797–846.
Dretske, Fred
    1972   Contrastive statements. *The Philosophical Review* 81: 411–437.
Dryer, Matthew S.
    1994   The discourse function of Kutenai inverse. In *Voice and Inversion*,
                Talmy Givón (ed.), 65–99. Amsterdam/Philadelphia: Benjamins.
É. Kiss, Katalin
    1998   Identificational vs. information focus. *Language* 74: 245–273.
Fanselow, Gisbert
    2009   Die (generative) Syntax in den Zeiten der Empiriediskussion. *Zeit-
                schrift für Sprachwissenschaft* 28: 133–139.
Featherston, Sam
    2005   The decathlon model: Design features for an empirical syntax. In
                *Linguistic Evidence: Empirical, Theoretical, and Computational Per-
                spectives*, Stephan Kepser and Marga Reis (eds.), 187–208. Berlin/
                New York: Mouton de Gruyter.
Featherston, Sam
    2009   Relax, lean back, and be a linguist. *Zeitschrift für Sprachwissen-
                schaft* 28: 127–132.
Ferreira, Victor S. and Hiromi Yoshita
    2003   Given-new ordering effects on the production of scrambled sen-
                tences in Japanese. *Journal of Psycholinguistic Research* 32(6):
                669–692.
Feyerabend, Paul
    1983   *Wider den Methodenzwang.* Frankfurt: Suhrkamp.

Forrest, Linda B.
   1997   Discourse goals and attentional processes in sentence production: The dynamic construal of events. In *Conceptual Structure, Discourse and Language*, Adele E. Goldberg (ed.), 149–162. Stanford, California: Center for the Study of Language and Information Publications.

Givón, Talmy (ed.)
   1994   *Voice and Inversion*. Amsterdam / Philadelphia: Benjamins.

Goodman, Nelson
   1954   *Fact, Fiction and Forecast*. London: Athlone Press.

Grosz, Barbara J. and Candace L. Sidner
   1986   Attentions, intentions, and the structure of discourse. *Computational Linguistics* 12: 175–204.

Gundel, Jeanette K.
   1974   The role of topic and comment in linguistic theory. Ph.D. dissertation, University of Texas.

Gundel, Jeanette K., Nancy Hedberg and Ron Zacharski
   2005   Pronouns without explicit referents: How do we know when a pronoun is referential? In *Anaphora Processing: Linguistic, Cognitive, and Computational Modelling*, Antonio Branco, Tony McEnery and Ruslan Mitkov (eds.), 351–364. Amsterdam: Benjamins.

Haspelmath, Martin
   2009   Welche Fragen können wir mit herkömmlichen Daten beantworten? *Zeitschrift für Sprachwissenschaft* 28: 157–162.

Herring, Susan C.
   1994   Afterthoughts, antitopics, and emphasis: The syntacticization of post-verbal position in Tamil. In *Theoretical Perspectives on Word Order in Asian Languages*, Miriam Butt, Tracy Holloway King and Gillian Ramchand (eds.), 119–152. Stanford: Center for the Study of Language and Information Publications.

Herring, Susan C. and John C. Paolillo
   1995   Focus position in SOV languages. In *Word Order in Discourse*, Pamela Downing and Michael Noonan (eds.), 163–198. Amsterdam: Benjamins.

Hörnig, Robin and Caroline Féry
   2009   Linguistic markers of discourse status in describing altered spatial layouts. Ms., University of Potsdam.

Horvath, Julia
   1986   *FOCUS in the Theory of Grammar and the Syntax of Hungarian*. Dordrecht: Foris.

Isaacs, Ellen A. and Herbert H. Clark
   1987   References in conversation between experts and novices. *Journal of Experimental Psychology* 116: 26–37.

Johnson-Laird, Philip N.
1968   The choice of the passive voice in a communicative task. *British Journal of Psychology* 59: 7–15.

Kaiser, Elsi
2006   Effects of topic and focus on salience. In *Proceedings of Sinn und Bedeutung* 10 (ZAS Working Papers in Linguistics vol. 44), Christian Ebert and Cornelia Endriss (eds.), 139–154. Berlin.

Keller, Frank
2000   Gradience in grammar: Experimental and computational aspects of degrees of grammaticality. Ph.D. dissertation, University of Edinburgh.

Keller, Frank and Theodora Alexopoulou
2001   Phonology competes with syntax: Experimental evidence for the interaction of word order and accent placement in the realization of information structure. *Cognition* 79 (3): 301–371.

Kempen, Gerard and Karin Harbusch
2005   The relationship between grammaticality ratings and corpus frequencies: A case study into word-order variability in the midfield of German clauses. In *Linguistic Evidence: Empirical, Theoretical, and Computational Perspectives*, Stephan Kepser and Marga Reis (eds.), 329–349. Berlin/New York: Mouton de Gruyter.

Kempen, Gerard and Karin Harbusch
2006   Comparing linguistic judgments and corpus frequencies as windows on grammatical competence: A study of argument linearization in German clauses. Ms., Nijmegen and Koblenz.

Krifka, Manfred
2002   For a structured meaning account of questions and answers. In *Audiatur Vox Sapientiae: A Festschrift for Arnim von Stechow*, Caroline Féry and Wolfgang Sternefeld (eds.), 287–319. Berlin: Akademie.

Krifka, Manfred
2007   The semantics of questions and the focusation of answers. In *Topic and Focus*, Chungmin Lee, Matthew Gordon and Daniel Büring (eds.), 139–150. Dordrecht: Kluwer.

Krifka, Manfred
2010   Varieties of semantic evidence. In *Handbook of Semantics*, Claudia Maienborn, Paul Portner and Klaus von Heusinger (eds.). Berlin/New York: Mouton de Gruyter.

Kuhn, Thomas S.
1970   Logic of discovery or psychology of research? In *Criticism and the Growth of Knowledge*, Imre Lakatos and Alan Musgrave (eds.), 1–23. Cambridge: Cambridge University Press.

Lambrecht, Knud
2001   A framework for the analysis of cleft constructions. *Linguistics* 39: 413–516.

MacWhinney, Brian and Elizabeth Bates
1978   Sentential devices for conveying givenness and newness: A cross-cultural developmental study. *Journal of Verbal Learning and Verbal Behavior* 17: 539–558.

Mathesius, Vilém
1975   *A Functional Analysis of Present Day English on a General Linguistic Basis* (ed. by J. Vachek). The Hague/Paris: Mouton.

Matić, Dejan
2003   Topics, presuppositions, and theticity: An empirical study on verb-subject clauses in Albanian, Greek, and Serbo-Croatian. Ph.D. dissertation, University of Cologne.

Matthewson, Lisa
2004   On the methodology of semantic fieldwork. *International Journal of American Linguistics* 70: 369–415.

Myachykov, Andriy, Russel S. Tomlin and Michael I. Posner
2005   Attention and empirical studies of grammar. *The Linguistic Review* 22: 347–364.

Newton-Smith, William H.
2000   Underdetermination of theory by data. In *A Companion to the Philosophy of Science*, William H. Newton-Smith (ed.), 532–536. Oxford: Blackwell.

Newmeyer, Frederick J.
2003   Grammar is grammar and usage is usage. *Language* 79: 682–707.

Onea, Edgar and Klaus von Heusinger
2009   Grammatical and contextual restrictions on focal alternatives. In *Focus and Background in Romance Languages*, Daniel Jacob and Andreas Dufter (eds.), 281–308. Amsterdam: Benjamins.

Paul, Hermann
1880   *Prinzipien der Sprachgeschichte*. Tübingen: Niemeyer.

Poesio, Massimo, Rosemary Stevenson, Barbara Di Eugenio and Janet Hitzeman
2004   Centering: A parametric theory and its instantiations. *Computational Linguistics* 30: 309–363.

Popper, Karl
1934   *Logik der Forschung*. Tübingen: Siebeck (11th ed. 2005).

Prat-Sala, Mercè
1997   The production of different word orders: A psycholinguistic and developmental approach. Ph.D. dissertation, University of Edinburgh.

Prat-Sala, Mercé and Holy P. Branigan
2000   Discourse constraints on syntactic processing in language production: A cross-linguistic study in English and Spanish. *Journal of Memory and Language* 42: 168–182.

Prentice, John L.
1967   Effects of cueing actor vs. cueing object on word order in sentence production. *Psychonomic Science* 8: 163–164.

Prince, Ellen
1981   Toward a taxonomy of given-new information. In *Radical pragmatics*,
         Peter Cole (ed.), 223–256. New York: Academic Press.
Quesada, Diego and Stavros Skopeteas
2010   The discourse functions of inversion: an experimental study on
         Teribe (Chibchan). *Journal of Pragmatics* 42: 2579–2600.
Roland, Katy
1994   The pragmatics of Modern Greek voice. In: Talmy Givón (ed.), *Voice
         and Inversion,* 233–260. Amsterdam / Philadelphia: Benjamins.
Rooth, Mats
1992   A theory of focus interpretation. *Natural Language Semantics* 1:
         75–116.
Sampson, Geoffrey R.
2007   Grammar without grammaticality. *Corpus Linguistics and linguistic
         Theory* 3: 1–32.
Schütze, Carson T.
1996   *The Empirical Base of Linguistics: Grammaticality Judgments and
         Linguistic Methodology.* Chicago: University of Chicago Press.
Skopeteas, Stavros and Gisbert Fanselow
2009   Effects of givenness and constraints on free word order. In *Informa-
         tion Structure from Different Perspectives*, Malte Zimmerman and
         Caroline Féry (eds.), 307–331. Oxford: Oxford University Press.
Skopeteas, Stavros and Gisbert Fanselow
2010   Focus types and argument asymmetries: A cross-linguistic study in
         language production. In *Comparative and Contrastive Studies of
         Information Structure*, Carsten Breul and Edward Göbbel (eds.),
         169–198. Amsterdam / Philadelphia: Benjamins.
Skopeteas, Stavros and Caroline Féry
2007   Contrastive topics in pairing answers: A cross-linguistic production
         study. In *Linguistic Evidence 2006*, Sam Featherston and Wolfgang
         Sternefeld (eds.), 327–347. Berlin / New York: Mouton de Gruyter.
Skopeteas, Stavros, Caroline Féry and Rusudan Asatiani
2009   Word order and intonation in Georgian. *Lingua* 119: 102–127.
Skopeteas, Stavros, Ines Fiedler, Sam Hellmuth, Anne Schwarz, Ruben Stoel,
Gisbert Fanselow, Caroline Féry and Manfred Krifka
2006   *Questionnaire on Information Structure.* (Interdisciplinary Studies on
         Information Structure, vol. 4). Universitätsverlag Potsdam, Germany.
Sloman, Steven A. and David A. Lagnado
2005   The problem of induction. In *Cambridge Handbook of Thinking
         and Reasoning*, Keith Holyoak and Robert Morrison (eds.), 95–116.
         Cambridge: Cambridge University Press.
Sorace, Antonella and Frank Keller
2005   Gradience in linguistic data. *Lingua* 115: 1497–1524.

Speyer, Augustin
    2007   Die Bedeutung der Centering Theory für Fragen der Vorfeldbesetzung
                im Deutschen. *Zeitschrift für Sprachwissenschaft* 26: 83–115.
Szabolcsi, Anna
    1981   Compositionality in focus. *Folia Linguistica* 15: 141–163.
Tomlin, Russell S.
    1995   Focal attention, voice and word order: An experimental, cross-lin-
                guistic study. In *Word Order in Discourse*, Pamela A. Downing and
                Michael Noonan (eds.), 517–554. Amsterdam: Benjamins.
Tomlin, Russell S.
    1997   Mapping conceptual representations into linguistic representations:
                The role of attention in grammar. In *Language and Conceptuali-
                zation*, Jan Nuyts and Eric Pederson (eds.), 162–189. Cambridge:
                Cambridge University Press.
Vion, Monique and Annie Colas
    1995   Contrastive marking in French dialogue: Why and how. *Journal of
                Psycholinguistic Research* 24: 313–331.
Vogel, Ralf
    2005   Degraded acceptability and markedness in syntax, and the stochastic
                interpretation of optimality theory. In *Gradience in Grammar*, Gisbert
                Fanselow, Caroline Féry, Matthias Schlesewsky and Ralf Vogel (eds.),
                246–269. Oxford: Oxford University Press.
Walker, Marilyn A., Aravind K. Joshi and Ellen F. Prince (eds.)
    1998   *Centering Theory in Discourse*. Oxford: Clarendon Press.
Ward, Gregory L. and Ellen F. Prince
    1991   On the topicalization of indefinite NPs. *Journal of Pragmatics* 16:
                167–177.
Weber, Andrea and Karin Müller
    2004   Word order variation in German main clauses: A corpus analysis.
                *Proceedings of the 20th International conference on Computational
                Linguistics*. Geneva, Italy, 71–77.
Wedgwood, Daniel, Gergely Pethő and Ronnie Cann
    2003   Hungarian 'focus position' and English *it*-clefts: the semantic under-
                specification of 'focus' readings. Ms., University of Edinburgh.
Weskott, Thomas and Gisbert Fanselow
    2009   Scaling issues in the measurement of linguistic acceptability. In *The
                Fruits of Empirical Linguistics, Volume 1: Process*, Sam Featherston
                and Susanne Winkler (eds.), 229–245. Berlin/New York: Mouton de
                Gruyter.
Weskott, Thomas, Robin Hörnig, Elsi Kaiser, Caroline Féry, Sabine Kern, Gisbert
Fanselow and Reinhold Kliegl
    2006   Information Structure and the Anticipation of Discourse Referents.
                Ms., University of Potsdam.

The prosodic investigation of information structure

Aoju Chen

1. Introduction

Many languages use prosody in addition to morpho-syntactic devices to encode information structural categories, such as topic, focus, and information states (e.g., new, given, accessible).[1] How exactly these categories are prosodically encoded has been a research issue in the field of prosody and pragmatics for decades. The following questions have been extensively addressed in a wide range of languages:

(1) How is the focused constituent realized relative to the pre- and post-focus sequence in an utterance?
(2) How is focus realized in differently sized constituents, i.e., narrow focus, such as a one word focus, compared to broad focus, such as a VP-focus or a whole sentence focus?
(3) How are different types of focus distinguished (e.g., non-contrastive focus vs. contrastive focus)?
(4) How is topic, either contrastive or non-contrastive, realized? Is topic realized differently from focus?
(5) What are the prosodic correlates of different information states of a referent?

In this chapter, I will consider the prosodic cues that have been examined in past work in order to address the above-mentioned questions using either a phonetic approach (Section 2) and or a phonological approach (Section 3). More specifically, I will illustrate how various prosodic cues are employed

---

[1] The term 'prosody' is often used synonymously with intonation in the literature. The traditional definition of prosody is however related to poetic metrics and alike and tends to focus more on the organization of sounds into larger constitutes or domains; intonation is sometimes narrowly defined as pitch alone or pitch, duration and intensity. For this reason, many authors prefer the term prosody when they are also concerned with features such as the rhythm and phrasing of a sentence. In this chapter, the term 'prosody' refers to intonation (by its narrow definition) and phrasing.

to mark information structural categories in light of the findings published on different languages, and discuss the methodological issues crucial to each approach. Furthermore, I will describe step by step how to use Praat (Boersma and Weenink 2010), a freeware program for speech analysis, to conduct phonetic and phonological analysis (Section 4). Finally, I will briefly consider the limitations in research on prosodic marking of information structure.

2. A phonetic approach

2.1. Relevant prosodic parameters

In a phonetic approach, researchers aim to establish the phonetic or acoustic correlates of information structural categories by mainly examining variations in three prosodic parameters: fundamental frequency (f_0), measured in Hertz (Hz), referring to the number of the complete cycles in the complex wave of a sound per second; duration, measured in seconds or milliseconds (s or ms); and to a lesser extent, intensity (or amplitude), measured in decibels (dB). These properties are also known as pitch, quantity, and loudness respectively. The difference between these two sets of terms is that the latter are the perceptual terms and the former are the physical forms of the latter. In the literature the two sets of terms are often used interchangeably. I will use the terms pitch, duration, and intensity in the following sections, as these terms appear to be more well-known than their counterparts.

Variations in pitch are commonly examined in the constituent of interest (hereafter referred to as the target constituent) along the following parameters: pitch maximum (or peak height), pitch minimum before and/or after pitch maximum, pitch range (the difference between pitch maximum and pitch minimum), also known as pitch span or pitch excursion, and mean pitch, also known as pitch level or pitch register (Cruttenden 1997, Ladd 1996), peak alignment (the timing of pitch maximum relative to a pre-determined segmental boundary, e.g., the end of the stressed vowel), and pitch elbow (the timing of pitch minimum relative to a pre-determined segmental boundary, e.g., the end of the word). For the sake of comparison, pitch maximum, pitch minimum, and pitch range are often obtained for the pre-focus and post-focus constituents as well. With respect to variations in duration, analyses can be performed over segments of different sizes, including word, syllable (both stressed and unstressed), stressed vowel, and less commonly, the onset and coda of the stressed syllable (e.g., Hanssen,

Peters and Gussenhoven 2008). In contrast to pitch and duration, intensity has only been examined in a small number of studies. This may be related to the fact that a reliable measurement of intensity is hard to obtain because intensity is highly sensitive to the quality of the microphone and the mouth-to-microphone distance.

In languages that use prosody to mark information structure, newness and categories like focus tend to be encoded with a wider pitch range, a longer duration, and a higher intensity, compared to givenness and categories like topic. The marking of contrast is similar to the marking of newness. Such cross-linguistic similarities in the use of prosody are argued to be the linguistic manifestation of the Effort Code (Gussenhoven 2004). According to the Effort Code, the speaker uses more articulatory effort to convey more important messages, leading to a wider pitch range. The increase in pitch range is most probably accompanied by an increase in duration and intensity. However, prosodic marking of information structure can be language-specific and even variety-specific in several interesting ways. First, certain prosodic parameters may be relevant to the marking of information structure in one language or variety but irrelevant in another language or variety. For example, peak height and peak alignment are used to distinguish broad focus, narrow (non-contrastive) focus (hereafter referred to as narrow focus) and contrastive focus in American English (Xu and Xu 2005) but only word duration is used for this purpose in British English (Sityaev and House 2003). Similarly, peak alignment is used to distinguish narrow focus from broad focus in Madrid Spanish (Face 2001) but word duration is used instead in Mexican Spanish (Kim and Avelino 2003). Furthermore, when languages use the same parameter for the same purpose, they can differ in the directionality of the form-function relation. For example, both German and Dutch use peak alignment to distinguish contrastive focus from broad focus. Interestingly, compared to broad focus, peak alignment is later in contrastive focus in German but earlier in Dutch (Baumann et al. 2007, Hanssen, Peters and Gussenhoven 2008). Moreover, languages can also differ in the domain of application of the prosodic changes accompanying the focused word. For example, in English all syllables within the focused word are lengthened (Cambier-Langeveld and Turk 1999), whereas in Swedish only the stressed syllable and the immediately following syllable within the focused word are lengthened (Heldner and Strangert 2001). In what follows, the uses of each of the parameters mentioned in the preceding paragraph will be illustrated in more detail with findings from a selection of published studies concerning the realization of broad focus, narrow focus, and contrastive focus.

Narrow focus vs. broad focus: Eady et al. (1986) found that in American English sentence-final nouns (e.g., *cat*) were spoken with both a longer duration and a higher pitch peak in narrow focus (e.g., *What did Jef give the ball to? Jef gave the ball to the cat.*) than in the VP focus (e.g., *What did Jef do? Jef gave the ball to the cat.*). Similarly, Xu (1999) found that in Mandarin Chinese, words (e.g., *mo* 'touching' in *mao-1mi-1 mo-1 mao-1mi-1* 'Kitty is touching kitty') are realized with a higher pitch level (in the case of tone 1, the high level tone, as in *mo*) or an expanded pitch span (in the case of tone 2 – mid-rise, tone 3 – low-dipping, and tone 4 – high-falling), and a longer duration in narrow focus (e.g., uttered as the answer to the question *mao-1mi-1 zen-3mo nong-4 mao1mi-1?* 'What is kitty doing to kitty?') than in the VP focus (uttered as the answer to the question *mao-1mi-1 gan-4ma-2 ne?* 'What is kitty doing?'). Regarding intensity, Vainio and Järvikivi (2007) examined variations in intensity in the pre-final word and the final word in Finnish sentence pairs like *Menemme laivalla Jimille* 'We go by boat to Jimi's' and *Menemme Jimille laivalla* 'We go to Jimi's by boat' at the point where the pitch maximum was reached in each word. They found that speakers used a higher intensity in the pre-final word than in the final word but the difference was larger when the pre-final word was focused (*Millä menette Lumille?* 'with what do you go to Lumi's?'; *Minne menette laivalla?* 'Where do you go by boat?') than when the verb + prepositional phrase was focused (*Mitä teette tänään* 'What do you do today?').

Contrastive focus vs. non-contrastive focus with different sizes: Baumann et al. (2007) reported that in German, object nouns (e.g., *Banane* in *Marlene will eine Banane schälen* 'Marlene wants to peel a banana') were fairly systematically realized with a higher and later pitch peak, a wider pitch span, and a longer stressed syllable in contrastive focus (uttered as the answer to the question *Will Marlene eine Kartoffel schälen?* 'Does Marlene want to peel a potato?') than in broad focus (uttered as the answer to the question *Was gibt's Neues?* 'What's new?'). Hanssen, Peters and Gussenhoven (2008) showed that in Dutch the word bearing the sentence accent (e.g., 'Manderen' in *we willen in Manderen blijven wonen* 'We want to stay in Manderen') was spoken with the stressed syllable having a longer onset and coda, an earlier peak alignment, a lower elbow (or a steeper fall), an earlier elbow, and with the vowel immediately following the stressed syllable having a lower onset pitch in contrastive focus (uttered as the answer to the question *Willen jullie in Montfort blijven wonen?* 'Do you want to stay in Montfort?') than in broad focus (uttered as the answer to *Wat is er met jullie?* 'What's the matter?'). Notably, in both studies, little difference was found in the realization of contrastive focus and narrow focus. This suggests that contrastivity and narrow scope have the same effect on the intonation of the focused constituent.

Information states of discourse referents: In a study on reference maintenance in a second language (L2), Chen (2009a) observed that intermediate Turkish learners of Dutch used duration and pitch span to express changes in information states, albeit not always like native speakers of Dutch. Regarding duration, both givenness (i.e., the second and subsequent mentions of a referent) and inferential accessibility (i.e., a referent inferable from a previously mentioned referent) led to a decrease in the duration of the referential expressions when compared to newness (the first mention of a referent) in both L1 and L2 Dutch. Regarding pitch span, givenness led to a decrease in pitch span of the referential expression in both L1 and L2 Dutch. But accessibility led to an increase in pitch span when compared to newness in L2 Dutch, but a decrease in pitch span in L1 Dutch.

2.2. Methodological issues

2.2.1. Choice of speech materials

When designing a production experiment, one needs to consider carefully what the sentences to be elicited should be like segmentally because the choice of speech materials will have direct consequences on the reliability of the prosodic analysis and eventually on the strength of the conclusions drawn from the experiment. For experiments mainly concerned with duration, preference should be given to materials that contain "the highest possible number of target segments whose durations can be reliably and accurately estimated" (Turk, Nakai and Sugahara 2006: 4). The reason for this is that reliable and accurate duration measurements are directly related to how reliably segmentable the materials are. According to Turk, Nakai and Sugahara (2006), materials that contain alternations of obstruents with salient oral consonantal constrictions, such as plosives, /p/, /t/, /k/, /b/, /d/, /g/; sibilants, e.g., /s/, /ʃ/, /z/, /ʒ/; affricates, e.g., /tʃ/, /dʒ/; clusters of consonants differing in both place and manner of articulation, e.g., /sn/, /pl/; and sonorant segments such as vowels are most suitable for duration measurements. For studies primarily concerned with pitch, it is often recommended to use sentences or at least target constituents consisting only or primarily of sonorant segments (i.e., vowels; nasals, e.g., /n/, /m/, and /ŋ/; or approximants, e.g., /l/, /r/, /w/, /j/). This choice of materials is motivated by three facts: (1) Voiceless obstruents have no pitch, leading to discontinuous pitch contours; (2) Voiced obstruents are plagued by irregularity in voicing and consequently in pitch periods; and (3) Obstruents can raise or lower the pitch of the adjacent vowels depending on their voicing status. However, this recommendation may put too much emphasis on the continuousness and neatness of the pitch contour. Reliable analyses on pitch-related measurements also entail reliable segmentation. For example, to measure peak alignment in Dutch, it is necessary to identify the end of the accented vowel of the target word (Ladd, Mennen and Schepman 2000). Materials consisting of alternations of nasals and vowels appear to satisfy both demands (Turk, Nakai and Sugahara 2006).

These guidelines for choosing experimental materials will work well for experiments designed to elicit data with predetermined lexical content. In these experiments, what the speaker is supposed to say is fixed and usually a relatively small number of sentences need to be composed. But difficulty can arise when a large number of sentences are needed, as these guidelines impose a lot of constraints on the usable words. Furthermore, it is not always possible to have control over what exactly speakers will produce, for example, in studies concerned with spontaneous production. Inevitably, the data obtained in a spontaneous sitting may not be ideal for pitch- or duration-related analyses. In this case, it is crucial to use annotation and segmentation criteria that have been tailored to the specific materials consistently across materials.

2.2.2. Segmentation

As mentioned in the preceding section, reliable segmentation is important in making both duration- and pitch-related measurements. It has long been noted that segmentation, particularly at the phoneme level, is a difficult task due to the overlap of articulatory gestures used to produce successive speech (Peterson 1955). In some cases, it is simply not possible to determine the exact boundaries between individual phonemes, such as the boundary between a vowel and a central or lateral approximant (e.g., /w/, /l/). Knowledge of phonetics and solid training are needed to be able to conduct reliable segmentation (as much as the speech materials allow) even in materials that have been composed following the guidelines described in Section 2.2.1. Typically, researchers use information from different sources in tandem to determine the boundaries of phonemes; such sources include the waveform, the spectrogram (a picture with various shades of grey showing how the frequencies of the components of a sound change with time), and the auditory impressions. Turk, Nakai and Sugahara (2006: 6), however, suggested that one should "rely primarily on spectrograms for first-pass segmentation decisions within an accuracy of 5–10 ms, and on waveforms for more fine-grained segmentation decisions, once general boundary regions have been defined". The cues used to determine the phoneme boundaries may be language-specific in certain cases. It is beyond the scope of this chapter to consider in detail how to segment a continuous stretch of speech into phonemes. Readers are referred to Turk, Nakai and Sugahara (2006) for segmentation criteria for sequences of segments in American English, Standard Scottish English, and to a lesser extent, Southern Standard British English, Standard Dutch, Northern Finnish, and Standard Japanese, Peterson and Lehiste (1960) and Naeser (1970) for more discussion on segmentation criteria in materials in American English, and van Zanten, Damen and van Houten (1993) for discussions on segmental criteria in Dutch materials.

2.2.3. Interpreting pitch tracks

To obtain reliable pitch maximum and pitch minimum in a selected region, one should be able to interpret pitch tracks correctly. Special attention should be paid to possible tracking errors, consonantal effects on pitch, and end of utterance effects on pitch, as these can lead to incorrect interpretations of the ups and downs in pitch (Gussenhoven 2004: 8–13). Below is a summary of the main points raised in Gussenhoven's discussion on how to interpret pitch tracks.

With respect to tracking errors, a pitch tracker may mistake voiceless friction for voicing and irregularly voiced signals for voiceless signals. Furthermore, it may pick up periodic background noise and display spurious pitch values. Moreover, the pitch tracker may not analyze the voiced signal correctly. It may confuse peaks in the signal that do not correspond with the periodicity of the signal and report a pitch value that is twice that of the actual pitch value (doubling errors). It may also miss every second periodicity peak and report a pitch value that is half of the actual pitch value (halving errors). With respect to consonantal effects on pitch, obstruents can raise or lower the pitch of the adjacent vowel. More specifically, voiceless obstruents raise the pitch at the onset of the following vowel. Both voiceless and voiced obstruents lower the pitch at the end of the preceding vowel, though the lowering caused by voiced obstruents is greater. Finally, utterance-final consonantal sonorants may lead to a reversed pitch movement (relative to the immediately preceding pitch movement) in the last part of the utterance where the signal fades out. When inserting pitch-related landmarks, one should not confuse ups and downs triggered by tracking errors, adjacent consonants, and utterance-final consonantal sonorants with the 'real' pitch maximum and minimum.

2.2.4. Scales of pitch

The perceived pitch depends directly on f_0. But the relation between pitch and f_0 is not linear. This is because the ear is more sensitive to changes in the lower range of f_0 (100 Hz–1000 Hz) such that the same change in f_0 is perceived to be larger between pitches in the lower range than between those in the higher range (1000 Hz–10000 Hz) (Ladefoged 1996). For example, while the perceived difference between 300 Hz and 450 Hz is almost the same as the perceived difference between 500 Hz and 600 Hz, the perceived difference between 1500 Hz and 3000 Hz is the same as the perceived difference between 4000 Hz and 8000 Hz. In terms of musical scales, while the difference between 100 Hz and 200 Hz will be perceived as an octave, the difference between 1000 Hz and 1100 Hz will be perceived as less than a minor second. Because of the nonlinearity of pitch, it is often suggested in the literature that the Hertz scale should be transformed into a psychoacoustic frequency scale providing steps corresponding to equal perceptual intervals, such as the musical semitone (ST) scale, the Bark scale, the mel scale, and the Equivalent Rectangular Bandwidth (ERB) scale. The semitone scale is a logarithmic transformation of the Hertz scale; the Bark scale and the mel scale are nearly linear below 500 Hz but logarithmic above 500 Hz; and the ERB-rate scale is between linear and logarithmic below 500 Hz but logarithmic above 500 Hz (Nolan 2003).

However, how well the psychoacoustic scales reflect our perception depends on the specific pitch parameter in question. With respect to the perceived pitch span, Nolan (2003) found that semitones and ERB-rate best reflected listeners' intuition about pitch span, with semitones being marginally better. This is similar to the finding of Traunmüller and Eriksson (1995), who examined the perception of pitch span in male and female voices via a liveliness judgment task. With respect to pitch register, Rietveld and Chen (2006) found that mels and Hertz reflected listeners' intuition about pitch register better than semitones and ERB-rate. With respect to the perceived prominence of a certain pitch movement, Rietveld and Gussenhoven (1985) found that differences in the perceived prominence as a function of differences in pitch span were more adequately described using the Hertz scale than the semitone scale. When the pitch register of the pitch movements was co-varied with their pitch span, prominence judgments followed the ERB-rate scale more closely than the Hertz scale or the semitone scale (Hermes and van Gestel 1991). Notably, representing pitch in semitones and Hertz is generally accepted by scientific journals, although there may be a preference for the semitone scale in some communities.

In Praat, pitch values can be obtained in the Hertz scale as well as the psychoacoustic scales. In the case of semitones, pitch values can be obtained with different reference values, including 1 Hz, 100 Hz, 200 Hz, and 440 Hz. If the reference value for a sound is too high, the pitch values that are lower than the reference value will be represented as negative values in semitones. It is therefore practical to choose a reference value that is lower than the lowest pitch in the data under investigation, for example, 1 Hz, or set the reference value for each speaker separately, whereby the lowest pitch of each speaker serves as the reference value (e.g., Xu and Xu 2005).

3.   A phonological approach

3.1. Phonological cues

In a phonological approach, researchers are interested in how the prosodic structure of an utterance is varied to express information structural categories. There are three aspects of the prosodic structure that can express information structural categories: location of pitch accent, also known as accent placement (i.e., presence vs. absence of accent on segments of different sizes, e.g., phoneme, syllable, and word), type of pitch accent (e.g., a falling accent vs. a rising accent), and phrasing (i.e., how an utterance is divided into smaller phrases). Note that not all three structural elements are present in every language. For example, accent placement and type of pitch accent are relevant to the prosodic structure of West Germanic languages but not to the prosodic structure of languages like Mandarin Chinese and Korean.

In West Germanic languages, the focused constituent is accented, typically with a falling accent (transcribed as H*L, pronounced as "high star low" or "h star l"; for further details on intonational transcription see Section 3.2.1); the post-focus sequence is usually deaccented (Ladd 1996, Gussenhoven 1984, Féry 1993), as illustrated in the example in Figure (1a), in which the subject NP is focused. Accenting in the prefocus sequence is usually rhythmically motivitated (Gussenhoven 1984, Horne 1990), as illustrated in the example

in Figure (1b), in which the unfocused subject noun is spoken with H*L
and forms the preferred strong-weak-strong rhythmic pattern with the verb
and the object noun. Other languages use phrasing to mark focus, such as
Seoul Korean (Jun 2006) and Tokyo Japanese (Pierrehumbert and Beckman
1988, Nagahara 1994). For example, in Seoul Korean, the focused constituent initiates a new intermediate phrase (ip) and the post-focus constituents
are included into the same phrase (post-focus dephrasing). In the example
in Figure (2), an intermediate phrase boundary starts at the focused word
Yeona-lul and the following words are dephrased (Jun 2009).

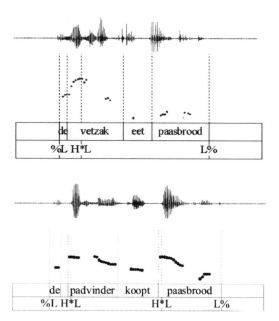

Figure 1. Pitch tracks and waveforms of *De vetzak eet paasbrood* 'The fatty is
eating Easter bread' (a) and *De padvinder koopt paasbrood* 'The scout
is buying Easter bread' (b) uttered in response to the question *Wie eet
paasbrood?* 'who is eating Easter bread?' and the question *Wat koopt
de padvinder?* 'what is the scout buying?' respectively. These examples were taken from production data obtained from native speakers of
Dutch (Chen 2007).

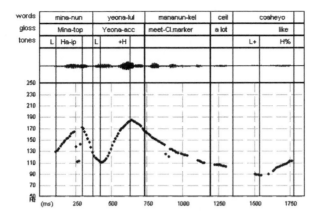

words	mina-nun		yeona-lul		mananun-kel	cell	coaheyo	
gloss	Mina-top		Yeona-acc		meet-Cl.marker	a lot	like	
tones	L	Ha-ip	L	+H			L+	H%

Figure 2. Pitch track and wave form of *Mina-nun Yeona-lul mannanun-kel ceil coaheyo* 'Mina likes meeting Yeona very much' with focus on the second word 'Yeona-lul' (Jun 2009)

In some Romance languages, narrow focus and broad focus are distinguished by means of choice of accent type. For example, in Palermo Italian (Grice 1995) and European Portuguese (Frota 2000), sentence-final constituents are spoken with a falling accent with a late peak (transcribed as H*+L) in narrow focus but a falling accent with an early peak (transcribed as H+L*) in whole sentence focus. In Neapolitan Italian, sentence-final constituents are spoken with a rising accent (L+H*) in narrow focus but a falling accent H+L* in whole sentence focus (D'Imperio 1999).

Finally, both accent placement and choice of accent type play a significant role in encoding information states of discourse referents in West Germanic languages. For example, in read speech in German, sentence-final referents that are new are frequently realized with H+L* and H+!H*, two falling accents differing in how the high tones step down, whereas sentence-final referents that are given are typically deaccented (Baumann 2006, de Ruiter 2010). Furthermore, sentence-final referents that are accessible are most frequently realised with H+L*, followed by H+!H* (de Ruiter 2010). [2,3]

---

[2] Accessible referents were operationalized as referents which were introduced earlier in the discourse and reoccurred after the mention of two other referents.

[3] The preference for certain types of accent to encode new and accessible referents is however not found in spontaneous speech, suggesting an interesting difference in the use of intonation between read speech and spontaneous speech (de Ruiter 2010). The general pattern of accenting non-given referents and deaccenting given referents still holds for spontaneous speech.

3.2.   Methodological issues

3.2.1. Intonational transcription

To study the phonological marking of information structural categories, researchers need to annotate the speech materials for accent placement, accent type, and phrasing, preferably following an existing transcription system developed for the language at issue. Over the past two decades, such a transcription system has been developed for a wide range of languages and different varieties of the same language within the autosegmental metrical (AM) framework, which is currently the most widely used framework in the field of intonational phonology (Pierrehumbert 1980, Beckman and Pierrehumbert 1986, Pierrehumbert and Beckman 1988, Ladd 1996).[4] In this framework, the intonation contour of a sentence is described as sequences of high (H) and low (L) tones. The tones function either as (parts of) pitch accents or as phrase tones marking the edges of two types of prosodic units, the intermediate phrase (phrasal accents) and the intonational phrase (boundary tones). Pitch accents can be made up of one or more tonal targets. The tone that is associated with the stressed syllable is demarcated with the '*' sign. The exact tonal events differ from language to language. For example, Korean and Mandarin Chinese have phrase tones but no pitch accents. The inventory of pitch accents and phrase tones and their definitions in a given language or a variety within a language are usually based on a rigorous analysis of the intonational phonology of that language or variety and are thus language- or variety-specific.

The transcription system for American English, ToBI (Tone and Break Indices), was the first one proposed in the AM framework (Beckman and Ayes 1994). In addition to using H and L tones to describe tonal events, ToBI uses break indices to mark the prosodic grouping of the words in an utterance. At the end of each word, the subjective strength of its association with the next word is labeled on a scale from 0 (for the strongest perceived association) to 4 (for the clearest perceived break). The locations of the two highest categories of association strength or break indices, 3 and 4, are also where the phrasal accent and boundary tone are located. In recent years, ToBI systems have been developed for a variety of languages (e.g.,

---

[4] Transcription systems which were developed in non-AM frameworks are still used, such as the discourse intonation approach (Brazil, Coulthard and Johns 1980), and the International Transcription System for Intonation (INSINCT) (Hirst and Di Cristo 1998).

Catalan, French, German, Greek, Spanish, Korean, Japanese, Portuguese, etc.). All these systems have their own homepage, where a manual for teaching the system to new transcribers is available, free of charge, together with recorded examples of transcribed utterances. The reader is referred to the ToBI homepage for more information on the existing ToBI systems (http://www.ling.ohio-state.edu/~tobi/).

Other transcription systems developed in the AM framework do not necessarily share all the conventions of ToBI. For example, the system for Dutch, ToDI (Transcription of Dutch Intonation), differs from the English ToBI in a number of aspects (Gussenhoven 2005). First, ToDI covers only the 'To' part of ToBI; only one phrase type is coded, namely, the intonational phrase, avoiding undesirable intermediate phrase breaks. Second, the final edge tone of the intonational phrase is optional. Third, accentless intonational phrases are allowed. Fourth, a pitch accent depicts the pitch contour starting from the stressed syllable and continuing to the next accented syllable; therefore, it has no leading tones (i.e., tones preceding a starred tone). Finally, the pitch accents H* and L* in ToDI describe high level (or weak rise) and low level pitch respectively; but H* and L* in ToBI represent a single high and low tonal target from which the pitch falls or rises. Transcription systems following the ToDI conventions have been developed for British English (Grabe 2004), French (Post 2000), and Russian (Odé 2008).

Note that not all transcription systems that use the AM framework claim the phonological identity of the tonal events. For example, Grice, Baumann and Benzmüller (2005) and Odé (2008) explicitly point out that their system is primarily aimed to give a phonetic description of the tonal events. How to determine whether a tonal event is phonetic or phonological is still an unsettled issue in the field of prosody. Different criteria and experimental methods have been proposed (see Gussenhoven 1999, and Prieto 2012 for an overview). Yet they appear not to always yield the same result for a given tonal event (e.g., Prieto, Torres and Vanrell 2008). It therefore makes sense to say that the phonological marking of information structural categories essentially consists of the use of tonal patterns with distinct shapes in different information structural conditions and the phonological identity of the tonal patterns is assumed in the absence of evidence against this assumption.

Recent years have seen growing interest in using the AM framework to study the intonation of second language learners (e.g., Ueyama 1997, Jun and Oh 2000, Jilka 2000, Chen and Mennen 2008, Gut 2009, Hellmuth 2010). Very recently, researchers have also begun using the AM framework to examine how young children use intonation (Prieto and Vanrell 2007 for

Catalan, Frota and Vigário 2008 for Portuguese, Chen and Fikkert 2007 for Dutch). A methodological concern applicable to both research areas is that the existing AM transcription systems were developed to describe the structural properties of 'mature' intonation patterns produced by adult native speakers of a language, and consequently may not be suitable for the purpose of transcribing the intonation of children and L2 learners, who may not yet have a full mastery of the intonational system of the target language. Applying these transcription systems to children's and L2 learners' intonation may therefore run the risk of shoehorning their intonation in categories typical for adult native speakers. To minimize such a risk, one can adopt an existing AM transcription system as a starting point and introduce additional symbols or additional categories to capture the patterns that either appear to differ phonetically from tonal patterns recognized in the existing model based on adult speakers (e.g., in the scaling of pitch or the alignment of tonal targets) or do not resemble any of the tonal patterns in the model for adult speakers. For example, Chen and Fikkert (2007) introduced extra symbols to code observable variations in pitch scaling and peak alignment in H*L and !H*L in utterances produced by two-year old Dutch-speaking children. Chen (2011) observed that some Dutch 4- to 5-year-olds sometimes pronounced compound nouns (e.g., *fietsclub* 'cyclist-club') with two distinct falling patterns, one on each noun. Native speakers of Dutch were still able to hear that the primary lexical stress was on the first noun. The double-fall is not a pitch accent type recognized in ToDI. It was transcribed as H*L HL, following the ToDI conventions. If these novel tonal patterns turn out to occur rather infrequently, one could consider either merging them with the existing tonal patterns that they resemble or merging them into one category for the sake of statistical analyses, which usually require a minimal number of data points for each category.

3.2.2. *Validating annotation*

Transcribing the intonation pattern of a stretch of speech in a given language is a process of mapping the tonal event of interest onto the descriptions and examples of tonal categories established in the phonology of the language, and then deciding which category it belongs to. This is a skill that comes with "a solid understanding of intonation theory ... and speech acoustics ... and good ear-training" (Grabe, Kochanski and Coleman 2007). Intonational transcription is also a process that inevitably involves judgments from the labelers, especially in ambiguous cases. It is therefore highly recommendable to provide independent evidence showing that the labeling is consistent and reliable, though such evidence is still lacking in the majority of published work based on hand-labeled data.

There are several ways to validate the consistency and reliability of the labels. First, one can analyze the phonetic realization of the tonal categories to establish whether the tonal categories are indeed distinguishable from each other along one or more phonetic parameters. This method is particularly useful in the case of pitch accents that may be easily confused with each other (e.g., H* vs. L*H). If pairs of similar pitch accents differ significantly along one or more parameters in which they are supposed to differ (e.g., the pitch span of the rise and the alignment of the lowest pitch from which the rise starts in the case of H* vs. L*H), then it can be concluded that the labels indeed represent what they stand for. For example, Braun and Chen (2010) analyzed the phonetic realization of accents in the adverb *now* in sentences like *Put the book in cell one. Now put the book in cell 2* with respect to pitch maximum, pitch minimum, duration, etc. in order to corroborate the phonological analysis of *now* – which was relatively difficult due to its shortness and the subsequent compression in the realization of the tonal targets (Grabe 1998). Phonetic analysis has also been used to corroborate the analysis of phrasing. For example, Frota (2002) examined whether the minimum pitch was reached after the falling accent on the subject noun in sentences like *The Angolans gave spices to the journalists* to decide whether there was a phrasal boundary after the subject noun in European Portuguese. She found that the falling accent fell lower when the subject noun was the topic of the sentence than when the subject noun was the focus of the sentence, leading to the conclusion that a phrasal boundary was present after the topical subject noun but not after the focused subject noun. Jun and Fougeron (2000) compared the duration of post-focus sequences (e.g., *at breakfast* in the sentence *Marion will eat some bananas at breakfast* with focus on *bananas*) to the duration of the same sequences in a neutral sentence (i.e., uttered without a context), and the duration of the final syllable of the focused word to the duration of the same syllable in the neutral sentence to determine whether the post-focus sequence was merged into the same phrase as the focused word in Parisian French (i.e., dephrased). They reported that the post-focus sequence was not consistently shorter in the focus condition than in the neutral condition. Further, the final syllable of the target word was not consistently longer in the focus condition than in the neutral condition. This led to the conclusion that the post-focus sequence in Parisian French was deaccented (i.e., spoken with a relatively flat tonal pattern) but not dephrased. It should be noted that such a use of phonetic analysis is practical and useful only when the speech materials lend themselves easily to reliable phonetic analysis of pitch- and duration-related parameters (see Sections 2.2.2 and 2.2.3).

Furthermore, mathematical modeling has been shown to be useful in assessing the phonetic basis of tonal categories (Grabe, Kochanski and Coleman 2007, Andruski and Costello 2004). Grabe, Kochanski and Coleman (2007) constructed polynomial models with four coefficients to capture the shape of seven types of accents in intonational phrase-final position, which is also sentence-final in their materials.[5] These accent types and following boundary tones (demarcated with the % sign) were detected by trained labelers in a selection of 700 read sentences in varieties of British English: H* H% (high rise), H*L % (fall), H*L H% (fall-rise), L*H L% (rise-(plateau)-fall), L*H H% (rise), L*H % (rise-plateau) and L* H% (late rise) (Grabe 2004).[6] The four coefficients described the average pitch of the accent, the slope of the rise and/or the fall of the accent, and two kinds of curvature, i.e., a parabola shape and a wave shape. The analysis window of each accent began 100 milliseconds before the midpoint of the lexically stressed syllable and extended to the end of the voiced part of the accented word. It was found that the models for all but L* H% differed significantly from each other in one or more of the first three coefficients. This indicated that six of the seven accent types were associated with a set of statistically different pitch patterns. The authors speculated that the late rise L* H% could not be distinguished from L*H H% or from L*H %, possibly due to the relatively small number of tokens of L* H% compared to the number of tokens of L*H H% and L*H %. Although Grabe, Kochanski and Coleman's (2007) work clearly demonstrates the usefulness of polynomial modeling as a tool to validate hand-labeled accent types, it should be pointed out that this approach is limited in several aspects. First, its application in speech materials containing some amount of unvoiced segments is potentially problematic. As the authors pointed out, a model with four polynomial coefficients can handle data with about only 10% unvoiced materials. Furthermore, human listeners appear to make use of not only pitch-related information, but also other acoustic information in the process of labeling

---

[5]   A polynomial is a mathematical expression of finite length constructed from variables and constants. It uses only the operations of addition, subtraction, multiplication, and non-negative integer exponents (retrieved from Wikipedia).

[6]   The '%' boundary symbol indicates that the pitch level associated with the last tone of the pitch accent in the intonational phrase is continued up to the edge of the phrase (Grabe 2004).

accents. Grabe, Kochanski and Coleman's (2007) approach is exclusively concerned with pitch. In addition, the frequency of a particular accent in particular dialects or varieties and associated listener expectations may also play a role in listeners' decision-making, as acknowledged by the authors. But these kinds of information are not dealt with in the models.

Finally, a more widely used validation method, compared to that of using supporting phonetic analysis and mathematical modeling, is the analysis of inter-transcriber agreement (Silverman et al. 1992, Pitrelli, Beckman and Hirschberg 1994, Grice et al. 1996, Syrdal and McGory 2000, Gut and Bayerl 2004, Chen 2011). This approach is relatively easy to implement as it neither imposes strict constraints on the speech materials nor requires knowledge of modeling. But two or more labelers are needed to transcribe the intonation patterns of at least a selection of the data. Two measures of inter-transcriber agreement have been used in past work, i.e., the percentage of agreements between pairs of transcribers (Silverman et al. 1992, Pitrelli, Beckman and Hirschberg 1994, Chen 2011), and Cohen's kappa coefficient (e.g., Gut and Bayerl 2004). The latter differs from the former in that it takes into account the agreement that occurs by chance (Cohen 1960). Studies using the two measures appear to yield similar results. That is, the highest inter-transcriber agreement has been found in the detection of an intonational phrase boundary (> 90%), followed by presence vs. absence of accent, and type of accent. This tendency reflects the degree of complexity of the corresponding phonological categories (Gut and Bayerl 2004).

3.3. Combining phonological analysis with phonetic analysis

In most of the work on the prosodic realization of information structural categories, either a phonetic approach or a phonological approach is adopted. However, adopting a solely phonetic approach may risk neglecting the role of phonological cues in some languages. For example, in English, if a word is realized with a longer duration when focused than when not focused, this can be because the word was accented when focused but unaccented when not focused. From a cross-linguistic perspective, adopting only a phonetic-approach can pose difficulties when making generalizations on the similarities and differences between languages. For example, an increase in duration may be related to accentuation in one language but phrasal boundary marking in another language (Frota 2000). It is therefore recommendable to take phonology into account when conducting a phonetic analysis by, for example, performing separate phonetic analyses on materials that belong to different phonological categories. This has been done in certain studies concerning tone languages, although such phonological categories are of a lexical nature. In these studies, the researchers have carefully controlled the choice of lexical tone or included it as an experimental variable, and have examined the phonetic parameters for words realised with different lexical tones separately (e.g., Xu 1999, Y Chen 2006).

In the same vein, a phonological approach alone may not fully address questions about the prosodic realization of information structural categories, as there can be phonetic differences in their realization in the absence of differences in their phonological realization. It can therefore be very useful to combine the two approaches, as has been done in some recent studies. For example, in a study on the prosodic realization of topic in German, Braun (2006) first examined the phonological realization of both contrastive and non-contrastive topics in sentence-initial position in short passages in German. She found that contrastive topics were not realised differently from non-contrastive topics and both types of topics were frequently realized with a rising accent (L+H* and L*+H). She subsequently conducted a phonetic analysis on the two types of topics, and found that contrastive topics were realized with a higher peak, a later peak and a larger pitch excursion than non-contrastive topics. Regarding the prosodic realization of focus and topic, Chen (2007) found that sentence-initial focus and topic were realised similarly in Dutch SVO sentences from a phonological perspective. In both conditions, the subject nouns were accented and the most frequently used accent was H*L. However, the H*L-accented subject nouns were pronounced with a lower pitch minimum, an earlier peak, and an earlier alignment of the pitch minimum in the focus condition than in the topic condition (Chen 2009b).

4. Doing prosodic analysis in Praat

In this section, a short tutorial on how to do prosodic analysis in Praat is given with a hypothetical research question as a starting point. No prior knowledge of Praat is required to follow the tutorial. Praat can be downloaded from the Praat website: www.praat.org. It can be used on different operating systems, e.g., Windows, Macintosh, Linux, etc. This short tutorial is based on Praat in Windows.

Suppose you want to find out how learners of Dutch with different native languages use intonation to distinguish narrow focus (on the object) from broad focus in read speech, and you plan to conduct a phonological analysis (i.e., choice of accent type) and a phonetic analysis on the object noun (i.e., duration of the word and the stressed syllable, pitch maximum, pitch minimum, and pitch span of the word) in cases where the two focus conditions are not distinguished phonologically. You have recorded a number of sentences (e.g., *De voetganger eet bieslook* 'The pedestrian is eating chives') spoken as answers to WHAT-questions (e.g., *Here is a pedestrian. He is eating something. What is the pedestrian eating?*) and as answers to questions like *What's happening?* All the sentences have been recorded in one .wav file. You have cut the file using programs like Adobe Audition, and saved the answer sentences as separate .wav files on your PC.[7] In what follows, I will describe how to annotate the sentences for the purpose of both the phonological and phonetic analyses using Praat in a step-by-step fashion.

4.1. Starting Praat

Click on the Praat icon to start Praat. Two windows will appear on your screen: The Objects window on the right and the Picture window on the left (Figure 3 on next page). The Picture window can be closed or minimized if no figures need to be drawn.

4.2. Reading in a sound file

▶ In the Praat objects window, click the heading 'Read', then 'Read from file...'
▶ This will open a browser. Browse in your folder and find the file that you have saved and want to annotate, select it, and then click on 'Open'. You can only read one file in at a time.[8]
▶ The file will appear on your Praat objects list in the objects window as a new object. At the same time a menu bar will appear on the right side of the objects window (Figure 4). You can listen to your file by selecting the file (as you would in Word) and then clicking on 'Play' on the right side.

---

[7] It is also possible to do the cutting in Praat, as will become clear in the rest of this section.

[8] Note that if a .wav file is too long to be opened via the 'Read from file' function, you can open it as a long sound file by clicking on 'Open long sound file' under the heading 'Read'. Whether a .wav file is large enough to count as a long sound file depends on the duration of the file, sampling rate, number of channels (mono vs. stereo), etc.

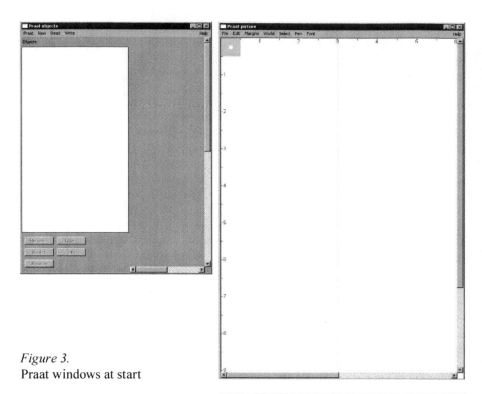

Figure 3.
Praat windows at start

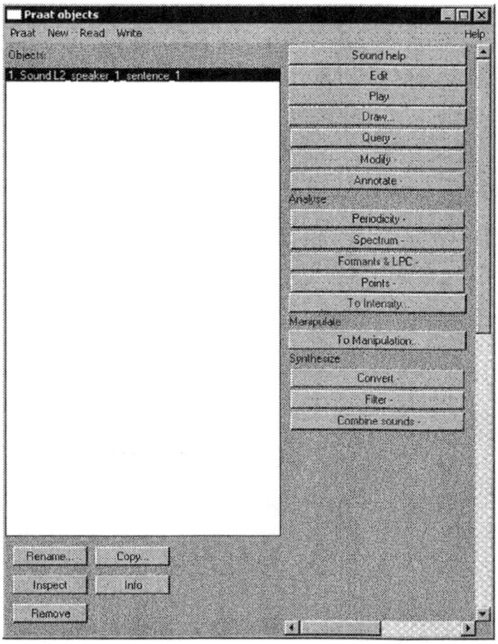

Figure 4.
Praat objects window with
a sound object read in

4.3. Creating a TextGrid

To annotate a sound file for further analyses, you need to create a TextGrid. The TextGrid file can have one or more tiers. There are two types of tiers, interval tiers and point tiers. The interval tiers are for annotations that apply for a stretch of sound, but do not need to align with a specific point in the signal, e.g., the orthographic transcription of sentences or words. The point tiers are for labels that need to be aligned with a particular point in the signal, which can either apply for a stretch of sound (e.g., a label specifying the accent type) or a particular point in the signal (e.g., a label indicating the time point at which the highest pitch is reached within a word). To create a TextGrid file:

▶ Select the sound file in your objects window.
▶ Click 'Annotate' (on the right side of the Objects window), then select 'To TextGrid…'
▶ A dialog box will appear, asking about the tiers you want to have in the TextGrid. In the cell following 'All tier names', specify the names of the tiers in the order in which you want them to appear from top to bottom in the TextGrid. For the above-mentioned hypothetical analyses, you need a tier for labels of pitch accents (tone tier), a tier for labels indicating the boundaries of the word (word tier), a tier for labels indicating the boundaries of the stressed syllable (syllable tier), and a tier for labels indicating the location of pitch maximum and pitch minimum in the word (pitch tier).[9] All the four tiers are point tiers. It is often convenient to include at least two other tiers, namely, an interval tier on which a sentence is segmented to words (sentence tier) and an interval tier for remarks, questions, or anything that may be relevant to your analysis (misc tier). You can order the tiers as follows: sentence, word, syllable, pitch, tone, misc.
▶ Specify the names of the point tiers in the cell corresponding to the question 'Which of these are point tiers'(Figure 5).
▶ Then click on 'OK'. A TextGrid object will appear in the Objects window as a new object following the sound file. It is automatically named after the sound file. You can view the TextGrid by selecting it and then clicking on 'Edit'. You will see the empty TextGrid with the tiers numbered on the left side and named on the right side.

---

[9] You can also merge the word tier and the syllable tier into one tier, for example, the segment tier. Instead of using landmarks like w1, w2, s1, and s2, you can use more neutral landmarks, such as b1, b2, b3 etc. to demarcate different boundaries.

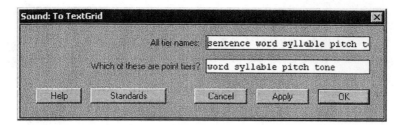

Figure 5. Defining the tier names and the order of their appearance

4.4. Annotating in the TextGrid

▶ Select the sound file and the corresponding TextGrid in the objects window, and then click on 'Edit' on the right side of the window.

▶ A TextGrid Editor will appear (Figure 6). In the upper panel, you see the waveform with pulses (blue vertical lines). In the middle panel, you see the pitch contour (in blue), the intensity contour (in light yellow), the spectrogram (in shades of grey), and the formant contours (in red, representing the acoustic consequences of the changing shapes of the mouth and pharynx). In the bottom panel, you see the TextGrid. For the current purposes, you only need to display the pitch contour and the spectrogram. To 'hide' any of these analyses, click on the corresponding heading in the Editor and unselect the 'show ...' function.

▶ The size of the Editor is adjustable in the usual way in which you would adjust the size of a table in Word. You can also maximize the size of the Editor by clicking on the square on the top right corner. To undo this, click on the double square on the top right corner.

▶ It is important to adjust the settings for each of the analyses appropriately. As the spectrogram and the pitch analyses are most relevant here, we will discuss their settings in more detail. You can view and change the settings by clicking on the corresponding function on the top of the TextGrid Editor and then selecting 'Spectrogram/Pitch settings'. In most cases, the standard settings of Praat are the best. However, the following variables in the Spectrogram and Pitch settings may be adjusted:

▷ The View range (Hz) setting in the Spectrogram settings: You need to set the maximum frequency to a value suitable for the speaker you are analyzing. For a child, 8000 Hz is desirable. For an average adult male speaker, use 5000; for an average adult female speaker, use 5500 Hz.

The range that you set here will be shown to the left of the Editor window.

▷ The Dynamic range (dB) in the Spectrogram settings: All values that are no more than the Dynamic range dB below the maximum will be drawn in white. The standard value is 50 dB. If there is substantial background noise in your recording, you can set the value at 30 dB or 40 dB. This way the frequencies of the background noise will be drawn in white, and not interfere with the display of the frequencies of the speech, which are drawn in grey.

▷ The Pitch range (Hz) setting in Pitch settings: This is the most important setting for pitch analysis. The standard range is from 75 Hz to 500 Hz, which means that the pitch analysis will be performed only on values that fall within this range. For a more accurate pitch analysis, you should adjust the range to the pitch range of the speaker(s) whose speech you are analyzing. The range that you set here will be shown on the right edge of the Editor window. For a male voice, you may want to set the floor to a value between 50 Hz and 80 Hz and the ceiling to a value between 200 Hz and 300 Hz, depending on the lowest and highest pitch of the speaker. For a female voice, you can set the floor to a value between 80 Hz and 100 Hz and the ceiling to a value between 300 Hz and 500 Hz. For a child's voice, the range can be set from 150 Hz to 600 Hz. In general, you should try different floor and ceiling frequencies to find out which range gives you the best display of the pitch contour. A rule of thumb is that the floor should not be too much lower (> 50 Hz) than the lowest pitch of an utterance and the ceiling should not be too much higher (> 100 Hz) than the highest pitch of the utterance.

▷ The Unit setting in the Pitch settings: The standard unit, or scale, is Hz. You can also choose to display the frequencies in semitones, mels, ERBs or Hz (logarithmic).

▷ The View range setting in the Advanced pitch settings: The standard value is 0.0 (= auto) for both cells following the variable 'view range'. This means that the view range is the same as the analysis range. You can choose a different view range than the analysis range, for example, when an utterance happens to have a narrower pitch range (e.g., 80 Hz~ 150 Hz for a male voice) than the chosen analysis range for the whole data set (e.g., 50 Hz~300 Hz).

▶ Now you are ready to annotate the sentence. You may want to start by segmenting the sentence into words in the sentence tier (interval tier).

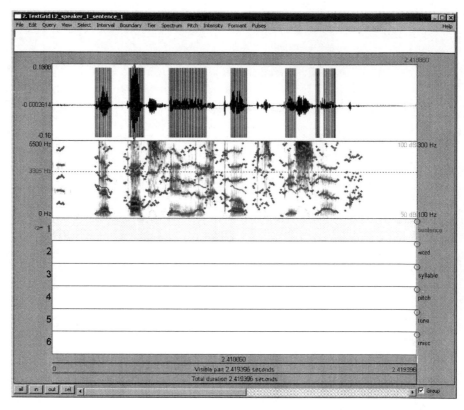

Figure 6. TextGrid Editor window displaying a sentence produced by a female

Assuming that you can get a sense for approximately where a word begins and ends by looking at the waveform and the spectrogram:

▷ Select the portion of the sound that you choose as the word to be segmented (e.g., *varken* in our example) as if you were highlighting a word in Word: Left click on the point in the waveform or the spectrogram where you think the word starts, then, keeping the mouse button pressed, move to the point where you think the word ends, and release the mouse button. If the word is selected, a pinkish colored shadow should cover the selected portion.

▷ Click on the shadowed part of the top horizontal bar at the bottom of the TextGrid Editor to hear the portion you have selected. You can adjust your selection by removing the pinkish shadow (by clicking in the waveform or the spectrogram) and try a new selection.

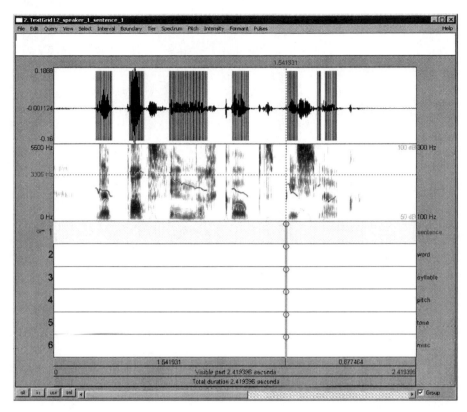

Figure 7. TextGrid Editor window with a vertical line indicating the beginning of the object noun

▷ Once you have a reasonably good selection, remember where the beginning and end points of the selection approximately are in the waveform or the spectrogram. Then insert the beginning and end boundaries in the sentence tier: Click on the beginning of the selection in the waveform or the spectrogram. A vertical line with small circles will appear in each of the TextGrid tiers (Figure 7). Click on the circle in the sentence tier to place a word boundary there. Repeat to place a word boundary at the end of the word.

▷ Click in the interval between the word boundaries to select the segmented word; this interval will be highlighted in yellow. Then click on the shadowed part of the top horizontal bar at the bottom of the TextGrid Editor to hear the word and check whether the segmentation is satisfactory.

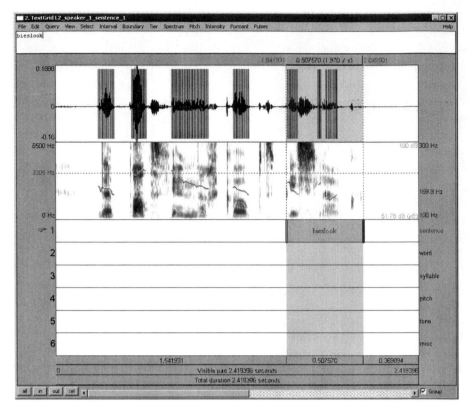

Figure 8. TextGrid Editor window with the word boundaries of the object noun
labeled on tier 1

▷ At this stage, you can improve the segmentation by zooming in on
the portion you have selected: Click on 'Sel' in the bottom left corner
of the TextGrid Editor, then inspect whether you want to move the
boundaries more to the left or to the right on the basis of details in
the waveform and the spectrogram. You can remove a boundary by
clicking on the heading 'Edit' in the TextGrid editor and then selecting
'Remove boundary'. You can click on 'Out' or 'All' in the bottom left
corner of the TextGrid Editor to get back to the entire sound file.

▷ If you are happy with the segmentation, click in the interval between
the word boundaries to type the label, in this case the transcription of
the word. Note that the text you type will appear both in between the
two boundaries and at the top of the Editor window (Figure 8).

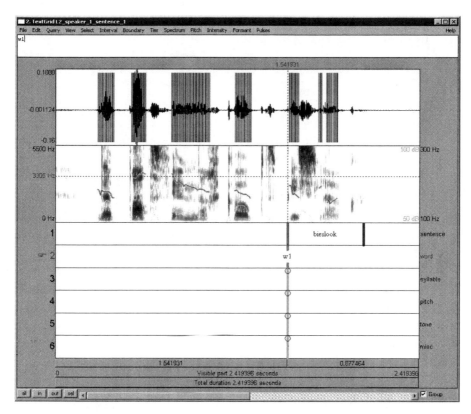

Figure 9. TextGrid Editor window with the beginning of the object noun labeled on tier 2

▷ To get the time values for the beginning, the end, and the duration of the word, click between the word boundaries. The word is then selected in the word tier and the corresponding portions in the other tiers of the TextGrid; the waveform and the spectrogram are also selected. The duration is displayed in seconds both in the selection at the top of the Editor Window and at the top play bar. The time values for the beginning and the end of the word are given in the selection at the top of the Editor Window (Figure 8).

▶ After you have placed word boundaries for all the words of the sentence and typed the labels in the sentence tier, you can 'copy' the word boundaries of the object noun into the word tier (point tier):

▷ Click on the beginning boundary of the object noun in the word tier, a vertical line with a small circle will appear in all tiers of the TextGrid.

▷ Click on the circle of the vertical line in the segment tier to place the beginning boundary of the word.

▷ Type the label name in the open space of the vertical line (e.g., w1) (Figure 9).

▷ Repeat the above steps to place and label the end boundary of the object noun (e.g., w2) in the segment tier.

▷ You can also get the time value of each boundary in this point tier: Click on the boundary. A vertical line extending from the boundary to the edges of the whole Editor window will appear, and the time value of the boundary will appear at the top edge of the Editor window.

▶ Continue by placing the boundaries of the stressed syllable of the object noun in the syllable tier. Follow the same procedure as described above to find the portion of the stressed syllable, place the boundaries, and put the label names (e.g., s1 and s2 for the beginning and end of the stressed syllable respectively) in the syllable tier. You can also get the time value of each boundary as described above.

▶ Next place the landmarks to indicate where the pitch reaches its maximum and minimum in the object noun in the pitch tier (point tier):

▷ Select the portion of the word where the pitch maximum occurs. Watch out for microprosodic effects (see Section 2.2.3)

▷ Click on the heading 'pitch' and then select 'move cursor to maximum pitch'. A vertical line with a small circle will appear in each of the TextGrid tiers. Click on the circle in the pitch tier to place a landmark there and then type the label for pitch maximum (e.g., H).

▷ Select the small portion of the word where the pitch minimum is reached. Click on the heading 'pitch' and then select 'move cursor to minimum pitch'. Again a vertical line with small circles will appear in each of the TextGrid tiers. Click on the circle in the pitch tier to place a landmark there and then type the label for the pitch minimum (e.g., L). If the contour in the word has a rise-fall shape, it is useful to insert a landmark indicating where the lowest pitch preceding the pitch maximum occurs and a second landmark to indicate where the lowest pitch following the pitch maximum is reached. This way, you can consider including both measures of the pitch minimum into your analysis.

▷ The pitch value of a landmark in the pitch tier can be read by clicking on the landmark. The pitch value is displayed on the right edge of the Editor window.

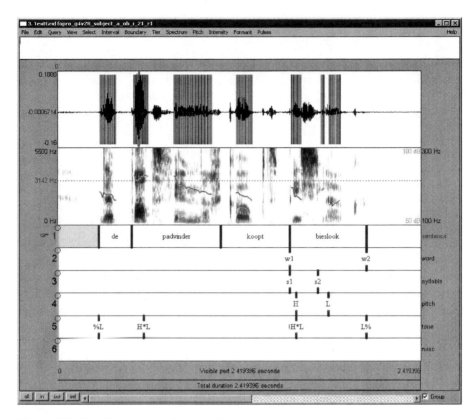

Figure 10. A fully annotated textgrid

▶ As the last step, annotate the intonation of the sentence in the tone tier (point tier). Even though only the intonation of the object noun is of interest in this hypothetical study, it is very useful to annotate the intonation of the rest of the sentence. In our example, the object NP was spoken with a downstepped falling pitch pattern, which entails a high tone in the preceding sequence (i.e., H*L in the subject noun). In the ToDI notation, this accent should be labeled !H*L, followed by a low boundary tone. Click on the highest point of the contour. A vertical line with a small circle will appear in each of the TextGrid tiers. Click on the circle in the tone tier to set the tone landmark and then type the accent label.

4.5. Saving the TextGrid

▶ You have now fully annotated the sentence (Figure 10). Save the TextGrid to a directory by clicking on the heading 'File' in the TextGrid editor and then selecting 'Write to text file...'. Normally the TextGrid is saved in the same directory as the .wav file.

▶ Follow the steps mentioned above from 'Reading in a sound file' to 'Saving the TextGrid' to annotate the rest of the answer sentences. Once you become familiar with this procedure, you will find other possible ways of doing the annotation in a different order than the one described above. For example, you may want to first annotate all the sentences phonologically and then to decide which phonetic parameters you will annotate.

4.6. Extracting information from TextGrids via Praat scripts

As you can imagine, it will get quite tedious to manually note down the time values, pitch values, and pitch accent labels in all the sentences for further analysis. Luckily, you can extract this information from a batch of .wav files and corresponding TextGrids often in one go by means of Praat scripts. You can either learn to write the scripts yourself or use scripts written and generously made available on the web by others. It is very likely that the analyses you want to do have been done by many others using scripts. Therefore, you can easily find scripts on the web that you can use with no or minor adaptation.[10] To learn how to write Praat scripts, you can follow the tutorial on Praat scripting at http://www.fon.hum.uva.nl/praat/manual/Scripting.html.

5.   Final remarks

As may have already become clear in Sections 2 and 3, published work on the prosodic realization of information structural categories mostly concerns relatively short declarative sentences with canonical word order (e.g., SVO, SV + Indirect Object + Direct Object, SV + Adverbial), which have been read out loud as responses to *Wh*-questions or *Yes/No*-questions in a

---

[10] Here are the URLs of two Praat script archives: the MacLab Praat Script Archive maintained by Joe Toscano at https://sites.google.com/site/praatscripts/ and the UCLA Praat script resources at http://www.linguistics.ucla.edu/faciliti/facilities/acoustic/praat.html. The Praat User Group also has handy scripts available in its archive at http://uk.groups.yahoo.com/group/praat-users/. You can also contact the author for scripts used to extract time values, pitch values and pitch accent labels.

lab setting. Research based on spontaneous speech is still sparse. Furthermore, in past work, the dimension topic-focus has usually overlapped with the dimension given-new, even though the referential expressions in the studies on information states were not necessarily the topic or focus constituent of an utterance. There has been some work done to examine differences in the prosodic realization of focus when it conveys given information as opposed to new information (e.g., Wang and Xu 2011), in sentences with different lengths (e.g., Wang and Xu 2011), in non-canonical word orders compared to canonical word orders (e.g., Kim and Avalino 2003), and in questions compared to declaratives (Eady and Cooper 1986). In addition, limited work has been done to address the prosodic realization of information structure among children learning a first language and adults learning a second language (see Dimroth and Narasimhan, this volume, Chen 2009, 2011 for an overview). These limitations however open up a range of interesting research questions for future work in this line of research.

References

Andruski, Jean E. and James Costello
    2004   Using polynomial equations to model pitch contour shape in lexical tones: an example from Green Mong. *Journal of the International Phonetic Association* 34: 125–140.
Baumann, Stefan
    2006   *The Intonation of Givenness – Evidence from German.* (Linguistische Arbeiten 508). Tübingen: Niemeyer.
Baumann, Stefan, Johannes Becker, Martine Grice and Doris Mücke
    2007   Tonal and articulatory marking of focus in German. In *Proceedings of the 16th International Congress of Phonetic Sciences, Saarbrücken, 6th 9th August 2007*, Jürgen Trouvain and William J. Barry (eds), 1029–1032. Dudweiler: Pirrot.
Beckman, Mary E. and Janet B. Pierrehumbert
    1986   Intonational structure in English and Japanese. *Phonology Yearbook* 3: 255–309.
Beckman, Mary E. and Gayle Ayers Elam
    1994   Guidelines for ToBI transcription (version 2.0, February 1994).
Boersma, Paul and David Weenink
    2010   Praat: doing phonetics by computer (Version 5.1.25) [Computer program]. http://www.praat.org/ (retrieved on 20 January 2010).
Braun, Bettina
    2006   Phonetics and phonology of thematic contrast in German. *Language and Speech* 49 (4): 451–493.

Braun, Bettina and Aoju Chen
    2010   Intonation of 'now' in resolving scope ambiguity in English and
            Dutch. *Journal of Phonetics* 38: 431–444
Brazil, David, Malcolm Coulthard and Catherine Johns
    1980   *Discourse Intonation and Language Teaching.* Harlow: Longman.
Cambier-Langeveld, Tina and Alice Turk
    1999   A cross-linguistic study of accentual lengthening: Dutch vs. English.
            Journal of Phonetics 27: 171–206.
Chen, Aoju
    2007   Intonational realisation of topic and focus by Dutch-acquiring 4- to
            5-year-olds. In *Proceedings of the 16th International Congress of
            Phonetic Sciences,* Jürgen Trouvain and William J. Barry (eds.), 1553–
            1556. Dudweiler: Pirrot.
Chen, Aoju
    2009a   Intonation and reference maintenance in Turkish learners of Dutch:
            A first insight. *Language, Interaction, and Acquisition* 2: 33–57.
Chen, Aoju
    2009b   The phonetics of sentence-initial topic and focus in adult and child
            Dutch. In *Phonetics and Phonology: Interactions and Interrelations,*
            Marina Vigário, Sónia Frota and M. João Freitas (eds.), 91–106.
            Amsterdam: Benjamins.
Chen, Aoju
    2011   Tuning information structure: intonational realisation of topic and
            focus in child Dutch. *Journal of Child Language* 38: 1055–1083.
Chen, Aoju and Paula Fikkert
    2007   Intonation of early two-word utterances in Dutch. In *Proceedings
            of the 16th International Congress of Phonetic Sciences,* Jürgen
            Trouvain and William J. Barry (eds.), 315–320. Dudweiler: Pirrot.
Chen, Aoju and Ineke Mennen
    2008   Encoding interrogativity intonationally in a second language. In *Pro-
            ceedings of Speech Prosody,* Plínio A. Barbosa, Sandra Madureira
            and Cesar Reis (eds.), 513–516. Campinas: Editora RG/CNPq.
Chen, Yiya
    2006   Durational adjustment under corrective focus in Standard Chinese.
            Journal of Phonetics 34: 176–201.
Cohen, Jacob
    1960   A coefficient of agreement for nominal scales. *Educational and
            Psychological Measurement* 20: 37–46.
Cruttenden, Alan
    1997   *Intonation.* (2nd edn.) Cambridge: Cambridge University Press.
De Ruiter, Laura
    2010   *Studies on Intonation and Information Structure in Child and Adult
            German.* (MPI Series in Psycholinguistics 54). Wageningen: Ponsen
            en Looien.

D'Imperio, Mariapaola
  1999   Tonal structure and pitch targets in Italian focus constituents. In *Proceedings of the 14ᵗʰ International Conference on Phonetic Science.*
Eady, Stephen J. and William E. Cooper
  1986   Speech intonation and focus location in matched statements and questions. *Journal of the Acoustical Society of America* 80: 402–415.
Eady, Stephen J., William E. Cooper, Gayle V. Klouda, Pamela R. Mueller and Dan W. Lotts
  1986   Acoustical characteristics of sentential focus: narrow vs. broad and single vs. dual focus environments. *Language and Speech* 29(3): 233–251.
Face, Timothy L.
  2001   Focus and early peak alignment in Spanish intonation. *Probus* 13: 223–246.
Féry, Caroline
  1993   *German Intonation Patterns.* (Linguistische Arbeiten 285). Tübingen: Niemeyer.
Frota, Sónia
  2000   *Prosody and Focus in European Portuguese: Phonological Phrasing and Intonation.* New York: Garland Publishing.
Frota, Sónia
  2002   The Prosody of Focus: a Case-Study with Cross-Linguistic Implications. *Proceedings of Speech Prosody* 2002, 319–322.
Frota, Sónia and Marina Vigário
  2008   Early intonation in European Portuguese. Talk given at the Third Conference on Tone and Intonation, Lisbon, September 2008.
Grabe, Esther
  2004   Intonational variation in urban dialects of English spoken in the British Isles. In *Regional Variation in Intonation*, Peter Gilles and Jörg Peters (eds.), 9–31. Tübingen: Niemeyer.
Grabe, Esther
  1998   *Comparative Intonational Phonology: English and German.* (MPI Series in Psycholinguistics 7). Wageningen: Ponsen en Looien.
Grabe, Esther, Greg Kochanski and John Coleman
  2007   Connecting intonation labels to mathmatical descriptions of fundamental frequency. *Language and Speech* 50: 281–310.
Grice, Martine
  1995   *The Intonation of Interrogation in Palermo Italian: Implications for Intonation Theory.* (Linguistische Arbeiten 334). Tübingen: Niemeyer.
Grice, Martine, Matthias Reyelt, Ralf Benzmüller, Jörg Mayer and Anton Batliner
  1996   Consistency in transcription and labeling of German intonation with GToBI. In *Proceedings of the 4ᵗʰ International Conference on Spoken Language Processing*, 1716–1719.

Grice, Martine, Stefan Baumann and Ralf Benzmüller
  2005   German intonation in aAutosegmental-metrical phonology. In
          Prosodic Typology: The Phonology of Intonation and Phrasing,
          Sun-Ah Jun (ed.), 55–83. Oxford: Oxford University Press.
Gussenhoven, Carlos
  1984   *On the Grammar and Semantics of Sentence Accents.* Dordrecht:
          Foris.
Gussenhoven, Carlos
  1999   Discreteness and gradience in intonational contrasts. *Language and
          Speech* 42: 281–305.
Gussenhoven, Carlos
  2004   *The Phonology of Tone and Intonation.* Cambridge: Cambridge Uni-
          versity Press.
Gussenhoven, Carlos
  2005   Transcription of Dutch intonation. In*Prosodic Typology: The Phonol-
          ogy of Intonation and Phrasing,* Sun-Ah Jun (ed.), 118–145. Oxford:
          Oxford University Press.
Gut, Ulrike
  2009   *Non-Native Speech: A Corpus-Based Analysis of Phonological and
          Phonetic Properties of L2 English and German.* Frankfurt: Peter
          Lang.
Gut, Ulrike and Petra Saskia Bayerl
  2004   Measuring the reliability of manual annotations of speech corpora.
          In *Proceedings of Speech Prosody*, 565–568.
Hanssen, Judith, Jörg Peters and Carlos Gussenhoven
  2008   Prosodic Effect of Focus in Dutch Declaratives. In *Proceedings of
          Speech Prosody*, Plínio A. Barbosa, Sandra Madureira and Cesar Reis
          (eds.), 609–612. Campinas: Editora RG/CNPq.
Heldner, Mattias and Eva Strangert
  2001   Temporal effects of focus in Swedish. *Journal of Phonetics* 29 (3):
          329–361.
Hellmuth, Sam
  2010   The contribution of accent distribution to foreign accentedness:
          causes and implications. In *Proceedings of New Sounds 2010.*
          Retrieved on 10th May, 2010, from http://ifa.amu.edu.pl/newsounds/
          Proceedings_guidelines.
Hermes, Dik J. and Joost C. van Gestel
  1991   The frequency scale of speech intonation. *Journal of the Acoustical
          Society of America* 90: 97–102.
Hirst, Daniel and Albert de Cristo
  1998   A survey of intonation systems. In *Intonation Systems*, Daniel Hirst
          Daniel and Albert de Cristo (eds.), 1–44. Cambridge: Cambridge
          University Press.

Horne, Merle
    1990   Accentual patterning in 'new' vs. 'given' subjects in English. In *Working Papers of Department of Linguistics, Lund University*, 81–97.

Jilka, Matthias
    2000   The contribution of intonation to the perception of foreign accent. Ph.D. dissertation, University of Stuttgart.

Jun, Sun-Ah
    2006   Intonational Phonology of Seoul Korean Revisited. *Japanese-Korean Linguistics* 14: 15–26, Stanford: Center for the Study of Language and Information. [Also printed in *UCLA Working Papers in Phonetics* 104: 14–25, 2005]

Jun, Sun-Ah
    2009   Focus domains and complex NP focus in Korean. Talk given at the 19th Japanese-Korean Linguistics Conference, Hawaii. Nov. 12th, 2009.

Jun, Sun-Ah and Cécil Fougeron
    2000   A Phonological model of French intonation. In *Intonation: Analysis, Modeling and Technology*, Antonis Botinis (ed.), 209–242. Dordrecht: Kluwer Academic Publishers.

Jun, Sun-Ah and Mira Oh
    2000   Acquisition of 2nd language intonation, In *Proceedings of the 6th International Conference on Spoken Language Processing*, 76–79.

Kim, Sahyang and Heriberto Avelino
    2003   An intonational study of focus and word order variation in Mexican Spanish. In *La tonía: Dimensiones fonéticas y fonológicas*, Esther Herrera and Pedro M. Butragueño (eds.), 357–374. Mexico City: Colegio de México.

Ladefoged, Peter
    1996   *Elements of Acoustic Phonetics* (2nd edition). Chicago: University of Chicago Press.

Ladd, D. Robert
    1996   *Intonational Phonology*. Cambridge: Cambridge University Press.

Ladd, D. Robert, Ineke Mennen and Astrid Schepman
    2000   Phonological conditioning of peak alignment in rising pitch accents in Dutch. *Journal of the Acoustical Society of America* 107: 2685–2696.

Naeser, Margaret
    1970   Criteria for the segmentation of vowels on duplex oscillograms. In *Technical Report 124, Wisconsin Research and Development Center for Cognitive Learning*.

Nagahara, Hiroyuki
    1994   Phonological phrasing in Japanese prosody. Ph.D. dissertation, UCLA.

Nolan, Francis
    2003   Intonational equivalence: an experimental evaluation of pitch scales. In *Proceedings of the 15th International Congress of Phonetic Sciences,* 771–774.

Odé, Cécilia
    2008   Transcription of Russian Intonation ToRI: an interactive research tool and learning module on the internet. In *Studies in Slavic and General Linguistics*, vol. 34, (Dutch Contributions to the Fourteenth International Congress of Slavists), Peter Houtzagers, Janneke Kalsbeek, Jos Schaeken (eds.), 431–449. Rodopi: Amsterdam and New York.

Peterson, Gordon E.
    1955   An oral communication model. *Language* 31: 414–427.

Peterson, Gordon E. and Ilse Lehiste
    1960   Duration of syllable nuclei in English. *Journal of the Acoustical Society of America* 32 (6): 693–703.

Pierrehumbert, Janet B.
    1980   *The phonetics and phonology of English intonation.* Ph.D. thesis, Massachusetts Institute of Technology. (Published by Garland Press, New York, 1990.)

Pierrehumbert, Janet B. and Mary E. Beckman
    1988   *Japanese Tone Structure.* Cambridge: Massachusetts Institute of Technology Press.

Pitrelli, John F., Mary E. Beckman and Julia Hirschberg
    1994   Evaluation of prosodic transcription labeling reliability in the ToBI framework. In *Proceedings of the 3rd International Conference on Spoken Language Processing.*

Post, Brechtje
    2000   *Tonal and Phrasal Structures in French Intonation.* The Hague: Thesus (Subsidiary of Holland Academic Graphics).

Prieto, Pilar
    2012   Experimental methods and paradigms for prosodic analysis. In *Handbook in Laboratory Phonology*, Abigail Cohn, Cécil Fougeron and Marie K. Huffman (eds.). Oxford: Oxford University Press.

Prieto, Pilar, Francesco Josep Torres and Maria del Mar Vanrell
    2008   Categorical perception of mid boundary tones in Catalan. Talk presented at the Third Conference on Tone and Intonation. Lisbon, 17th September, 2008.

Prieto, Pilar and Maria del Mar Vanrell
    2007   Early intonational development in Catalan. In *Proceedings of the 16th International Congress of Phonetic Sciences*, Jürgen Trouvain and William J. Barry (eds.), 309–314. Dudweiler: Pirrot GmbH.

Rietveld, Tony and Aoju Chen
2006   How to obtain and process perceptual judgments of intonational meaning. In *Methods in Empirical Prosody Research*, (*Language, Context, and Cognition*; Series editor: Anita Steube) Stefan Sudhoff, Denisa Lenertová, Roland Meyer, Sandra Pappert, Petra Augurzky, Ina Mleinek, Nicole Richter and Johannes Schließer (eds.), 283–320. Berlin/New York: Mouton de Gruyter.

Rietveld, Tony and Carlos Gussenhoven
1985   On the relation between pitch excursion size and prominence. *Journal of Phonetics* 13: 299–308.

Sityaev, Dimitry and Jill House
2003   Phonetic and phonological correlates of broad, narrow and contrastive focus in English. In *Proceedings of the 15th International Congress of Phonetic Sciences*, 1819–1822.

Silverman, Kim, Mary Beckman, Mori Ostendorf, Colin Wightman, Petti Price and Janet P. Pierrehumbert
1992   *ToBI: a standard for labeling English prosody*. In *Proceedings of the 2nd International Conference on Spoken Language Processing*.

Syrdal, Ann and Julia McGory
2000   Inter-transcriber reliability of ToBI prosodic labeling. In *Proceedings of the 6th International Conference on Spoken Language Processing*.

Traunmüller, Hartmut and Anders Eriksson
1995   The perceptual evaluation of F0 excursions in speech as evidenced in liveliness estimations. *Journal of the Acoustical Society of America* 97: 1905–1914.

Turk, Alice, Satsuki Nakai and Mariko Sugahara
2006   Acoustic segment durations in prosodic research: a practical guide. In *Methods in Empirical Prosody Research*, Stefan Sudhoff, Denisa Lenertová, Roland Meyer, Sandra Pappert, Petra Augurzky, Ina Mleinek, Nicole Richter and Johannes Schließer (eds.), 1–28. Berlin/New York: Mouton de Gruyter. In *Language, Context, and Cognition*. Series editor: Anita Steube.

Ueyama, Motoko
1997   The phonology and phonetics of second language intonation: the case of "Japanese English". In *Proceedings of the 5th European Conference on Speech Communication and Technology*, 2411–2414.

Vainio, Martti and Juhani Järvikivi
2007   Focus in production: Tonal shape, intensity, and word order. *Journal of the Acoustical Society of America* 121 (2): EL 55–61.

van Zanten, Ellen, Damen Laurens and Els van Houten
1993   Collecting data for a speech database. In *Analysis and Synthesis of Speech: Strategic Research Towards High-Quality Text-to-Speech Generation*, Vincent J. van Heuven and Louis C. W. Pols (eds.), 207–222. Berlin/New York: Mouton de Gruyter.

Wang, Bei and Yi Xu
    2011   Differential prosodic encoding of topic and focus in sentence-initial position in Mandarin Chinese. *Journal of Phonetics* 37: 502–520.
Xu, Yu
    1999   Effects of tone and focus on the formation and alignment of F0 contours. *Journal of Phonetics* 27: 55 105
Yi Xu and Ching X. Xu
    2005   Phonetic realization of focus in English declarative intonation. *Journal of Phonetics* 33: 159–197.

The psychology of information structure

Heidi Wind Cowles

In this chapter we will examine the influence that information structure has on the processing of language, both production and comprehension. One way in which to view information structure is as a mediator between the form of language and the mental states of interlocutors (and thus between linguistic structure and psychological states). Under this type of approach, the information status of referents in a sentence can potentially have a very important role to play in both the processing of a sentence as it unfolds in real time and the ultimate interpretation of it. Psycholinguistic approaches to information structure have primarily concentrated on the influence of focus status, although there has also been some work looking at the influence of topic status as well.

As with other approaches to information structure, there is a certain amount of terminological confusion, particularly as regards the use of the term *focus*. While many linguistic approaches make a key distinction between contrastive and informational focus (e.g., Kiss 1998, see also chapter 1.2 in this book), many psycholinguistic studies do not make this distinction explicitly, and studies of focus are often studies of contrastive focus, either implicitly or explicitly. Further, *focus* in psycholinguistic studies may also be used to mean focus of attention or the most prominent or salient referent in a sentence, which crucially does not correspond to the notion of focus used in linguistics in general and particularly in this book. This mixed use of the term *focus* has lead to some uncertainty about the nature of the influence of focus on sentence and discourse processing. While it is clear that focus plays an important role in this process, it is not entirely clear how it does so.

Work on topic, too, has some issues related to identifying topic and confounding this status with grammatical subject: in psycholinguistic work, topic has often been operationalized as the grammatical subject of a sentence, and while this allows for interesting and productive research, it does create questions about which effects are due to topic status and which are due to subject (or first mention) status. This creates a two-fold problem, in fact, because subject position is considered a prominent syntactic position that may give the subject's referent a prominent or highly salient status. Topic is thus equated with a prominent syntactic position, yet, the notion of prominence (and salience) is also associated with focus status, particularly focus of attention. Indeed, topic status is often associated with an increase in accessibility, with specific effects on the form of reference as one outcome of this (Lambrecht 1994, Ariel 1990, and others).

Thus, the issue of comparing topic and focus as well as how both of these concepts may be linked to more basic psychological constructs is somewhat tricky. Other information structural concepts that have been examined and compared are given and new information, which have sometimes been linked to topic and focus status, respectively.

In this chapter we will first consider information structure influences on sentence production, and in particular the influence of givenness and topic on the encoding of sentence structure. Next, we will turn to comprehension, where research has largely centered on focus status. Research in this area has examined how and when focused information is processed and what influence focus status has on the interpretation of syntactically ambiguous sentences. There is also work looking at the nature of focus with respect to the processing system, and how it might influence representations in memory. Finally, we will turn to the issue of information structure and the processing of coreferring expressions, particularly pronouns.

1. Information structure in sentence production

In most models of language production the processes that underlie production are divided into three major types, those related to message generation, grammatical encoding and phonological encoding. There are important differences between models about how these processes interact and what the flow of information is like between them, but for our purposes we can discuss them at a level of abstraction that overlooks these differences. Message generation precedes encoding processes and is considered by most approaches to be pre-linguistic in the sense that it involves representations that are not necessarily linguistic in nature, but rather conceptual. It is at this level that a speaker selects what information he or she will produce, and this is then encoded grammatically and phonologically. Levelt (1999) proposed that it is also at this level that topic and focus status are determined and marked, and that this status then causes particular encoding processes later on. Levelt argues that these statuses come about in the message level as a means to guide the addressee to key information in the speaker's utterance: what the utterance is about (and thus what any new information should be added to) and what part of it the addressee should attend to. For example, Levelt argues that when an utterance contains a predication about some referent, then that referent is marked as topic at the message level. Similarly, speakers will mark what is the "new focus" in the message, which Levelt defines as the information that the speaker believes his/her addressee was not previously attending to, but should now. These message-level statuses then influence the formulation of the utterance itself: items with topic status will be placed in a syntactically prominent position, such as subject.

Focus is more complicated in part because the notion of focus used by Levelt corresponds most closely to attentional focus, rather than information that is pragmatically unrecoverable (e.g., Lambrecht 1999) or information to which the presence of alternatives is relevant for the interpretation of linguistic expressions (Krifka and Musan, this volume). However, both focused and new referents and predications are *conceptually prominent* according to Levelt's model, and he makes a three-way distinction between the following status types (which are independent of topic status): "in focus", "accessible", and "in discourse model." Levelt notes that different languages encode these statuses in different ways.

Generalizing away from the particulars of Levelt's model, it seems clear that models of language production conceive of information structure status as a reflection of the mental representations of the speaker, and what the speaker intends to communicate to an addressee. Yet, information structure is but one of a large number of competing influences on sentence production, and so other factors (such as lexical frequency and conceptual availability independent of message intention) may influence the final encoding. Thus, while topic status at the message level tends to result in subject encoding, it is not a guarantee. Levelt does not fully articulate the syntactic structures associated with focus, but one recent hypothesis (Carlson et al. 2009) is that in otherwise unmarked utterances, focus is predicted to occur post-verbally. In terms of prosody, both topic and focus appear to also impact sentence production, with focus being encoded with particular pitch accents and longer duration. However, as we shall see below, there do not appear to be any one-to-one correspondences between acoustic encoding and information statuses. Thus, in this area as well there are almost certainly multiple factors that influence the final acoustic form of the sentence (cf. Ferreira 2007), of which information status may be one.

Nonetheless, these findings and observations leave us with the basic pattern in which topic status is associated with subject or early mention and focus status is associated with post-verbal mention. Related to this are numerous observations that sentences often follow a given-new pattern in which given information precedes new information, even when that means shifting the order or syntactic structure of the constituents in the sentence away from their usual, canonical positions. From a processing perspective, this ordering of topic and focus (as well as given and new information) makes a certain amount of sense. Language is processed in a largely incrementally way, such that when we encounter or produce a sentence we begin to process it right away, at the beginning, without waiting for the entire sentence to be available for either production or comprehension. If topics tend to come early or first in sentences, this gives speakers the opportunity to produce words that have been previously mentioned (or refer to referents that are already available) before potentially more difficult, new information. From a comprehension perspective, the benefit is even clearer: knowing the topic early on allows for any following information to be applied or integrated with that topic and thus the beginning of the sentence serves as a grounding point for further information (e.g., Gernsbacher 1990). However, while both topic and given information are often found early in sentences, this may not be only cause of creating non-canonical structures or word orders; as noted above, there appear to be many factors that influence the ordering of information in a sentence. One recent study of German has found that under certain circumstances new information may even be ordered first (Hörning et al. 2006).

Related to this notion of the given-new ordering of information, there has been work looking specifically at contextual influences on structural encoding that has focused particularly on the production of given *vs.* new information. Several studies have experimentally confirmed a givenness effect in sentence production: things that have been previously introduced in recent discourse or context are more likely to come earlier in sentences than things that have not been previously introduced (Bates and Devescovi 1989, Bock and Irwin 1980, Flores d'Arcais 1975, Prentice 1967, Turner and Rommetveit 1968). However, it isn't clear to what degree such effects are due to givenness itself (including increases in either conceptual or lexical accessibility) or topic status. Bock and Irwin (1980), for example, looked at the order of constituent recall in memorized sentences. In this experiment, speakers would first hear a set of context questions and then a set of answers that allowed alternative word orders (such as dative alternation). Then, they would hear the questions one by one and need to provide the correct answer from the list they had just heard. So, for example, a speaker might hear *A rancher received an inquiry from a cowboy about something he needed for his act. What did the rancher do?* and then reply with a memorized answer such as *The rancher sold the cowboy the horse.* Bock and

Irwin found that speakers were more likely to place a noun earlier when it or a related noun (e.g., *Roy Rogers*) was used in the preceding context, although this effect was larger when the noun was repeated. They also found that giving identical words in isolation as prompts for sentence recall created the same effect. They argue that in this case the prompt words had no context to provide referents for the nouns and thus lexical accessibility alone can influence word order.

In another study looking at givenness and accessibility, Prat-Sala and Branigan (2000) compared inherent accessibility (based on intrinsic features like animacy, imageability, and prototypicality) to context-derived accessibility using a picture-description task in which subjects heard a setup sentence followed by the wide-focus question, *What happened?* and then described a picture. The preceding setup sentence made the target argument more prominent to the speaker by placing it first in a *there*-construction with a demonstrative determiner (*this*) with adjectival modification. Additional properties were then predicated of it. An example is shown below in (1), with the target argument underlined.

(1)   *There was this old rusty <u>swing</u> standing in a playground near a <u>scooter</u>, swaying and creaking in the wind.*

Their results showed that the more richly described referent (*swing*) was mentioned earlier in speakers' picture descriptions than the less richly described referent (*scooter*), suggesting that prominence leads to a temporary increase in the derived accessibility of the corresponding concepts from memory. Interestingly, results from a Spanish version of their materials suggest that this increased conceptual accessibility influences word order rather than grammatical role assignment: Spanish speakers were more likely to produce dislocated actives, which are constructions that allow a (typically) post-verbal object argument to be mentioned pre-verbally and a (typically) pre-verbal subject argument to be mentioned post-verbally. However, unlike passive constructions, in which the active object becomes the passive subject, the grammatical roles do not change in Spanish dislocated actives. Thus, the authors argue, these dislocated actives show that it is possible that speakers leave grammatical role assignments unchanged and simply move the prominent element to the beginnings of sentences. This further suggests that the type of mention/given status may simply alter accessibility, which in turn influences order of mention rather than grammatical status. Thus, any apparent influence of topic could simply be due to increased accessibility rather than topic status.

Cowles (Cowles 2003, Cowles and Ferreira 2012) explicitly tested for topic effects by examining the influence of referents mentioned in *about*-phrases on the syntactic structure of spoken utterances. The use of *about*-phrases made it possible to manipulate topic status without using the grammatical subject position. In one experiment, speakers first listened to sentences that contained a target noun that was mentioned either in a post-verbal *about*-phrase (*A nurse noticed something about the lightning*) or as the object of an embedded sentence complement (*The nurse noticed something as she watched the lightning*). After each sentence, speakers saw a theme-experiencer verb (e.g., *frightened*) followed by two nouns (e.g., *baby, lightning*) and needed to verbally produce a sentence that used these three words and fit with the sentence that they just heard. Responses were coded according to whether the target noun was mentioned before (and in a higher syntactic position than) the other target noun. Cowles found a topic-mention advantage in which *about*-phrase targets were more likely to be produced early in an utterance compared with non *about*-phrase targets. These results were replicated in a written production task, with a much more robust topic advantage effect (Cowles 2007). Further, Cowles and Ferreira (2012) found that other tasks with spoken materials that tried to find accessibility differences between topic and non-topic referents, such as lexical decision, failed to find them. Taken together, these results suggest that either topic status exerts an influence on sentence production that is more than simply a manipulation of accessibility or that such an influence is only seen when speakers engage the sentence production system. These results support the idea that manipulations of topic status via *about*-phrases can have an impact specifically on sentence production.

Thus, we are left with a picture of information structure influence on sentence production in which it appears that topic status may be assigned at the pre-linguistic message level and then encoded linguistically, and there is some evidence that topic status has an influence that cannot be reduced to changes in the accessibility of referents. However, givenness (and the corresponding increase in accessibility) does appear to be highly relevant in sentence production as well and it may still be that the apparent influence of topic is linked in many cases with givenness. As we shall see later in this chapter, this issue of givenness, accessibility, and topic status is also examined in studies looking at coreference and coreferential form.

2. Information structure in sentence comprehension

As a bridge between mental states and linguistic form, information structure serves as a means of signaling the mental states of the speakers with respect to the information they intend to convey, and thus provides comprehenders with information that could help guide the processing and interpretation of sentences. A key question for psycholinguistics is how and when this information is used. For example, Carpenter and Just (1977) proposed that clefts and pseudoclefts guide readers to process new information and then integrate it with their model of the discourse. However, other structures and cues to information structure status should also influence processing, and a similar, though broader, proposal was made by Cowles (2003) in which it is not only clefts or other specialized syntactic structures that provide this guide, but rather that the prosodic, structural, and referential encoding of information in a sentence provides cues to information structure that can be used to guide both initial processing and later integration.

Another key question is how information structure is identified, which is not a trivial issue: as other chapters in this book have highlighted (see, e.g., chapters 1, 2, and 4), prosody is one of the key cues to focus structure in many spoken languages. Related to this, pitch accents that mark focus appear to particularly influence processing and are thought to make the expression carrying the pitch accent as well as their corresponding referents more prominent or salient. For example, Cutler and Fodor (1979) showed that focus pitch accent aids in a phoneme monitoring task, causing faster response times. However, there may not be any one-to-one mapping between prosody and information status. Hedberg and Sosa (2007) argue that while there is some systematic relationship between intonational cues and information structure categories, it is not as simple as a one-to-one mapping. In particular, they did not find any particular prosodic cue that could be used to unambiguously distinguish topic from focus in spontaneous English dialogue. For example, they found that the L+H* pitch accent, argued elsewhere to be strongly linked to contrastiveness (e.g., Pierrehumbert and Hirschberg 1990), also occurred on non-contrastive topics. Other pitch accents, including H*, L*, and H*+L occurred at least once on both topics and foci, thus calling into question whether these can be used to distinguish these statuses. Other researchers (Gundel and Fretheim 2001) have also argued that other languages, like Norwegian, have no prosodic cues that enable hearers to uniquely identify topic and focus in an utterance. Also, while prosody provides at least partial cues to focus status, in written language prosody is not overtly available and so structural cues are needed. Thus, it is a fundamental challenge for researchers to understand how comprehenders determine information status based on possibly unreliable cues from prosody and syntax. In general, researchers have dealt with this issue by using prosody and structures that are as informationally unambiguous as possible, such as cleft structures and focus particles such as *only*. Another major question is how information statuses like topic and focus influence the online comprehension of sentences, and what the nature of this influence is. The majority of experimental work in comprehension has focused on these two questions, and has largely looked at focus status, and in particular on several key areas where focus status may play a critical role. Another area where information structure has been applied to language processing is in coreference, where both topic and focus have been examined as factors in resolving antecedents. We shall consider both of these areas, starting with the influence that focus has on attention and the representation of the focused referent in memory.

2.1. Focus influence on memory, attention, and information encoding

While focus is associated with auditory cues that are likely to make it stand out with respect to other parts of the sentence, there are also structural positions that allow focus to stand out in written language. Birch and Garnsey (1995) used two types of constructions to investigate focus, which for them crucially meant "the most important and emphasized constituent in the sentence" (Birch and Garnsey 1995: 233). Because of this somewhat different definition of focus, they used both *it*-clefts (which are dealt with in Winkler's chapter on information structure in English, this volume) and *there*-insertions, which are not generally considered to mark focus in the information structural sense discussed above and elsewhere in this book, but present new information. Examples of their materials are given below in (2) and (3).

(2)   *It was the lion that stole the show at the circus this year.*

(3)   *There was this trinket that the little girl wanted to get at the fair.*

Interestingly, Birch and Garnsey found that these constructions produced the same results, but crucially for our purposes, they found that participants were both faster and more accurate at recognizing a word when it had been focus in a previous sentence compared to when it was not. A questionnaire study also confirmed that participants selected the target word as the most important more when it was in a focus position (73%) than when it was not (17%; the non-focus condition placed target words in several different syntactic positions, including direct object, object of a preposition, and subject of a relative clause). Further, they also found that this focus position appeared to make phonological information about the focused element more readily available, but did not find clear results for semantically related information. From this, Birch and Garnsey suggest that while cleft structures may emphasize a referent, focus may highlight only particular aspects of it, perhaps those that are specific to the context it is used in.

Another study (Birch, Albrecht and Myers 2000) also looked at the influence of *it*-cleft and *there*-insertion structures using a speeded probe recognition task, in which participants needed to report as quickly as possible whether they had seen a given probe word in an immediately preceding sentence. For example, after reading a set of sentences like the one in (4) below, participants would be presented with a word such as "mayor" and asked to respond as quickly as possible with whether the word had occurred in the previous set of sentences.

(4)   *Betty was covering local and state races. She was at City Hall for a press conference. Minutes into the conference, an argument erupted. It was the mayor who refused to answer a reporter's question.*

The authors made two key discoveries. First, when focus status was compared against a 'neutral' context (in which the target word appeared in subject position, such as *The mayor refused to answer a reporter's question*) there was no difference in response times to probe words that occurred immediately after the sentence containing the focused referent. However, when they compared focus status against a defocused context (in which the target occurred post-verbally) then focus status prompted faster response times. Second, they found that focus status did cause faster responses compared to a neutral context when the probe point was delayed by 10 seconds. Taken together, these results suggest that placing a referent in a focusing structure such as a cleft does influence the representation and availability of a referent in memory, but that it does so primarily by increasing the amount of time the referent is available/activated in memory. In the short term, both syntactic focus and subject mention appear to provide an equal increase in availability of the representation in memory, but the increase continues only for focus. Given the common link between topic and subject status, it is tempting to see this as a way in which focus and topic both impact processing, and we shall see below in the discussion about coreference that there is other evidence for this. However, while Birch et al. (2000) only provide a couple of examples, their materials do not appear to confer topic status on the subject target and the authors consider the advantage for subjects in their materials to be due to first mention advantage (e.g., Gernsbacher, Hargreaves and Beeman 1989).

Data from eye-movements also suggest that the effects of focus may be felt most strongly in later processing. Birch and Rayner (1997) tracked eye movements while participants read sentences that contained either an *it*-cleft or *there*-insertion to sentences without these structures. They found no difference in initial processing measures at the focused word compared to the non-focused. However, there were differences in measures of reprocessing, with participants more likely to reread previous text after encountering a focused word. Further, second-pass rereading times were longer on focus compared to non-focus. Birch and Rayner also used *wh*-question-answer pairs to manipulate the assignment of wide *vs.* narrow focus in the answer. An example is given in (5)–(7) below.

(5)   Wide-focus question: *What was the danger from?*

(6)   Narrow-focus question: *What might catch fire?*

(7)   Answer: *The danger from the poisonous gases was that the laboratory might catch fire.*

In the wide-focus case, the focus in the answer appears to be a prepositional phrase modifying the subject noun, in the narrow-focus case it appears to be the object of the main verb or part of the second clause in a pseudo-cleft. Birch and Rayner found that these conditions produced complementary effects on reading patterns: the narrow focus showed reprocessing but not initial processing differences and the wide focus caused longer initial reading times but not longer rereading times. The authors suggest that this is because the larger focus region allowed readers to realize they were reading the focus before they reached the end of it. These results show that focus assigned from *wh*-questions has an impact that is not necessarily different from that caused by syntactic marking of focus, and also that focus caused extra reading time of the focused constituent, either in initial reading or in rereading. They argue that focus information is encoded more carefully. Related to this, Foraker and McElree (2007) argue that clefted structures cause an increase in the strength of the antecedent's representation in memory rather than selecting a particular referent to be placed into a special attentional focus status. Other supporting evidence for a more careful initial encoding for focus followed by later easier processing comes from an eye-tracking study in Hindi by Shaher et al. (2008), who found longer initial reading times at the focus position followed by faster times.

The idea that focus status causes a more careful encoding in memory is also supported by work examining the Moses Illusion, in which comprehenders are likely to answer "two" when asked a question like "How many of each animal did Moses take on the ark?" In looking at the effect of focus status on the effectiveness of this illusion, Bredart and Modolo (1988) found that placing the incorrect information (e.g., Moses, who did not put animals in an ark) in a cleft caused people to catch the error more often. Sturt et al. (2004) also used cleft constructions to examine the influence of focus on comprehension with a change detection task in which participants would first read a short passage and then see a passage that was either identical or differed by a single word. Participants were asked to tell the experimenter if they had noticed a change, and if so, what it was. In critical passages, the changed word was either clefted using an *it*-cleft, or it was the non-clefted element in a pseudocleft. The changed word could also either be closely related to the original word (e.g., *beer* for *cider*) or unrelated (e.g., *music* for *cider*). Sturt et al. found that when the changed word was unrelated, focus made no difference; participants were very good at noticing changed words in this case. However, when the changed word was semantically related to the original word, then focus made participants significantly more accurate at detecting the change. They found the same effect when they manipulated focus using prior context with the presence or absence of a discourse-linked *wh*-phrase, as shown in (8) below. In this type of context, the discourse-linked *wh*-phrase (e.g., *which man*) questions which member of a previously established or inferable set of possibilities is the correct one (i.e., which man out of a set of men got into trouble). The authors compared (8) to (9) as a context sentence for the target sentence, (10), in which the changed word is underlined.

(8) *Everybody was wondering which man got into trouble.*

(9) *Everybody was wondering what was going on that night.*

(10) *In fact, the man with the hat was arrested.*

Participants were significantly more accurate at detecting the change in sentences like (10) when they were preceded by sentences like (8) compared to (9). These results also suggest that focusing constructions like clefts, as well as focusing contexts in which discourse-linked *wh*-questions are used, cause more attention to be paid to the focus. Taken together with the previous studies, this work suggests that linguistic focus status plays an important part in directing attentional focus as well as in the availability of information in memory and the degree to which it continues to be activated.

2.2. Detecting focus violations

Some work has used question-answer pairs to examine how and when mismatches in focus disrupt processing, with the majority of this work done using an Event-related brain potentials (ERP) methodology (e.g., Hruska et al. 2000, Johnson et al. 2003, Magne et al. 2005). In this method, the electrical activity of the brain (EEG) is recorded at the scalp and then differences in the changes of amplitude, electrical polarity (positive or negative), timing, and scalp distribution of brain waves are measured in response to external events, such as reading or listening to language. ERP studies examining prosodic cues in both English (Johnson et al. 2003) and German (Hruska et al. 2000) found an increased N400 response at words that should, but do not, have focus pitch accent. The N400 response is a characteristic change in brain wave activity in which there is a negative shift in polarity that is largest (often with a sharp peak) around 400 milliseconds after the beginning of the stimulus that elicited it. The N400 response appears to occur to some degree after every word, but the size of the amplitude changes depending on a number of factors, including those related to lexical and semantic processing (see Kutas et al. 2006 for a review). Thus, these results suggest that focus status may influence lexical processing during auditory sentence processing. Using written materials, Cowles et al. (2007a) tested short passages in English that included question-answer pairs. In their study, participants would read a short two-sentence passage that introduced three discourse participants and ended with a *wh*-question; an example is given in (11) below.

(11)   Setup: *A queen, an advisor and a jester were in the throne room. Who did the queen silence with a word, the advisor or the jester?*
        Focus-violation Answer*: It was the queen that silenced the jester.*
        Congruent Answer: *It was the jester that the queen silenced.*

They reported two main findings: first, at the focus position in the answer, the focus violation (*queen*) produced a greater negative amplitude than the non-violation. Second, this position in both conditions was markedly more positive than any other word position in the sentence, except for the final word. This second finding is similar to results reported in German by Bornkessel, Friederici and Schlesewsky (2003) and complicates the interpretation of their results: the first finding is highly suggestive of an N400 modulation in which a focus anomaly influences the semantic processing of the word in focus position. However, because the focus position elicits a large late positivity that has been associated with information integration (Bornkessel, Friederici and Schlesewsky 2003), it is possible that the focus anomaly influences the amplitude of this late positivity instead of the N400. Focus would then modulate information integration (as indexed by this late positivity) rather than lexical semantic processing (as indexed by the N400). The results from Cowles et al. did not allow them to distinguish between these possibilities, but taken all together, ERP evidence from written and spoken language suggests that focus status influences processes related to both lexical semantic interpretation and information integration.

Turning back to spoken language, Birch and Clifton (1995) were interested in the interaction of focus pitch accent and scope during processing. They presented participants with short, spoken question-answer dialogues in which pitch accent was manipulated to place focus accent on either the verb or the object of the verb (underlined in the example below). The preceding question then varied in order to place focus on either the object of the verb (12b), or the entire predicate (12a).

(12)   a.   *What did Tina do while her neighbors were away?*
       b.   *What did Tina do with her neighbor's dog?*
       c.   *She walked the dog.*

Thus, the pitch accent would either match or mismatch the scope of the focus of the question. Birch and Clifton found that participants were sensitive to focus pitch accent with respect to the preceding question – participants preferred dialogues in which the pitch accent matched the focus specified by the question. Further, they found that accented NPs can project focus: participants also found dialogues sensible when the object (e.g., *dog*) was given pitch accent following questions like (a) as well as when it followed (b). These results provide experimental evidence in favor of previous observations and proposals about focus assignment and focus spread (Gussenhoven 1983, Selkirk 1984, 1996)

Birch and Clifton (2002) looked at placing pitch accent on adjuncts, as opposed to arguments. Like arguments, new or informative adjuncts should receive focus pitch accent in question-answer pairs, however they should not allow focus to project upwards in the same way that arguments can (see, for instance, also Section 2.7 in the introductory chapter and the chapter on the prosodic investigation of information structure). So, in a sentence pair like (13), placing accent only on *speedily* should be unacceptable. Also, if new information conferred in adjuncts should be given focus pitch accent, then only placing accent on *drove* should also be unacceptable, or at least less acceptable than placing accent on both *drove* and *speedily*.

(13)   *How did Ted get to Minnesota?*
       He drove speedily.

In a series of experiments, they confirmed the well-discussed observation of the linguistics literature that adjuncts cannot project focus, including post-verbal ones like that are seen above as well as postnominal and pro-nominal modifiers.

Bader and Meng (1999) looked at focus revision using different types of structures in canonical and non-canonical word orders in German. While German, like English, has a canonical word order in which the subject precedes the object in a sentence, it also allows the object to precede the subject, although sentences may be temporarily ambiguous between canonical and non-canonical word orders. Bader and Meng used a speeded grammatical judgment task and found that while readers had the most difficulty with non-canonical structures, this effect was strongest when the structure also required a focus revision, suggesting that the processes involved in revising focus are in addition to other revision processes, such as the need to revise structure. Stolterfoht and Bader (2004) also examined focus in German using canonical and non-canonical word orders. In particular, they were interested in whether it is possible to dissociate focus-related processes from syntactic ones using an ERP methodology. They compared sentences that required structural revision or focus revision and found that sentences with non-canonical word orders elicited both an early positivity (around 300ms after the disambiguating word) and a late one (starting around 700ms). The early positivity was not sensitive to presence or absence of a focus participle, but the late positivity was. The authors interpret the early positivity as a correlate of syntactic reanalysis, which is insensitive to focus differences. The later positivity is more difficult to interpret, but the authors argue that regardless of the precise process that the later positivity indexes, their results also show that focus influences can be distinguished from structural ones.

Paterson et al. (2007) used focus incongruence to investigate whether the position of the focus particle *only* in a sentence influences online focus identification, which is relevant both to the timing of focus processing and the extent to which an overt marker like *only* impacts processing. In a series of eye-tracking experiments, they looked at sentences like the following:

(14) Congruent Focus, DO: *At dinner, Jane passed only the salt to her mother but not the pepper as well because she couldn't reach.*

(15) Congruent Focus, IO: *At dinner, Jane passed the salt to only her mother but not her father as well because she couldn't reach.*

(16) Incongruent Focus, DO: *At dinner, Jane passed only the salt to her mother but not her father as well because she couldn't reach.*

(17) Incongruent Focus, IO: *At dinner, Jane passed the salt to only her mother but not the pepper as well because she couldn't reach.*

They found that readers showed difficulty with incongruent versions of the sentence, where there was a mismatch between the argument that the focus particle preceded and the type of argument present in the contrast clause (*but not the X*). In particular, readers took longer overall to read the clause following the contrast clause and spent longer looking back into the earlier part of the sentence. Interestingly, this effect is not seen immediately at the incongruity, suggesting that while focus status plays an important role in online sentence processing, it is not necessarily immediate, but instead may influence integrative processes. Also of note from their results, they conducted an off-line sentence completion task in which participants would read the beginning of the sentences until (and including) the word *not*. They found that while participants supplied an appropriate contrast constituent, this effect was notably weaker when the focus participle occurred early in the sentence. This suggests that there may be a difference in the online interpretation of focus particles (in which they are associated with the immediately adjacent phrase) and off-line interpretation, when grammatical alternatives (such as associating the participle to both phrases) are also considered.

2.3. Interaction of focus with syntactic phenomena

Focus status has also been used in the examination of ambiguous structures, including ellipsis and reduced relative clauses. One key question has been whether focus status is a factor that can guide initial interpretation and provide a means to avoid ambiguity. Another question has been a more general one of whether and how focus interacts with structural processing. We will consider work on two types of syntactic phenomena: ellipsis and reduced relative clauses.

2.3.1. Focus effects on ellipsis

Stolterfoht et al. (2007) used a type of elliptical structure, replacives, which imply contrast (see also Section 2.7 in the introductory chapter), to study implicit prosody (e.g., prosodic effects during silent reading) and focus assignment during online sentence processing in German using ERPs. Implicit prosody has been argued to have an impact on sentence processing (Fodor 1998, 2002), and Stolterfoht et al. were interested in the potential online influence of implicit prosodic information on focus interpretation during silent reading. They used replacive structures with and without focus particles to manipulate focus and implicit prosodic structure independently, and constructed several types of sentences, examples of which are shown in (18) and (19) below. When the sentences included focus particles (shown in parentheses in the examples), they were not ambiguous and did not require revision of either focus structure or implicit prosody. However, when the same sentences did not have a focus particle, then this created a temporary ambiguity that either required a later revision to focus interpretation alone (as in (18)) or to both focus and prosodic interpretations (as in (19)).

(18) Object replacive, focus revision only

   Am Dienstag hat der Direktor   (nur) [den SCHÜler]$_F$
   On Tuesday has the principal$_{NOM}$ (only) the pupil$_{ACC}$
   getadelt,   und nicht [den LEHrer]$_F$
   criticized, and not   the teacher$_{ACC}$
   'On Tuesday, the principal criticized (only) the pupil, and the principal did not criticize the teacher.'

(19) Subject replacive, focus, and prosodic revision

   Am Dienstag hat (nur) [der DiREKtor]$_F$ den Schüler
   On Tuesday has (only) the principal$_{NOM}$ the pupil$_{ACC}$
   getadelt,   und nicht [der LEHrer]$_F$
   criticized, and not   the teacher$_{NOM}$
   'On Tuesday, (only) the principal criticized the pupil, and the teacher did not criticize the pupil.'

Based on previous work on focus interpretation in German (Bader and Meng 1999, Stolterfoht and Bader 2004) they assumed that without a focus particle, the first conjunct has a wide focus interpretation in which the entire phrase (e.g., *On Tuesday, the principal criticized the pupil*) is focused and the nuclear accent is on the object, *the pupil*. When the sentence continues with an object replacive then there is no need to revise the prosodic interpretation (*the pupil* still carries nuclear stress), but it is necessary to revise the focus interpretation to have a narrow focus on *pupil*. When the sentence continues with a subject replacive, then there is both a focus revision required and a prosodic revision. When there is a focus particle, then neither type of revision is necessary. Stolterfoht et al. (2007) found two different types of ERP responses for the focus and prosodic revisions. For focus revision, they found an increased positivity between 350 and 1100ms. The prosodic revision they found in increased negativity with a wide distribution across the scalp between 450 and 650ms. The precise interpretation of these ERP components is still not entirely agreed upon, but the positivity is consistent with other studies that have found increased positivities associated with focus processing (Bornkessel, Friederici and Schlesewsky 2003, Cowles et al. 2007a). Importantly, these results show that focus interpretation is distinct from implicit prosody, despite the fact that focus is often marked by prosodic cues. This provides experimental, processing support for the idea that information structure is not subsumed under structural representation, but is its own independent level of representation (e.g., Lambrecht 1994, and many others).

Carlson et al. (2009) looked at focus influences on interpretation of *wh*-remnants in sentences with another type of ellipsis: sluicing. An example of a sentence with sluicing is given in (20) below:

(20) *The mayor insulted the reporter, but I don't remember who else.*

As in many cases of ambiguous language, there is an ambiguity here that is caused by omitted material. The sluicing construction means that it is not specified whether the speaker doesn't remember who else *the mayor insulted* or who else *insulted the reporter*. Frazier and Clifton (1998) found that there is a bias in comprehenders toward choosing the object as the antecedent of the remnant (*who else*), but that placing pitch accent on the subject (e.g., *mayor*) could cause participants to choose the subject instead. Some linguistic analyses of ellipsis have proposed that the omitted part of the sentence corresponds to given, non-focus information and that the antecedent of the *wh*-remnant corresponds to focused material (e.g., Merchant 2001).

Carlson et al. (2009) provide experimental, processing evidence to support this claim in a series of four experiments. Their results showed that the preference for object interpretation was not affected by whether the object was at the end of a clause, nor by the amount of intervening material between the object and the *wh*-remnant, suggesting that the preference for object antecedents cannot be reduced to recency or the distance from the *wh*-remnant (i.e., the *wh*-remnant is not simply being interpreted with the referent of the closest noun). Further, placing contrastive pitch accents on either subject, object or both replicated Frazier and Clifton's (1998) results, and also extended them to establish that participants noted when pitch accent occurred on both subject and object, such that they continued to show a preference for object interpretation, but it was much weaker when the subject was also accented. When there was an *it*-cleft in the clause preceding the sluice, participants preferred the referent of the clefted noun as the antecedent of the *wh*-remnant. Their data also provide other insights into the interpretation of focus: first, they found remarkably similar results for both acoustically-marked contrastive focus and syntactically-marked contrastive focus, suggesting that focus status is indeed distinct from any particular formal instantiation of it. Most interestingly, the results from their final, fourth experiment suggest that focus status may be assigned preferentially as low as possible in the verb phrase: when they presented participants with pre-sluice clauses that contained an object and indirect object, as in (21), they found that people preferred the indirect object as the antecedent of the *wh*-remnant, such that people interpreted the elided material as *what occasion Lucy bought the present for.*

(21)   *Lucy bought some present for some occasion, but I don't know what.*

If it is indeed the case that the remnant preferentially links to the focus of the preceding clause, as their other experiments suggest, then it would appear that the final indirect objects in this case are given focus status. Further work is needed to compare both orders of DO and IO to see whether position is truly the cause of the preference or whether there is something about the grammatical status of IO itself that attracts focus.

2.3.2. Reduced relative clauses

Another ambiguous structure that has been intensively examined is the reduced relative clause. Of particular interest is how this ambiguity is resolved – when the correct interpretation is reached, and what information drives this process. A full account of the debate over this process is outside the scope of this chapter, but focus has been considered as one possible factor, with several studies examining what influence focus status might have on the interpretation of reduced relative clauses.

First, it is important to see whether focus can influence ambiguous interpretation of this type at all. Schafer et al. (2000) looked at whether focus pitch accent would influence the interpretation of sentences that were otherwise ambiguous between an embedded question and relative clause interpretation, such as *I asked the pretty little girl who's cold.* They controlled prosodic boundaries and the length of the ambiguous clauses and then either placed pitch accent on *who's* or *cold.* Participants listened to the sentences and then were asked to press a button as soon as they understood the sentence and supply a verbal paraphrase on the sentence in response to a written prompt, *What happened?* Schafer et al. found that placing focus pitch accent on the *who* lead to significantly more embedded question interpretations than when pitch accent was placed on *cold.* There was no difference in how quickly participants decided they understood the question. These results are important because they show that focus status (via pitch accent) can influence the interpretation of otherwise structurally ambiguous sentences.

With respect to whether focus can guide interpretation during the processing of temporarily ambiguous sentences, Ni, Crain and Shankweiler (1996) examined whether the use of the focus particle *only* could allow readers to avoid initial misinterpretations of reduced relative clause sentences. For example, in (22) below, the lack of an overt *that* between *businessmen* and *loaned* means that the initial part of the sentence could easily (and preferentially) be parsed such that *loaned* is the main verb rather than the beginning of a relative clause. It is only at the disambiguating point, the actual main verb, *were,* that it becomes clear that this is not the correct structure for the sentence, and many studies have found that comprehenders experience difficulty at this point – this is often referred to as a garden path effect (Frazier 1987).

(22) *The businessmen loaned money at low interest were told to record their expenses.*

Ni et al. (1996) compared sentences like (22) with sentences like (23), in which the focus particle *only* replaced the definite determiner.

(23) *Only businessmen loaned money at low interest were told to record their expenses.*

Their hypothesis was that because *only* presupposes that the following focus is being considered against a set of implicit alternatives, readers encountering (23) would be more likely to avoid the misinterpretation of *loaned* as the main verb because it would be referentially more appropriate to follow the focus with an identifying phrase to distinguish which businessmen are being referred to (businessmen who were loaned money versus those who were not). Thus, Ni et al. predicted that while (22) would show a garden path effect, (23) would not. This is precisely what they found, while there were increases in reading times in a self-paced reading task at *were* in sentences like (22) compared to an unambiguous control, sentences like (23) did not show this garden path effect. Further, in an additional eye-tracking study, a measure of early, initial processing – first-pass reading time – showed the same pattern, suggesting that it is not simply the case that *only* allowed readers to rapidly reanalyze the sentence after an initial misinterpretation. Thus, from these data it appears that focus information may prevent readers from initially misanalyzing reduced relative clauses. Crucially, this also means that focus information may be rapidly calculated during on-line processing, at least when a focus particle is used.

However, these results have proved problematic. While Sedivy (2002) replicated Ni et al.'s findings, Clifton, Bock and Rado (2000) failed to do so. Clifton, Bock and Rado (2000) also looked at the influence of *only* comparing low-contrast and high-contrast nouns; nouns like *actress* and *conservative* have clear conceptual contrasts (actor and liberal), and so may more easily meet the contrast set requirements of *only* as compared with nouns that do not have this built-in contrast. Their eye-tracking results show that sentences with *only* combined with a high contrast noun did not show initial disruption in first-pass reading times, but did show disruptions in measures of later processing. They argue that the influence of *only* is to help with the reinterpretation necessary to recover from an initial misinterpretation, but not guide the initial processing of the reduced relative clause.

Interestingly, it may be that the influence of focus on initial relative processing interacts with the type of the relative clause. Paterson, Liversedge and Underwood (1999) looked at what they term 'short' relative clauses in which the first verb is followed by a noun phrase (e.g., *The men passed the salt smiled.*) and found that focus particles influenced later reanalysis processes, but did not affect initial parsing. Liversedge, Paterson and Clayes (2002) looked at 'long' relative clauses in which the first verb is followed by a prepositional phrase instead of a noun phrase, such as *The/Only motorists stopped in the car park received a warning about their outdated permits.* In this case, their eye-tracking results show no evidence of a garden path effect in early measures of processing (first pass and first pass regression), and participants also spent less time re-reading reduced relative clause sentences overall when they contained *only*. Both papers account for the influence of *only* based on preferences for structural interpretation: in 'short' relative clauses, there is a strong preference to interpret the noun following the verb as a direct object and the presence of *only* cannot influence this strong preference. However, when the noun is embedded in a prepositional phrase then the direct object analysis is not available and so then it is possible for a focus particle like *only* to guide interpretation in the absence of a strong preference. This account is further supported by results from Filik, Paterson and Liversedge (2005), who examined whether the addition of a biasing context could eliminate the garden path effect in short relative clauses using *only*. To do this, they used an eye-tracking methodology to compare the use of *only* with short reduced and unreduced relative clauses following a context sentence that contained a discourse-linked or non-discourse-linked *wh*-question. For example,

(24)   *Tom wondered [who/which builders] fitted a kitchen.*

(25)   *Only builders (who where) paid a deposit fitted a kitchen within the week.*

They argue that the discourse-linked *which* contexts should cause readers to anticipate modifying information after *builder* to specify *which builder*. However, while the discourse-linked contexts did speed reading times, they did not influence initial processing times at the disambiguating verb. In a second experiment, they compared the same types of context with long relative clauses and found evidence that in this case context did mitigate the garden path effect and that in the discourse-linked context influenced parsing toward a relative clause rather than a main clause.

Taken together, these results suggest that focus particles like *only* can have an impact on initial sentence processing and may play a role in guiding syntactic processing. However, as with sentence production, other factors may mitigate this influence, such as a stronger preference toward interpreting a post-verbal noun phrase as a direct object.

3. Studies of information structure in anaphora and (co)reference

Another area in which the effect of information structure on processing has been studied is coreference, and pronoun resolution in particular. When comprehenders encounter a coreferring expression, they need to correctly match it to an antecedent referent (see Garnham 2001 for an overview). This is not necessarily a trivial process, particularly for pronouns, because it can be the case that there is no syntactic, morphological or semantic information available at the point of the pronoun that allows one antecedent referent to be definitively chosen. Previous work has shown that there are a number of factors implicated in the pronoun resolution process, including thematic-role parallelism (e.g., Stevenson, Nelson and Stenning 1995), syntactic constraints like binding theory (e.g., Badecker and Straub 2002, Sturt 2003), coherence relations (e.g., Kehler 2002; Kertz, Kehler and Elman 2006) and implicit causality (e.g., Garnham et al. 1996). The relative accessibility of possible antecedents is another key factor that is commonly proposed in approaches to reference form and pronoun resolution, with high accessibility leading to increased likelihood of pronoun antecedent status (Ariel 1988; Ariel 1990; Gundel, Hedberg and Zacharski 1993) Other work has also proposed that different types of coreferring expressions may be sensitive to different cues and that this sensitivity may vary cross-linguistically (e.g., Kaiser and Trueswell 2008). Thus, as with sentence production and comprehension, there are a number of competing factors at work in coreference processing.

There have been a large number of studies looking at the role of discourse prominence on the selection of antecedents for both pronominal and reflexive coreferring expressions. One way to view such accessibility is that within the mental model of the discourse that is constructed during comprehension (e.g., Johnson-Laird 1983), certain entities in the model are more prominent, more at the center of attention or more salient than others. In general, the consistent finding is that higher accessibility of a referent leads to an increased likelihood of it being interpreted as the antecedent of a pronoun (Arnold et al. 2000) as well as a coreferring expression referring to a prominent/accessible antecedent referent being most easily processed when it is pronominal (Gordon, Grosz and Gilliom 1993). This appears to be true both for linguistic and non-linguistic context and introduces the idea that the main way in which information structure may have an influence is by changing the accessibility of referents. While many studies have used subject position as a means to make a potential antecedent prominent or accessible, there are relatively few studies that have tried to address the influence of topic (or focus) status on coreference processing directly.

Arnold (1998) did so by comparing the influence of topic and focus on ambiguous pronoun resolution. In this study, participants rated the naturalness of three-sentence paragraphs in which the second sentence crucially varied the way in which the antecedent was encoded. She found that when a cleft construction was used to focus the antecedent, the paragraphs were rated more natural when the focused element was subsequently referred to by a pronoun compared to a name. Paragraphs were also rated higher when non-focus elements were referred to by a name rather than by a pronoun. When a simple declarative was used instead of a cleft construction in the second sentence, the rating was higher when the topic (i.e., the grammatical subject of the second sentence) was referred to by a pronoun rather than by a name, and also when the non-topic was referred to by a name rather than by a pronoun. Arnold concludes that topic and focus serve the similar function of making their referents cognitively prominent.

Cowles, Kluender and Walenski (2007b) found similar results in an online test of the same question. They used a cross-modal lexical priming task in which participants listened to three-sentence passages and then needed to say aloud a name that appeared on a computer screen during the passage. The passages were of three kinds, one in which there was a discourse topic (a name given in subject position for two consecutive sentences), one with a sentence topic (an initial scene-setting sentence followed by a name given in subject position in the second sentence) and one with a contrastive focus (an initial scene-setting sentence followed by a name given in an *it*-cleft). There were two versions of each of these passages, one in which the target name (topic/focus) was the first-mentioned person in the sentence and one in which it was the second-mentioned person. The final sentence contained a pronoun whose antecedent referent was ambiguous between the previously mentioned target (topic/focus) and another name. The visual probe named either of these two potential antecedents and appeared on the screen at the offset of a pronoun in the final sentence. Cowles et al. found that participants named the probe faster when it referred to a topic or focus referent compared to a non-topic/focus, and that the order of mention didn't have an effect – topic/focus status was more important than whether the name was mentioned first or second. Further, this initial online bias was also matched in an off-line task that measured which referent is ultimately preferred as the actual antecedent for the pronoun. These results suggest that topic and contrastive focus have a similar influence on pronoun antecedent selection, which the authors suggest is due to the fact that both information statuses require that the referent is already part of the model of the discourse at the time it is referred to. This requirement may cause increased accessibility of the referents within a mental model of the discourse.

Looking at other forms of coreference, Almor (1999) found that coreference to a contrastive focus referent (encoded by *it*- and *wh*-clefts) with a repeated name is less natural than when the referent is not the contrastive focus, supporting the idea that contrastive focus causes a preference for a less-specific reference. In the same study, Almor also found that placing an antecedent in a clefted position caused an inverse typicality effect in which participants took longer to read a coreferring category noun phrase like *the bird* when it referred unambiguously to *robin* than when it referred to *penguin*. This somewhat counterintuitive pattern was also found when the antecedent was the subject of an active sentence compared to when it was the object of a passive *by*-phrase (Cowles and Garnham 2005). Thus, again, it appears that both clefts and grammatical subject play similar roles during coreference processing, regardless of the type of coreferring expression.

Turning for a moment to production, there has been some work looking at the production of pronouns, particularly with respect to the lexicalization process – how to get from a concept to the production of the corresponding word (Jescheniak, Schriefers and Hantsch 2001) as well as feature agreement (Bock, Eberhard and Cutting 2004). Work looking at the influence of focus status on written production (Birch, Albrecht and Myers 2000) found that focus status increased the likelihood that participants would make at least one reference to the focused noun in a discourse continuation task in which participants read short passages and then write a logical continuations of them. Further, the form of this coreference was more likely to be pronominal. Work looking at the influence of topic status on the written production of coreference found a similar effect for topic: higher percentages of pronominal coreference were made to post-verbal antecedents when they occurred in *about*-phrases compared to when they did not (Cowles 2007). The use of post-verbal *about*-phrases in this study allows us to decouple topic status from subject position, and suggests that topic status may have an effect on the production of pronouns independently of subjecthood. However, it does not rule out that topic status (as with contrastive focus) influences coreferential form principally by influencing the accessibility of the referent in the mental model of a discourse.

In the end, it appears that while topic status is often associated with attenuated forms of reference, like pronouns, it appears that subsequent reference to both topic and (contrastive) focus antecedents is also linked to pronominal forms. It may be the case that both topic and contrastive focus serve to make their referents more accessible and are thus better referents for pronominal reference.

4. Conclusions

All of the results in this chapter highlight the importance of information structure on sentence processing, and taken together show that both specific formal (syntactic, prosodic) encoding and certain types of prior context (e.g., *wh*-questions) that influence information status can have an important influence during processing, either directly or by changing the accessibility of corresponding referents. Topic status appears to have an impact on both the grammatical encoding of a sentence and the reference forms that are chosen. In comprehension, different types of focus have been studied in many contexts, and the overall picture is that focus status appears to have both immediate and long lasting effects on sentence comprehension. Focus, particularly when encoded using clefts, appears to increase the accessibility of referents in memory and, when marking focus using particles like *only*, also aids in guiding structure building and interpretation processes in ambiguous sentences. However, focus does not need to be encoded using clefts or focus particles to have an impact: several studies have found focus effects in *wh*-question-answer pairs, with focus anomalies interacting with both lexical processing and larger integration processing. Further, wide vs. narrow scope appears to be calculated and used during online processing. Thus, focus status appears to play an important role in comprehension, both when it is overtly marked with particular syntactic or prosodic cues, but also when prior context provides indications of how to assign focus.

There is still an outstanding issue concerning the relationship of topic and focus status (and especially contrastiveness) to the accessibility of referents in a discourse model. All of these types of status appear to increase the accessibility of referents, yet each serves different informational functions and so more work is needed to develop a clearer idea of how these statuses truly influence accessibility.

It is worth noting that these results indicate that there are practical implications for work on the processing of information structure related to how easy or difficult it is to process information in a text. While many modern word processing programs possess grammar checking functions that, for example, advise against the use of passive constructions under any circumstances, research from processing studies of information structure show that using non-canonical structures like passives or clefts can serve an important function in providing cues about which information an utterance is about and which information is previously unknown. In principal, an understanding of how information structure influences processing can provide a basis for writing clearer texts, in which the form in which information is conveyed matches expectations about what should be topic or focus.

References

Almor, Amit
1999   Noun-phrase anaphora and focus: The informational load hypothesis. *Psychological Review* 106: 748–765.
Ariel, Mira
1988   Referring and accessibility. *Journal of Linguistics* 24: 65–87.
Arnold, Jennifer E.
1998   Reference form and discourse patterns. Ph.D. dissertation, Stanford University.
Arnold, Jennifer E., Janet G. Eisenband, Sarah Brown-Schmidt and John C. Trueswell
2000   The rapid use of gender information: evidence of the time course of pronoun resolution from eyetracking. *Cognition* 76: B13–B26.
Badecker, William and Kathleen Straub
2002   The processing role of structural constraints on the interpretation of pronouns and anaphors. *Journal of Experimental Psychology: Learning, Memory, and Cognition* 28: 748–769.
Bader, Markus and Michael Meng
1999   Subject-object ambiguities in German embedded clauses: An across-the-board comparison. *Journal of Psycholinguistic Research* 28: 121–143.
Bates, Elizabeth and Antonella Devescovi
1989   *Competition and Sentence Production. Cross-linguistic Studies of Sentence Processing.* Cambridge: Cambridge University Press.
Birch, Stacy, Jason E. Albrecht and Jerome L. Myers
2000   Syntactic focusing structures influence discourse processing. *Discourse Processes* 30: 285–304.
Birch, Stacy and Charles Clifton
1995   Focus, accent, and argument structure: Effects on language comprehension. *Language and Speech* 38: 365–391.
Birch, Stacy and Keith Rayner
1997   Linguistic focus affects eye movements during reading. *Memory and Cognition* 25: 653–660.
Bock, Kathryn J. and David E. Irwin
1980   Syntactic effects of information availability in sentence production. *Journal of Verbal Learning and Verbal Behavior* 19: 467–484.
Bock, Kathryn J., Kathleen M. Eberhard and J. Cooper Cutting
2004   Producing number agreement: how pronouns equal verbs. *Journal of Memory and Language* 51: 251–278.
Bornkessel, Ina, Angela Friederici and Matthias Schlesewsky
2003   Contextual information modulated initial processes of syntactic integration: the role of inter- versus intrasentential predictions. *Journal of Experimental Psychology: Learning, Memory and Cognition* 29: 871–882.

Bredart, Serge and Karin Modolo
  1988   Moses strikes again: Focalization effect on a semantic illusion. *Acta
            Psychologica* 67: 135–144.
Carlson, Katy, Michael Walsh Dickey, Lyn Frazier and Charles Clifton
  2009   Information structure expectations in sentence comprehension.
            Quarterly Journal of Experimental Psychology 62: 114–139.
Carpenter, Patricia A. and Marcel A Just (eds.)
  1977   *Reading Comprehension as Eyes see it. Moses strikes again. Cognitive
            Processes in Comprehension.* Hillsdale, NJ: Erlbaum.
Clifton, Charles Jr., Jeannine Bock and Janina Rado
  2000   Effects of the focus particle *only* and intrinsic contrast on the com-
            prehension of reduced relative clauses. In *Reading as a Perceptual
            Process*, Alan Kennedy, Ralph Radach, Dieter Heller and Joël Pynte
            (eds.), 591–619. Amsterdam: North-Holland.
Cowles, H. Wind
  2003   Processing information structure: Evidence from comprehension and
            production. Ph.D. dissertation, University of California, San Diego.
Cowles, H. Wind
  2007   The influence of "aboutness" on pronominal coreference. *Zentrum
            für Allgemeine Sprachwissenschaft, Working Papers in Linguistics* 48:
            23–38.
Cowles, H. Wind and Victor Ferreira
  2012   The influence of information structure on sentence production.
            Discourse Processes 49: 1–28.
Cowles, H. Wind and Alan Garnham
  2005   Antecedent focus and conceptual distance effects in category noun-
            phrase anaphora. *Language and Cognitive Processes* 20: 725–750.
Cowles, H. Wind, Robert Kluender, Marta Kutas and Maria Polinsky
  2007   Violations of information structure: An electrophysiological study of
            answers to wh-questions. *Brain and Language* 102: 228–242.
Cowles, H. Wind, Matthew Walenski and Robert Kluender
  2007   Linguistic and cognitive prominence in anaphor resolution: topic,
            contrastive focus and pronouns. *Topoi* 26: 3–18.
Cutler, Anne and Jerry Fodor
  1979   Semantic focus and sentence comprehension. *Cognition* 7: 49–59.
d'Arcais, Flores G. B.
  1975   *Some Perceptual Determinants of Sentence Construction. Studies in
            Perception.* Milan: Martello.
É. Kiss, Katalin
  1998   Identificational focus versus information focus. *Language* 74: 245–273.
Ferreira, Fernanda
  2007   Prosody and performance in language production. *Language and
            Cognitive Processes* 22: 1151–1177.

Filik, Ruth, Kevin B. Paterson and Simon Liversedge
    2005   Parsing with focus particles in context: Eye movements during the processing of relative clause ambiguities. *Journal of Memory and Language* 53: 473–495.
Fodor, Janet Dean
    1998   Learning to parse? *Journal of Psycholinguistic Research* 27: 285–319.
Fodor, Janet Dean
    2002   Prosodic disambiguation in silent reading. *Proceedings of the 32nd Annual Meeting of the North East Linguistic Society 32*. Amherst: GSLA.
Foraker, Stephani and Brian McElree
    2007   The role of prominence in pronoun resolution: Active versus passive representations. *Journal of Memory and Language* 56: 357–383.
Frazier, Lyn
    1987   Sentence processing: A tutorial review. In *Attention and Performance XII: The Psychology of Reading.*, M. Coltheart (ed.), 559–586. Hove, UK: Lawrence Erlbaum.
Frazier, Lyn and Charles Clifton, Jr.
    1998   Comprehension of sluiced sentences. *Language and Cognitive Processes* 13: 499–520.
Garnham, Alan, Matthew Traxler, Jane Oakhill and Morton Ann Gernsbacher
    1996   The locus of implicit causality effects in comprehension. *Journal of Memory and Language* 35: 517–543.
Garnham, Alan
    2001   *Mental Models and the Interpretation of Anaphora* Hove, UK: Psychology Press.
Gernsbacher, Morton, David Hargreaves and Mark Beeman
    1989   Building and accessing clausal representations: The advantage of first mention versus the advantage of clause recency. *Journal of Memory and Language* 28: 735–755.
Gernsbacher, Morton Ann
    1990   *Language Comprehension as Structure Building.* Hillsdale, NJ: Erlbaum.
Gordon, Peter C., Barbara J. Grosz and Laura A. Gilliom
    1993   Pronouns, names, and the centering of attention in discourse. *Cognitive Science* 17: 311–348.
Gundel, Jeanette K.
    1974   The role of topic and comment in linguistic theory. Ph.D. dissertation, University of Texas.
Gundel, Jeanette K., Nancy Hedberg and Ron Zacharski
    1993   Cognitive status and the form of referring expressions in discourse. *Language* 69: 274–307.

Gundel, Jeanette K. and Thorstein Fretheim
    2004   Topic and focus. In *The Handbook of Contemporary Pragmatic Theory*, Laurence Horn and Gregory Ward (eds.), 175–196. Oxford, UK: Blackwell.

Gussenhoven, Carlos
    1983   Focus, mode, and the nucleus. *Journal of Linguistics* 19: 377–417.

Hedberg, Nancy and Juan Sosa
    2007   The prosody of topic and focus in spontaneous English dialogue. In *Topic and Focus: Cross-Linguistic Perspectives on Meaning and Intonation*, Chungmin Lee, Matthew Gordon and Daniel Büring (eds.), 101–120. Dordrecht: Springer.

Hörnig, Robin, Thomas Weskott, Reinhold Kliegl and Gisbert Fanselow
    2006   Word order variation in spatial descriptions with adverbs. *Memory and Cognition* 34: 1183–1192.

Hruska, Claudia, Kai Alter, Karsten Steinhauer and Anita Steube
    2000   Can wrong prosodic information be mistaken by the brain? *Journal of Cognitive Neuroscience* (Supplement 122). E82.

Jescheniak, Jorg, Herbert Schriefers and Ansgar Hantsch
    2001   Semantic and phonological activation in noun and pronoun production. *Journal of Experimental Psychology: Learning, Memory and Cognition* 27: 1058–1078.

Johnson, Shaun, Charles Clifton, Mara Breen, A. Martin and Joanna Morris
    2003   ERP investigation of prosodic and semantic focus. Paper presented at the Annual Meeting of the Cognitive Neuroscience Society, New York.

Johnson-Laird, Philip N.
    1983   *Mental Models.* Cambridge, UK: Cambridge University Press.

Kaiser, Elsi and John C. Trueswell
    2008   Interpreting pronouns and demonstratives in Finnish: Evidence for a form-specific approach to reference resolution. *Language and Cognitive Processes* 23: 709–748.

Kehler, Andy
    2002   *Coherence, Reference and the Theory of Grammar.* Stanford, CA: Center for the Study of Language and Information Publications.

Kertz, Laura, Andrew Kehler and Jeffrey Elman
    2006   Grammatical and coherence based factors in pronoun interpretation. *Proceedings of the 28th Annual Conference of the Cognitive Science Society*, Vancouver, Canada.

Kutas, Marta, Cyma van Petten and Robert Kluender
    2006   Psycholinguistics electrified II (1994–2005). In *Handbook of Psycholinguistics*, Morton Ann Gernsbacher and Matthew Traxler (eds.), 659–724. New York: Elsevier.

Lambrecht, Knud
    1994   *Information Structure and Sentence Form. Topic, Focus, and the Mental Representation of Discourse Referents.* Cambridge: Cambridge University Press.
Liversedge, Simon P., Kevin B. Paterson and Emma L. Clayes
    2002   The influence of *only* on syntactic processig of "long" relative clause sentences. *The Quarterly Journal of Experimental Psychology* 55: 225–240.
Magne, Cyrille, Corine Astesano, Anne Lacheret-Dujour, Michel Morel, Kai Alter and Mireille Beckman
    2005   On-line processing of "pop-out" words in spoken French dialogues. *Journal of Cognitive Neuroscience* 17: 740–756.
Merchant, Jason
    2001   *The Syntax of Silence: Sluicing, Islands, and Identity in Ellipsis* Oxford, UK: Oxford University Press.
Ni, Weija, Stephen Crain and Donald Shankweiler
    1996   Sidestepping garden paths: assessing the contributions of syntax, semantics and plausibility in resolving ambiguities. *Language and Coginitive Processes* 11: 283–334.
Paterson, Kevin B., Simon Liversedge and Geoffrey Underwood
    1999   The influence of focus operators on syntactic processing of short relative clasuses. *The Quarterly Journal of Experimental Psychology* 52A: 717–737.
Paterson, Kevin B., Simon P. Liversedge, Ruth Filik, Barbara J. Juhasz, Sarah J. White and Keith Rayner
    2007   Focus identification during sentence comprehension: Evidence from eye movements. *The Quarterly Journal of Experimental Psychology* 60: 1423–1445.
Pierrehumbert, Janet and Julia Hirschberg
    1990   The meaning of intonational contours in the interpretation of discourse. In *Intentions in Communication*, Philip R. Cohen, Jerry L. Morgan and Martha E. Pollack (eds.), 271–311. Cambridge, MA: Massachusetts Institute of Technology Press.
Prat-Sala, Mercé and Holy P. Branigan
    2000   Discourse constraints on syntactic processing in language production: A cross-linguistic study in English and Spanish. *Journal of Memory and Language* 42: 168–182.
Prentice, John L.
    1967   Effects of cueing actor vs. cueing object on word order in sentence production. *Psychonomic Science* 8: 163–164.
Schafer, Amy J., Katy Carlson, Charles Clifton and Lyn Frazier
    2000   Focus and the interpretation of pitch accents: Disambiguating embedded questions. *Language and Speech* 43: 75–105.

Sedivy, Julie
  2002   Invoking discourse-based contrast sets and resolving syntactic ambi-
            guities. *Journal of Memory and Language* 46: 341–370.
Selkirk, Elisabeth O.
  1984   *Phonology and Syntax: The Relation between Sound and Structure.*
            Cambridge, Massachusetts: Massachusetts Institute of Technology
            Press.
Selkirk, Elisabeth O.
  1995   Sentence prosody: Intonation, stress and phrasing. In *Handbook of
            Phonological Theory*, John Goldsmith (ed.), 550–569. Cambridge,
            MA: Blackwell.
Shaher, Rukshin, Pavel Logacev, Felix Engelmann, Shravan Vasishth and Narayanan
Srinivasan
  2008   Clefting, topicalization and the given-new preference: Eyetracking
            evidence from Hindi. Paper presented to the Architectures and
            Mechanisms of Language Processing, Cambridge, U.K.
Stevenson, Rosemary J., Alexander W. R. Nelson and Keith Stenning
  1995   The role of parallelism in strategies of pronoun comprehension.
            Language and Speech 38: 393–418.
Stolterfoht, Britta and Markus Bader
  2004   Focus structure and the processing of word order variations in German.
            In *Information Structure: Theoretical and Empirical Aspects*, Anita
            Steube (ed.), 259–275. Berlin/New York: Mouton de Gruyter.
Stolterfoht, Britta, Angela Friederici, Kai Alter and Anita Steube
  2007   Processing focus structure and implicit prosodyduring reading: dif-
            ferential ERP effects. *Cognition* 104: 565–90.
Sturt, Patrick, Anthony J. Sanford, Andrew Stewart and Eugene J. Dawydiak
  2004   Linguistic focus and good-enough representations: an application of
            the change-detection paradigm. *Psychonomic Bulletin and Review*
            11: 882–88.
Turner, Elisabeth and Ragnar Rommetveit
  1968   Focus of attention in recall of active and passive sentences. *Journal
            of Verbal Learning and Verbal Behavior* 7: 543–548.

The acquisition of information structure

Christine Dimroth and Bhuvana Narasimhan

1. Introduction

The linguistic expression of information structure, i.e., the formal reflexes of an utterance's co(n)text integration, have recently gotten quite some attention in the study of first as well as second language acquisition. The primary dimensions of information structure that are often addressed in the acquisition literature include givenness (maintained vs. new information), aboutness (topic vs. comment) as well as emphasis and highlighting (e.g., contrastive topic, focus). Core questions that have been addressed in this area involve the following:

1. Do first and second language learners adapt their utterances to their hearer's informational needs from early on?
2. When do language learners home in on language-specific preferences for information selection and distribution in longer stretches of discourse? Can adult L2 learners ever become native-like in this respect?
3. Do language learners express the same kinds of information structure relations as adult native speakers (e.g., topic, comment, given, new, focus, contrast) using the same devices (e.g., word order, referential devices, intonation, particles)?

Child and adult learners begin to use linguistic devices such as pronouns, word order, prosody, particles, ellipses, and so on at a relatively early stage of acquisition. However, the use of these elements for marking information structure, e.g., for the expression of discourse integration or their interpretation does not always correspond to their use in the target language, i.e., the language spoken in the learners' social environment.

Most studies have either considered first or second language acquisition separately. Direct comparisons are the exception, but the general assumption is that the two types of acquisition follow a different logic and, in particular, are typically characterized by different outcomes:

> Children usually seem to reach the target, whereas adults are observed as not reaching the target, whereby the question might be raised of how to determine what the target is. (…) adults are generally assumed to start

from a disadvantageous position, as compared to children. It seems obvious, however, that children may also start with some disadvantages in comparison with adults. They must go through their whole cognitive development, which to some extent will take place simultaneously and in interaction with their linguistic development. (...) Apart from simply acquiring the language, children have to construe an understanding of space, time, relationships between speech partners, and speech situations in general. (Hendriks 2000: 369–370)

In what follows we will summarize findings concerning the role of information structure in first language acquisition (Section 2) and second language acquisition (Section 3) and thereby take the earliest manifestations of information structure marking as our starting point (Sections 2.1 and 3.1). The following sections (Sections 2.2 and 3.2) deal with the development of language-specific devices for the expression of information structure and consider those formal devices that have gotten the most attention in the acquisition literature, namely the form of referring expressions, word order, and information distribution in discourse. Sections 2.3 and 3.3 discuss the role of information structure at different stages in first and second language acquisition. Section 4 presents an overall summary and conclusions.

2. Information structure in first language acquisition

In acquiring a first language, children face the formidable task of learning the lexical and grammatical forms in the ambient language and homing in on the range of semantic and pragmatic distinctions that these forms encode. The remarkable rapidity and ease with which very young children acquire language suggest that they have powerful abilities to detect patterns in the input (Tomasello 2003) in ways that some linguists suggest are innately constrained (Pinker 1989). At the same time, children also bring to the task of language-learning communicative and cognitive abilities that are still in the process of development (Bates 1976). The issue of which factors are influential when, and how they interact, remains deeply mysterious even after several decades of research.

In exploring how children acquire information structure, we are entering territory that is the least understood in the field of language acquisition. Information structure involves notions such as 'topic' and 'comment', 'given' and 'new' information that have to do with how referents are represented in mental models of the situational/discourse context. The 'given-new' distinction has to do with accessibility (see also Cowles, this volume): how available a referent is in the minds of speakers and hearers in a particular communicative context. Several factors influence accessibility, including prior mention of referents in the discourse, as well as their prototypicality (Kelly, Bock and Keil 1986) and imageability (Bock and Warren 1985), among others. The term 'topic' refers to what the utterance is about, whereas the term 'comment' refers to what is said about the topic (Hockett 1958, Firbas 1964, Daneš 1970, Sgall et al. 1986). Although the topic is typically accessible to the speaker and hearer and the comment is often inaccessible and 'new', in principle, the two distinctions are orthogonal (Ertel 1977, MacWhinney and Price 1980, von Stutterheim and Klein 2002).

The acquisition of these basic dimensions of information structure present daunting challenges to the learner of a first language. First, these notions involve particular construals of a given situation that are signalled, and sometimes created, primarily through language, and are therefore (by definition) subject to contextual variability. For instance, the topicality and givenness of the same referent can fluctuate within the same communicative context, often with no perceptual correlates of these changes. Second, the correlation between the pragmatic notions and their linguistic expression is probabilistic. For instance, adults tend to treat the subjects or first-mentioned noun phrases in preceding utterances as prominent for the purposes of computing pronominal reference (Song and Fisher 2005). However, Arnold (1998) found that only 64% of subject pronouns in a sample of children's storybooks referred back to the subject of the preceding clause. So while children may frequently encounter associations between forms and functions that are informative about the relevant distinctions in the adult language, such associations are not invariant. One implication is that children may require a good deal of exposure to patterns of use in the input language before they can acquire adult-like conventions, although other researchers have argued otherwise (Song and Fisher 2005).

Further, the acquisition of information structure involves an additional dimension, viz. the development of children's sensitivity to the informational needs of the listener. Prior research suggests that children's capacity to read the intentions of their communicative partners develops remarkably early and, along with a motivation to share psychological states with others, may well be instrumental in their ability to acquire language (Tomasello et al. 2005). Yet there is evidence that this understanding does not automatically lead to adult-like use of the appropriate linguistic forms, such as pronouns, that require the ability to infer the knowledge states of the listener (Campbell, Brooks and Tomasello 2000). So how does children's developing linguistic knowledge interact with their emerging social cognitive abilities?

In the following sections, we will explore the developmental trajectory in the acquisition of information structure in children, focusing on two key themes: (a) the acquisition of linguistic devices that signal information structure distinctions at the utterance and discourse-level (e.g., word order, referential forms, discourse organization), and (b) children's developing socio-cognitive and communicative abilities that influence their use of specific linguistic conventions.

2.1. Early precursors to the development of information structure

When do children begin to adapt their communicative expressions according to the context and the informational needs of their listeners? There is no easy answer to this question since it depends on how we construe the terms "communicative expression", "needs of the listener", and "adapt". Since we are concerned in this survey with how *linguistic* devices are used to convey information structure distinctions, we may consider beginning our exploration at the stage when children first begin to produce one-word utterances, roughly around 12 months of age. Yet the socio-cognitive and communicative capabilities that children exhibit at the stage of one-word utterances start have their roots much earlier, in the early stages of infancy.

There is considerable behavioral evidence that very early social interactions involve a high degree of mutual responsiveness between caregiver and child. Infants only a few months old exhibit turn-taking behavior, in the sense of acting when the adult is passive, and being passive when the adult is acting (Trevarthen 1979). They also engage in proto-conversations, involving an exchange of emotions and bouts of mutual gazing (Stern 1985). By the age of 12 months, infants are also already aware that others may or may not visually perceive objects. Brooks and Meltzoff (2002) found that infants at this age turned significantly more often to an object when an adult had turned toward it with eyes open than with eyes closed.

Further, infants between the ages of 9–18 months are able to infer that adults' actions are goal-directed. When an adult tried to give them a toy across a table, but was unable to do so (e.g., could not extract it from a container), infants show less signs of impatience than when the adult was able but unwilling to give the toy over (Behne, Carpenter and Tomasello 2006). At around the same time, children are also engaging in triadic activities involving the child, an adult, and some outside entity, and by 12–15 months, children not only share goals but coordinate roles, e.g., placing blocks on a tower while the adult holds it steady, with the shared goal of building a block tower (Tomasello et al. 2005). These studies show a high level of awareness of the mental states of others as well as the motivation to collaborate in joint activities with shared goals and action plans, all of which abilities also underlie the appropriate co-construction of meaning during language use in various communicative situations.

The use of pointing as a referential device is an important milestone in children's communicative abilities. Recent research shows that children as young as 12 months of age use pointing gestures to inform another person of the location of an object that the person is searching for. So children on the cusp of producing words can already conceive of others as intentional agents with informational states, and have the motivation to provide such information to their interlocutors (Liszkowski et al. 2006). In a related study, O'Neill (1996) invited 2-year-old children to find hidden objects that they then had to obtain with the help of their mothers. In one condition, the mothers witnessed the hiding event whereas in another condition, they did not (because they were out of the room or covered their eyes). Children, especially the older 2-year-olds, provided more information verbally and with pointing gestures when the mothers had not witnessed the hiding event than when they had. This study suggests that children can make inferences about the knowledge state of their interlocutors based on their physical co-presence and/or their level of perceptual access to a given situation.

While the findings from individual studies can be debated, when taken together they provide evidence that well before children begin to use language in any productive way, they already possess considerable socio-cognitive and communicative abilities. It is reasonable to assume that these abilities interact with children's growing understanding of the linguistic conventions of the ambient language in the early stages of development. In the following sections, we examine this interaction more closely starting with children's acquisition of referring expressions (Section 2.2.1) and word order (Section 2.2.2) and the development of their abilities to produce connected discourse such as narratives (Section 2.2.3). Owing to space limitations, our survey does not include discussion of the acquisition of other linguistic devices that are used to mark information structure, including particles such as Japanese *wa* and *ga*, use of various construction types (e.g., left dislocations, cleft constructions), and intonation, among others (but see Chen, this volume for a discussion of intonation in acquisition).

2.2.   The L1 acquisition of language-specific devices for the expression of information structure

2.2.1. Referring expressions

When children first begin to use one-word utterances, aspects of their developing pragmatic knowledge become manifest in various ways. For instance, Baker and Greenfield (1988) suggest that children have a capacity to attend to new or changing (versus old) information from the time they are young infants. Children at the one-word stage will verbalize the novel or changing element in a given context, and take for granted constant, unchanged, or unique elements (even when the names for such elements are part of the child's vocabulary).[1]

Leaper and Greenfield (1980) conducted an experiment to investigate children's spontaneous utterances produced when performing purely nonverbal imitation tasks. The researchers first ascertained the child's vocabulary using parental interview, and then created a script for the nonverbal imitation tasks based on the child's available vocabulary and toys. The script consisted of a series of episodes where one semantic function varied while others remained the same. For example:

1. Toy cat eats a banana;
2. Toy cat eats a cookie;
3. Toy dog eats a banana;
4. Toy cat eats a banana.

During the imitation task, the mother acted out each episode and solicited the child's nonverbal imitation by repeating, "Do what I do" or an equivalent phrase. The parents were told not to label the toys or mention the action events. The researchers predicted that the child would spontaneously verbalize selected portions of the scripted event, viz. the variable or changing elements of the event (e.g., 'cookie' in Step 2 of the episode in the script outlined above). Leaper and Greenfield found that at the one-word stage of language development (17–19 months of age), children were encoding the new or variable aspects of the situation. These results confirmed prior research proposing that children will verbalize the most 'informative' element of the situation (Bates 1976, Greenfield and Smith 1976).

---

[1]   Note that the use of 'old' and 'new' information as used here is somewhat different from our formulation of the 'given' vs. 'new' distinction in the introduction, where the key notion is that of accessibility.

Interestingly, children are not only sensitive to whether elements of a situation are 'new' for themselves, but also exhibit awareness of whether an entity is new for their interlocutor. This kind of sensitivity has been investigated in a study on word learning by Akhtar, Carpenter and Tomasello (1996). The word learning study involved a somewhat different situation than the one in the word use study conducted by Leaper and Greenfield (1980). Rather than studying the influence of discourse novelty on children's use of known labels, the word learning study investigated the role of discourse novelty in children's ability to learn and understand words. Twenty-four-month-old children and two adults played with three novel objects that did not have names. Then the children played with a fourth novel (and nameless) object while the adults were absent. The four objects were then placed in a clear box. The adults then reappeared and displayed excitement about the contents of the box and modeled a new word (e.g., *Look, I see a gazzer!*). At the time of the use of the new word, the fourth nameless object (the target object) was novel only to the adults, not to the children. Nevertheless, children displayed significant learning of the new word, associating the word 'gazzer' with the nameless object that had been discourse-new for the adult at the time that they produced the novel word. These findings suggest that 24-month-olds understand that adults use language for entities that are novel to the discourse context, and that this novelty is determined from the speaker's point of view.

The evidence from the pointing studies mentioned in Section 2.1 (Liszkowski et al. 2006, O'Neill 1996), and from findings on children's early word learning and production of one-word utterances, among others, suggest that children have an early sensitivity to discourse novelty and a precocious ability to infer the informational needs of the listener. These abilities are also manifested in later stages of development in children's use and comprehension of a variety of referential forms to talk about 'given' and 'new' referents.

Much of the work on referring expressions suggests that children are influenced by discourse context in their choice of referential form from an early age (Hickmann 2002). For instance, increased givenness results in increased pronominalization in children aged 3–5 years (MacWhinney and Bates 1978). Further, studies of spontaneous language production demonstrate that children flexibly vary their choice of referential form (null, pronominal, and lexical forms) based on a variety of discourse-pragmatic factors. Children acquiring Hindi, Inuktitut, Italian, and Korean tend to use lexical noun phrases to label new referents and reduced (null/pronominal) forms to talk about referents that have been mentioned in prior discourse.

Other pragmatic factors that also play a role include the presence of competing referents in the discourse or situational context, whether the referent label is provided in response to a wh-question, and the animacy of the referent, among others (Clancy 1997; Allen 2000; Narasimhan, Budwig and Murthy 2005; Serratrice 2005). Children's patterns of argument realization are also influenced by whether or not they are jointly attending to referents in the context with their interlocutor (Skarabela 2007). A keen sensitivity to local discourse context has also been demonstrated in experimental studies of children's comprehension of pronouns. Findings show that children, like adults, interpret a pronoun subject as coreferential with the subject or first noun phrase of the preceding sentence (Song and Fisher 2005).

Other experimental studies have addressed the issue of whether children can assess listener knowledge states independently of their own by investigating the communicative conditions under which children use pronouns as a substitute for other types of referring expressions. In a series of two experiments, an adult asked 2.5- and 3.5-year-old children acquiring English about an event that had just happened (Campbell, Brooks and Tomasello 2000). In one condition, the adult had witnessed the target event together with the child, whereas in the other condition the adult had not been present in the room for the event. In both cases, the adult then asked a specific question such as "What did X do?" (suggesting that she knew that X had done something, although not what the nature of the action was), or a general question such as "What happened?" (suggesting that she only knew that something happened, but did not know either the event or the actor). Findings from this research show that children vary their choice of referential form depending on how adults queried children about events. The youngest children (2;5 years) made more full noun references in response to the generic question "What happened?" than to the specific question "What did X do?" to which children tended to respond with more pronouns and null references.

Yet, other factors that are likely to play a role in adult language use, e.g., whether or not the adult had witnessed the target event, did not influence younger children's choice of referring expressions. This fact suggests that children may be aware that things can be 'given' or 'new' for other people but may take more time to learn how differences in information status correspond to different linguistic forms. Similar conclusions have been drawn with respect to children's use of word order in recent research, a topic to which we turn in the next section.

2.2.2. Word order and information structure

During sentence production, adults typically order previously mentioned referents ('given' or accessible information) first, before they introduce referents that have not yet been mentioned in the discourse ('new' or inaccessible information) (Wundt 1900, Halliday 1967, Chafe 1976, MacWhinney 1977, Bock 1977, Levelt 1989). From an early age, children are sensitive to the predominant ordering patterns in the language to which they are exposed (Slobin 1985). We know that children begin to order constituents in systematic ways as early as the age of 24 months, when they are just beginning to produce multiword utterances (Brown 1973, Braine 1976). But how do children's cognitive and communicative preferences interact with their developing knowledge of language-specific ordering conventions during the process of speech production?

In her research on the development of the topic-comment distinction in children acquiring Italian, Bates (1976) observed that the child sometimes blurted out the novel information first, later adding the other units, a pattern that was characterized as the 'comment-topic' ordering (it should be noted that the predicate was taken to be the 'comment' in this study). In related research examining children's word order preferences to encode 'new' vs. 'old' (or 'given') elements, Baker and Greenfield (1988) examined children's spontaneous production in nonverbal imitation tasks when they were at the two-word stage. Children at this stage continue to use one-word utterances to encode new or uncertain information (as discussed in Section 2.2.1). In addition, children also exhibited a tendency to begin with new information in their two-word utterances.

But in surveying the research on the role of information status on word order in children, we find contradictory results, suggesting that children have a "given-new" preference, a "new-given" preference, or no ordering preference at all (Bates 1976, MacWhinney and Bates 1978, MacWhinney 1982, Schelletter and Leinonen 2003). For instance, MacWhinney and Bates (1978) conducted a study in which child and adult speakers of English, Hungarian, and Italian described nine triplets of pictures whose elements varied along the pragmatic dimension of givenness vs. newness. In the first picture of each series, all elements were new. In the second and third pictures, one element increased in newness and the remaining elements increased in givenness. The results revealed no strong relation between word order and givenness or newness. Further, Goldin-Meadow and Mylander (1984) found no evidence of new-given or given-new ordering in deaf children of hearing, non-signing parents, children who created language

without a model. These findings suggest that children may have no systematic ordering preferences influenced by the information status of referents.

But in more recent research investigating ordering preferences within
conjunct noun phrases, it was found that 3- to 5-year-old children acquiring
German exhibit an ordering preference that is opposite to that of adults:
"new-given" (Narasimhan and Dimroth 2008). These findings shed light on
previous findings showing a "new-given" ordering preference at the sentential level (Baker and Greenfield 1988, Bates 1976, MacWhinney 1985) by
demonstrating that prior mention in the discourse is not only sufficient to
influence children's ordering preferences at the phrasal level, independently
of sentence-level factors such as topicality, agentivity, or subjecthood, but
continues to influence children's non-adult-like ordering preferences well
beyond the early period of multi-word utterances.

The research showing a "new-given" preference is surprising since it
demonstrates that the processing and/or communicative considerations
influencing linear ordering in adults do not play the same role in children's
early word combinations. If the "given-new" order facilitates retrieval and
planning processes in adult language production, it might be expected to
play an even greater role in children, who have more limited processing
capacities than adults. The findings are also unexpected in light of acquisition research showing children's early conformity to ordering patterns in
the input when conveying semantic distinctions, "who does what to whom"
(Akhtar and Tomasello 1997). The rarity of deviant word orders in child
language raises the issue of the nature of children's cognitive and communicative biases that result in a non-adult-like preference for the "new-given"
order.

Children's systematic "new-given" ordering preference may be related
to their selection preferences at an early age. As discussed in Section 2.2.1,
children tend to encode the novel or changing aspects of a situation in
their single-word utterances, and even when they are capable of producing
longer utterances at the two-word stage, prefer to omit elements known to
the speaker and the hearer (Baker and Greenfield 1988, Bates 1976). Such
a selection preference is suggestive of what children consider worthy of
mention, and may well play an important role in explaining the non-adult-
like ordering biases found in the phrasal conjunct study. It is also important to note that the 'new-given' preference may not be global, but may be
construction-specific. Research by Stephens (2010) suggests that children
acquiring English prefer the 'given-new' order in producing the postverbal
arguments of dative and locative alternation verbs in an elicited production
task (e.g., *spray **the wagon with paint*** versus *spray **paint on the wagon***).

So far, we have examined studies investigating the influence of given-ness on linear ordering. We turn now to two classic studies investigating the relationship between topic-comment marking and word order in acquisition. As part of a larger study examining children's comprehension and use of different linguistic devices to mark the topic-comment distinction, Hornby (1971) asked children aged 6, 8, and 10 years to say which of two pictures (e.g., *one picture showed a girl riding a horse while the other depicted a boy riding a bicycle*) the experimenter was talking about when s/he used a sentence that matched neither of the pictures completely (e.g., *The boy is riding the horse*). Hornby's prediction was that the children would point to the picture containing (what they construed to be) the topic (e.g., a boy) when they had to match pictures with sentences belonging to a variety of construction types such as actives (with or without contrastive stress on the subject or the verb), passives, clefts, and pseudoclefts. In addition, children were also asked to produce descriptions of the pictures.

Findings from the study suggest that word order is not the sole determinant of the topic-comment distinction at any age. Children in all three age groups were more likely to select pictures containing the topic irrespective of sentence type, even in the case of clefts and sentences with contrastive stress on the verb or the subject, where the topic is linearly ordered *after* the comment. But there are developmental changes in the role of word order in the marking of topic-comment structure between the ages of 6 years and 10 years. At the age of 6 years, children did not show any tendency to select the picture containing the element mentioned earlier in an active declarative sentence, nor did they produce many active sentences in which the topic preceded the comment that were not also marked by contrastive stress. But the pattern changed by the time children were 8 years of age, with word order playing a greater role. Many more picture selections were made on the basis of the element that appeared earlier in the active sentences, and active sentences with a topic-comment order were also produced more frequently in the picture descriptions. Additionally, children were more likely to select the element mentioned early in the sentence in pseudocleft and passive sentences as well. By the age of 10 years, the importance of word order declined, perhaps owing to an increase in their ability to use other devices by this time, and children selected the active construction with the topic-comment order less frequently. They also more frequently selected the later mentioned elements as the topic in pseudoclefts and in constructions which had stress on the early-occurring element. Hornby also found that although the importance of word order changes over time, contrastive stress was the predominant device used at all three age levels.

However, MacWhinney and Price (1980), who conducted a study using the same picture-matching task as in Hornby (1971), propose that the methodology employed in the Hornby study might not reflect children's tendency to select pictures containing topics. Rather in their own study, they found that 6–7-year-olds were pointing to whichever element was stressed in the sentence they heard, especially in the case of clefts. MacWhinney and Price suggest that although distinctions such as 'given' vs. 'new' might be amenable to investigation using isolated sentences, it is much more difficult to investigate the processing of topic-comment structure in individual sentences. They conjecture that the processing of topicality in isolated sentences versus in connected discourse may have different developmental trajectories. It is the issue of information structure at the discourse-level that we turn to next.

2.2.3. Learning to produce narrative discourse

Children first learn to produce connected discourse in the context of conversation, as they learn to link their utterances with those that occurred in prior conversational turns. In communicative contexts, children have the benefit of the conversation management skills of highly cooperative adult partners. The set of skills required to produce connected discourse in the form of a narrative is arguably more demanding, and research on this topic suggests that it is acquired gradually and continues to develop into later childhood (Hoff-Ginsberg 1997).

Children's acquisition of narrative skills is often investigated using wordless picture books to elicit narratives at different ages (Hickmann and Hendricks 1999, Karmiloff-Smith 1986, Bamberg 1987, Berman and Slobin 1994). For instance, research by Karmiloff-Smith (1986) shows that children's use of pronouns in narratives develops in several stages. When asked to narrate a story from a sequence of pictures, children under the age of 5 years tend not to use pronominalization to link utterances, but to describe each picture separately. Between the ages of 5 and 8 years, children use pronouns to refer to the main character of the story but not any of the other characters (the 'thematic subject strategy'). Only after the age of 8 years do children use pronouns anaphorically to maintain reference, and nominal forms to introduce new characters or to switch reference. However, children's use of anaphoric reference shows a great deal of crosslinguistic and individual variation, and the nature of the task used to elicit narratives may play a role as well. As discussed in Hoff-Ginsberg (1997), children acquiring German, who were under age 5, were able to use anaphoric reference appropriately after they heard a story several times before telling it (Bamberg 1987).

Children's acquisition of articles has also been investigated in a variety of studies (Brown 1973, Maratsos 1974, 1976, Warden 1976). This research suggests that children acquiring English initially employ the definite (vs. the indefinite) article when introducing a referent known to themselves but unknown to the listener. The use of the indefinite article to introduce new referents did not emerge until around the age of 9 years. On the other hand, some studies show that children's overuse of the definite article in production may be an artifact of the experimental design (e.g., Emslie and Stevenson 1981). In a study of children acquiring French, Karmiloff-Smith (1979) notes children's tendency to overuse definite reference and interprets this tendency, not as egocentrism, but as arising from children's incomplete knowledge of how the morphemes are related to each other within the system of referring expressions in the language (see also Garton 1983).

The use of a range of other linguistic devices to mark information structure distinctions in narrative discourse is also acquired only gradually. Hickmann and Roland (1990) show that there is a developmental progression in how children acquiring French employ dislocations. The use of dislocation in adult French is as a topic-promoting device to promote non-active (but known) referents to active status (Hendriks 2000). Children at the age of 4 years however use dislocations to promote *new* referents to topic status. By the age of 7 years, such uses of dislocation are less frequent, and by the age of 10 years, their use as topic-promoting devices for new referents has dropped considerably. The use of such constructions, typically with definite determiners that are inappropriate for new referents (e.g., *Le cheval il court* 'the horse he runs') suggests that children may be struggling with the given-new distinction rather than the dislocated form itself.

In a study with children acquiring Chinese, Hendriks (2000) showed that 5-year-old children and adults use the topic marker *ne* differently. The use of *ne* in the child data is correlated with temporal information in topic positions, whereas in the adult data *ne* is correlated with agentive topics. Hendriks notes that German children also tend to organize most of their discourse around temporal and spatial topics, with many utterances in their stories starting with *und dann* 'and then' or *und da* 'and there' (see Klein 2008 for the notion of 'topic time' and 'topic place').

These findings suggest that children's use of devices to mark information structure distinctions in discourse may start out with different functions than they are used for in adult language, and only gradually approach the conventions found in adult language.

2.3. Discussion

Our survey of children's acquisition of information structure, while necessarily brief, reveals certain interesting patterns that crosscut our discussion
of the various linguistic devices used to convey distinctions such as 'topic'
vs. 'comment' or 'given' vs. 'new'. First, in their use of linguistic forms
to convey information structure distinctions, children exhibit sensitivity to
the informational needs of the listener at an early age. This main finding
is based on research investigating children's pointing gestures, their word
learning, and their use of referring expressions.

Second, despite evidence of early sensitivity, children do not always use
the linguistic forms in the input in appropriate ways from an early age. For
instance, children's use of pronouns is not influenced by the listener's co-
presence and ability to perceive the target event although the immediate
discourse context does exert a significant influence. German-speaking children's use of word order in phrasal conjuncts demonstrates their sensitivity
to the distinction between 'new' and 'old' information, yet their propensity
to order 'new' information first is not adult-like. Children's use of the topic
marker *ne* in Chinese also suggests that children do not use linguistic forms
in the same way as adults do despite their sensitivity to the relevant distinctions.

Third, the developmental trajectory involves gradual rather than discrete
changes over time, although this needs to be investigated much further. For
instance, children's use of word order to convey or infer topic-comment
structure appears to follow a protracted U-shaped developmental curve
wherein word order is initially limited in its use, then (over)extended, and
finally restricted again as children work out the conventions governing the
use of this device.

In each of these cases one can ask whether children learn to encode
information structure distinctions based on their experience of form-function associations in the input; or whether they rely on 'natural' associations
between entities that are prominent in their mental models of the discourse
and a hierarchy of prominence in grammatical relations (Arnold et al. 2001,
Song and Fisher 2005). Further, if one assumes the latter position, one can
query whether prominence hierarchies in the mental models that children
construct are similar to those of adults. On the other hand, if there is indeed
continuity in the cognitive architecture of children and adults, then further
questions arise: does any non-adult-like performance in children's comprehension or performance arise because of limited processing capacities
(cf. Valian and Eisenberg 1996), (non-) availability of adult-like syntactic

representations (Grinstead 2000), or developmental delays in the mappings in the interface between pragmatics and syntax (Grinstead 2004)? The answers to these intriguing questions await further research.

3. Information structure in second language acquisition

For a long time, research on second language (L2) acquisition has focused on the development of core morpho-syntactic properties in a new language and largely ignored the potential impact that categories of information structure might have on this process. Whether L2 speakers attempt to adapt the form of their utterances to the informational needs of their interlocutors in a given discourse context, and how they do so, has only lately attracted more interest by L2 researchers.

This also holds for the possible influence of the relevant form-function-mappings in the learners' source language, which is the more remarkable given that the role of prior linguistic knowledge that the learners bring to the task of L2 acquisition has traditionally played an important role for this research. The transfer of L1 knowledge has been studied extensively and often been put forward as an explanatory factor for the observed differences between the learner language and the target language. Prior knowledge of L1-specific or (partly) language-neutral principles of information structure, on the other hand, has been largely ignored in this context.

In order to investigate the information structure of L2 discourse, learner varieties must be studied as communicative systems in their own right and not as imperfect imitations of the target language. Since researchers started to adopt such a perspective and to study production or comprehension in context, a whole array of interesting results has shown that information structure plays an important role in shaping the structure of learner utterances and the process of L2 acquisition. The bulk of this research focuses on adult L2 learners. Child L2 learning is a relatively recent field of interest and much less is known about the role of information structure in L2 acquisition (but see Haberzettl 2003). In a way, child L2 learners have to cope with both: the difficulties of young children to home in on the informational needs of the listener (see Section 2) and the challenges of marking information structure and organizing discourse in a new language.

The current report concentrates on studies involving tutored and untutored adult L2 learners. Most researchers assume that the means to express information structure are rarely explicitly taught in language classes. Tutored as well as untutored learners therefore have to deduce the target adequate form-function correspondences from the target language input plus the context in which they are exposed to the relevant utterances.

At first glance it looks as if the literature on information structure in L2 acquisition came to a somewhat paradox overall conclusion. On the one hand, information structural principles are said to have an important impact on the form of learner utterances from the beginning of the acquisition process onwards. On the other hand it is claimed that the target adequate expression of information structure is very hard if not impossible to achieve even by very advanced learners and fluent bilinguals because it involves a so-called *interface* between different modules of linguistic competence (syntax and discourse).

A closer look at the relevant studies reveals, however, that what is understood by "information structure" can differ quite dramatically. Some studies are concerned with the impact of very general and potentially language neutral principles of information structure whereas others are dealing with language specific preferences for information selection and distribution that interact closely with grammatical properties of the target language. Furthermore, some researchers are interested in finding out if and how L2 learners express basic information structure dimensions in a developing language whereas others want to know if learners manage to exactly match the distribution of native speakers' probabilistic preferences for certain structures in certain contexts at ultimate attainment.

3.1. Information structure in elementary learner varieties

Adult L2 learners are – by definition – competent (native) speakers of at least one first, or source, language. Their command of this source language(s) includes the mastery of the language specific means for the expression of information structure, as well as more general knowledge about the fact that we constantly adapt the way in which we communicate certain contents to the informational needs of our hearers. As competent language users adult learners implicitly know that information can be new or given for the hearer, or that one part of an utterance can be a more direct answer to an interlocutor's question than another part, and they know from experience that distinctions like these are somehow expressed in language.

When acquiring a new language, L2 learners can rely on this implicit (language neutral) knowledge, e.g., the general tendency to overtly verbalize information that is new and unknown to the hearer, and reduce or elide forms referring to maintained or given information. This does of course not mean that adult beginners would immediately know about the target language's formal constraints on reduction, elision (ellipsis), or other information structure devices. But it can be assumed that as skilled and co-operative communicators they develop some learner specific ways to signal how the content of their utterances relates to the preceding context and the informational needs of the hearer.

Thus it is all the more surprising that to date only a few studies have systematically investigated how L2 learners adapt the form of their utterances to the particular context of use and the knowledge states of their interlocutors. But some exceptions include studies that have provided detailed analysis of beginning L2 learners' utterances in context, and have thereby not viewed them as a largely insufficient copy of the target language but as constituting an independent learner variety in its own right (see Klein and Perdue 1992 for an overview).

The earliest manifestation of untutored adult L2 learners' attempts to communicate in the target language was labeled *Pre-Basic Variety* (Perdue 1996), the more stable linguistic system formed at the following developmental stage was called *Basic Variety* (Klein and Perdue 1997). Both stages are characterized by a small number of organizational principles that are largely independent of source and target language properties. Principles that serve the expression of information structure categories and reflect the learners' general assumptions about context integration play an important role at both stages and will be briefly discussed below.

Speakers of the *Pre-Basic Variety* (Perdue 1996) are true beginners who know only around 50 words (mainly nouns, some adverbials, and prepositions) of the target language and are therefore largely dependent on support provided by their native interlocutors when, for example, trying to report an event. The 'scaffolding' spontaneously provided by the native speakers mainly consists of concrete and targeted questions, often guiding the information structure of the answers towards focus-only ellipsis.

But beginning learners are also capable of expressing fuller information structures on their own. As shown in Klein and Perdue (1992) mainly two types of patterns are used. The first pattern consists of the juxtaposition of two NPs or, alternatively, an NP and a PP/an adverbial. Utterances following this pattern are typically attested in contexts in which the first NP refers to the topic whereas the second constituent encodes the comment (utterances predicate a property of a topic); see the examples under (1a) below. The second utterance pattern consists of an NP optionally preceded by an adverbial and is used to introduce a new referent (examples under (1b)).

(1)   Beginning learner utterances with a topic-comment structure
       (Klein and Perdue 1992)

    a. *one man*   – *for the window*

       meisje   – *honger*
       girl   – hunger

       les deux   – *content*
       the two of them – happy

    b. *aujourd'hui ici* – *quatre familles*
       today here   – four families

       vandag   – *hoofdpijn*
       today   – headache

The form of beginning learner utterances can also reflect other dimensions of information structure. In many European languages contrastive topics followed by focused answer particles are attested from early on. Contrastive topics are typically drawn from the preceding native speaker utterance and are often marked by a rising intonation contour (see Andorno 2008, for a detailed analysis), whereas the following negative or affirmative particle carries a falling pitch accent. Examples from L2 Italian, German, and English are given in (2). In the English example (2c) the contrastive topic is produced by the learner and not taken over from the native speaker utterance.

(2)   Beginning learner utterances with contrastive topics and focused answer particles

    a. Learner Markos, L1 Erytrean   (Andorno 2008)
       Int: *hai visto qualcosa di nuovo, qualche: cinema – qualcosa alla*
             televisione?
             'did you see something new, some cinema – something on TV?'
       MK: *televisione sì*
             'TV yes'

    b. Learner Marcello, L1 Italian   (Becker 2005)
       Int: *reparieren sie selbst fahrrad oder auto?*
             'Do you yourself repair bicycle or car?'
       Mo: *auto nein, fahrrad ja*
             'car no, bicycle yes'

    c. Learner Santo, L1 Italian   (Silberstein 2001)
       Int: *'do you have your driving license?'*
       San: *original copy no.*

These examples illustrate that at the *Pre-Basic Variety* stage, where learners only possess a limited number of (mainly) content words, utterances are already adapted to the hearer's knowledge state with the help of word order and supra-segmental means. At the subsequent stage, the *Basic Variety*, learners extend their lexical repertoire and the need to rely on the interlocutor's scaffolding is reduced. This is mainly achieved through the integration of verb phrases in the learner variety (functional elements or inflectional morphology are still not used productively). Word order is now no longer exclusively motivated by information structure principles but gains an additional function: it is used to signal the argument structure of verbs (learners obey the so called 'Agent First Constraint').

But the 'Topic First Constraint' known from the preceding stage is still valid and is one of the few general principles determining word order at the *Basic Variety*.[2] Example (3) from Klein and Perdue (1992), is an extract of a film retelling produced by a Punjabi learner of English. Expressions characterizing the topic situation precede the focal information that is answering the underlying question (*What happened then to Charlie?*). In the last utterance, the two *Basic Variety* word order principles are in conflict, because the referent "girl" is at the same time the agent and in focus (what the gaffer is telling the policeman is the answer to the question *Who stole the bread?*). The learner places the NP referring to the focal agent in utterance final position.

(3)   Extract from an L2 learner's film retelling:
      Charlie Chaplin: Modern Times.

      girl stealing one shop (...)
      girl go (...)
      shop gaffer telephoning police
      police coming
      charlie and girl accident
      charlie bread come pickup
      police telling charlie "you bread stealing"...
      gaffer telling charlie "sorry policeman
      he don't stealing bread
      stealing bread girl"

---

2   This word order principle is called "Focus Last Constraint" in Klein and Perdue (1997).

Here, the learner violated the 'Agent First Constraint' for the benefit of the 'Topic First Constraint'. Other *Basic Variety* speakers have opted for the opposite solution, i.e., keeping the NP referring to the agent in first position, maybe with a focal pitch accent. The need to resolve such conflicts between default constraints and the need to express more complex information structures has been interpreted as a pushing factor in L2 development, motivating the acquisition of more target language word order patterns like dislocations and clefts (Klein and Perdue 1997).

It generally seems that the topic-comment distinction is more frequently marked than the given-new distinction in elementary learner varieties. Reference maintenance, for example, is usually not marked with pronouns or zero-anaphora and early definite or indefinite articles/numerals are not used systematically (compare example (3) above). Does this mean that elementary L2 learners do not mark givenness at all?

Chen (2009) wondered if *Basic Variety* speakers rely on other means to mark the givenness of discourse referents, more precisely, if their subsequent mentions of a given NP differ from the first one in intonation. She selected NPs that were produced up to eight times in a learner narrative and compared two parameters, duration, and pitch range. The results show that increasing givenness or availability is reflected in both shorter duration and a shallower pitch excursion (compare also Gullberg 2003, for a study on the role of gesture for the compensatory expression of anaphoric linkage).

Up to here we saw that early L2 learners can rely on their knowledge of communicative-pragmatic principles from early on. Language neutral principles of information organization shape utterance structure in elementary learner varieties, even though learners still lack the grammatical means that native speakers of their target language employ to this end. Does this mean that adult L2 learners have an easy time with information structure throughout? A series of studies show that this is not the case. Learning problems arise when information structure principles interact with the acquisition of sentence grammar (Benazzo 2003, Dimroth 2002, Schimke et al. 2008), and when language specific information structure distinctions differ from those encoded in the L1 – in particular whenever such distinctions have consequences beyond the sentence, e.g., for the way information is distributed in discourse. These issues are addressed in the next section.

3.2. The L2 acquisition of language specific devices for the expression of information structure

This section presents a selection of features that have received much attention in the literature.[3] Section 3.2.1 is about the form of referring expressions and anaphoric linking devices as a means to distinguish maintained from new information and to enhance discourse cohesion; Section 3.2.2 treats the acquisition of word order and the way learners use it to signal the information status of parts of speech, and 3.2.3 summarizes findings concerning the acquisition of the partly language specific information distribution in discourse, in particular the mapping of conceptual domains (e.g., time, space, entities) onto information structural categories (e.g., the selection of only one main protagonist as a discourse topic vs. the eligibility of other agents in topic role).[4]

Many empirical studies focus on L2 learners' production of certain information structural markings, but data from comprehension and judgements as well as on-line processing under real time conditions will also be treated.

3.2.1. The form of referring expressions

Most languages have an array of referring expressions like indefinite and definite NPs,[5] different types of pronouns, and/or zero-anaphora, the selection of which depends, among other factors, on the degree of givenness, or accessibility, of the intended referent for speaker and hearer. Accessibility is, among other things, a function of the number and the recency of prior mentions, and also of the antecedent's grammatical role and information status. Even though there seems to be a universal tendency of the type 'the more accessible the referent – the lighter the referring expression' there are

---

[3] Some additional topics like for example the second language acquisition of adverbials, negation, and focus particles have to be neglected for reasons of space (but see Benazzo et al. 2004, Dietrich and Grommes 1998, Dimroth and Klein 1996, Giuliano 2003, Schlyter 2005, Silberstein 2001, Véronique 2005.)

[4] For the acquisition of supra-segmental means for the expression of information structure see Chen, this volume.

[5] For the L2 acquisition of definiteness see Liu and Gleason (2002), Robertson (2000), Sleeman (2004).

numerous language specific ways to map a gradual increase in accessibility onto discrete forms.

How do L2 learners adapt the form of referring expressions in order to signal givenness and anaphoric linking? Studies on L2 production have revealed a development from under-explicit to over-explicit expression of reference maintenance. After an early phase in which maintained referents are often left implicit (Ahrenholz 2005), L2 learners typically favor full NPs over pronouns and zero-anaphora even in contexts where referents are accessible and uniquely identifiable (Chini 2005, Extra et al. 1988, Hendriks 2000). The reasons might not relate to the acquisition of information structure alone, but also have to do with the fact that lexical means are acquired before grammatical ones. Pronominal forms are particularly complex and error-prone (typically encoding gender, number, case) and learners avoid ambiguous reference that could be created by deviant pronominal forms.

Studies have, however, not only investigated L2 learners' overuse of lexical nouns, they have been particularly interested in figuring out how more advanced learners acquire the target-like use and interpretation of potentially ambiguous anaphoric expressions (e.g., personal pronouns vs. zero-anaphora) in their L2, in particular when their first language does not make a similar distinction (Belletti et al. 2007, Sorace 2005).

In so-called pro-drop languages like Spanish or Italian an overt subject pronoun is characteristically interpreted as referring to an antecedent that was newly introduced in the discourse ('topic shift'). Null-pronouns, in contrast, typically refer to given, topical antecedents, often encoded as lexical subjects in preverbal position. A series of recent studies (e.g., Belletti et al. 2007, Sorace and Filiaci 2006) indicate that advanced and even near-native L2 learners with a source language that does not encode such differences rely on target deviant pronoun resolution strategies. In a picture verification task, for example, near-native English learners of L2 Italian had to interpret pronouns in ambiguous contexts (Sorace and Filiaci 2006: 352).

(4)   *La mamma dà   un bacio alla   figlia,   mentre lei/0*
       The mother gives a   kiss   to-the daughter, while   she
       se mette   il   cappotto.
       wears [= puts on] the   coat
       'The mother kisses her daughter, while she/0 is putting on her coat.'

Results showed that learners had acquired a target-like interpretation of null pronouns. Like the native speakers[6], their preferred antecedent was the subject of the main clause. The learners' interpretation of overt pronouns, however, was not target-like in that they had significantly more subject choices than the native speakers.

Sorace and Filiaci (2006: 361) conclude that L2 learners have "a wider range of interface mappings for pronominal subjects than native speakers". Whereas native speakers associate null pronouns with topic maintenance and overt pronouns with topic shift, an overt pronoun can also be interpreted as referring to a maintained topic by an L2 learner. It is, however, an open question if this is due to representational differences, versus a consequence of the additional processing load that L2 speakers face, especially in ambiguous contexts. Evidence for the latter interpretation comes from differences in structures with forward vs. backward anaphora (pronouns in pre-posed vs. post-posed subordinate clauses) indicating that learners' pronoun resolution strategies are partly mediated by overall processing costs.

In a study by Roberts et al. (2008) on intermediate to advanced learners of Dutch (non-prodrop) with L1 Turkish (prodrop) or L1 German (non-prodrop) it was shown that cross-linguistic differences of this kind do indeed cause learning problems. But constraints on limited processing resources matter independently. In an on-line task (eye tracking while reading) both learner groups experienced difficulties integrating syntactic and discourse information and showed a processing disadvantage whenever two potential antecedents for a pronoun (a sentence internal and a sentence external one) were available in the preceding discourse. In an off-line task, Turkish learners differed from German learners of Dutch in that they interpreted Dutch pronouns in line with overt pronouns in their source language and favoured a sentence-external antecedent. The German learners like the Dutch native speakers had a sentence-internal subject preference.

Whereas advanced L2 learners are able to produce anaphoric referring expressions they might not always come to a target-like interpretation of the intended referent, when encountering ambiguous anaphors in their L2, and might be particularly likely to rely on L1 strategies when the processing load is high.

---

[6]   There was an unexpected amount of variability in the native speakers that was, however, matched by learners.

3.2.2. Word order

This section deals with the L2 acquisition of language specific word order patterns to express information structure distinctions, in particular the topic-comment or focus-background dimension. As in the case of referring expressions, there is an ongoing debate concerning questions of learnability versus the acquisition process proper. Empirical studies are either based on spontaneous production data (where identifying information units like topic is not a trivial task; cf. Chini and Lenart 2008), or on more controlled on-line and off-line comprehension tasks (e.g., contextualized acceptability judgements) that run the risk of being less natural, which might be particularly problematic for investigating information structure. Partly divergent findings concerning L2 learners' achievements in mapping word order on information structure are summarized and exemplified below.

Some studies (e.g., Hendriks 2000, Trévise 1986) have explored when L2 learners learn to map discourse functions that they know from their source language onto hitherto unknown syntactic constructions encountered in the L2 input. Hendriks (2000) studied production data from Chinese immersion learners of L2 French and focused on the form and function of left dislocations that play an important role as a topic promoting device (reintroducing topics or disambiguating them from other potential candidates) in spoken French (Lambrecht 1994, Klein this vol.). In their retellings of picture stories the L2 speakers used left dislocations (with only one exception) for the target adequate function (see example (5)).

(5)   *La vache, finalement, elle a   bandé   la patte du   cheval.*
       The cow   finally   she has bandaged the foot of-the horse.
       'Finally, the cow bandaged the horse's foot.'

Hendriks concludes that the L2 learners "clearly know the functions that topic-promoting devices can have, and they transfer all possible functions from the source language into the target language." (2000: 392). Even though the form of their utterances (e.g., the resumptive pronoun) is not always target like, the L2 learners clearly understand the construction's discourse function (see also Hendriks' discussion of L1 learners' acquisition of the same construction in Section 2). Trévise (1986), studying the acquisition of L2 English by French speakers, comes to a similar conclusion.

Other researchers, addressing the so-called *Interface Hypothesis*, wonder if L2 learners' ultimate attainment in the domain of word order and information structure is really fully target-like (e.g., Belletti et al. 2007, Hertel

2003, Hopp 2009, Lonzano 2006, Sorace 2005). Despite the fact that learners seem to understand the discourse function of the constructions they produce in their L2, the quantitative distribution of certain patterns does not always correspond to the native speaker use. Proponents of the *Interface Hypothesis* assume that advanced L2 learners can achieve native-like competence with purely syntactic properties (e.g., word order as a function of argument structure) whereas syntax reflecting information structure (so-called syntax-discourse interface phenomena) is "persistently problematic" (Lonzano 2006: 158). Research in this context has focused on the acquisition of split intransitivity in Spanish and Italian and predicts that there is a phase of target adequate word order differentiation as a function of verb class (unergative vs. unaccusative verbs, see (6a) vs. (6b) below), but not as a function of information structure (VS with both verb types with focused subject; see (6c)).

(6) Word order variation in Spanish intransitive sentences
(examples from Lonzano 2006)

Q1: What happened last night in the street?
  a. *Una mujer gritó.* ('A woman shouted'; unergative – SV)
  b. *Vino la policía.* ('Arrived the police'; unaccusative – VS)

Q2: Who shouted last night in the street?
  c. *Gritó [UNA MUJER]*$_F$ ('Shouted a woman'; unergative with subject focus – VS)

Q3: Who arrived last night at the party?
  d. *Vino [LA POLICÍA]*$_F$ ('Arrived the police'; unaccusative with subject focus – VS)

L2 learners have to deduce such preferences from the native speaker input that is, however, relatively confusing because it is probabilistic and not categorical ((6a) is not ungrammatical after Q2). Empirical studies using contextualized judgement or production tasks take quantitative results from native speakers as a yard stick. Results are partly contradictory.[7]

Lonzano (2006) compared native-speakers' and learners' preferences in broad focus contexts (Q1 in example (6) above) to subject focus contexts (Q2). The advanced L2 learners (with L1 Greek and English) behaved in a target like manner in the broad focus contexts, where their preferences

---

[7] In one experimental condition investigated in a study by Hertel (2003), native speakers of Spanish produced only 39% of the predicted word order.

depended on the verb class, but not in subject focus contexts in which "the English and Greek groups accept optionally both VS and SV, which results in optionality, a type of divergence" (Lonzano 2006: 174). Hertel (2003), who also assumed that word order reflecting information structure would be hard or impossible to acquire, investigated the same phenomenon in English learners of Spanish. In her study, however, "the prediction, that discourse-related word order would be acquired after lexically determined word order was not born out." (Hertel 2003: 295).

Hopp (2009) investigates the acquisition of German scrambling (OS order in the so-called *middlefield*) by learners with L1 English (no scrambling), Russian (scrambling with information structure effects analogous to German), and Dutch (scrambling with a slightly different function) and comes to the conclusion that "convergence at the syntax-discourse interface is possible for L2 learners, irrespective of whether the L1 encodes identical information structure-to-syntax mappings (Russian) or not (English)." (Hopp 2009: 477). The findings are based on an off-line and an on-line task (judgements and self-paced reading) involving sentences with scrambled word order in appropriate (given object, focused subject, cf. (7)) and inappropriate contexts.

(7)   *Wer hat den Vater geschlagen?*
       ('Who beat the father?'; inducing subject focus)

       Ich glaube, dass den   Vater der   [Onkel]$_F$ geschlagen hat.
       I   think   that the.ACC father the.NOM uncle   beaten   has.
       'I think that the uncle hit the father.'

Hopp found L1 effects: at less advanced proficiency levels only the Russian learners showed target-like command of the morpho-syntactic and the information structure constraints of German scrambling. At a more advanced level the English learners did so as well. But even the most advanced learners with L1 Dutch differed in their judgements of the scrambled sentences. In an on-line experiment (self-paced reading) it was found that scrambling slowed all readers down, but the degree to which it did so differed as a function of the syntax-to-information structure match. Native speakers as well as L2 learners with Russian and English as source languages showed facilitatory effects when the sentences appeared in contexts licensing the scrambled word order, whereas the L1 Dutch group treated all contexts alike. Despite these L1 effects, however, "these findings indicate that phenomena at the syntax-discourse interface may not present insurmountable difficulty in adult L2 acquisition, neither in off-line comprehension, nor in on-line processing, and, in consequence, that this particular area of L2 acquisition is not constrained by representational deficits" (Hopp 2009: 478–479).[8]

Interestingly, the Dutch learners had the greatest difficulties with the acquisition of German scrambling, despite the fact that Dutch has a very similar syntactic option. Unlike German, Dutch OS scrambling in the middlefield is however restricted to deictic NPs functioning as contrastive topics (*dat [zulke boeken]$_{CT}$ selfs [Jan]$_F$ niet koopt*; 'that not even Jan buys such books')[9]. The resemblance might make it particularly hard to acquire the target-like interpretation of the word order pattern.

Similar effects have been observed in other cases in which closely related languages use similar word orders for only slightly different information structure purposes. Bohnacker and Rosén (2008) compared the constituents occurring in the prefield in the V2 languages Swedish and German. Based on corpus data they found that Swedish has a stronger tendency than German to reserve the clause-initial position for subject pronouns and expletive elements and to avoid the fronting of objects or heavier adverbials. In their study of very advanced Swedish L2 learners of German they found that "the learners largely apply the information-structural and word-order frequency patterns of their L1 Swedish to German, which results in an unidiomatic, non-native discourse structure." (Bohnacker and Rosén 2008: 514). Such L1 influence was also attested in a series of studies focusing on the way in which near native L2 speakers organize complex information beyond the clause.

3.2.3. Information distribution and perspective taking in discourse

A number of cross-linguistic studies with L2 learners of different source and target language combinations indicate that even very advanced L2 speakers show traces of L1 influence in that the macro-structure of their L2 discourse is influenced by L1 related principles of information selection and organization (Carroll and Lambert 2003, Stutterheim and Lambert 2005). L2 learners not only have to learn the target language forms and meanings, they also have to cope with the consequences that grammaticized concepts can have for language specific preferences in discourse

---

[8] For a critical discussion of the discourse-pragmatics deficit ascribed to adult L2 learners by the *Interface Hypothesis* see also Domínguez and Arche (2008).

[9] Example quoted after Hopp (2009: 467).

organization. The grammaticized features of a language (e.g., the +/– grammaticized expression of temporal aspectual distinctions) can lead to differences in the conceptual organization and representation of information for expression in coherent discourse. According to this view information structure does not only matter for the structure of learner utterances (e.g., word order, or the form of referring expressions), but also for the macro-planning of a discourse, i.e., the selection of information to be expressed and its segmentation into propositional units.

A prominent example has to do with the acquisition of language-specific preferences for information organization in narrative discourse. Like other types of discourse, narration can be conceived of as an answer to a global discourse question (or *quaestio*; Stutterheim and Klein 2002) that determines the information distribution in and across individual utterances. The temporal domain plays a particularly important role in narrative discourse, and L2 learners not only have to learn the target specific formal means and the temporal distinctions that are obligatorily marked (e.g., the temporal category of aspect), but also their consequences for discourse organization.[10] In a study comparing film-retellings produced by very advanced learners of English with German or French as source languages, Stutterheim and Lambert (2005) find L1 influences at the level of information selection and distribution. Native speakers of English prefer an 'observer anchored' perspective in which the temporal intervals talked about ('topic time') are established in relation to the deictic *now* of the perceived event. The events that are linked to these time intervals tend to be presented as unbounded. The German learners, in their source language, prefer an event-based perspective in which the topic time is linked to the situation-time of a preceding event and often explicitly shifted from utterance to utterance (*dann* 'then'). Events are mainly presented as bounded, i.e., their endpoints are explicitly mentioned. A quantitative analysis of texts produced by highly advanced German learners of English indicates that the learners have moved into the direction of the target language on a number of features (temporal adverbials, number of unbounded events, etc.), without, however achieving a complete shift of the overall perspective.[11]

---

[10] Cf. Carroll and Lambert (2003) who showed that even very advanced L2 learners remained in the macro-level planning preferences found in their L1.

[11] See Carroll and Natale (2010) for a related study of the organization of temporal continuity and learners' choice between a protagonist vs. a narrator oriented perspective and Benazzo and Andorno (2010) for a study showing how learners mark topic discontinuity in narrative discourse.

Similar differences between near-native L2 speakers and native speakers were also found in the organization of spatial descriptions. Carroll et al. (2000) studied the organization of picture descriptions produced by highly advanced L2 speakers of German after 8–22 years of immersion and found that they had managed to reorganize the role played by conceptual domains like objects and space in their discourses, albeit to different degrees. The English, but not the Spanish learners, switched from their preferred existential strategy for reference introduction (*there is a fountain*) towards the locational strategy preferred by German speakers (*auf dem Platz ist ein Brunnen*; 'on the square is a fountain'). However, both learner groups had difficulties with the discourse consequences of the proadverbial forms used for reference maintenance in German (*Daneben ist ein Baum.* 'Beside-there is a tree'). Thus they failed to achieve an overall target-like discourse organization, and to adapt to a unifying principle of information organization. "It would thus seem that one of the core factors driving language acquisition is the goal of consistency in pairing form-function relations on a systematic scale. Perspective taking may therefore constitute a driving force in promoting the grammaticalization of form-function relations in both learner and fully-fledged languages" (Carroll et al. 2000: 464).

3.3. Discussion

Despite partly inconsistent findings researchers seem to converge on the view that native-like competence in the domain of information structure is very hard to achieve, from information selection and distribution all the way to the on-line use of language-specific means to mark the information status and the context relatedness of certain units in connected discourse. The approach inspired by the *Interface Hypothesis* assumes that this is due to the fact that it is generally easier to acquire target like knowledge of narrow syntax than syntactic knowledge that has to be synchronized with knowledge in other areas of linguistic competence, e.g., semantics or pragmatics.

The discussion of this hypothesis also addressed the question of whether interface problems were due to representational deficits of interlanguage grammars or rather to L2 processing difficulties. In the discussion of his findings, Lonzano (2006: 177) points out that representational deficits would imply that "adult L2 learners are insensitive to information packaging" and concludes that this is unlikely, given the presumed universality of information structure dimensions like the topic-comment distinction and the fully-fledged discourse capacities of adult speakers. The early L2 data that were discussed in Section 3.1 equally speak against this view. Some researchers therefore reinterpret the observed difficulties in processing terms and assume that the problems are due to the fact that learners do "not have the necessary processing resources to integrate multiple sources of information consistently" (Sorace and Filiaci 2006: 361, compare also the discussion in Hopp 2009).

Representational deficit or processing constraints – the general view is still that the problems at the syntax-discourse interface, in other words, the problems with information structure are bigger than those that have to do with 'narrow syntax'. Whereas the latter suffices for 'neutral' utterances, marked discourse contexts make too high demands on the computation at the interface (Belletti et al. 2007, Lonzano 2006).

Under a more functional perspective, however, all utterances in context have an information structure, i.e., so-called unmarked structures should be considered as having an 'interface' as well. Why, then, is the acquisition of certain features so difficult? "The task faced by learners in uncovering these patterns is formidable." (Carroll et al. 2000: 462). The patterns that they are trying to deduce from the input are preferred patterns, not categorical distinctions – as mentioned occasionally in the preceding sections, the native speaker control data in many studies was much less clear than expected. It is not always entirely clear what determines the choice of one linguistic option over another in on-line discourse production and categories such as the preceding context, the level of activation or accessibility of knowledge, etc. do not always fully account for native speakers' preferences and their intuition for a unifying information structural perspective.

The literature reviewed in this section has shown that potentially universal principles of information structure shape the structure of learner utterances from early on – i.e., even before syntactic constraints are acquired. At more advanced stages of acquisition, however, language specific form-function relations in the domain of information structure can remain problematic for a long time, in particular concerning their influence on the construction of connected discourse and the precise quantitative match of native speaker preferences. On-line processing under real time conditions remains difficult where the target-like interpretation of ambiguous forms is based on a discourse-dependent preference.

But the knowledge of language-general information structure principles and the experience as users of language in context that adults bring to the task allow them to be communicatively successful even with the very restricted linguistic resources available at the beginning of the L2 acquisition process.

4. Conclusions

In order to achieve adult native-like competence in the domain of information structure, both first and second language learners are faced with a similar learning challenge: they have to acquire the often subtle form-function relations specific for their target language that allow the expression of information structure at the utterance and discourse levels. This presupposes knowledge about the basic principles of information organization that are relevant for discourse organization, and here child and adult learners might approach the learning task with somewhat different preconditions.

In the introduction to this survey and in the sections devoted to first and second language acquisition respectively we have addressed the following dimensions:

1) Givenness (maintained vs. new information)
2) Aboutness (topic – comment)
3) Emphasis and highlighting (e.g., contrastive topic, focus)

Adults must have acquired some knowledge about these dimensions through the acquisition of their first language (Hendriks 2000), whereas young children have to learn what the relevant distinctions are in parallel with their general cognitive development. The question that arises is: what kinds of knowledge do adults versus children bring to the language learning task and does it help or hinder their acquisition of information structure? There are at least the following possibilities:

A. Adult L2 learners have somewhat of an advantage compared to child L1 learners. As cognitively mature language users they know that dimensions like givenness, aboutness, and emphasis matter for communication and are likely to be formally reflected in language. They are therefore going to pay attention to the means that native speakers use for their expression in the target language right from the start. Nothing seems to speak against this view, although there is evidence from L1 acquisition showing that children show early sensitivity to the relevance of these basic dimensions. The pointing gestures produced by young infants for example indicate that they are aware of the need to take into account what is given or new for their interlocutor at an early age (cf. Section 2.1).

B. Adult L2 learners have a large advantage compared to child L1 learners. From first language acquisition adults not only know <u>that</u> factors such as givenness, aboutness, and emphasis are relevant for communication, but also <u>how</u> they are implemented in their native language. Under the assumption that this implementation (mapping of functions to forms) is at least partly universal (e.g., "lighter" expressions for maintained information; given before new, topic before comment, intonational highlighting of contrastive/focal information, etc.), adults can transfer their knowledge of these regularities to their target language. For L1 acquisition on the other hand research, such as Narasimhan and Dimroth (2008) suggests that children may not start out with function to form mapping regularities such as 'given-before-new' but have to learn them.

Findings like the ones discussed in relation to the *Basic Variety* (Section 3.1) seem to speak in favor of positive transfer in adult L2 acquisition for some regularities (e.g., topic before focus), but only partly for others ('lighter' expressions for maintained information). In the early stages of L2 acquisition this kind of positive transfer seems to be mediated by grammatical complexity, e.g., use of word order for expressing information structure may present an easier challenge than other devices, for instance, pronouns which take different forms as a function of person, number, gender, etc.

C. Child L1 learners have an advantage over adult L2 learners. Even though the basic information structure dimensions might be universally relevant, different languages express them to different degrees, and the principles interact with the grammatical categories of the target language in crucial ways. Learning a new language would then result in a re-organization of entrenched information structure principles for adult L2 learners, which might be more difficult than acquiring grammar and information structure together during child L1 acquisition. This seems to be the view proposed by Slobin: "For the child, the construction of the grammar, and the construction of semantic/pragmatic concepts go hand in hand. For the adult, construction of the grammar often requires a revision of semantic/pragmatic concepts, along with what may well be a more difficult task of perceptual identification of the relevant morphological elements." (Slobin 1993: 242).

The kind of revision that L2 learners have to make might become relevant when it comes to more subtle reflexes of information structure than the ones mentioned so far (word order, referring expressions). In this paper we have only briefly dealt with the question of how children and adults learn to structure more complex discourse types (e.g., narrations, see sections 2.2.3 and 2.2.3). Information distribution and perspective taking in discourse depend in a very subtle way on the categories that are grammaticalized in some languages but not in others (Stutterheim and Nüse 2003, Dimroth et al. 2010). The acquisition of these kinds of discourse reflexes of sentence level structural properties in a second language is indeed very difficult, as ultimate attainment studies (Stutterheim and Carroll 2006) show. Child L1 learners do eventually home in on the target preferences, but it takes them a long time. Even 14 year olds have often not yet fully acquired adult-like ways of information organization in L1 discourse (Stutterheim, Halm and Carroll 2012).

Investigating how children and adults learn to encode information structure is of fundamental importance as it offers important insights into the nature of language, mind, and communication. Yet, perhaps owing to the complexity of the domain and the heterogeneity of phenomena that it encompasses (from word learning to discourse organization, from intonation to morphology and syntax), research in this field is surprisingly sparse. Our survey, encompassing early contributions as well as more recent research, suggests however that it is possible to find answers to deep questions about the nature of the early communicative systems that learners construct, and how these systems develop over time under the influence of the ambient language. We anticipate that further research will continue to deepen our understanding of this intriguing field of inquiry.

References

Ahrenholz, Bernt
  2005   Reference to persons and objects in the function of subject in learner varieties. In *The Structure of Learner Varieties*, Henriette Hendriks (ed.), 19–64. Berlin / New York: Mouton de Gruyter.
Akhtar, Nameera and Michael Tomasello
  1997   Young children's productivity with word order and verb morphology. *Developmental Psychology* 33: 952–965.
Akhtar, Nameera, Malinda Carpenter and Michael Tomasello
  1996   The role of discourse novelty in early word learning. *Child Development* 67: 635–645.
Allen, Shanley
  2000   A discourse-pragmatic explanation for argument representation in child Inuktitut. *Linguistics 38*: 483–521.
Andorno, Cecilia
  2008   Entre énoncé et interaction: le rôle des particules d'affirmation et négation dans les lectes d'apprenant. *Acquisition et Interaction en Langue Etrangère* 26: 173–190.
Arnold, Jennifer
  1998   Reference form and discourse patterns. Unpublished Dissertation, Stanford University.

Arnold, Jennifer, Jared Novick, Sarah Brown-Schmidt, Janet Eisenband and John Trueswell
   2001   Knowing the difference between girls and boys: The use of gender during online pronoun comprehension in young children. *Proceedings of the BU Child Language Conference*, 59–69. Boston, MA.
Baker, Nancy and Patricia Greenfield
   1988   The development of new and old information in young children's early language. *Language Sciences* 10: 3–34.
Bamberg, Michael
   1987   *The Acquisition of Narratives*. Berlin/New York: Mouton de Gruyter.
Bates, Elisabeth
   1976   *Language and Context: The Acquisition of Pragmatics*. New York: Academic Press.
Becker, Angelika
   2005   The semantic knowledge base for the acquisition of negation and the acquisition of finiteness. In *The Structure of Learner Varieties*, Henriette Hendriks (ed.), 263–314. Berlin/New York: Mouton de Gruyter.
Behne, Tanya, Malinda Carpenter and Michael Tomasello
   2005   One-year-olds comprehend the communicative intentions behind gestures in a hiding game. *Developmental Science* 8: 492–99.
Belletti, Adriana, Elisa Bennati and Antonella Sorace
   2007   Theoretical and developmental issues in the syntax of subjects: Evidence from near-native Italian. *Natural Language and Linguistic Theory* 25: 657–689.
Benazzo, Sandra
   2003   The interaction between the development of verb morphology and the acquisition of temporal adverbs of contrast: A longitudinal study in French, English and German L2. In *Information structure and the Dynamics of Language Acquisition*, Christine Dimroth and Marianne Starren (eds.), 187–210. Amsterdam: John Benjamins.
Benazzo, Sandra, Christine Dimroth, Clive Perdue and Marzena Watorek
   2004   Le rôle des particules additives dans la construction de la cohésion discursive en langue maternelle et en langue étrangère. *Langages* 155: 76–105.
Benazzo, Sandra and Cecilia Andorno
   2010   Discourse cohesion and topic discontinuity in native and learner production. In *Eurosla Yearbook* 10, Leah Roberts, Martin Howard, Muiris Ó Laoire and David Singleton (eds.), 92–118. Amsterdam: John Benjamins.
Berman, Ruth and Dan I. Slobin
   1994   *Relating Events in Narrative: A Crosslinguistic Developmental Study*. Mahwah, New Jersey: Lawrence Erlbaum.

Bock, Kathryn
  1977   The effect of a pragmatic presupposition on syntactic structure in
          question answering. *Journal of Verbal Learning and Verbal Behavior*
          16: 723–734.
Bock, Kathryn and Richard Warren
  1985   Conceptual accessibility and syntactic structure in sentence formu-
          lation. *Cognition* 21: 47–67.
Bohnacker, Ute and Christina Rosén
  2008   The clause-initial position in L2 German declaratives: Transfer of
          information structure. *Studies in Second Language Acquisition* 30:
          511–538.
Braine, Martin
  1976   *Children's First Word Combinations.* Chicago: University of Chicago
          Press
Brooks, Rechele and Andrew Meltzoff
  2002   The importance of eyes: How infants interpret adult looking behavior.
          Developmental Psychology 38: 958–966.
Brown, Roger
  1973   *A First Language: The Early Stages.* Cambridge, MA: Harvard Uni-
          versity Press.
Campbell, Aimee, Patricia Brooks and Michael Tomasello
  2000   Factors affecting young children's use of pronouns as referring
          expressions. *Journal of Speech, Language, and Hearing Research*
          43: 1337–1349.
Carroll, Mary, Jorge Murcia-Serra, Marzena Watorek and Alessandra Bendiscoli
  2000   The relevance of information organization to second language acqui-
          sition studies: The descriptive discourse of advanced adult learners
          of German. *Studies in Second Language Acquisition* 22: 441–466.
Carroll, Mary and Monique Lambert
  2003   Information structure in narratives and the role of grammati-
          cised knowledge: A study of adult French and German learners of
          English. In *Information Structure and the Dynamics of Language
          Acquisition*, Christine Dimroth and Marianne Starren (eds.), 267–
          288. Amsterdam: John Benjamins.
Carroll, Mary and Silvie Natale
  2010   Macrostructural planning and patterns in reference management in
          narratives of native speakers of German, Italian, and advanced L2
          speakers (L1 German L2 Italian). In *Topic, struttura dell'informa-
          zione e acquisizione linguistica*, Marina Chini (ed.), 197–218. Milano:
          Franco Angeli Edizione.
Chafe, Wallace
  1976   Givenness, contrastiveness, definiteness, subjects, topics, and point
          of view. In *Subject and Topic*, Charles N. Li (ed.), 25–56. New York:
          Academic Press.

Chen, Aoju
    2009   Intonation and reference maintenance in Turkish learners of Dutch:
              A first insight. *Acquisition et Interaction en Langue Etrangère –
              Langage, Interaction et Acquisition* 2: 67–92.
Chini, Marina
    2005   Reference to person in learner discourse. In *The Structure of
              Learner Varieties*, Henriette Hendriks (ed.), 65–110. Berlin/New
              York: Mouton de Gruyter.
Chini, Marina and Ewa Lenart
    2008   Identifier le topique dans une tâche narrative en italien et en français
              chez les natifs (L1) et les apprenants (L2). *Acquisition et Interaction
              en Langue Etrangère* 26: 129–148.
Clancy, Patricia
    1997   Discourse motivations of referential choice in Korean acquisition.
              In *Japanese/Korean Linguistics* 6, Ho-min Sohn and John Haig
              (eds.), 639–659. Stanford: Center for the Study of Language and
              Information Publications.
Daneš, Frantisek
    1970   One instance of the Prague school methodology: Functional analysis
              of utterance and text. In *Method and Theory in Linguistics,* Paul
              Garvin (ed.), 132–146. Paris/The Hague: Mouton.
Dietrich, Rainer and Patrick Grommes
    1998   „Nicht". Reflexe seiner Bedeutung und Syntax im Zweitspracherwerb.
              In *Eine zweite Sprache lernen. Empirische Untersuchungen zum
              Zweitspracherwerb*, Heide Wegener (ed.), 173–202. Tübingen: Narr.
Dimroth, Christine
    2002   Topics, assertions and additive words: How L2 learners get from infor-
              mation structure to target language syntax. *Linguistics* 40: 891–923.
Dimroth, Christine, Cecilia Andorno, Sandra Benazzo and Josje Verhagen
    2010   Given claims about new topics. How Romance and Germanic speakers
              link changed and maintained information in narrative discourse.
              Journal of Pragmatics 42: 3328–3344.
Domínguez, Laura and María J. Arche
    2008   Optionality in L2 grammars: the acquisition of SV/VS contrast in
              Spanish. In Harvey Chan, *Proceedings of the 32nd Annual Boston
              University Conference on Language Development*, Heather Jacob
              and Enkeleida Kapia (eds.), 96–107. Somerville, USA, Cascadilla.
Emslie, Hazel C. and Rosemary J. Stevenson
    1981   Pre-school children's use of the articles in definite and indefinite
              referring expressions. *Journal of Child Language* 8: 313–328.
Ertel, Suitberg
    1977   Where do the subjects of sentences come from? In *Sentence Pro-
              duction: Developments in Research and Theory*, Sheldon Rosenberg
              (ed.), 141–167. Hillsdale, New Jersey: Erlbaum.

Extra, Guus, Sven Strömquvist and Peter Broeder
    1988   Pronominal reference to persons in adult second language acquisi-
            tion. In *Processes in the Developing Lexicon*, Peter Broeder, Guus
            Extra, Rouland van Hout, Sven Strömqvist and Kaarlo Voionmaa
            (eds.), 86–113. Strasbourg, Tilburg, Göteborg: European Science
            Foundation.

Firbas, Jan
    1964   On defining the theme in functional sentence analysis. *Traveaux
            Linguistique de Prague* 1: 267–280.

Garton, Alison
    1983   An approach to the study of determiners in early language develop-
            ment. *Journal of Psycholinguistic Research* 12: 513–525.

Giuliano, Patrizia
    2003   Negation and relational predicates in French and English as second
            languages. In *Information Structure and the Dynamics of Language
            Acquisition*, Christine Dimroth and Marianne Starren (eds.), 119–158.
            Amsterdam: John Benjamins.

Goldin-Meadow, Susan and Carolyn Mylander
    1984   The development of morphology without a conventional language
            model. *Papers from the Chicago Linguistic Society* 20: 117–133.

Greenfield, Patricia and Joshua H. Smith
    1976   *The Structure of Communication in Early Language Development*,
            New York: Academic Press.

Grinstead, John
    2000   Constraints on the computational component vs. grammar in the lex-
            icon: A discussion of Bates & Goodman. *Journal of Child Language*
            27: 737–743.

Grinstead, John
    2004   Subjects and interface delay in Child Spanish and Catalan. *Language*
            80: 40–72.

Gullberg, Marianne
    2003   Gestures, referents, and anaphoric linkage in learner varieties. In
            Information Structure and the Dynamics of Language Acquisition.
            Christine Dimroth and Marianne Starren (eds.), 311–328. Amsterdam:
            John Benjamins.

Haberzettl, Stefanie
    2003   "Tinkering" with chunks: Form-oriented strategies and idiosyncratic
            utterance patterns without functional implications in the IL of
            Turkish speaking children learning German. In *Information Struc-
            ture and the Dynamics of Language Acquisition*, Christine Dimroth
            and Marianne Starren (eds.), 45–64. Amsterdam: John Benjamins.

Halliday, Michael K.
    1967   Notes on transitivity and theme in English, part 2. *Journal of Lin-
            guistics* 3: 199–244.

Hendriks, Henriette
   2000   The acquisition of topic in Chinese L1 and French L1 and L2. *Studies in Second Language Acquisition* 22: 369–397.
Hertel, Tammy J.
   2003   Lexical and discourse factors in the second language acquisition of Spanish word order. *Second Language Research* 19: 273–304.
Hickmann, Maya and Henriette Hendriks
   1999   Cohesion and anaphora in children's narratives: A comparison of English, French, German, and Chinese. *Journal of Child Language* 26: 419–452.
Hickmann, Maya and Francoise Roland
   1990   Topiques et sujets dans les récits d'enfants français [Topics and subjects in the narratives of French children]. Paper presented at the Third Conference of the Re´seau Europe´en de Laboratoires sur l'Acquisition des Langues, Bielefeld.
Hickmann, Maya
   2002   *Children's Discourse: Person, Space and Time Across Languages.* Cambridge Studies in Linguistics 98. Cambridge: Cambridge University Press.
Hockett, Charles
   1958   *A Course in Modern Linguistics.* New York: Macmillan.
Hoff-Ginsberg, Erika
   1997   *Language Development.* Pacific Grove, California: Brooks/Cole.
Hopp, Holger
   2009   The syntax-discourse interface in near-native L2 acquisition: Offline and on-line performance. *Bilingualism: Language and Cognition* 12: 463–483.
Hornby, Peter
   1971   The role of topic-comment in the recall of cleft and pseudocleft sentences. *Papers from the Seventh Regional Meeting of the Chicago Linguistic Society*, 445–453.
Karmiloff-Smith, Annette
   1979   *A Functional Approach to Child Language.* London: Cambridge University Press.
Karmiloff-Smith, Annette
   1986   Some fundamental aspects of language acquisition after five. In *Studies in Language Acquisition*, 2nd revised edition, Paul Fletcher and Michael Garman (eds.), 455–474. Cambridge: Cambridge University Press.
Kelly, Michael H., Kathryn J. Bock and Frank C. Keil
   1986   Prototypicality in a linguistic context: Effects on sentences structure. *Journal of Memory and Language* 25: 59–74.

Klein, Wolfgang
    2008   The topic situation. In *Empirische Forschung und Theoriebildung: Beiträge aus Soziolinguistik, Gesprochene-Sprache- und Zweitspracherwerbsforschung: Festschrift für Norbert Dittmar*, Bernt Ahrenholz, Ursula Bredel, Wolfgang Klein, Martina Rost-Roth and Romuald Skiba (eds.), 287–305. Frankfurt am Main: Lang.

Klein, Wolfgang and Clive Perdue
    1992   *Utterance Structure: Developing Grammars again.* Amsterdam: John Benjamins.

Klein, Wolfgang and Clive Perdue
    1997   The Basic Variety (or: Couldn't natural languages be much simpler?). *Second Language Research* 13: 301–347.

Lambrecht, Knud
    1994   *Information Structure and Sentence Form: Topic, Focus, and the Mental Representations of Discourse Referents.* Cambridge: Cambridge University Press.

Leaper, Campbell and Patricia Greenfield
    1980   A perceptual and situational analysis of the use of single-word utterances. *Paper presented at the Western Psychological Association*, Honolulu.

Levelt, Willem. J. M.
    1989   *Speaking: From Intention to Articulation.* Cambridge, MA: Massachusetts Institute of Technology Press.

Liszkowski, Ulf, Malinda Carpenter,Tricia Striano and Michael Tomasello
    2006   Twelve- and 18-month-olds point to provide information for others. *Journal of Cognition and Development* 7: 173–187.

Liu, Dilin and Johanna I. Gleason
    2002   Acquisition of the article the by nonnative speakers of English: An analysis of four non-generic uses. *Studies in Second Language Acquisition* 24: 1–26.

Lozano, Cristobal
    2006   Focus and split intransitivity: The acquisition of word order alternations and unaccusativity in L2 Spanish. *Second Language Research* 22: 145–187.

MacWhinney, Brian
    1977   Starting points. *Language* 53: 152–168.

MacWhinney, Brian and Elizabeth Bates
    1978   Sentential devices for conveying givenness and newness: A cross-cultural developmental study. *Journal of Verbal Learning and Verbal Behavior* 17: 539–558.

MacWhinney, Brian
    1982   Basic syntactic processes. In *Language Acquisition: Syntax and Semantics*, Vol. 1, Stan A. Kuczaj (ed.), 73–136. Hillsdale, NJ: Erlbaum.

MacWhinney, Brian
    1985   Hungarian language acquisition as an exemplification of a general
            model of grammatical development. In *The Crosslinguistic Study of
            Language Acquisition.* Dan I. Slobin (ed.), 1069–1156. Hillsdale, NJ:
            Erlbaum.
MacWhinncy, Brian and Derek Price
    1980   The development of the comprehension of topic-comment marking.
            In *Proceedings of the First International Congress for the Study of
            Child Language*, David Ingram, Fred Peng and Philip Dale (eds.).
            Lanham, MD: University Press of America.
Narasimhan, Bhuvana, Nancy Budwig and Lalita Murty
    2005   Argument realization in Hindi caregiver-child discourse. *Journal of
            Pragmatics* 37: 461–495.
Narasimhan, Bhuvana and Christine Dimroth
    2008   Word order and information status in child language. *Cognition* 107:
            317–329.
Perdue, Clive
    1996   Pre-basic varieties: the first stages of second language acquisition.
            Toegepaste Taalwetenschap in Artikelen 55: 135–150.
Pinker, Steven
    1989   *Learnability and Cognition: The Acquisition of Verb-Argument
            Structure.* Cambridge, MA: Harvard University Press.
Roberts, Leah, Marianne Gullberg and Peter Indefrey
    2008   On-line pronoun resolution in L2 discourse: L1 influence and general
            learner effects. *Studies in Second Language Acquisition* 30: 333–357.
Robertson, Daniel
    2000   Variability in the use of the English article system by Chinese
            learners of English. *Second Language Research* 16: 135–172.
Schelletter, Christina and Eeva Leinonen
    2003   Normal and language-impaired children's use of reference: syntactic
            versus pragmatic processing. *Clinical Linguistics and Phonetics* 17
            (4/5): 335–343.
Schimke, Sarah, Josje Verhagen and Christine Dimroth
    2008   Particules additives et finitude en néerlandais et allemand L2.
            Acquisition et Interaction en Langue Etrangère 26: 191–210.
Schlyter, Suzanne
    2005   Adverbs and functional categories in L1 and L2 acquisition of French.
            In *Focus on French as a Foreign Language: Multidisciplinary
            Approaches*, Jean-Marc Dewaele (ed.), 36–62. Toronto: Multilingual
            Matters.
Serratrice, Ludovica
    2005   The role of discourse pragmatics in the acquisition of subjects in
            Italian. *Applied Psycholinguistics* 26: 437–462.

Sgall, Peter, Eva Hajičová and Jarmila Panevová
  1986   *The Meaning of the Sentence in Its Semantic and Pragmatic Aspects.*
          Dordrecht: Reidel/Prague: Academia.
Silberstein, Dagmar
  2001   Facteurs interlingues et spécifiques dans l'acquisition non-guidée
          de la négation en anglais L2. *Acquisition et Interaction en Langue
          Etrangère* 14: 25–59.
Skarabela, Barbora
  2007   Signs of early social cognition in children's syntax: The case of
          joint attention in argument realization in child Inuktitut. *Lingua* 117:
          1837–1857.
Sleeman, Petra
  2004   The acquisition of definiteness distinctions by L2 learners of French.
          In *Linguistics in the Netherlands*, Leonie Cornips and Jenny Doetjes
          (eds.), 158–168. Amsterdam: John Benjamins.
Slobin, Dan. I.
  1985   Crosslinguistic evidence for the language- marking capacity. In *The
          Cross-Linguistic Study of Language Acquisition*, Dan. I. Slobin (ed.),
          1157–1249. Hillsdale, NJ: Erlbaum.
Slobin, Dan. I.
  1993   Adult language acquisition: A view from child language study. In
          Adult Language Acquisition: Cross-Linguistic Perspectives, Clive
          Perdue (ed.), 239–252. Cambridge: Cambridge University Press.
Song, Hyun-joo and Cynthia Fisher
  2005   Who's "she"? Discourse prominence influences preschoolers' com-
          prehension of pronouns. *Journal of Memory and Language* 52:
          29–57.
Sorace, Antonella A.
  2005   Syntactic optionality at interfaces. In *Syntax and Variation: Recon-
          ciling the Biological and the Social*, Leonie Cornips and Karen P.
          Corrigan (eds.), 46–111. Amsterdam: John Benjamins.
Sorace, Antonella and Francesca Filiaci
  2006   Anaphora resolution in near-native speakers of Italian. *Second Lan-
          guage Research* 22: 339–368.
Stephens, Nola M.
  2010   Given-before-new: The effects of discourse on argument structure in
          early child language. Ph.D. dissertation, Department of Linguistics,
          Stanford University.
Stern, Daniel. N.
  1985   *The Interpersonal World of the Infant.* New York: Basic Books.
Tomasello, Michael
  2003   *Constructing a Language: A Usage-Based Theory of Language
          Acquisition.* Cambridge, MA: Harvard University Press.

Tomasello, Michael, Malinda Carpenter, Joseph Call, Tanya Behne and Henriette Moll
    2005   Understanding and sharing intentions: The origins of cultural cogni-
                tion. *Behavioral and Brain Sciences* 28: 675–691.
Trevarthen, Colwyn
    1979   Communication and cooperation in early infancy: A description
                of primary intersubjectivity. In *Before Speech: The Beginning of
                Interpersonal Communication*, Margaret M. Bullowa (ed.), 321–347.
                New York: Cambridge University Press.
Trévise, Anne
    1986   Is it transferable, topicalization? In *Cross-Linguistic Influence in
                Second Language Acquisition*, Eric Kellerman and Mike Sharwood
                Smith (eds.), 186–206. Oxford: Pergamon.
Valian, Virginia and Zena Eisenberg
    1996   The development of syntactic subjects in Portugese-speaking children.
                Journal of Child Language 23: 103–128.
Véronique, Daniel
    2005   Syntactic and semantic issues in the acquisition of negation in
                French. In *Focus on French as a Foreign Language*, Jean-Marc
                Dewaele (ed.), 114–134. Clevedon: Multilingual Matters.
von Stutterheim, Christiane and Wolfgang Klein
    2002   Quaestio and L-perspectivation. In *Perspecive and Perspectivation
                in Discourse*, Carl. F. Graumann and Werner Kallmeyer (eds.), 59–88.
                Amsterdam: John Benjamins.
von Stutterheim, Christiane and Ralf Nüse
    2003   Processes of conceptualisation in language production: Language
                specific perspectives and event construal. *Linguistics* 41: 851–881.
von Stutterheim, Christiane and Monique Lambert
    2005   Cross-linguistic analysis of temporal perspectives in text produc-
                tion. In The *Structure of Learner Varieties*, Henriette Hendriks (ed.),
                203–230. Berlin / New York: Mouton de Gruyter.
von Stutterheim, Christiane and Mary Carroll
    2006   The impact of grammatical temporal categories on ultimate attain-
                ment in L2 learning. In *Educating for Advanced Foreign Language
                Capacities*, Heidi Byrnes, Heather Weger-Guntharp and Katie
                Sprang (eds.), 40–53. Georgetown: Georgetown University Press.
von Stutterheim, Christiane, Ute Halm and Mary Carroll
    2012   Macrostructural principles and the development of narrative com-
                petence in L1 German: The role of grammar. In *Comparative
                Perspectives to Language Acquisition: A tribute to Clive Perdue*,
                Marzena Watorek, Sandra Benazzo and Maya Hickmann (eds.),
                559–585. Clevedon: Multilingual Matters.

Warden, David
    1976   The influence of context on children's use of identifying expressions and references. *British Journal of Psychology* 67: 101–112.

Wundt, Wilhelm. M.
    1900   *Die Sprache.* Leipzig: Engelmann.

Computation and modeling of information structure

Manfred Stede

1. Introduction and overview

Generally speaking, research in *Computational Linguistics* strives to devise models of language processing that are formal and can at least potentially be implemented as computer software. These models need not be intended as processing models of the human mind (in which case they would fit into the emerging neighbor discipline of *computational psycholinguistics*); instead, they are most often conceived as merely providing an input/output relation that is adequate either from a descriptive perspective, or for some particular practical purpose. Nowadays, if computer implementation is the central goal and applications for the "real world" are to be built, this type of work is subsumed under the label of *language technology.*

In this chapter, we are concerned with the role that information structure (IS) plays in such computational models of language understanding and production. Our aim is twofold: On the one hand, we introduce some specific research issues and methodologies that computational linguists employ; on the other hand, we characterize the state of the art of these methodologies when applied to various aspects of IS. Most of the work surveyed here does not aim at modeling human mental processes, but some of it is concerned with real-world application, i.e., it is relevant for language technology. We will mention these differences in orientation when discussing the respective research, since different aims often lead to specific methodological choices.

The majority of models built in computational linguistics are intended to characterize language processing *in context* – which may be a situational context (as in human-machine interaction) or merely the co-text. Regarding the information structure, the overall goal, therefore, is to project certain features of the *discourse structure* onto certain features of individual utterances, where the word *discourse* can refer to a spoken dialogue or to a written monologue. The notion of a *discourse model* – a representation of that part of the context that is relevant for the processing task – will thus play an important role in this chapter. For example, assume that we want to devise a model of text understanding for the particular genre of newspaper reports. The computer is supposed to build up a representation of the content of an input report, so that it can be used for some specific purpose such as automatically summarizing the report, answering questions about the content, or translating it to another language. At any rate, the text will be processed sentence by sentence, and – depending on the underlying semantic theory – some kind of representation of the meaning will be constructed. Along the way, several issues regarding the information structure play a role: Sentences will often contain pronominal expressions whose antecedents need to be found for the semantic representation to be completed; this task of *anaphora resolution* is related to different degrees of *givenness* or *familiarity* of potential antecedents. Furthermore, it might be important to break the text up into sections dealing with different topics (in a general sense), so that signals for topic shifts need to be detected, which also relates to the topics (in the IS sense) of sentences. And finally, if one of the tasks for our system were converting the text to *speech* (as in programs for reading web pages aloud), producing an appropriate intonation would, in part, depend on recognizing the *focus/background* structure of sentences in the input text, so that accents are placed on the right words in the output.

In the following sections, we will be looking at different scenarios where computational models of discourse structure can or must deal with information structure. Beginning with written language, we first examine the above-mentioned problem of text understanding (Section 2) and then turn to its "reverse", the task of automatic text generation (Section 3). Regarding spoken language, we investigate the role of IS in dialogue systems, and present some work on integrating IS in the understanding and the generation of speech (Section 4). Finally, we will draw a few conclusions (Section 5).

2. Text understanding

An "ideal" automatic text understanding system that tries to recover the meaning of an input text as thoroughly as possible, would move from sentence to sentence, and determine the meaning of each, as well as possible relationships between the meanings of the individual sentences (such as underlying temporal or causal relationships). It would try to compute the underlying intentions of the writer, answering questions such as: Why is the writer saying this, and what is she trying to accomplish? To do all this, the system would carefully track what the text is "about" at any point, taking hints from, for example, non-canonical word order that may have been employed to emphasize a certain point, or to indicate a change of topic. While this ideal and perfect text understanding system is out of reach for the time being, there are many interesting approaches that are moving in this direction and achieving results that are useful for a variety of purposes.

When computing the meaning of texts in some way or another, one inevitable task is *reference resolution*: In order to form a representation of the proposition expressed by a sentence, the entities being referred to need to be known. Accordingly, reference resolution has received a lot of attention in computational linguistics, especially in the discourse processing community. We will review the state of the art in the following subsection, and thereafter turn to the much smaller body of research devoted to other aspects of the analysis of information structure in text understanding.

2.1. Reference resolution

When a text is processed sentence by sentence, and a meaning representation is to be computed for each sentence, this will usually be a variant of the form $F(R,P)$ suggested by John Searle in his work on speech acts, where R represents the referents mentioned in the sentence, P the predication stated over the referents, and F some operator indicating the illocutionary force. The referents, however, may be realized by anaphoric expressions: words or phrases that refer only indirectly by pointing to another linguistic expression in the previous discourse. The clearest cases, of course, are pronouns of various kinds. A sentence containing one or more pronouns cannot be understood in isolation, and that is why *pronoun resolution* is a very prominent task in automatic text understanding. It has figured prominently in computational linguistics, and major theoretical proposals have emanated from it (cf. Webber 1980, and work cited below). The other problem of reference resolution, definite noun phrases of various kinds, can, in fact, be much more difficult, as their understanding often requires non-linguistic background knowledge.

In the case of pronoun resolution, the role of information structure is particularly obvious: Since they carry almost no information about their referent, they have to be resolved by computing the most "prominent" antecedent at the time of their occurrence in a discourse. For this task, two families of approaches have been proposed: *Centering* and *salience*-based models. *Centering* is (at least in its original formulation) based on the idea that grammatical roles are primarily responsible for assigning different degrees of prominence to discourse referents, whereas *salience*-based models take a variety of factors into consideration and determine antecedents by computing numerical salience scores for the possible referents.

These approaches have their roots in computational linguistics, but are now also widely used as models of anaphoric processing in human language processing. We will discuss the two approaches in turn.

2.1.1. Grammatical analysis: Centering

The basic idea underlying this influential line of research is the *discourse center hypothesis*, which states that at any point in processing a discourse there is always a distinguished, most "central" entity that the discourse is currently "about". This entity is often called the "focus of attention" – not to be confused with the IS notion of focus, as characterized in Chapter 1. Experimental evidence for discourse centers in human language processing has been provided, for instance, by Hudson, Tanenhaus and Dell (1986), who measured reading times for variants of a text and found that a sentence is processed fastest when the current center is realized as a pronoun; they also demonstrated that the subject of a clause is particularly important for controlling the focus of attention. With similar methods, Guindon (1985) showed that hearers take longer to process a pronoun referring to a non-center than one referring to the center, while processing a non-pronominalized noun phrase that is central takes longer than processing one that is not central.

Now, the crucial question is how the property of being central arises in the reader's mind, i.e., which linguistic devices are responsible for maintaining or shifting the focus of attention. Centering theory, which was conceived in its original version in the 1980s and published by Grosz, Joshi and Weinstein (1995), claims that center management is achieved by an interaction between the form of the referring expressions (most importantly: pronoun versus full NP) and their mapping to grammatical roles. The model uses three components:

- A list of *forward-looking centers* for a sentence S_n, written as $C_f(S_n)$. This is a partially-ordered set of the discourse referents mentioned in S_n. The ordering is determined by grammatical role:[1] subject–direct object–others (indirect object, obliques).[2]

---

[1] Grosz, Joshi and Weinstein (1995) acknowledge that other factors (text position, lexical semantics) may play a role, but in effect admit only grammatical roles into their model.

[2] In the version of Brennan, Walker and Pollard (1987), the ordering is more elaborate: subject–direct object–indirect object–other subcategorized elements–adjuncts.

- The *preferred center* of S_n, written as $C_p(S_n)$, is the discourse referent at the first position of $C_f(S_n)$.
- The *backward-looking center* $C_b(S_n)$ is the highest-ranking referent of the preceding sentence (i.e., from the $C_f(S_{n-1})$ list) that is also realized in S_n.

Thus, the C_f's predict possible connections to the subsequent sentence, whereas the C_b represents the connection to the previous sentence – which is "the" center, i.e., the focus of attention when processing S_n.

Managing the center is now a matter of arranging the referring expressions in such a way that the transition from one sentence to the next minimizes the processing effort for the reader. What types of such transitions can be distinguished? The key issues are whether C_b stays the same, and how C_b relates to the preferred center C_p of the utterance. We show here the proposal of Brennan, Walker and Pollard (1987), which is slightly more elaborate than that of Grosz, Joshi and Weinstein (1995).[3]

	$C_b(S_n) = C_b(S_{n-1})$	$C_b(S_n) \neq C_b(S_{n-1})$
$C_b(S_n) = C_p(S_n)$	CONTINUE	SMOOTH SHIFT
$C_b(S_n) \neq C_p(S_n)$	RETAIN	ROUGH SHIFT

A text usually changes its topic once in a while, and thus centers have to be shifted – the claim of Centering theory is that this can be done in successful and less successful ways, which can be characterized by the transition types. Brennan, Walker and Pollard (1987) posit the following ranking for the four transitions: CONTINUE > RETAIN > SMOOTH SHIFT > ROUGH SHIFT. According to this, other things being equal, a writer should keep the C_b constant and realize it as subject; if that seems inappropriate, the writer should choose a RETAIN, or if necessary a SMOOTH SHIFT, and only in the worst case a ROUGH SHIFT.

In order to capture the phenomenon of intuitively correct pronoun choice, Grosz, Joshi and Weinstein (1995) proposed the following rule: If any element of $C_f(S_n)$ is realized as a pronoun in the following sentence S_{n+1}, then the $C_b(S_{n+1})$ must also be realized as a pronoun. This rule formalizes the intuition (and the experimental findings, such as those mentioned above) that pronouns are used for central referents; some non-central referent(s) may be pronominalized in addition, but not in isolation.

---

[3] Brennan, Walker and Pollard (1987) used the terms SHIFTING and SHIFTING-1 instead of SMOOTH SHIFT and ROUGH SHIFT. The latter terms were introduced by Walker, Joshi and Prince (1994) and have since become more popular in the literature.

Let us now illustrate this approach with a short example, taken from Brennan, Walker and Pollard (1987):

"Brennan drives an Alfa Romeo. She drives too fast. Friedman races her on weekends. She often beats her."

Assuming that for the first sentence, C_b is to be set to C_p (in the absence of a preceding utterance), the center assignment is the following. (We denote a discourse referent by a label for the semantic entity (in upper case letters) followed by the linguistic unit realizing it.)

U_1: Brennan drives an Alfa Romeo.
C_b: [BRENNAN:Brennan]
C_f: ([BRENNAN:Brennan] [ALFA:Alfa Romeo])

In the second sentence, the pronoun can only refer to Brennan, who is also (still) the C_b. Note that the linguistic realization in the description is that of the preceding sentence; whereas for the C_f, we use the word from the current sentence:

U_2: She drives too fast.
C_b: [BRENNAN:Brennan]
C_f: [BRENNAN:she]

From the table given above, we see that the transition from U_1 to U_2 is a CONTINUE. Moving on to U_3, we again find a reference to Brennan, who thus remains the C_b. She does not head the C_f list, though, and therefore the transition is of type RETAIN.

U_3: Friedman races her on weekends.
C_b: [BRENNAN:she]
C_f: ([FRIEDMAN:Friedman] [BRENNAN:her] [WEEKEND:weekends])

In U_4, the subject pronoun is preferably interpreted as referring to Friedman, who is the new C_b and again heads the C_f list; the ensuing transition is a SMOOTH SHIFT, i.e., now the topic of the discourse has changed from Brennan to Friedman.

U_4: She often beats her.
C_b: [FRIEDMAN:Friedman]
C_f: ([FRIEDMAN:she] [BRENNAN:her])

From a computational standpoint, in order to make use of the predictions of Centering theory for the purpose of reference resolution, the theory needs to be operationalized. To this end, Brennan, Walker and Pollard (1987) proposed an algorithm that works in a "generate and test" fashion: Given an utterance U_n of the discourse, it first (i) constructs all possible pairs of a C_b and a C_f list, then (ii) applies several filters to reduce the set, and finally (iii) ranks the remaining pairs in order to determine the best hypothesis, which entails referent assignments to the pronouns in U_n (if any).

We illustrate this procedure by showing how U_4 in the example given above would be processed. Phase (i) would build C_f lists consisting of possible referents for the subject pronoun followed by possible referents for the direct object pronoun (as prescribed by the ranking proposed in Centering theory). Applying morphological constraints, Brennan and Friedman are possible antecedents in both cases; thus the two candidate C_f lists are:

([FRIEDMAN:she] [BRENNAN:her])
([BRENNAN:she] [FRIEDMAN:her])

The algorithm considers all entities from $C_f(U_{n-1})$ as possible backward centers and adds NIL as a term denoting that no C_b can be found for the current utterance. Hence, for our example utterance U_4, the C_b candidates are ([FRIEDMAN:Friedman] [BRENNAN:her] [WEEKEND:weekends] NIL). The cross-product of this list and the two C_f lists is the result of Phase (i): in our case, eight different $<C_b, C_f>$ pairs.

In Phase (ii), three filters are employed to reduce the set of candidate pairs. One removes pairs that would assign the same antecedents to pronouns that have been indexed as incompatible in a previous phase of syntactic/semantic analysis. The second filter implements the constraint requiring C_b to be the highest-ranked element of $C_f(U_{n-1})$ that is realized in U_n. Any $<C_b, C_f>$ pair violating this condition is eliminated; in our example, this applies to pairs having a C_b that differs from FRIEDMAN, and, thus, we are left with only two pairs:

P1: $<$[FRIEDMAN:Friedman], ([FRIEDMAN:she] [BRENNAN:her])$>$
P2: $<$[FRIEDMAN:Friedman], ([BRENNAN:she] [FRIEDMAN:her])$>$

The third filter implements the "pronominalization rule" and eliminates pairs where some element from $C_f(U_{n-1})$ is realized as a pronoun in U_n but the C_b is not. In our example utterance U_4, both entities on C_f are realized as pronouns, and so both P1 and P2 survive the filter.

Finally, Phase (iii) is in charge of ranking the remaining $<C_b, C_f>$ pairs – this is the step in which the preference hierarchy over transitions comes into play. The algorithm finds that P1 would amount to a SMOOTH SHIFT, while P2 would be a ROUGH SHIFT, and thus P1 is chosen as the preferred solution, whereby the pronouns are being assigned their antecedents as shown.

These examples discussed in the early Centering literature focus on linguistically interesting phenomena of pronominalization, but they are, of course, relatively simple. When moving from laboratory examples to authentic text, some additional factors need to be considered, such as that of avoiding boredom: Should the topic of the discourse, i.e., the center, stay the same across many sentences, an author usually would *not* repeatedly mention it as a pronoun in subject position. And some further complications need to be dealt with, e.g., how to apply the theory in cases of complex sentences with various kinds of clause embedding (see Kameyama 1998). In fact, following the early work in the 1980s, much research was conducted within the framework of Centering theory, and variants of several aspects of the theory have been explored.[4] Here, we will concentrate on the ordering of forward-looking centers, about which Brennan, Walker and Pollard (1987: 156) already observed that their ranking of grammatical roles "usually coincides with surface constituent order in English" and that it would be "of interest to examine data from languages with relatively freer constituent order (e.g., German) to determine the influence of constituent order upon centering."

2.1.2. Anaphora and familiarity status

One of the studies which takes up this idea is that conducted by Strube and Hahn (1999), which claims that the ordering of the C_f list should not be determined by grammatical roles but by differences in *familiarity status* of referents in the sense of Prince (1981, 1992). In her early work, Prince had proposed a fairly complex taxonomy of categories, shown in Figure 1. "Evoked" referents are readily accessible to the reader, because they were present in the prior discourse or in the utterance situation. "Inferable"

---

[4] An early synopsis was provided in (Walker, Joshi and Prince 1998), and a more recent survey, specifically from the perspective of computational linguistics, is given by Poesio et al. (2004). Beaver (2004) rephrases centering theory within an optimality-theoretical framework in which a set of constraints evaluate pairs of possible anaphoric forms and interpretations.

referents are related to evoked ones, and Prince distinguishes between whether this relation is one of "containment" (as in "one of these eggs") or a different one (e.g., part-whole). Among the "new" referents, we find those that are known to the reader in principle, but have not yet been used in the discourse (e.g., "the sun"); others are brand-new, and the subcategory "anchored" covers those immediately derived from a known entity (e.g., "a friend of mine").

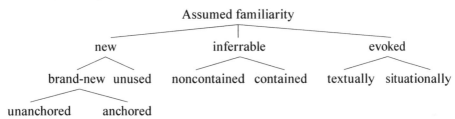

Figure 1. Taxonomy of "familiarity status" categories (Prince 1981)

For their pronoun resolution algorithm, Strube and Hahn require only a coarse-grained version of this taxonomy, by which the entities referred to in an utterance can either be "hearer-old" or "hearer–new" (a distinction introduced in (Prince 1992)). The former are further separated into "evoked" (pronominal and nominal anaphora, previously mentioned proper names, etc.) and "unused" referents (proper names and titles of entities that are discourse-new but hearer-old). Hearer-new entities, in contrast, are entities that have been newly introduced in the discourse, and correspond to the category "brand-new" in the original taxonomy.

The general idea of Strube and Hahn's approach, which they call "Functional Centering", is primarily to order the C_f list for an utterance by familiarity: Hearer-old discourse entities are ranked higher than hearer-new discourse entities. Further, if two entities have the same familiarity status, then their relative order mirrors that of linear precedence in the sentence. Stated more formally, let ◀ denote the ordering relation on C_f and pos a function yielding the position of an expression in the utterance; then the rules are as follows:

1. If $x \in$ OLD and $y \in$ NEW, then $x \blacktriangleleft y$
2. If $x, y \in$ OLD or $x, y \in$ NEW, then $x \blacktriangleleft y$, if $pos(x) < pos(y)$

Strube and Hahn make this point in particular for German, but they also present some evidence, which supports the application of their ranking criteria to English data, i.e., a language with less freedom in constituent ordering.

Their pronoun resolution procedure, then, relies only on this particular C_f ordering – it does not require the notion of a backward-looking center, nor that of transition types:

Process utterance U_n:

(i) If a pronoun is encountered in U_n, test the elements of $C_f(U_{n-1})$ in the given order until an element satisfies all the required morphosyntactic, binding, and sortal criteria. This element is chosen as the antecedent of the pronoun.

(ii) When utterance U_n is completely read, generate $C_f(U_n)$; rank the elements by familiarity and linear precedence.

Using a corpus consisting of portions of German newspaper and fictional texts, the authors report that their pronoun resolution (for 3rd person and possessive pronouns) based on Functional Centering achieves 9% more accuracy (83.7% versus 74.8%) than the algorithm proposed by Brennan, Walker and Pollard (1987), which was sketched in the previous subsection. This indicates that for languages with less-restricted word order, familiarity status and linear precedence are more predictive features for pronominal accessibility than the grammatical functions are.

In addition, Strube and Hahn provide an extension of their approach for texts where the main problems of anaphora resolution are not caused by the pronouns but by indirect anaphora with definite NPs (also called "inferables" or "bridging anaphora"), by using the more fine-grained familiarity status labels from Prince (1981) as shown in Figure 1, and a more elaborate ranking and resolution procedure.

The corpus annotation of familiarity status was done manually by Strube and Hahn, in order to enable them to perform a simulation of their algorithm and determine the figures given above. From a computational perspective, the question arises whether this type of annotation can also be done automatically, so that an anaphora resolution module could profit from this pre-processing. Before trying to build such a system, however, it is methodologically sensible to first investigate whether human annotators can perform such an annotation reliably. This can be done by having multiple annotators work on the same data and then checking the degree of their agreement. In general, such studies have to be received and compared carefully, since a lot depends on the level of "difficulty" provided by the particular data set, the precise formulation of the annotation guidelines, the amount of "training" that annotators have received, and a variety of other factors. However, there is evidence that humans can work quite reliably with the category familiarity status.[5] For example, Nissim et al. (2004) proposed a classification that combines elements from Prince's original taxonomy, her later distinction of discourse/hearer-old/new, along with some new categories. The top level consists of "old" (defined as discourse-old and hearer-old), "mediated" (discourse-new but inferable), and "new"; "old" is then split into six subtypes, and "mediated" into nine. For this fairly complex tag set, the annotation guidelines provide a decision tree that establishes priorities for cases where more than one tag seems to apply. With this provision, the authors report kappa values[6] of 0.845 for the basic three-way distinction and 0.788 for the full taxonomy, which can be regarded as a good level of agreement, indicating that the task can be accomplished without too much guesswork. The data used in the study were transcriptions of three dialogues from the Switchboard corpus of telephone conversations (cf. Section 4.1).[7]

The ability to determine familiarity status automatically is important for anaphora resolution, where handling definite noun phrases (as opposed to pronouns) is particularly challenging. While the general rule of thumb suggests that an indefinite NP is used to introduce new referents into the discourse while definite NPs take up known referents, Vieira and Poesio (2000) found that 50% of the definite NPs in their corpus of newspaper articles were, in fact, not anaphoric but discourse-new, usually because the referent was known to be unique by world knowledge. Hence, an anaphora resolution module considering the analysis of a definite NP needs to know whether it should look for an antecedent at all. The idea that this decision can be made *without* relying on world knowledge goes back to Hawkins (1978), who identified several correlations between discourse-new definite NPs and features of their syntactic environment. He thus proposed a list of "special predicates" that license definiteness because they are semantically functional (e.g., "the fact that X", "the conclusion that X", etc.), because they contain superlatives or adjectives such as "first", "last", "maximum", etc., or because the nouns denote temporal entities ("morning", "afternoon",

---

5   For an overview of annotation schemes, including a critique and a new proposal, see Riester (2008).

6   For a discussion of Cohen's kappa as a measurement of inter-annotator agreement in computational linguistics, see Artstein and Poesio (2008).

7   The importance of the role of text type was demonstrated by Ritz, Dipper and Götze (2008), who applied the same annotation guidelines to three different German data sets. With seven categories, kappa was 0.55 for newspaper commentary, 0.61 for "maptask" dialogues, and 0.73 for question-answer pairs elicited by a questionnaire.

etc.). Further, Hawkins proposed some rules for distinguishing restrictive from non-restrictive modification, which is another major factor in the distinction discourse-new/old. A computational implementation of his observations was presented by Vieira and Poesio (2000), who defined syntactic patterns for their parser (also adding some rules for appositions and proper names); the implementation achieved 72% precision and 69% recall in identifying discourse-new descriptions in their newspaper corpus.

Several other researchers tackled the non-/anaphoricity problem with machine learning approaches rather than with hand-coded rules. For example, Ng and Cardie (2002) coded 37 different features with a decision tree induction system, which applied to all types of nominals, not just to definite NPs. The features belonged to four groups: lexical (string or head matching), grammatical (syntactic type of NP, various properties, some specific forms), semantic (lexical relationship), and positional (is the NP located at the beginning of the text). The authors report accuracies of 84% and 86.1% for two different data sets. Note that the figures cannot be compared to those of Vieira and Poesio, as Ng and Cardie also classified pronouns, which are almost always anaphoric, and hence the overall task was somewhat easier.

The binary decision problem (old versus new NP referent) is of course considerably more coarse-grained than Prince's taxonomy with its seven categories. A few studies have employed at least the top-level three-way distinction, thus adding a category for referents that can be inferred from old referents. Working with transcribed spoken dialogues, Nissim (2006) used only seven features to train her decision tree model, including one fairly "deep" one (the grammatical role), the syntactic type of the NP and the determiner, and measurements of previous mentions. The overall accuracy achieved is 79.5%, which includes a rather bad performance on new referents (precision 62.3%; recall only 23.4%). Nissim then re-calculated the results with a conflation of the categories "mediated" and "new", which leads to a much higher accuracy of 93.1%; not surprisingly, the "mediated" category is thus creating considerable difficulty for the automatic classification.

2.1.3. Salience-based approaches to pronoun resolution

The step from "Classical" (Section 2.1.1) to "Functional" Centering (beginning of Section 2.1.2) and related approaches was quite significant: Instead of only examining discourse segments in pairs and assigning the main responsibility for coreference decisions to grammatical roles, Functional

Centering posited that familiarity status be the decisive phenomenon; determining this status, then, can depend on quite a variety of factors, as we have seen. One way of modeling this situation computationally is to abandon discrete, categorical distinctions of familiarity and move to a continuous numerical scale instead. In this line of research, the term *salience* is often used to denote the degree to which a referent is accessible at a particular point during discourse processing. Such models can be developed from a cognitive perspective, i.e., as simulation of mental processes, or from the practical needs of anaphora – in particular, pronoun resolution. The latter approach is exemplified by a well-known algorithm from Lappin and Leass (1994), which we will briefly introduce here. They focused on personal pronouns and on inter-sentential anaphora; thus, in the following, considerations of syntactic binding are ignored.[8]

Similar to the discourse center hypothesis, the basic idea of Lappin and Leass's (1994) procedure is to associate a pronoun with the antecedent expression that morphosyntactically agrees with the pronoun and whose referent is currently the most salient. Processing a discourse thus means keeping a list of referents and their salience values, and updating these salience values when moving from one unit of discourse to the next. So, Lappin and Leass (1994) claim that an ordered C_f list, as implemented in Centering theory, is not powerful enough to capture the interplay of various factors contributing to relative degrees of salience, and hence they introduce numerical weights. Whenever a referent is mentioned in a sentence, its weight increases by a certain amount, which depends largely on grammatical features. Thus, a referent mentioned in subject position receives 80 points, whereas the direct object receives 50, and other complements only 40 points. A referent introduced in a presentational construction (e.g., "There was...") gains 70 points. Subsequently, "structural" prominence is additionally rewarded: Referents that are *not* mentioned within an adverbial phrase receive another 50 points, and those realized as head nouns another 80 points. Processing a sentence in this fashion amounts to accumulating points for the various referents, which are supposed to capture the differences in salience. Furthermore, the algorithm encodes a recency preference: When moving from one sentence to the next, all the salience values are reduced by 50%, but the referents in the previous sentence receive an extra 100 points. The resulting ordering of referents according to their weights is

---

[8]   A similar approach with a somewhat broader scope, a more thorough grounding in syntactic theory, and greater emphasis on evaluation methodology was later proposed by Stuckardt (2001).

then taken as the basis for resolving pronouns. Naturally, one may ask: How did Lappin and Leass (1994) arrive at precisely those weights? The answer to this question is, that they studied a corpus of expository texts, devised their general algorithm, and then adjusted the weights in such a way that performance of the algorithm became optimal for that particular corpus.

Nowadays, one would automatically derive the optimal weights from an annotated corpus by using machine learning techniques. In this way, it is possible to detect genre-specific differences by allowing the algorithm to learn from different corpora. More importantly, the optimal weights are likely to differ between languages, and which of the dimensions of salience induction are language-universal and which have to be adapted to the grammatical properties of a particular language is an interesting research issue.

2.2. Automatic analysis of topic and focus

Due to its immediate relevance for anaphora resolution, the computation of familiarity status is highly important for computational approaches to text understanding. Other IS dimensions, in particular the topic/comment or focus/background structure, have received much less attention in computational linguistics; and besides being less relevant for practical applications, their treatment is also considerably more difficult. That is the reason why most of the work in this context has been done on the basis of existing *treebanks*, i.e., corpora that have been manually annotated with syntactic structure (and possibly on other levels, too). In particular, the *Prague Dependency Treebank (PDT)*, a corpus of Czech texts from various genres, has played a central role in this type of research. The annotations are divided in three layers: morphology, surface syntax (dependency trees with grammatical roles), and deep syntax, which includes fewer nodes than the surface syntax layer (function words are omitted), but also adds traces for deleted material. Furthermore, on this layer (which is called the "tecto-grammatical" layer), the nodes are labeled with thematic roles.

The PDT was used in early experiments on the automatic detection of topic and focus (see Hajičová, Skoumalovà and Sgall 1995, which also contains a proposal for English), and later on, the tectogrammatical layer was extended with manual annotations of "topic-focus articulation" or "TFA" for short (Buranová, Hajičová and Sgall 2000). Here, topic is meant in the sense of aboutness-topic, and focus represents the information asserted about the topic, thus leading to a partitioning of the sentence. TFA, in turn, builds on distinguishing contextually-bound (CB) and unbound (UB) material, which is determined by using the familiar question test: Given a sentence, construct a question that the sentence serves as an answer to; then, label material in the sentence that provides a reproduction of material from the question as CB. Now, the TFA annotation of nodes on the tecto-grammatical layer uses three values: t for non-contrastive CB items; c for contrastive CB items; f for UB items. Buranová, Hajičová and Sgall (2000) provide rules (which are too complex to be reproduced here) for assigning these labels, using features of structural configurations, word order, and intonation. The rules were further developed into annotation guidelines, which were then evaluated for inter-annotator agreement (Vesela, Havelka and Hajičová 2004). When three annotators work with the three categories, the agreement is 82.24%; when the t and c values are conflated, the number rises to 86.42%.

When moving from working with a treebank to "raw" or minimally-processed text, the situation becomes more difficult. The aforementioned annotation study by Ritz, Dipper and Götze (2008) dealt not only with familiarity but also with identifying topic and focus. The guidelines they used (Dipper, Götze and Skopeteas 2007) treat these two as independent: one as part of a topic-comment distinction and the other as part of a focus-background distinction. Similar to the PDT, two types of focus are distinguished in these guidelines: contrastive and new-information. For topic, there are also two subcategories – aboutness and frame-setting (see Section 5.1 in Chapter 1) – that can occur in a sentence simultaneously: "[Physically]$_{fs}$, [Peter]$_{ab}$ is doing very well." Annotators were given texts with pre-labeled NPs (defining the set of "markables" to choose from) and had to independently identify topics and foci in different types of German text. For topic, kappa values were between 0.46 (newspaper commentary) and 0.91 (question-answer pairs elicited in an experiment); for foci, the respective values were 0.41 and 0.62. These values indicate that the task is either hard to define, or inherently difficult, or both. One would expect that focus is easier to recognize in spoken than in written language – an issue we will address later in Section 4.1.

3. Text generation

While text understanding amounts to constructing an adequate representation of meaning for some input text, text generation solves the (to some extent reverse) problem of producing an adequate text from a specification of its meaning. The nature of this specification depends heavily on the scenario of its application: Some text generators take raw data as input, for instance when generating reports from time-series data; others expect full-fledged, structured semantic representations (in some logical or frame-based formalism), possibly supplemented by a specification of the under-lying communicative goal(s) that are to be achieved with the text. To give a concrete example, in a book recommendation application (Stede 2002), the system asks the user to provide attributes of the book being sought (spe-cific topic, length, language, etc.), then it retrieves suitable books from the database, and finally it generates a description for each book based on the database entry plus the information on which attributes actually match the expectation of the user. Furthermore, thanks to the dynamic generation process, comparisons between similar books can be included. The degree of matching between user preferences and book features, in turn, affects the communicative goal: Should the system, for instance, *highly recom-mend* a book (because it is an almost perfect match) or merely *describe* the book in more neutral terms (because it barely matches the expectations)? In this case, inserting evaluative adjectives or choosing suggestive verbs are among the means of achieving the communicative goal.

In general, text generators tend to follow a three-step architecture as described in detail by Reiter and Dale (2000):

1. *Text planning* decides what information is to be communicated, and how it is to be arranged – the discourse structure is fixed (at least to some extent).
2. *Sentence planning* breaks the overall information down into sentence-size chunks, chooses the content words that are to be used for each projected sentence, and decides on the sentence structure to be used.
3. *Surface realization* maps each "sentence plan" to a well-formed sentence in the target language, using grammatical knowledge; it also selects cer-tain function words (prepositions, determiners).

Nowadays, actual implementations typically produce short texts within domains that lend themselves to formal models (of both the content and the structure of the texts); many systems produce reports of various kinds (e.g., weather reports, stock market reports, or project reports based on data from respective software tools). A popular area of application is medicine, where research prototypes have been developed for producing medication leaflets, clinical documents such as discharge summaries, or personalized "stop smoking" recommendation letters.

Natural language generation (NLG) has always been conceived as a matter of serialized *choices under constraints:* In addition to the constraint that the output faithfully present the meaning encoded in its input, many generators try to find the *most suitable* sequence of sentences in the given context. Often, the factors influencing generation decisions are in conflict with one another, such that the overall process is modeled as one of *weighted-constraint satisfaction,* i.e., as an optimization problem.[9] Since information structure is a major factor of differentiation between similar sentences (and texts), IS-related considerations have always played a significant role in the NLG choice processes.

3.1. Focus of attention in text planning

In most generators, the linear order of the information to be presented is being arranged in the first phase, i.e., during text planning. Accordingly, research on text planning has, from the beginning, been concerned with discourse-level aspects of information structure, that is, how to linearize the (at this stage pre-verbal) content in such a way that the text will move smoothly from topic to topic, rather than irregularly jumping back and forth. Consider the following short example from Kibble and Power (2004: 401) who argue that the two variants communicate the same information, but that a generator should strive to produce variant (a) rather than (b):

(1) a. *Elixir is a white cream.*
It is used in the treatment of cold sores.
It contains aliprosan.
Aliprosan relieves viral skin disorders.

b. *Elixir contains aliprosan.*
Viral skin disorders are relieved by aliprosan.
Elixir is used in the treatment of cold sores.
It is a white cream.

The crucial concept here is the "focus of attention", which we introduced in Section 2.1.1 above when discussing Centering. In this particular respect, generation can, in fact, be seen as the converse of understanding: While Centering tries to infer the discourse center from the grammatical roles and types of referring expressions, text generation (when planning the sentences) actively *selects* grammatical roles, word order, and types of referring expressions, so that the reader will be able to correctly identify the

---

[9] However, in the actual implementations, not all approaches formally solve an optimization problem; sometimes, the search for the best solution is merely guided by heuristics that do not guarantee an optimal result.

object in the center. This, of course, presupposes that the generator has an idea of what the central entities of the text are and how they ought to be distributed as "most" central in the various portions of the text. This arrangement, which applies globally across the entire text, needs to be determined in the text planning stage, so that the sentence planner, then, has the relevant information at its disposal.

To this end, in the pioneering work by McKeown (1985) on *schema*-based text generation, text planning was performed by first selecting a schema from a library of pre-fabricated ones (which would cover different types of discourse) and then sequentially filling this schema with propositions from the set of propositions-to-be-communicated. To guide this choice, the planner maintained three registers of past, current, and potential focus in order to achieve an adequate linear sequence. It applied four focusing rules in the following order: try to shift the focus to an entity mentioned in the previous proposition; maintain the current focus; resume a past focus; and shift focus to an entity most related to the current focus.[10]

Later on, more flexible approaches to text planning were developed. The idea of Hovy and McCoy (1989) was to abandon pre-fabricated text schemata and instead build the "rhetorical structure" of the text by combining propositions via coherence relations in the sense of Rhetorical Structure Theory (Mann and Thompson 1988). Two propositions can be linked by a relation (e.g., Sequence, Circumstance, Purpose), and the resulting three-node tree can in turn be combined with another proposition or another tree, so that a complete tree is produced recursively (this tree represents the text plan and is then given to the sentence planner). Again, one has to make sure that an adequate linear ordering is achieved; Hovy and McCoy (1989) employed a *focus tree* for this purpose, which served as a structured representation of the entities-in-focus and allowed for more elaborate ordering procedures than the three lists used by McKeown (1985).

For purely descriptive or expository text, where relationships between entities are basically static, such relatively simple models of maintaining focus of attention are often sufficient. For narrative text, when it comes to verbalizing more complex event structures, however, the notion of discourse focus needs to be augmented, as argued by Maybury (1991). The input to his system is a network of events and states produced by simulation software (in this case, for military missions). Events and states are represented as predicate-argument structures with time stamps, and they can

---

[10] This last step obviously requires some sort of semantic network knowledge in order to compute "relatedness" of entities.

be connected to one another by causal or temporal relations. In order to map such a network to a text plan and thereby decide how the information is to be ordered, the system computes the "saliency" of each event on the basis of (i) the number of links it has to other events, (ii) the frequency of its occurrence, and (iii) some domain-specific knowledge of its importance (i.e., the relevance of event types in the particular domain). The text planner can be parameterized so that the events are recounted either by similarity of topic, in temporal order, reflecting causal relationships, or in terms of spatial proximity. In order to achieve this, Maybury's system uses different focus lists for topic, temporal, and spatial focus, where each individually plays the same role as in the earlier approaches.

The division of labor between text planning and sentence planning is not without its problems. The question of how to order the propositions is related quite closely to how the constituents are to be ordered in the sentences; after all, a single badly constructed sentence can completely spoil the thematic development of the text. When the strong modularity is to be maintained, i.e., when no interaction is allowed between the two stages, the text planner can mark elements of the propositions as "to be topical", so that the sentence planner can try to make decisions that realize this specification. In effect, as Kibble and Power (2004) point out, one has to make the assumption that the text planner can predict certain options for syntactic realization on the basis of the argument structure of predicates – to some extent it needs to anticipate the lexicalization decisions (in particular the choice of the verb). These authors formulate the problem in terms of Centering: Propositions need to be arranged in such a way that "good" transitions can be achieved. However, the transition types (as proposed by Brennan, Walker and Pollard (1987), see above) need to be *operationalized* for the generation task: We need to actively decide which transition to use under what circumstances. Kibble and Power (2004: 406) cite a lack of conclusive empirical evidence for the preference of certain transitions (e.g., Retain over Smooth Shift) and replace them in their generation system with four individual constraints. Their text planner enumerates all possible linearizations of the discourse structure and then determines which one incurs the least violations of these constraints (which in practice can be weighted to fit particular applications). The constraints are:

Cohesion: $\quad C_b(U_{n-1}) = C_b(U_n)$

Salience: $\quad C_p(U_n) = C_b(U_n)$

Cheapness: $\quad C_p(U_{n-1}) = C_b(U_n)$

Continuity: $\quad C_f(U_{n-1}) \cap C_f(U_n) \neq \emptyset$

3.2.   Information structure in sentence planning and realization

After the linear order in which propositions are to be communicated has been fixed and an assignment of propositions to (future) sentences has been decided, the remaining sentence planning tasks that are immediately relevant to IS are: choosing the lexical units for verbalizing the information, constructing adequate referring expressions (including pronouns), and fixing the order of the constituents. Since approaches to text generation differ somewhat on the question of where to draw the line between sentence planning and realization, for our purposes here we will leave this distinction aside and discuss the two stages in tandem.

In order to make well-motivated information structural decisions when planning and realizing sentences, the generator needs to maintain a *discourse model* that keeps track of entities and propositions that are being referred to, so that each realization – for example, of a referring expression – will be appropriate in the given context. In the following, we first discuss the role of such discourse models in generation research, and then the task of "translating" the information from the discourse model into generation decisions.

3.2.1.   Discourse models in sentence planning

For many practical applications where only relatively "simple" text is produced, it is sufficient to limit the discourse model to a list of the entities that the text so far has referred to, augmented by their respective familiarity status (for instance, using Prince's (1992) categories, as introduced in Section 2), so that pronouns can be produced where appropriate – which is probably the minimum IS requirement for a text to be acceptable. After planning and generating a sentence, the familiarity status of those entities that have been mentioned needs to be updated.

Beyond this basic step, a number of more elaborate models have been proposed. In the SPUD sentence planner (Stone et al. 2001), entities are given both a newness value in Prince's terms (hearer-old/new and discourse-old/new) and a salience assignment, which amounts to a partial order indicating how accessible the entities are for reference in the current context. Furthermore, a certain amount of non-linguistic background knowledge is necessary in order to make decisions on some non-canonical syntactic constructions, as will be shown in the next subsection. This background knowledge is needed to supply information on how the entities are being related to each other, in particular whether they stand in a *partial-order set relation* (*poset*, for short) to one another. Such poset relations include part – whole, subset – superset, and class membership.

Endriss and Klabunde (2000) proposed a model that is similarly rich in information, and whose mechanics are derived from Discourse Representation Theory (Kamp and Reyle 1993). Their discourse model thus consists basically of a pair <R,K>, where R is a set of mutually known discourse referents, and K a set of DRS conditions (essentially predications on the referents), which represent the propositions to be communicated in a decomposed form. Since their primary interest lay in the role of IS in sentence production, Endriss and Klabunde (2000) subsequently made a number of finer distinctions. First, they split R into two subsets R_A and R_N, consisting of referents that appeared in the directly preceding sentence, and in the remaining previous sentences, respectively. Then, they added three sets to the discourse model, which record specific attributes of the referents:

- *Ref* records the discourse status of referents: It can be *new* (not mentioned yet), *maintained* (meaning that it is currently "active"), or *re-established* (meaning that it was mentioned earlier on in the discourse).
- *Id* derives information on the identifiability of the referents from *Ref*; its values are *unidentifiable* (for a new referent), *identifiable* (usually for re-established referents that can be realized with a definite description), *anaphorically identifiable* (for maintained referents).
- *Alt* stores alternative sets for referents: If two referents in R are both instances of the same superordinate concept, they are treated as potential alternatives (which may be relevant for focus marking decisions).

Obviously, *Alt* is to be supplied by background knowledge, and constitutes a static component of the discourse model. The other parts are subject to being updated when a sentence has been produced: Any new referents mentioned in the sentence are added to R_A; referents that were mentioned in the last sentence but are not mentioned in the current one are moved from R_A to R_N; and in the case in which an "old" referent is being re-established, it is moved from R_N to R_A. Similarly, the *Ref* and *Id* sets are brought up to date, and the propositional content of the new sentence is added in the form of DRS conditions to K.

A recording of this kind represents the informational state that the writer assumes the reader to have constructed at a particular point of text production/reception, and hence it is essentially backward looking. A complementary aspect, which, so far, has received less attention in generation research (or in discourse research in general), is that of looking *forward*: A speaker or writer knows which entities are going to remain relevant in the subsequent discourse, and this private knowledge can be expected to have effects on sentence planning decisions as well. Pattabhiraman and Cercone (1990) use the terms "salience" and "relevance" for the two dimensions; Chiarcos (2010) speaks of "hearer-salience" and "speaker-salience". In contrast to the structured, symbolic discourse models described above, Chiarcos proposes a numerical model, where "salience scores" for both dimensions are recorded for all the entities and updated after a sentence has been generated (quite similar to the numerical models of anaphora resolution mentioned in Section 2). In any case, the role of the discourse model is to assist IS-related production decisions in the upcoming sentence, to which we turn next.

3.2.2. Making IS-related generation decisions

Maybe the most important decision to be made by a sentence planner, in general, is *lexical choice*: the mapping from pre-verbal propositions to lexical units of the target language. Choosing the verb and possibly one of its alternations, in particular, has consequences for information structure because of the associated role linking (the assignment of grammatical roles to arguments of the predicate in the proposition). However, discussing general lexical choice, with its manifold non-IS-related aspects, would lead us too far away from our subject; for our purposes here, we concentrate, instead, on two sentence planning tasks that also have immediate relevance for the information structure: deciding on the word order, and on the form of referring expressions.

3.2.2.1. Word order

For many languages, a common generation strategy is to assume a "standard" word order as prescribed by grammatical rules, and to depart from this order only when faced with special circumstances. Whether or not these circumstances hold, is something the generator needs to derive from the current state of the discourse model. The good news is that existing descriptive-functional work on the licensing conditions of "non-canonical constructions" provides a good starting point for implementing these decisions in a sentence planner. For example, Prince (1998) argued that left-dislocation (as in "The new John Irving novel, I read it already") is possible only when the initial NP stands in a salient *poset* relation (see above) with some previously evoked entity in the discourse model. For the example sentence, this condition is met when the preceding sentence is "Five books were offered to me", so that there is a set-member relation between "five books" and "the new John Irving novel". Birner and Ward (1998) proposed that the same condition hold for topicalization, and that in addition the open proposition expressed by the main clause, which is constructed by replacing the constituent receiving tonic stress by a variable, is salient to the hearer.

One such generator implementing constraints of this kind is the above-mentioned SPUD (Stone et al. 2001). Using the formalism of Lexicalized Tree Adjoining Grammar (Yang, McCoy and Vijay-Shanker 1991), SPUD constructs a syntactic tree for a sentence from a set of candidate elementary trees encoding lexical items and their syntactic behavior, with variant trees for specific syntactic constructions. For instance, a transitive verb is associated with a tree for the canonical word order, with one for the topicalized form, etc. All elementary trees are paired with semantic/pragmatic representations (in analogy to compositional semantic analysis in language understanding), so that the generator can successively enumerate those complete syntactic trees that faithfully express the given input specification of the meaning. The constraints associated with elementary trees have different degrees of specificity, and SPUD aims at building the sentence tree from elementary trees whose semantic/pragmatic representation is maximally specific; in this way, IS constraints can be encoded. SPUD thus produces a topicalization whenever the specific pragmatic conditions are met: The referent stands in a poset relation to a referent that has just been mentioned, and there is a salient open proposition, as characterized by Birner and Ward (1998). A similar approach, albeit in a different formal framework, was implemented by Klabunde and Jansche (1998), whose generator produces left-dislocation or a hanging-topic construction when specific pragmatic conditions are met, and a "simple" canonical construction otherwise.

However, as noted by Valduvi (1990) and elaborated for NLG by Cresswell (2002), one should be aware of the fact that while licensing conditions of the kind given above are *necessary*, they are by no means *sufficient*. In authentic text material, the corresponding constructions are clearly not used in each case in which the conditions are satisfied. The consequence is that algorithms based on just encoding the licensing conditions will *overgenerate*, i.e., produce the non-canonical constructions much too often.[11] Cresswell (2002) argues that one should be careful to distinguish these three cases:

- The non-canonical construction is entirely optional.
- The non-canonical form is odd even though the necessary conditions hold.
- The non-canonical form is obligatory, because different inferences are triggered when using it.

Cresswell (2002) suggests that a sentence planner based on pragmatic goals, like SPUD, ought to be extended by three additional goals: (i) With *attention-marking* goals, speakers employ a non-canonical construction to indicate what entity is particularly relevant in the current context. (ii) *Discourse relation* goals can trigger the usage of a non-canonical form whenever the continuation of the discourse somehow violates the default expectation (e.g., in terms of temporal development, when the discourse relation is not NARRATIVE but PARALLEL). (iii) *Focus-marking* goals can be responsible for the usage of a non-canonical form in order to disambiguate the focus-background structure. Cresswell (2002) did not go so far as to offer a computational solution, though, which means that her proposal still is an open research issue.

Generation through the combination of lexicalized trees that pair syntactic with semantic/pragmatic information is a thorough and systematic way by which the production decisions may be made. For languages with less-restricted word order, however, the search space becomes quite large, and selecting the most appropriate realization among many alternatives becomes increasingly difficult. An alternative production model for such languages is that of "grammatical competition",[12] where (possibly weighted) constraints on linear order are posited by various modules of the system, and during realization, the order that violates the lowest number of constraints is selected. Endriss and Klabunde (2000) proposed to integrate certain IS-related word order preferences into such a model. The *topic* should precede the *focus*, and topic candidates are taken from the intersection of the R_A list of the discourse model (i.e., the referents realized in the previous

---

[11] Cresswell performed an empirical study and found that in her 750.000 word corpus of transcribed oral histories, the four non-canonical forms topicalization, left-disclocation, *it*-cleft, and *wh*-cleft occur 850 times in total.

[12] For a comprehensive proposal of handling German word order with a (computational) competition model, see Uszkoreit (1987).

sentence) and the referents of the proposition to be realized. Then, they propose ordering rules for "referential movement": Maintained referents are to precede re-established ones, which in turn precede new referents (recall the definitions from the discourse model). And finally, anaphorically identifiable referents are to precede definite descriptions, which in turn precede nonidentifiable referents. These preferences are added to the pool of linearization constraints/preferences, which the surface realizer evaluates to determine the optimal overall linear order; ultimately, the success of such a model depends to a good extent on the weights associated with the various preferences – and these weights need to be individually motivated in one way or another. A common method is to derive them from an annotated corpus, i.e., to set them by using empirical evidence. An interesting study along these lines was presented by Cahill and Riester (2009), who also address the task of ranking candidate linearizations, in their case couched in the framework of Lexical-Functional Grammar (LFG). In this two-level framework, the generation task is the production of a constituent structure (c-structure for short) from a given functional structure (f-structure), which represents the "semantic input" to the sentence generator. Given the free word order, the generator may produce a whole range of well-formed sentence candidates; Cahill and Riester (2009) investigated the role of information status in ranking those candidates.

3.2.2.2. *Referring expressions*

The construction of referring expressions has enjoyed much attention in NLG research, since it is quite important for the successful production of acceptable text, and, in comparison to other aspects of text and sentence planning, it is relatively easy to isolate: Algorithms for choosing referring expressions can be developed, tested, and compared independently of a complete generation system. Probably the most research has been concerned with finding *minimal distinguishing* descriptions: Given a set of objects and one of them to be identified, what is the minimal linguistic description that serves to pick it out? Let us focus here on the problem of *pronoun generation*, which is – at least to a good extent – driven by IS-related factors.[13] As long as fairly short texts of limited complexity are to be generated, a straightforward solution is to implement the rules of Centering theory, as

---

[13] For an interesting extension of a classical "minimal distinguishing description" algorithm with saliency factors, see Krahmer and Theune (2002).

introduced earlier. This method was used, for instance, in the ILEX generator (Oberlander et al. 1998) and in ICONOCLAST (Kibble and Power 2004); these systems always pronominalize the backward-looking center C_b.

There are two problems with this simple approach: For one thing, the pronominalization rule (a referent can be referred to with a pronoun only if the C_b is also pronominalized) applies only in cases where two subsequent utterances share two (or more) referents, and it does not offer any rule or explanation for why the non-C_b might be pronominalized. The second problem surfaces when studying authentic text of non-trivial complexity: It turns out that a large number of C_bs are *not* pronominalized, which means that more specific rules are needed. Building on earlier work by McCoy and Strube (1999), these questions were tackled by Henschel, Cheng and Poesio (2000), who studied a corpus of museum labels of different kinds (catalogue texts, etc.). Their 5000-word corpus contained 1450 NPs, 23% of which formed reference chains, i.e., they were mentioned at least twice in the text. Henschel, Cheng and Poesio (2000) disregard locally bound pronouns, as they can be handled by the surface realizer on the grounds of grammatical rules. Subsequently, they studied those features of the context that seemed to influence the pronominalization decision for the remaining class of 101 pronouns in the corpus, which they called discourse pronouns.

The first of these features is *distance*. As the unit of measurement, Henschel, Cheng and Poesio (2000) use an "utterance", which they define as a finite clause; relative clauses and complement clauses are not counted as distinct utterances. The "previous utterance" is then defined as that preceding utterance which is on the same level of embedding as the utterance. Using this definition, it turns out that 97% of discourse pronouns have their antecedent in the same or in the previous utterance; henceforth these will be called "short-distance pronouns". The second feature is discourse status. Following Prince (1992), Henschel, Cheng and Poesio (2000) posit that pronominalization is governed by the distinction discourse-old/new, whereas definiteness is determined by information status (hearer-old/new). In the corpus, 66% of all the short-distance discourse pronouns have a discourse-old antecedent. The third and final feature is subjecthood. Not surprisingly for any proponent of Centering Theory, for 63% of the short-distance pronouns, the antecedent is realized as subject.

Based on these figures, Henschel, Cheng and Poesio (2000) define *local focus* – to be understood as the set of referents available for pronominalization, and to be updated at each utterance boundary – as the union of (i) discourse-old referents and (ii) those that were just realized as subject. Most often, both are the same singleton set, corresponding to the "classical" C_b.

As a step beyond Centering, though, the authors observe that newly introduced referents are not immediately pronominalized in the following utterance, unless they have been introduced as subject (which was also noted by Brennan 1998). This is understood as a reflection of two typical strategies for introducing a new referent into the discourse. Let X be a referent that is introduced in u_1 and referred to again in u_2. The first strategy introduces X in the new, non-subject part of u_1, and in that case, it is usually not pronominalized in u_2. An example from the corpus (Henschel, Cheng and Poesio 2000: 310):

> *Shortly after inheriting the building in 1752, he commissioned the architect Pierre Contant d'Ivry to renovate **the main rooms**. The engravings for **these rooms**, showing the wall lights in place, were reproduced in...*

The second strategy introduces X in subject position in u_1, which is often regarded as typical for the onset of a discourse segment, or for the beginning of the text. In this case, X is usually pronominalized in u_2. Thus, the subject position seems to function as creating a givenness allocation for the denoted referent. A corpus example:

> **Scottish born, Canadian based jeweller, Alison Bailey-Smith**, *constructs elaborate and ceremonial jewellery from industrial wire.* **Her** *materials are often gathered from sources such as abandoned television sets...*

Using this definition of local focus, it was found that 91% of all short-distance pronouns in the corpus are licensed. Most of the non-licensed pronouns occur in contexts of "strong parallelism", where the subject or object role in subsequent utterances is filled by the same referent. In the generation algorithm that Henschel, Cheng and Poesio (2000) derived from their observations, strong parallelism always overrides the local focus criterion and allows for the pronominalization of referents with discourse-new antecedents in non-subject position.

What remains to be clarified are the reasons for *not* pronominalizing a member of the local focus. Henschel, Cheng and Poesio (2000) point out that this sometimes happens as a means of avoiding ambiguity: When there is a competing referent for a pronoun besides the intended antecedent, a definite description is often preferred. In the corpus, though, half of the NPs in ambiguous contexts are, nevertheless, pronouns. The authors conclude that referents of the previous utterance which are *not* in the local focus do not disturb pronominalization, even if they have the same gender and number. Only if the actual referent has a competitor in the local focus, is pronominalization blocked. A second factor that impedes pronominalization may be the discourse structure. It has often been observed that definite descriptions (sometimes called "overspecified NPs") are employed to signal the reader that a new discourse segment is starting. Now, in a generation scenario, a text plan (as characterized above) does contain the boundaries of the intended discourse segments. The pronominalization algorithm can thus set the local focus to ∅ at each segment boundary, thereby disallowing pronominalization for all discourse entities of the first utterance in the segment. Figure 2 shows the algorithm given by Henschel, Cheng and Poesio (2000), which combines the insights just described. When simulating its performance on the corpus, its decisions agree with the original realizations in 87.8% of the cases.

Let X be a referent to be generated in utterance (u2), and *focus* be the set of referents of the previous utterance (u1) which are

   (a) discourse-old, or
   (b) realized as subject.

(1) X has an antecedent beyond a segment boundary	def description
(2) X has an antecedent two or more utterances distant	def description
(3) X has an antecedent in (u1), and	
(3a) X occurs in strong parallel context	pronoun
(3b) X ∉ *focus*	def description
(3c) X ∈ *focus* and	
• X has a competing referent Y ∈ *focus*	def description
• X has a competing referent Y in (u1) amplified with apposition or nonrestrictive relative clause	def description
• else	pronoun

The repetition blocking rule overrides the pronominalization suggested in (3c) to a definite description.

Figure 2. Pronominalization algorithm by Henschel, Cheng and Poesio (2000: 311)

As noted at the end of Section 3.2.1, most discourse models and their exploitations encode only backward-looking features; this is also the case for Henschel, Cheng and Poesio's (2000) algorithm. Chiarcos (2010) argues that the generation of referring expressions should also depend on looking forward, i.e., on the speaker's knowledge of the subsequent non-/importance of referents. In his algorithm for generating referring expressions, which extends a well-known proposal by Dale and Reiter (1995), the backward-looking salience is still the main criterion – referents have to be identifiable by the reader! – but an additional preference is added: When an entity is particularly speaker-salient, which means that it will remain highly promi-nent in subsequent utterances, Chiarcos's algorithm prefers a more marked realization of the nominal expression; his markedness hierarchy ranges from personal pronouns (unmarked) via demonstrative pronouns to definite pronouns, and finally to indefinite NPs.

As a final remark, it should be pointed out that in text generation, too, rule-based algorithms compete nowadays with statistical methods for solving certain problems. This started with the idea that surface realizers determine word order on the basis of statistical (*n-gram*) models learned from cor-pora (Langkilde and Knight 1998) and was also later extended to sentence planning. We mentioned the corpus-based approach of Cahill and Riester (2009) above; similarly, Stent, Prasad and Walker (2004) show how a good mapping from a text plan (tree of rhetorical relations and propositions) to a sequence of sentence plans can be obtained by learning a model from a set of pre-fabricated sentence plans, whose corresponding linguistic realizations have been judged for relative comprehensibility by human readers.

4. Spoken dialogue systems

Language understanding and language generation come together in the field of spoken dialogue systems, a very active research area in computational linguistics, which has also gained prominence in real-world applications (voice banking, travel information, package tracking systems, etc.). The current state of the art, however, allows for a certain amount of free interac-tion between user and computer (often illustrated by the initial system utterance being a general "How can I help you" rather than a very specific "Name the destination of your trip" or the like). In these cases, IS becomes important especially on the speech production side – which is also some-what easier to computationally implement than speech recognition.

4.1. Data annotation

Processing spoken language is a matter of statistical modeling, and hence it fundamentally relies on annotated corpora for training and evaluating these models. For American English, a standard resource is the *Switchboard* corpus, which is comprised of 2430 recorded telephone conversations.

Portions of it have been semi-automatically annotated with prosodic information, in particular with pauses and pitch accents, which were distinguished as *nuclear* (defined as structurally most prominent) and *plain* accents (Ostendorf et al. 2001). Also, some basic syntactic information (parts of speech, phrase boundaries) was added to the data. The interesting question, then, is how this information correlates with IS features. In order to study this, several researchers have proposed IS annotation schemata and applied them to portions of the Switchboard data; the familiarity categories (new, mediated, old) annotated by Nissim et al. (2004) have already been described in Section 2.1.2 of this chapter.

Calhoun et al. (2005) added two more levels of annotation. For one thing, prosodic phrases were marked as *theme* if they only contained information that linked the utterance to the preceding discourse, and *rheme* otherwise. The test for themes includes a prosodic feature: The utterance must sound appropriate when the theme phrase is said with a marked intonation such as L+H* LH%. An example given by Calhoun et al. (2005) is "I lived over in England for four years. [Where I lived]$_{theme}$ [was a town called Newmarket]$_{rheme}$." Here, it should be appropriate to place an L+H* accent on "Where" and/or "lived", and a final LH%. The second new level is Background/Contrast. Noting that the notion of "contrast" and its supposed prosodic correlates are fairly disputed in the literature, Calhoun et al. (2005) propose a rather "pre-theoretic" annotation that assigns to each content word the first appropriate label from this ordered list: *correction* (speaker uses word for correction or clarification), *contrastive* (speaker intends to contrast the word with a previous one), *subset* (speaker highlights one member of a set that is a current topic), *adverbial* (speaker uses a focus particle to highlight that word, and not another in the natural set), *answer* (the word or its phrase fills an open proposition set up in the context). If none of these labels apply, annotators are to mark the word as *background*. The authors argue that the data labeled with this *contrast* information can then be fruitfully exploited to investigate correlations with discourse structure or with more abstract speaker intentions.

4.2. Information structure in speech recognition

The basic problem of automatically detecting IS-relevant features in spoken language is the enormous variability that a speech recognizer has to deal with in the first place: Speakers have very different voices and articulation habits, which the recognizer needs to adapt to when encountering input, and in addition, it would be desirable to find markers of prominence or non-prominence that are relative to the general pattern of the speaker's voice. For human beings, this is usually unproblematic, but for a computational model operating in real-time, it presents a great challenge. One way to reduce the complexity, which is often pursued in theory-oriented work, is to work with controlled experiments or with *read* speech, for example with broadcast news. For practical applications (dialogue systems), however, such simplifications are not possible.

In practice, the accuracy of speech recognizers nowadays is far from perfect, so that efforts are clearly concentrated on "just" computing the most likely word sequence the speaker has uttered – leaving little room for attending to information structure. However, some work in this direction has been done on the basis of the above-mentioned Switchboard corpus, whose annotations can be used to train and evaluate statistical models. The overall problem is commonly split in two subtasks: The first is to detect mere "prominence" in the auditory signal, usually on the basis of pitch accents. This is a relatively well-studied task; for example, Sridhar et al. (2008) report an accuracy of 78% on the Switchboard data. The second subtask is to form a hypothesis about the underlying motivation of such "prominence", i.e., to interpret it as signaling some aspect of information structure (or not).

Using the Switchboard data with annotated pitch accents, givenness, and focus as described in the previous subsection, Sridhar et al. (2008) tried to automatically distinguish between new and old items occurring in natural conversational speech (as exemplified in Switchboard), based on their acoustic properties. The latter were modeled with 26 features representing pitch contour, duration, and energy. The authors performed only a binary classification by joining the categories "new" and "mediated" (thus contrasting them with "old"), which resulted in an accuracy of 79% across all noun phrases. Computing this across all types of NPs is, however, a somewhat artificial problem, as pronouns are almost always used to refer to "old" entities anyway. Thus, Sridhar et al. (2008) were also interested in the distribution of pitch accents across the full nouns only, and found that 82% of the "new" nouns bore a pitch accent, while the figures for "mediated" and "old" were 78% and 73%, respectively, a statistically significant difference. Hence not only in controlled speech (for which these factors have been analyzed in many earlier studies) are there measurable acoustic and prosodic differences between nouns with different givenness status, but also in spontaneous conversation. In particular, they found duration to be the most useful acoustic feature for separating "new" noun phrases from the others, while no feature could be found to predict the difference between "old" and "mediated" NPs.

Work on the automatic recognition of focus has also begun only very recently. Exploiting the whole spectrum of different annotations in the Switchboard corpus, Calhoun (2007) tested the hypothesis that focus can be modeled probabilistically: Focus should be more likely to occur on a word if it is more prominent, both structurally and acoustically, than would be expected given its syntactic and discourse features. He found that a binary focus/background distinction (thus merging the various focus categories in the corpus) can be predicted with 72.6% accuracy using only prosodic features (phrase breaks, accents); when information status and basic syntactic features (part of speech, position in phrase) are added, the figure increases to 74.8%; an additional measurement of acoustic prominence, combining duration and pitch features, leads to a further increase by 2.6%. Calhoun found that prosody alone is not sufficient to predict focus – it needs to be combined with syntax and familiarity status.[14] Finally, the question arises whether any measurable differences between the various subcategories of focus can be detected. Sridhar et al. (2008) used the categories *adverbial*, *contrastive*, *subset*, and *other*, and found that different acoustic characteristics distinguish them from the background class. In particular, acoustic features turn out to be useful for classifying *adverbial* and *other* correctly, while the remaining categories do not seem to profit from acoustic features, and, instead, may be classified more reliably by considering their part of speech.

4.3. Information structure in spoken language generation

In application oriented Computational Linguistics, the majority of work on producing spoken language deals with *text-to-speech synthesis*, where a written input, taken as just a string of surface words, is converted to speech on the basis of context-dependent grapheme-to-phoneme conversion. For many practical purposes, these surface based methods produce quite good results; however, it is precisely the information-structural considerations that are necessarily ignored in such approaches. In contrast, the "deeper"

---

[14] As for the interaction between acoustic prominence and prosodic structure, Calhoun also gives results on phonetic differences in the realization of nuclear versus pre-nuclear accents, which we do not report here.

models are often called *concept-to-speech synthesis* and try to utilize different kinds of linguistic information to improve the output quality. The crucial task here is the placement of accents. If this goes wrong, the speech may sound odd or even suggest the wrong meaning, if, for example, an underlying semantic contrast relation has not been brought to the surface, or if a noun phrase denoting an entity that has already been referred to has been made to sound as if it were "new".

In particular, the last-mentioned problem inspired the early research on moving beyond plain text-to-speech mapping. A first step is the automatic production of a syntactic analysis for the input sentences and the mapping of particular structural features to specific prosodic features of the utterance (see, e.g., Dorffner, Buchberger and Kommenda 1990). For the "givenness problem", a fairly straightforward and purely surface-oriented approach was suggested by Hirschberg (1990): Any content word except for those whose root matches a word in the preceding context receives an accent. This detection of "givenness" through the use of a word repetition rule already leads to a significant improvement over a monotonous equal distribution of accents, but for acceptable results in connected discourse, it is clear that syntax and word-repetition are not enough and that pragmatics should directly influence the prosodic realization.

The "ideal" situation for concept-to-speech mapping is given in an NLG scenario as introduced in Section 3: One can draw upon both static linguistic resources and dynamic context information, as represented in the discourse model. The *communicative intentions* are an important factor influencing prosody in speech synthesis, especially in dialogues (see Teich et al. 1997); the other important factor, to which we attend here, is information structure. The overall architecture, then, is usually quite similar to that shown in Figure 3, taken from Van Deemter and Odijk (1997). The generation module draws upon the database for the content which is to be communicated, and on linguistic knowledge – either in the form of explicit grammatical knowledge, as in the case of "deep" generation, or on a set of sentence templates. Further, the generator inspects the context model (in our words: discourse model) in order to form an adequate utterance string, and the Prosody module adds prosodic annotations to it. The annotated string is then given to the speech synthesizer, which converts it to acoustic output. Excercising such direct influence on a speech synthesizer has become technically much easier in recent years through the development and standardization of "markup languages" – tag sets for annotating a sentence string with instructions for the synthesizer on adjustments in prosodic features, in particular on the placement of accents and pauses. One of these efforts is the *Speech Synthesis Markup Language*[15] defined by the World Wide Web Consortium (W3C).

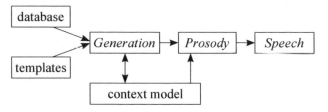

Figure 3. Architecture of a spoken-language generator (Van Deemter and Odijk 1997: 5)

The accenting model proposed by Van Deemter and Odijk (1997) uses the given/new distinction as the only influencing factor. Their implementation generates short descriptive texts for an interactive music player, hence the domain comprises composers and their works. The general approach to accents is similar to that of Hirschberg (1990), namely to compute deaccenting on the basis of givenness. There are two significant differences, though: Hirschberg used a word-based heuristic detection of givenness, whereas Van Deemter and Odijk (1997) compute it on the basis of the discourse model's representation of the underlying referents. And, since the generator has a syntactic representation of the target utterance, accent placement is supported by knowledge on phrase boundaries. Thus the system first determines which phrases are to receive an accent, and then a set of focus-accent rules determines what particular word in the constituent should receive the accent (i.e., the focus exponent). In the first step, all noun phrases in the syntax tree are marked as +A (to be accentuated). Then, in a second step, accent-blocking rules can overwrite the label to –A under four different conditions: (i) the referent was mentioned recently; (ii) the referent is an overall discourse-topic; (iii) the referent semantically subsumes an earlier mentioned referent (e.g., "This piece was written by [Mozart]+A. He was [a very successful composer]-A"); (iv) the candidate leaf node is "lexically unfit" to carry an accent (e.g., it is a pronoun).

A more elaborate model, both of syntactic structure and of accents (distinguishing between a nuclear and a prenuclear accent) was used in the generation system of Endriss and Klabunde (2000), which we already introduced in Section 3.2.2.1. Their "focus principle" was derived from a corpus study of oral retellings of a short animated movie, which revealed

---

[15] http://www.w3.org/TR/speech-synthesis11/ (accessed 22 May 2012)

the following regularities that are related to the focus projection rules of Gussenhoven (1983) and Selkirk (1984):

1. In phrases with a head daughter and adjunct daughter, the focus exponent is in the head daughter, and a prenuclear accent is in the adjunct daughter.
2. In phrases with a head daughter and complement daughter:
    a. if the head-daughter is a verbal projection, the focus exponent is in the head daughter, and a prenuclear accent is in the complement daughter.
    b. else the accents are in the complement daughter.

Endriss and Klabunde (2000) were concerned with the computation of the focus-background structure of sentences, which generalizes over the role of givenness as it had been used in the earlier work. The authors propose three reasons for placing information into the foreground, i.e., focusing it: (i) The information has been selected from a set of alternative beliefs ascribed to the listener; (ii) it is a revision of certain beliefs (in case of contrastive focus); (iii) the focused phrase expresses new information that the listener does not know or is not able to infer from his beliefs. While (iii) basically amounts to givenness and can be computed from a relatively simple discourse model (as in Van Deemter and Odijk's 1997 approach), knowledge about alternatives and contrasts requires both a more sophisticated dynamic discourse model, and static background knowledge (cf. Section 3.2.1). In the DRS-based model of Endriss and Klabunde (2000), a contrastive focus is realized if some property of an activated discourse referent in the R_A list (referents mentioned in the previous sentence) contradicts a property of a referent (of the same sort) in the semantic input for the current sentence. This rule would, for example, solve a problem that Van Deemter and Odijk (1997: 25) pointed out for their music-describing system: *Mozart wrote few string quartets. Haydn wrote many.* Here, both *Haydn* and *many* should receive an accent on the basis of the contrast to the first sentence.[16]

Contrast and its role in focusing decisions in spoken language generation (in particular, for descriptions) were studied in depth by Prevost (1995, 1996), whose work is couched in the IS model proposed by Steedman (2000). This is a two-tiered model, in which the upper tier breaks a clause into theme and rheme, and the lower tier assigns focus exponents: an obligatory one within the rheme, and an optional one within the theme. Here,

---

[16] Notice, however, that "Haydn" might not be accented if in the wider context it is currently a discourse topic; this illustrates the potential interactions of different focusing rules, which computational models ought to pay attention to.

"theme" is meant as a conflation of aboutness-topic and linking to previous utterances, i.e., givenness. According to Prevost, a relatively simple mapping of theme/rheme to prosodic tunes can account for many simple declarative sentences that generators deal with: The theme is realized with a rise-fall-rise tune (L+H* LH%) and the rheme with a rise-fall tune (H* LL%). Placing the pitch accents within these tunes is then a matter of deciding on the theme-focus and rheme-focus, respectively, which serve to "differentiate properties or entities in the current utterance from properties or entities established in prior utterances." (Prevost 1996: 295) Again, the challenge is to operationalize this intuition by means of an explicit discourse model and a background knowledge base (KB), which allows for the decision of whether two referents can be regarded as "alternatives". Following common practice, Prevost assumes a taxonomy of concepts, with discourse referents being instantiations of concepts (or, in other words, the KB provides the "sorts" of the referents). Within the taxonomy, one has to define cutoff points for deciding whether two concepts are still "similar"; Prevost defines this similarity by describing concepts as having either the same parent or grandparent concept. Since his generator produces object descriptions, the contrastive focus algorithm is in charge of determining the minimal set of properties of an object that serve to distinguish it, i.e., that contrast with the same property of objects mentioned earlier in the discourse. This task is very similar to that of generating a discriminative referring expression (cf. Section 3.2.2.2). We illustrate his approach with a simple example taken from (Prevost 1996: 299). Assume the system has just produced a description of an object e1, which is a "solid state amplifier"; now, the user asks about the type of a different object, e2, which bears the name "X5" and which the system knows to be a "tube amplifier". The system first considers the type and properties of e2 and determines (i) that it is in contrast to e1 (since they are both amplifiers), and (ii) that the property "tube" is discourse-new, whereas the type "amplifier" is discourse-old. Then the contrastive focus algorithm – shown in Figure 4 – finds that "tube" is in contrast with the corresponding property of the amplifier mentioned before and that mentioning it is sufficient for identifying the amplifier. The sentence planner thus produces a description of the sentence, stating that the theme is a definite NP whose head is "X5" (which also carries the theme-focus), and the rheme is a verb phrase with the predicate "be-amplifier" (indefinite) and the property "tube" (which carries the rheme-focus because it contrasts with the previous solid-state amplifier). The surface realizer maps the description to the output sentence plus the intonation markup, which is then given to the synthesizer:

The	*X5*	*is a*	*TUBE amplifier.*
L+H*$_c$	L(H%)	H*$_c$	LL\$

For more detailed (and more interesting) examples, see Prevost (1995, 1996). A combination of the Steedman/Prevost approach to IS and prosody with a more elaborate discourse model (the information state update model as implemented in GoDIS (Larsson 2002)) was described by Kruijff-Korbayová et al. (2003). The theme/rheme partitioning is computed by means of the "question under discussion" approach (Ginzburg 1996; see also Section 2.4 of Krifka and Musan, this volume), and focus/background within the theme and rheme are determined by checking for semantic parallelism (i.e., which entities are alternatives to one another, similar to Prevost's proposal). A slightly simpler approach, which is, however, embedded in a complete travel information dialogue system, is used by White, Clark and Moore (2010), who specify the theme of an utterance as the most important unit of information in terms of the user's preferences. For instance, if the system has begun to describe one particular flight option, and the user has indicated that she desires a quick, direct flight, then the next sentence can be generated as "(This direct flight)$_{theme}$ (departs at 9.30)$_{rheme}$". The realization module, based on Combinatory Categorial Grammar, decides on the type and placement of pitch accents and edge tones, and thus makes sure that the intonational phrases produced by the synthesis module accurately reflect the theme/rheme partitioning of the utterance.

DElist := list of discourse entities mentioned recently
Props(x) := {P | P(x) is true in KB}, properties of entity x
ASet(x) := {y | alt(x,y)}, x's alternatives
RSet(x,{}) := {x} ∪ {y | y ∈ ASet(x) & y ∈ DElist}, evoked alternatives
CSet(x,{}) := {}, subset of properties to be accented for contrasting

S := {}
for each P **in** Props(x)
    RSet(x, S ∪ {P}) := {y | y ∈ RSet(x,S) & P(y)}
    if RSet(x, S ∪ {P}) = RSet(x,S) **then** CSet(x, S ∪ {P}) := CSet(x,S)
    else CSet(x, S ∪ {P}) := CSet(x,S) ∪ {P})
    endif
    S := S ∪ {P}
endfor

Figure 4. Contrastive Focus algorithm from Prevost (1996: 296)

5. Summary and conclusions

As we have seen, in automatic text understanding, anaphora resolution and the role of givenness associated with it are quite essential aspects of the overall task. Other facets of information structure, however, are often to be seen as things that are "nice to have" rather than indispensible. Computational text analysis, even in its "deepest", most thorough forms, largely amounts to constructing the propositional content of sentences (and then processing them further), and IS in general has little to contribute to this process. In automatic text generation, however, the situation is rather different. Apart from the most simple applications, where only single sentences or very short text is required, the quality of the output is a major concern, and information packaging plays an important role in achieving this objective. That is, by the way, the reason why text generation and understanding in computational linguistics should not be regarded simply as converses of each other. Text understanding abstracts from nuances of meaning and reduces the sentence to the underlying proposition or logical form; text generation maps a logical form to a sentence and thereby faces the problem of selecting among the multitude of possible realizations – it is thus a matter of well-motivated choice. We emphasized the important role of the discourse model in making generation decisions: Sentences are produced in context, and they should enable the human reader to process them effectively. As a result, information structure is much more prominent in text generation than in text understanding (notwithstanding the initial work on identifying focus-background structure that we saw in Section 2.2).

The two sides of the coin come together in machine translation (MT), where both an analysis and a generation component are required. In principle, IS should be of great interest here, especially when translating between languages that employ quite different means of realizing it. This is acute, for instance, when translating from a language with rigid word order to one with free word order; see Steinberger (1994), Hoffman (1996), or Budzikovska (2000). Apart from this early work in the 1990s, however, MT has largely neglected information structure. The reason is a paradigm shift from symbolic, rule-based approaches to statistical ones relying on huge amounts of bilingual data, which was initiated in the 1990s; today, the vast majority of MT research is based on statistical models.[17] These models

---

[17] This is not the case for the commercially available translation software, which (still) largely implements rule-based transfer approaches based on syntactic analysis.

translate sentence by sentence, with no or minimal consideration of context, and with only minimal linguistic analysis involved. The huge advantage is their robustness, which most readers will have enjoyed when playing with an online translator on the web (such as those supplied by the major search engines). The models are still struggling with getting the basic message across, though, and do not attend to nuances yet – thus, IS as a phenomenon so far has not received attention in statistical MT.

With regard to spoken dialogue systems, we found a situation very similar to that described above for understanding and generation: Speech recognition is still a difficult computational problem, which means aspects of IS are only just starting to become a prominent research topic; in contrast, in spoken language generation one needs to employ at least simple models of IS in order not to produce bad or misleading intonation in the utterances. However, with more and more spoken dialogue systems being employed, the desire for a means of handling features of the information structure will grow.

In conclusion, let us emphasize once more that most work in computational linguistics requires dealing with "real" language use, be it spoken or written. Accordingly, the information structure cannot be investigated here on the basis of simplified sample utterances that neatly illustrate relevant phenomena – instead, the models have to account for it being part of the "big picture" of language use in context. That is why *empirical* research plays such an important role in computational approaches. For IS, we have cited studies demonstrating the difficulty that humans have when annotating notions like topic and focus in authentic written or spoken language; not surprisingly, it is even more difficult for machines to perform this task. As the reader will have noted, the level of detail implemented in computational models of IS often does not match the sophistication of specific accounts developed in theoretical linguistics, but this does not come as a surprise, given the multitude of problems that need to be addressed simultaneously when automatically processing written or spoken language. However, progress is being made: For example, models of grammatical knowledge, which are embodied in symbolic, statistical, or hybrid *parsers*, have seen great improvements in both robustness and accuracy in recent years. Accordingly, with better syntactic analyses being available, text understanding systems will have the chance to treat information structure more thoroughly. Some interesting problems at the sentence-discourse interface still await solution, though: The precise contents of discourse models, their updating mechanisms, and the "translation" of the current state of the discourse model into the interpretation or generation of the upcoming sentence are challenging for theoretical, descriptive, and computational research alike.

References

Artstein, Ron and Massimo Poesio
2008   Inter-coder agreement for computational linguistics. *Computational Linguistics* 34: 555–596.
Beaver, David
2004   The optimization of discourse anaphora. *Linguistics and Philosophy* 27: 1–53.
Birner, Betty and Gregory Ward
1998   *Information Status and Noncanonical Word Order in English.* Amsterdam: John Benjamins.
Brennan, Susan
1998   Centering as a psychological resource for achieving joint reference in spontaneous discourse. In *Centering Theory in Discourse*, Marilyn Walker, Aravind K. Joshi and Ellen Prince (eds.), 227–250. Oxford: Clarendon Press.
Brennan, Susan, Marilyn Walker and Carl Pollard
1987   A centering approach to pronouns. In *Proceedings of the 25th Conference of the Association for Computational Linguistics*, Stanford, CA: Association for Computational Linguistics, 152–162.
Budzikowska, Margo
2000   Information structure transfer: Bridging the information gap in structurally different languages. In *Envisioning Machine Translation in the Information Future. Proceedings of the 4th Conference of the Association for Machine Translation in the Americas*, John S. White (ed.), 80–88. Berlin/Heidelberg: Springer.
Buráňová, Eva, Eva Hajičová and Petr Sgall
2000   Tagging of very large corpora: topic-focus articulation. In *Proceedings of the 18th International Conference for Computational Linguistics*, 139–144.
Cahill, Aoife and Arndt Riester
2009   Incorporating information status into generation ranking. In *Proceedings of the Joint Conference of the 47th Meeting of the Association for Computational Linguistics and the 4th International Joint Conference on Natural Language Processing, Singapore. Association for Computational Linguistics*, 97–100.
Calhoun, Sasha
2007   Predicting focus through prominence structure. In *Proceedings of Interspeech*, 622–625. Antwerp, Belgium.
Calhoun, Sasha, Malvina Nissim, Mark Steedman and Jason Brenier
2005   A framework for annotating information structure in discourse. In: *Proceedings of the Association for Computational Linguistics Workshop on Frontiers in Corpus Annotation II: Pie in the Sky*, Ann Arbor/Michigan.

Chiarcos, Christian
    2010   Mental salience and grammatical form: Toward a framework for salience metrics in natural language generation. Ph.D. dissertation, University of Potsdam.

Creswell, Cassandre
    2002   Syntactic form and discourse function in natural language generation. In *Proceedings of the 2nd International Conference on Natural Language Generation*, Harriman / New York.

Dale, Robert and Ehud Reiter
    1995   Computational interpretation of the Gricean Maxims in the generation of referring expressions. *Cognitive Science* 19: 233–263.

Dipper, Stefanie, Michael Götze and Stavros Skopeteas (eds.)
    2007   *Information Structure in Cross-Linguistic Corpora: Annotation Guidelines for Phonology, Morphology, Syntax, Semantics, and Information Structure* (Interdisciplinary Studies on Information Structure 7). Potsdam: Universitätsverlag.

Dorffner, Georg, Ernst Buchberger and Markus Kommenda
    1990   Integrating stress and intonation into a concept-to-speech system. In *Proceedings of the 13th International Conference on Computational Linguistics, Helsinki. Stroudsburg, Pennsylvania: Association for Computational Linguistics*, 89–94.

Endriss, Cornelia and Ralf Klabunde
    2000   Planning word-order dependent focus assignments. In *Proceedings of the First International Conference on Natural Language Generation 2000*, Israel, Mizpe Ramon, 156–162.

Ginzburg, Jonathan
    1996   Interrogatives: Questions, facts and dialogue. In *The Handbook of Contemporary Semantic Theory*, Shalom Lappin (ed.), 385–422. Oxford: Blackwell.

Grosz, Barbara, Aravind Joshi and Scott Weinstein
    1995   Centering: A framework for modelling the local coherence of discourse. *Computational Linguistics* 21: 103–164.

Guindon, Raymond
    1985   Anaphora resolution: Short-term memory and focusing. In *Proceedings of the 23rd Annual Meeting of the Association for Computational Linguistics*, 218–227.

Gussenhoven, Carlos
    1983   Focus, mode and the nucleus. *Journal of Linguistics* 19: 377–417.

Hajičovà, Eva, Hana Skoumalovà and Petr Sgall
    1995   An automatic procedure for topic-focus identification. *Computational Linguistics* 21: 81–94.

Hawkins, John
    1978   *Definiteness and Indefiniteness*. London: Croom Helm.

Henschel, Renate, Hua Cheng and Massimo Poesio
   2000   Pronominalization revisited. In *Proceedings of the 18th International Conference on Computational Linguistics*, 306–312. Saarbrücken: Morgan Kaufmann.
Hirschberg, Julia
   1990   Accent and discourse context: assigning pitch accent in synthetic speech. *Proceedings of the Conference of the American Association for Artificial Intelligence*, 953–957.
Hoffman, Beryl
   1996   Translating into free word order languages. In *Proceedings of the International Conference on Computational Linguistics*, 556–561.
Hovy, Eduard and Kathleen McCoy
   1989   Focusing your RST: A step toward generating coherent multisentential text. In *Proceedings of the 11th Annual Meeting of the Cognitive Science Society*. Ann Arbor, Michigan.
Hudson, Susan, Michael Tanenhaus and Gary Dell
   1986   The effect of the discourse center on the local coherence of a discourse. In *Proceedings of the Eighth Annual Conference of the Cognitive Science Society*, 96–101. Hillsdale, NJ: Erlbaum.
Kameyama, Megumi
   1998   Intrasentential centering: A case study. In *Centering Theory in Discourse*, Marilyn Walker, Aravind K. Joshi and Ellen Prince (eds.), 89–112. Oxford: Clarendon Press.
Kamp, Hans and Uwe Reyle
   1993   *From Discourse to Logic*. Dordrecht: Kluwer.
Kibble, Rodger and Richard Power
   2004   Optimizing referential coherence in text generation. *Computational Linguistics* 30: 401–416.
Klabunde, Ralf and Martin Jansche
   1998   Abductive reasoning for syntactic realization. In *Proceedings of the Interational Workshop on Natural Language Generation*. Canada: Niagara-on-the-Lake.
Krahmer, Emiel and Mariet Theune
   2002   Efficient context-sensitive generation of referring expressions. In *Information Sharing: Reference and Presupposition in Language Generation and Interpretation*, Kees van Deemter, Rodger Kibble (eds.), 223–264. Stanford: Center for the Study of Language and Information Publications.
Kruijff-Korbayová, Ivana, Stina Ericsson, Kepa J. Rodrigues and Elena Karagjosova
   2003   Producing contextually appropriate intonation in an information-state based dialog system. In *Proceedings of the Conference of the European Chapter of the Association for Computational Linguistics*, Budapest, Hungary. Stroudsburg, PA: Association for Computational Linguistic.

Langkilde, Irene and Kevin Knight
    1998   Generation that exploits corpus-based statistical knowledge. In *Proceedings of the 17th International Conference on Computational Linguistics and 36th Annual Meeting of the Association for Computational Linguistics*, 704–710. Montréal.

Lappin, Shalom and Herbert Leass
    1994   An algorithm for pronominal anaphora resolution. *Computational Linguistics* 20: 535–561.

Larsson, Staffan
    2002   Issue-based dialogue management. Ph.D. dissertation, University of Göteborg.

Maybury, Mark
    1991   Topical, temporal, and spatial constraints on linguistic realization. *Computational Intelligence* 7: 266–275.

McCoy, Kathleen and Michael Strube
    1999   Generating anaphoric expressions: Pronoun or definite description? In *Proceedings of the Workshop on Reference and Discourse Structure of the Association for Computational Linguistics*, 63–71.

McKeown, Kathleen
    1985   *Text Generation.* Cambridge: Cambridge University Press.

Mann, William C. and Thompson, Sandra A.
    1988   Rhetorical structure theory. Toward a functional theory of text organization. *Text* 8: 243–281.

Ng, Vincent and Claire Cardie
    2002   Identifying anaphoric and non-anaphoric noun phrases to improve coreference resolution. In *Proceedings of the International Conference on Computational Linguistics*, 730–736.

Nissim, Malvina
    2006   Learning information status of discourse entities. In *Proceedings of the Conference on Empirical Methods in Natural Language Processing, Sydney.* Stroudsburg, PA: Association for Computational Linguistics.

Nissim, Malvina, Shipra Dingare, Jean Carletta and Mark Steedman
    2004   An annotation scheme for information status in dialogue. In *Proceedings of the 4th Language Resources and Evaluation Conference, Lisbon*, 1023–1026. Stroudsburg, Pennsylvania: Association for Computational Linguistics.

Oberlander, Jon, Michael O'Donnell, Alistair Knott and Chris Mellish
    1998   Conversation in the museum: Experiments in dynamic hypermedia with the intelligent labelling explorer. *New Review of Multimedia and Hypermedia* 4: 11–32.

Ostendorf, Mari, Izhak Shafran, Stefanie Shattuck-Hufnagel, Leslie Carmichael and William Byrne
2001   A prosodically labeled database of spontaneous speech. In *Proceedings of the Interantional Speech Communication Association Workshop on Prosody in Speech Recognition and Understanding*, 119–121.

Pattabhiraman, Thiyagarajasarma and Nick Cercone
1990   Selection: Salience, relevance and the coupling between domain-level tasks and text planning. In *Proceedings of the 5th International Workshop on Natural Language Generation, Dawson/Pennsylvania*, Kathleen McKeown, Johanna Moore and Sergei Nirenburg (eds.).

Poesio, Massimo, Rosemary Stevenson, Barbara di Eugenio and Janet Hitzeman
2004   Centering: A parametric theory and its instantiations. *Computational Linguistics* 30: 309–363.

Prevost, Scott
1995   A semantics of contrast and information structure for specifiying intonation in spoken language generation. Ph.D. dissertation, University of Pennsylvania.

Prevost, Scott
1996   An information structural approach to spoken language generation. In *Proceedings of the 34th Annual Meeting of the Association for Computational Linguistics*, Morristown, NJ. Stroudsburg, PA: Association for Computational Linguistics, 294–301.

Prince, Ellen
1981   Toward a taxonomy of given-new information. In *Radical Pragmatics*, Peter Cole (ed.), 223–255. New York: Academic Press.

Prince, Ellen
1992   The ZPG letter: Subjects, definiteness, and information status. In *Discourse Description: Diverse Linguistic Analyses of a Fund-Raising Text*, William Mann and Sandra Thompson (eds.), 295–325. Amsterdam: John Benjamins.

Prince, Ellen
1998   On the limits of syntax, with reference to topicalization and left-dislocation. In *The Limits of Syntax. Syntax and Semantics* 29, Peter Culicover and Louise McNally (eds.), 281–300. New York: Academic Press.

Reiter, Ehud and Robert Dale
2000   *Building Natural Language Generation Systems*. Cambridge: Cambridge University Press.

Riester, Arndt
2008   A semantic explication of "information status" and the under-specification of the recipients' knowledge. In *Proceedings of Sinn und Bedeutung* 12, Atle Grønn (ed.). Oslo: Institutt for litteratur, områdestudier og europeiske språk, 2008.

Ritz, Julia, Stefanie Dipper and Michael Götze
    2008   Annotation of information structure: an evaluation across different types of text. In *Proceedings of the 6th Language Resources and Evaluation Conference.* Marrakech, Morocco.

Selkirk, Elisabeth O.
    1984   *Phonology and Syntax: The Relation between Sound and Structure.* Cambridge, MA: MIT Press.

Sridhar, Vivek Kumar Rangarajan, Ani Nenkova, Shrikanth Narayanan and Dan Jurafsky
    2008   Detecting prominence in conversational speech: pitch accent, givenness and focus. In *Proceedings of the Speech Prosody Conference.* Campinas, Brazil.

Stede, Manfred
    2002   Polibox: Generating descriptions, comparisons, and recommendations from a database. In *Proceedings of the 19th International Conference on Computational Linguistics, Taipei.* Stroudsburg, PA: Association for Computational Linguistics.

Steedman, Mark
    2000   Information structure and the syntax-phonology interface. *Linguistic Inquiry* 31: 649–689.

Steinberger, Ralf
    1994   Treating 'free word order' in machine translation. *Proceedings of the International Conference on Computational Linguistics*, 69–75.

Stent, Amanda, Rashmi Prasad and Marilyn Walker
    2004   Trainable sentence planning for complex information presentation in spoken dialog systems. *Proceedings of the 42nd Annual Meeting of the Association for Computational Linguistics, Barcelona*, 79–86.

Stone, Matthew, Christine Doran, Bonnie Webber, Tonia Bleam and Martha Palmer
    2001   Microplanning with communicative intentions: the SPUD system. Technical report RuCCS TR 65, Dept. of Computer Science, Rutgers University.

Strube, Michael and Udo Hahn
    1999   Functional centering – grounding referential coherence in information structure. *Computational Linguistics* 25: 309–344.

Stuckardt, Roland
    2001   Design and enhanced evaluation of a robust anaphor resolution algorithm. *Computational Linguistics* 27: 479–506.

Teich, Elke, Eli Hagen, Brigitte Grote and John Bateman
    1997   From communicative context to speech: Integrating dialogue processing, speech production and natural language generation. *Speech Communication* 21: 73–99.

Uszkoreit, Hans
  1987   *Word Order and Constituent Structure in German.* Center for the Study of Language and Information: Lecture Notes. Stanford, CA. Stanford University.
Vallduvi, Enric
  1990   The informational component. Ph.D. dissertation, University of Pennsylvania.
van Deemter, Kees and Jan Odijk
  1997   Context Modeling and the Generation of Spoken Discourse. *Speech Communication* 21: 101–121.
Vesela, Katerina, Jiri Havelka and Eva Hajičová
  2004   Annotators' agreement: The case of topic-focus articulation. In *Proceedings of the 4th Language Resources and Evaluation Conference*, 2191–2194. Lisbon: European Language Resources Association.
Vieira, Renata and Massimo Poesio
  2000   An empirically-based system for processing definite descriptions. *Computational Linguistics* 26: 539–593.
Walker, Marilyn, Massayo Iida and Sharon Cote
  1994   Japanese discourse and the process of centering. *Computational Linguistics* 20: 193–232.
Walker, Marilyn, Aravind K. Joshi and Ellen Prince (eds.)
  1998   *Centering Theory in Discourse.* Oxford: Clarendon Press.
Webber, Bonnie Lynn
  1980   *A Formal Approach to Discourse Anaphora.* New York: Garland.
White, Michael, Robert Clark and Johanna Moore
  2010   Generating tailored, comparative descriptions with contextually appropriate intonation. *Computational Linguistics* 36: 159–201.
Yang, Gijoo, Kathleen McCoy and K. Vijay-Shanker
  1991   From functional specification to syntactic structures: systemic grammar and tree-adjoining grammar. *Computational Intelligence* 7: 207–219.

Information structure and theoretical models of grammar

Ingo Reich

1. Relevance to grammar

The title of this chapter strongly suggests that information structural notions like topic, comment, focus or background should, in some way or other, form an integral part of any adequate theory of grammar. But why should this actually be so? After all, information structural notions such as focus heavily depend on their context of use. Consider (1) and (2).

(1) a. *Who did you sell your typewriter to?*
     b. *I sold my typewriter* to CLYDE.

(2) a. *What did you sell to Clyde?*
     b. *I sold* my TYPEwriter *to Clyde.*

If the sentence *I sold my typewriter to Clyde* is uttered as an answer to (1a), the PP *to Clyde* is stressed, with an accent on *CLYDE*. However, if it is uttered as an answer to (2a), stress 'shifts' to the NP *my typewriter*, with an accent on *TYPEwriter*. Thus it seems that the locus of the pitch accent cannot be predicted without taking the context of use into account. And what is more, the difference in focal stress affects neither the sentence's syntax nor its semantics: Any situation in which I sold my typewriter *to CLYDE* is a situation in which I sold *my TYPEwriter* to Clyde, and vice versa. Thus, apparently, a shift in focus leaves the truth-conditions of the sentence untouched and only concerns the level of pragmatic interpretation.

1.1. Relevance to semantics

Or so it seems. Dretske (1972), from whom I borrowed and slightly adapted the above *typewriter*-example, argues, first of all, that even though (1b) and (2b) are truth-conditionally equivalent, these statements differ in contrast: Intuitively, (1b) contrasts with statements like *I sold my typewriter to Alex*, whereas (2b) contrasts with statements like *I sold my adding machine to Clyde*. This intuition is supported by the observation that it is perfectly fine to continue (1b) with the phrase *not to Alex*, but somehow inadequate to continue it with *not my adding machine*. And what is more, Dretske (1972: 412) argues that "if *C(U)* is a linguistic expression in which *U* is embedded, and *U* can be given different contrastive foci (say U_1 and U_2), then it often makes a difference to the meaning of *C(U)* whether we embed $C(U_1)$ or $C(U_2)$". Consider (3).

(3)   a. *I only sold my typewriter* to CLYDE.
       b. *I only sold* my TYPEwriter *to Clyde.*

In (3), the contrastive statements (1b) and (2b) are part of the slightly more complex statements (3a) and (3b) respectively, which contain, in addition, the particle *only*. The latter two, of course, differ in truth-conditions: Suppose I am in desperate need of money, and therefore I sold, with the intent to defraud, my typewriter (but nothing else) to two different people, namely Clyde and Alex. In this situation, (3a) is false, but (3b) is true. As Dretske (1972: 423) rightly points out, this truth-conditional effect is not to be taken to show that focus is a semantic phenomenon, but it strongly suggests that there are expressions in natural language that are in one way or another sensitive to focus: "We could easily take it as an argument for the view that certain pragmatic differences [...] are relevantly involved in the semantical [sic] analysis of certain expressions in which they can appear." Thus it is not necessarily focus itself but rather its interaction with focus-sensitive expressions like *only* that matters to semantics.

With respect to particles like *only* it is common to say that *only* 'associates' with the focus in its scope, leaving unsettled the question of how direct the connection between *only* and the focus in fact is. Another, more direct way to put it is to say that *only* 'binds' the focus in its scope (similar to the way in which a quantifier binds a pronoun). The foci in (3a) and (3b), then, are called 'bound' foci, while the foci in (1b) and (2b) are instances of 'free' focus. By and large, this difference in terminology corresponds to a distinction between 'weak' and 'strong' approaches to focus (see especially Beaver and Clark 2003, 2008), a distinction that is, as we will see in detail below, at the heart of the debate on association with focus.

Within the range of free foci, it might be necessary to further distinguish contrastive or, more generally, alternative focus from focus that is determined so to speak 'ex negativo' by a phenomenon usually called deaccentuation. Consider (4).

(4) *Where's your typewriter?*
    a. *I (#only)* SOLD *my typewriter.*
    b. *I (#only) sold my typewriter* to CLYDE.

As an answer to the question *Where's your typewriter?*, (4a) is most naturally pronounced with stress on *sold*. Intuitively, this accent pattern is very similar, if not identical, to the accent pattern (4a) receives as an answer to the question *What did you do with your typewriter?*. The latter case, like the cases in (1)–(3), is one which we have already seen as a case of contrastive focus. The former case, however, seems to be different in several respects: First, there is no intuition whatsoever that *sold* in (4a) contrasts with, say, *gave*. It rather seems that *sold* is stressed simply because *my typewriter* is not; and *my typewriter* is not stressed simply because it has already been mentioned in the context of the question. This is corroborated by two observations: First, in (4b) the stress shifts back to the end of the sentence, falling on *Clyde* rather than on *sold*. Second, neither in (4a) nor in (4b) is it possible to associate the focus with *only*. But if we relate (4a) and (4b) to the question *What did you do with your typewriter?*, association with *only* seems to be possible again.

    Alternatively, one may consider the stress pattern in (4a) as evidence that the question *Where's your typewriter?* is not answered directly, but rather indirectly by directly answering an implicit question like *What did you do with your typewriter?*, the answer to the latter question implying an answer to the former question. Similarly in (4b). This allows, on the one hand, for a uniform treatment of all focus phenomena. On the other hand, it requires an elaborate theory of (implicit and explicit) context questions or 'questions under discussion' (see also the introduction to this book and Section 3.1 below) which furthermore needs to provide an explanation for the fact that *only* does not associate with the relevant focus in more indirect cases.

    Whatever the correct analysis, the latter fact suggests that the foci in (4) should not be dealt with within semantics proper. Similar considerations apply to the notion of topic: Intuition tells us that an utterance of (4a) in the context of the question *Where's your typewriter?* is a statement about the typewriter (e.g., Reinhart 1981). The notion of aboutness, however, encodes some specific perspective on or processing of a given state of affairs, and thus does not affect truth-conditions. There may be one exception, though: contrastive topics. Consider (5).

(5)   a. *All of my friends didn't* COME.

       b. √ALL *of my friends* DID\n't *come.*

An utterance of (5a) with a default accent on the sentence-final verb *come* is preferably taken to be about *all of my friends* and to state for all of them that they didn't come. (5b), however, with (rising) stress on *all (of my friends)* as well as (falling stress) on *did* is also understood to be about *all of my friends*, but its interpretation differs crucially from that of (5a): (5b) states that it is not the case that all of my friends came (suggesting that in fact most did), i.e., the negation *not* outscopes the universal quantifier *all (of my friends)* (e.g., Büring 1997, Jacobs 1997).

1.2. Relevance to phonology

As is apparent from the preceding section, sentence accents are (in many languages) a prominent means to indicate relevant aspects of information structure, and thus intonational phonology plays a crucial role in any theory on information structure (see, e.g., Pierrehumbert and Hirschberg 1990). This is most evident with contrastive topics. As (5b) suggests, contrastive topics typically have two different pitch accents, a rising accent (on *all*), and a falling accent (on *did*). The rising accent – also called a B accent in Bolinger (1965) and Jackendoff (1972) – is in fact special in that it is – more precisely – a fall rise or 'root' contour, as indicated with the math root symbol $\sqrt{}$ in (5b). This B accent (marking contrastive topics) needs to be distinguished from the pitch accent marking contrastive (alternative) focus in English, which is called an A accent in Bolinger's terminology. Also consider Jackendoff's (1972: 261) famous 'Fred ate the beans'-example (6).

(6)   a. *Well, what about* Fred*? What did* he *eat?*
       b. $\sqrt{}$FRED (B) *ate the* $\overline{\text{BEANS}}$\ (A).

In (6b) we find a fall-rise (B accent) on *Fred*, and a fall (A accent) on *beans*. Together they form a so-called hat or bridge contour (Cohen and 't Hart 1967, Féry 1993, Jacobs 1997). As Jackendoff (1972: 262) observes, B accents are also found in 'topicalized' phrases as in (7).

(7)   a. BAgels (B), *I don't like to* EAT (A).
       b. *As for* FRED (B), *I don't think* HE (B) *can* MAKE (A) *it.*

Jackendoff (1972: 262) further observes that A accents are, in a sense, secondary: "The B accent occurs on the variable whose value is chosen first, the one which [the] speaker [...] is asking about. The A accent occurs on the variable whose value is chosen second, so as to make the sentence true for the value of the other variable." The fact that A and B accents differ in phonetic realization as well as in semantic interpretation strongly suggests that they are genuinely different. If this is in fact correct, then both notions – contrastive topic *and* contrastive focus – are of immediate relevance to phonology.

On the other hand, both accents are pitch accents. And, what is more, B accents seem to be parasitic on A accents in the sense that they are realized only if an A accent is realized as well; see (8b) vs. (8c). A accents, in contrast, can very well lead a life of their own (8a).

(8) a. BAgels (A), *I don't like.*
     b. *BAgels (B), *I don't like.*
     c. BAgels (B), *I* DON'T (A) *like.*

Note also that B accents (almost) always precede A accents, and that the relevant intonational pattern is well known from other phenomena, like gapping or answers to multiple *wh*-questions. So the chances are good that A and B accents are in fact two sides of the same coin, the observed differences in their realization being due to linearization or hierarchization effects (see, e.g., Pierrehumbert and Hirschberg 1990, Bartels 1999, Féry 2007 for discussion).

Following the above arguments, let us suppose that contrastive topics are in fact (semantically and phonologically) special instantiations of the phenomenon called contrastive (or alternative) focus above. If we are on the right track with this, then it is entirely sufficient to mark contrastively focused phrases with an F in syntax, see (9b) below, and to state corresponding rules for semantic interpretation and phonological realization.

(9) a. *I sold* my TYPEwriter *to Clyde.*
     b. *I sold [my typewriter]$_F$ to Clyde.*

On the level of semantic or pragmatic interpretation, F-marked constituents give rise to contrastive (alternative) interpretations. Details will be given below. On the level of phonological interpretation each F-marked constituent is – in languages like English, German or French – assigned a pitch accent, which is realized according to independently given rules for stress assignment, which are partly language specific (including the poorly understood rules for 'focus projection'. For reasons of space and due to the strong focus on semantic aspects in this article, I cannot go into detail about this subject here; but see, e.g., Selkirk 1996 for a discussion of this matter).

This is essentially what is proposed in Jackendoff (1972) and what has become standard within generative approaches to information structure since then. Jackendoff himself calls this F-marker "artificial" and one may wonder whether we could in fact do without such a marker for contrastive focus, all the more, since we have just argued above that there is (probably) no need for a special T-marker to indicate contrastive topics (though it might turn out to be neccesary to mark *aboutness* topics this way). There would be no need for a special F-marker for contrastive focus, of course, if contrastive focus were just an epiphenomenon of deaccentuation and, thus, givenness. As the discussion of the data presented in (4) suggests, this seems quite unlikely. Further evidence comes from so-called *second occurrence focus* (SOF). Consider (10), taken from Beaver et al. (2007), who adapted it from Partee (1999).

(10) a. *Me: Everyone already knew that Mary only eats [vegetables]$_F$.*
      b. *You: If even [Paul]$_F$ knew that Mary only eats [vegetables]$_{SOF}$, then he should have suggested a different restaurant.*

In (10a) the object *vegetables* is contrastively focused, and associates with the focus particle *only*. The contrastive focus on *vegetables* is, as usual, marked by a pitch accent. (10b) echos the VP *knew that Mary only eats vegetables* as part of a larger utterance, and, in this sense, the VP is given in (10b). What we observe is that this second occurrence of the VP is completely deaccented, i.e., no pitch accent is assigned to or within the VP. This comes somewhat as a surprise if we assume that contrastive focus and deaccentuation are in fact two (strictly) independent phenomena. However, in an experimental study, Beaver et al. (2007) showed that the contrastive focus on second occurrence expressions like *vegetables* in (10b) is still marked phonologically, though by a significant increase in length and intensity rather than by an increase in pitch. This, in turn, would be completely unexpected if contrastive focus were only to be negatively construed as that part of a sentence which escapes deaccentuation, simply because it is neither known nor given in the relevant context. Rather, it seems that deaccentuation of second occurrence expressions forces contrastively focused phrases to be phonologically marked in a way consistent with the process of deaccentuation. These experimental results thus support the consideration of contrastive focus and deaccentuation as two essentially different (but nevertheless related) phenomena.

1.3. Relevance to syntax

Whether this also implies the existence of F-markers in syntax is a completely different matter. But as long as syntax is seen as mediating between semantics and phonology, F-markers are a handy technical device to ensure that contrastively interpreted phrases receive phonological prominence, even though semantics and phonology do not 'talk to each other' directly.

In a feature-driven syntax, of course, F-markers could play a crucial role in accounting for genuinely syntactic phenomena such as movement processes. In Hungarian, for example, contrastively focused constituents are moved to a preverbal position; compare the postverbal neutral *Marival* in (11a) with the preverbal focused *Marival* in (11b) (see, e.g., Kiss 1987, 2007 and Gyuris, this volume). The preverbal focus is interpreted exhaustively (see, e.g., Szabolsci 1981).

(11)　a. *össze veszett János Marival*
　　　　out　fell　John　Mary-with
　　　　'John fell out with Mary.'

　　　b. *János Marival　veszett össze*
　　　　John　Mary-with fell　out
　　　　'It was Mary who John fell out with.'

Similar observations have been made for other languages. In Italian, see (12a), as well as in English, see (12b) (see also Winkler, this volume, for discussion), the contrastively focused constituent may be moved to a left-peripheral sentence position, where it is typically interpreted as the sole alternative for which the predication is true (see Rizzi 1997).

(12)　a. Il tuo libro *ho letto (non il suo).*
　　　b. Your book, *I have read (not his).*

In fact, not only contrastively focused phrases move to a left-peripheral sentence position, but also topics like *János* in (11b). In languages such as Italian or German left dislocation is one of the most prominent means of marking topics syntactically; see (13).

(13)　a. *Il tuo libro, lo ho letto. (Your book, I have read it)*
　　　b. *Dein Buch, das habe ich gelesen. (Your book, I have read it)*

This tendency to push topical and focal expressions towards the sentence's left periphery may suggest that this position's primary task is to interface

with discourse. As Rizzi (1997: 283) puts it "we can think of the comple-
mentizer system as the interface between a propositional content (expressed
by the IP) and the superordinate structure (a higher clause or, possibly, the
articulation of discourse, if we consider a root clause). As such, we expect
the C system to express at least two kinds of information, one facing the
outside and the other facing the inside." Rizzi (1997, 2004) proposes that
propositional contents are integrated into discourse via two functional projections, the topic phrase TopP and the focus phrase FocP:

(14)   a.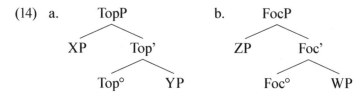

The functional head Top° defines, according to Rizzi (1997: 286), some
kind of 'higher predication', where YP comments on the topic XP. The head
Foc° is seen by Rizzi as partitioning the projection FocP into a focal part
ZP and a presuppositional part WP. Reconsidered from this perspective,
the Hungarian data discussed above suggest that TopP is systematically to
the left of FocP. To substantiate this proposal, Rizzi (1997) argues in great
detail that this structural refinement of the left periphery helps to explain,
for example, the relative distribution of finite (e.g., Italian *che*) and infinite
(e.g., Italian *di*) complementizers and topics in Romance languages as well
as several adjacency effects. In a similar vein, Frey (2000, 2004) argues
for a topic position in German, located at the left periphery of the 'middle
field' to the right of the C system and to the left of sentence adverbials like
wahrscheinlich ('presumably'); see (15).

(15)   I'll tell you something about Otto.

    a.   *Nächstes Jahr wird Otto wahrscheinlich Anna heiraten*
       next   year will Otto presumably   Anna marry
       'Next year, Otto will presumably marry Anna.'

    b.   *#Nächstes Jahr wird wahrscheinlich Otto Anna heiraten.*

Since (the topmost) TopP is located above FocP, this "cartographic" approach put forward by Rizzi and others does not necessarily imply topics to
be old information. This is different in Vallduví's (1990, 1992) information
packaging approach, which partitions sentences into focus and ground, and
ground into link and tail. Roughly speaking, Vallduví's ground corresponds

to the presuppositional part of a sentence, and his link to the topic. More precisely speaking, "[t]he knowledge encoded in the ground portion of a communicated proposition is knowledge the speaker assumes that the hearer already possesses [...] A link is an address pointer in the sense that it directs the hearer to a given address [...] in the hearer's knowledge store under which the information carried by the sentence is entered. Pointing to this address is part of the information anchoring role of the ground. By starting a sentence with a link speakers indicate to hearers that the focus must be entered under the address denoted by that link, i.e., that hearers must go to that address [...] and enter the information under its label" (Vallduví 1990: 58). According to Vallduví (1990, 1992) links are always left peripheral (though structurally subordinate); see (16).

(16)

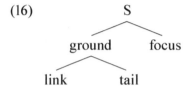

It should be noted, however, that in contrast to the cartographic approach of Rizzi (1997) the partitioning of a sentence into a focus, a link, and a tail as given in (16) does not parallel the syntactic structure of the sentence. Rather, Vallduví (1990, 1992) stipulates another level of syntax, information structure (IS), which builds on S-structure and feeds logical form (LF), which in turn feeds semantics. On the level of IS, focus constitutes the core of the sentence (the core IP), while link and tail are detached.

Like Vallduví (1990, 1992), Erteschik-Shir (1997, 2007) also argues for an information structural level of syntax, which she calls f-structure. In contrast to Vallduví (1990, 1992), however, she further argues that f-structure should in fact be considered a substitute for LF, it being directly interpreted by semantics (and phonological form). Consider (17) and (18).

(17) a. *Who ate the candy?*
     b. *TOP$_i$ [[the children]$_{FOC}$ ate [the candy]$_i$]*

(18) a. *Who did everyone talk to?*
     b. *Who did everyone$_{TOP}$ [talk to t]$_{FOC}$?*

On the level of f-structure, topics and foci are marked syntactically. In the context of (17a), for example, the answer *the children ate the candy* is assigned the f-structure in (17b): *the candy* is marked as topic, *the children* is marked as focus, and *ate* is presupposed. Even though the topic *the candy* stays in situ, it is given wide scope by relating it to the topic operator TOP. The generalization that topics always get widest scope also accounts for the tricky pair-list reading ("Tell me for everyone: Who did she talk to?") of (18a). This suggests that matters of quantifier scope can in fact be taken care of on the level of f-structure.

Since focus is not intimately tied to the left periphery of the sentence in Vallduví's as well as in Erteschik-Shir's approach, these approaches are rather well suited to deal with scrambling in languages described as having a free word order such as Russian, German or Hindi. Consider (19).

(19)   a. *[Wem]$_{IO}$ hast du [das Geld]$_{DO}$ gegeben?*
          'Who did you give the money to?'

       b. *Ich habe [das Geld]$_{DO}$ [dem Kassier]$_{IO}$ gegeben.*
          'I gave the money to the treasurer.'

German *geben* ('give') is usually considered to have 'indirect object (IO) before direct object (DO)' as its unmarked word order; see, e.g., Höhle (1982). Still, in the context of (19a), the inverse word order is perfectly fine; see (19b). This could be due to two reasons. Either the direct object *das Geld* ('the money'), being the topic of the sentence, pushes to the left, or *dem Kassier* ('the treasurer'), being its focus, pushes to the right. Anyway, the fact of the matter is that the focus ends up at the right periphery of the German middle field (see also Musan 2010).

This is somewhat unexpected within Rizzi's (1997, 2004) cartographic approach, since pushing the focus to the right increases the distance between its overt position and the position of the specifier of FocP, to which the focus needs to be moved covertly for matters of semantic or pragmatic interpretation (with the focus syntactically partitioning the projection FocP into a focal and a presuppositional part). This is not to say, of course, that it is impossible to account for scrambling within the cartographic approach. Rather, the facts suggest that we are dealing with two essentially independent phenomena, each requiring a different treatment, i.e., contrastive focus and, once again, deaccentuation. Left-dislocated foci systematically show a contrastive interpretation that can be strengthened to an exhaustive interpretation in some syntactic contexts. If we suppose that there is in fact some functional projection FocP at the sentence's left periphery (but see, e.g., Fanselow 2007, Sternefeld 2006 for discussion), it thus seems straightforward to restrict the movement to the specifier position of FocP to contrastively interpreted foci. Technically, this can be made sense of by restricting F-markers such that they only indicate contrastive foci, and by letting Foc attract F-features. Focus negatively determined by deaccentuation, on the other hand, is not subject to direct interpretation, but is rather an epiphenomenon of marking other, surrounding constituents in a sentence as given (in the relevant context). Again, technically, we could stipulate a givenness feature G, marking discourse given constituents in syntax (see, e.g., Sauerland 2004, Wagner 2007). Second occurrence expressions like, for example, *vegetables* in (10) above are, then, both F-marked (since they are associated with a focus particle) and G-marked (since they are reduced in pitch).

2.   Focus and background in semantics and pragmatics

2.1. Alternative semantics

This again raises the crucial question of how exactly to interpret F- or G-marked constituents and how to relate them to discourse. To this end, reconsider Dretske's typewriter example:

(20)   a.   *What did you sell to Clyde?*
       b.   *I sold [my typewriter]$_F$ to Clyde.*

As we saw in Section 1 above, the focus in (20b) heavily depends on the choice of the question that (20b) is supposed to answer, and roughly corresponds to the question's *wh*-phrase. According to Hamblin (1973), question (20a) essentially presents a set of possible answers of the form *I sold x to Clyde* (*x* being any salient object, e.g., *my typewriter*), of which the addressee is supposed to specify all and only the answers that are true. From this perspective, the focus in (20b) is quite naturally interpreted as relating (20b) to this contextually given set of possible answers, an utterance of (20b) asserting that the proposition *I sold my typewriter to Clyde* is actually a true possible answer to the question (20a), while suggesting that all other alternatives are wrong.

   This is in essence the fundamental idea of alternative semantics as proposed in several works by Rooth (1985, 1992, 1996) as a means to interpret focus. In contrast to *wh*-phrases, however, focus, by itself, does not (directly) affect truth-conditions, which is why Rooth suggests interpreting focus on a second level of interpretation $[[\cdot]]_F$, different from, but related to the usual level $[[\cdot]]$. On this second level, focused constituents like [*my typewriter*]$_F$ locally introduce a set of alternatives to (the denotation) of *my typewriter,* including (the denotation of) *my typewriter* itself. This second dimension of interpretation is (typo)graphically indicated in (21) by setting the denotation's elements in gray italics. These alternatives are, then, recursively passed on to the sentence level, where they give rise to a set of propositional alternatives; see (22).

...	...
my adding machine	*I sold my adding machine to Clyde*
(21) *[my typewriter]$_F$*	(22) *I sold [my typewriter]$_F$ to Clyde.*
my blue convertible	*I sold my blue convertible to Clyde*
...	...

This close relationship to the semantics of *wh*-interrogatives thus enables us to state a (necessary) well-formedness condition on question–answer pairs: A is a well-formed or congruent answer to Q if and only if the denotation [[Q]] of Q is a subset of the focus value [[A]]$_F$ of A.

Of course, this approach not only copes with matters of question–answer congruence, but also with the semantics of focus-sensitive particles, as Rooth (1985) shows in detail. To keep things simple, suppose (contrary to fact) that on LF, *only* operates on a propositional level; see (23b). The particle *only* thus has local access to both the ordinary semantic value (the proposition *that I sold my typewriter to Clyde*) and the focus semantic value (the set of propositions indicated in (22) above) of its sister node *I sold [my typewriter]$_F$ to Clyde*, and essentially states that of all relevant alternatives, the asserted proposition is the only one that is true; see (23c).

(23) a. *I only sold [my typewriter]$_F$ to Clyde.*
      b. *only [I sold [my typewriter]$_F$ to Clyde]*
      c. *only* $([[\alpha]]_F)$ $([[\alpha]])(w) = 1$ iff $\forall p \in [[\alpha]]_F (p(w) = 1 \rightarrow p = [[\alpha]])$

In Rooth (1992) the hitherto implicit link between the focus semantic value of a constituent α and the ordinary semantics of a focus-sensitive particle like *only* is made explicit by way of anaphora. Suppose that *only* is not directly restricted by the focus semantic value $[[\alpha]]_F$ of α, but more generally by some restrictor variable C ranging over sets of propositions. This boils down to the claim that the particle *only* may in fact be restricted by several sources and in different ways at the same time. The crucial task, then, is to find some systematic and empirically adequate way of linking the restrictor variable C to the focus semantic value $[[\alpha]]_F$ of α. This is exactly where the squiggle operator ~ comes in. By assumption the squiggle operator adjoins to some constituent α in LF, and relates this constituent to some anaphor Γ

of a suitable logical type. The relevant LF of example (23a) is, thus, rather something like (24b) below: The squiggle operator ~ adjoins to the sister of *only*, and introduces an anaphor Γ ranging over sets of propositions.

(24) a. *I only sold [my typewriter]$_F$ to Clyde.*
    b. *only* (C_7) *[[I sold [my typewriter]$_F$ to Clyde] ~ Γ_7]*
    c. *only* (C_7) $([[\alpha]])(w) = 1$ iff $\forall p \in C_7(p(w) = 1 \rightarrow p = [[\alpha]])$

If we suppose further that the variables C and Γ are anaphorically related to each other by way of coindexing (in a Q/A sequence, it is of course the question itself that is coindexed with Γ), we force C and Γ to denote exactly the same set of propositions. But what set of propositions does Γ actually denote? The basic idea is that the squiggle operator ~ locally retrieves the focus semantic value $[[\alpha]]_F$ of its sister node α, and requires Γ to denote a subset [!] of this focus semantic value. Since by assumption the coindexed variables C and Γ denote exactly the same set of propositions, C is indirectly restricted to the same subset of the focus semantic value $[[\alpha]]_F$ as Γ is, and *only* can be taken to quantify over this very subset; see (24c).

This way of construing the semantics of focus-sensitive particles like *only* naturally raises many questions, for example: Why don't we require Γ to be in fact *identical to* the focus semantic value $[[\alpha]]_F$ of α? (After all, this is what the semantics of *only* in (23c) suggests.) And, are there any restrictions on the distribution and interpretation of the squiggle operator? Regarding the first question, note that one of the benefits of the above maneuver is that C is, at least in principle, independent from Γ, and thus may (also) be determined by other sources. For example, in a given context, we may want C to only include the *salient* propositional alternatives. But if we were to fix the denotation of C by requiring it to be identical to the semantic value $[[\alpha]]_F$ of α, we would loose exactly this flexibility in determining the denotation of C. As for the second question, Rooth (1992) explicitly mentions three constraints on the squiggle operator: First of all, the squiggle operator requires an (unbound) F-marker within its syntactic scope (or, in semantic terms, the cardinality of its sister's focus value is required to be greater than 1). Second, the squiggle operator is an unselective focus binder, i.e., the focus semantic value of its mother node is set to the singleton containing its ordinary semantic value. And, last but not least, the squiggle operator has no effect whatsoever on the ordinary semantic interpretation of the LF tree.

One of the strengths of alternative semantics as proposed by Rooth certainly is the fact that focus is interpreted in situ. This correctly predicts island-insensitivity of association with focus; see (25) and e.g. Anderson (1972) and Jackendoff (1972) for discussion.

(25)   a.   *Dr. Jones only rejected [the proposal that [Bill]$_F$ submitted]*
       b.   **Who$_i$ did Dr. Jones reject [the proposal that t$_i$ submitted]?*

However, as Kratzer (1991) argues, this prediction of alternative semantics is not always borne out. There are relevant counterexamples. Consider her argument based on (26).

(26)   A.   *What a copycat you are! You went to Block Island because I
             did. You went to Elk Lake Lodge because I did. And you went to
             Tanglewood because I did.*
       B.   a.   *No, I only went to [Tanglewood]$_F$ because you did Δ*
             b.   *only(C$_7$) [[[I went to [TW]$_F$] because [you went to [TW]$_F$]] ~ Γ$_7$]*
             c.   *only(C$_7$) [[[TW]$_F$ λ1 [I went to t$_1$ because you went to t$_1$]] ~Γ$_7$]*

Suppose B rejects A's utterance in (26) with an utterance of (26a). (26a) is a case of VP ellipsis, and from what we know about VP ellipsis, it is rather straightforward to assume that something along the lines of (26b) represents its logical form (within alternative semantics). Since focus is interpreted locally, the focus value of the squiggle's sister node in (26b) contains not only propositions of the form *I went to Elk Lake Lodge because you went to Elk Lake Lodge*, but also propositions of the form *I went to Tanglewood because you went to Block Island*. However, all the latter propositions of the form *I went to x because you went to y*, where *x* is not identical to *y*, are clearly not salient alternatives in the present context. Therefore, the set of alternatives needs to be further restricted. One way to do this is to raise the focused constituent across the board; see (26c). But if we do so movement is involved, and we expect to observe island violations in more complex cases like the one in (27). However, we do not.

(27)   *You always contacted every responsible person before me. – No, I only
        contacted the person who chairs [the zoning board]$_F$ before you did.*

Is there some alternative way of dealing with examples like (27), one that does not involve focus movement? As Kratzer (1991) shows, there is. Suppose that there is not only one F-marker marking focus, but in fact a countable set of F-indices F1, ..., Fn. Suppose further that the interpretation of focus is in fact a two-step process: First, we need to build a representation that Jackendoff (1972) calls a "presupposition skeleton" by substituting each F-index Fi with a focus variable v_i; see (28b). In a second step, alternatives are derived with the help of focus variable assignments h that interpret (exclusively) focus variables v_i along the lines of (28c).

(28)   a. *[[I went to [TW]$_{FI}$] because [you went to [TW]$_{FI}$]]*
      b. *[[I went to v$_1$] because [you went to v$_1$]]*
      c. $[[(28b)]]_F = \{p; \exists\, h\!: p = [[I\ went\ to\ v_1\ because\ you\ went\ to\ v_1]]^h\}$

As is apparent from (28c), deriving alternatives from a presupposition skeleton mimics variable binding if two or more focus variables within the scope of h are identical. Though in general we want any two F-indices in a given tree to be distinct, identity requirements on VP ellipsis force identical F-indices in the case of (26) and (27). The representational view of alternative semantics proposed in Kratzer (1991) thus elegantly derives the correct reading from the properties of VP ellipsis that interact with the properties of focus interpretation.

    Unfortunately, this is not yet the end of the story. As Krifka (1991) points out, the interpretation of second occurrence focus as in (29b) requires selective binding.

(29)   a. *John only$_{FI}$ introduced [Bill]$_{FI}$ to Mary.*
      b. *John also$_{F2}$ only$_{FI}$ introduced [Bill]$_{FI}$ to [Sue]$_{F2}$.*

But both Rooth's denotational and Kratzer's representational variants of alternative semantics are unselective in nature, and consequently need to move the focus [Sue]$_{F2}$ to a position above and outside of the scope of *only* in order to prevent this focus from being bound by *only*. This, again, predicts island-sensitivity (see Rooth 1996 for further discussion).

    The lesson we learn from this discussion is that some mechanism of focus interpretation is needed that, first, mimics variable binding, and, second, does so in an essentially selective fashion. A variant of alternative semantics that meets these requirements is proposed in Wold (1996). Suppose, following Kratzer, that focus is marked with F-indices. Suppose further that each focus is selectively bound by some focus-sensitive operator like *only* or *also* as in (29). From Kratzer's proposal we know that it is straightforward to interpret focused constituents as variables. This can be done via the usual variable assignment g in the following way: When interpreting an indexed focus-sensitive expression like *only*$_{F1}$ in (29a), let us suppose that g is not yet defined for the index 1, i.e., variable assignments are, in general, partial. Suppose further that if g is not yet defined for the index 1, the variable assignment is assumed to simply ignore the index F1 on *Bill*, and to return the ordinary semantic value of the focused constituent. In this way, *only* has local (and distinguished) access to the ordinary semantic value of its sister node, i.e., to the proposition *that John introduced Bill to Mary*. If, however, g *is* defined for the index 1, we suppose that g interprets the focused constituent $[\text{Bill}]_{F1}$ as denoting the value of g at this very index (see the definition in (30) below): If g returns the individual John at index 1, the focused constituent $[\text{Bill}]_{F1}$ is taken to denote John; if g returns the individual Mary at index 1, the focused constituent $[\text{Bill}]_{F1}$ is taken to denote Mary; and so on, and so forth.

(30) $[[\text{ } [Bill]_{F1}]]^g = \begin{cases} g(1) \text{ if } 1 \in dom(g) \\ Bill \text{ if } 1 \notin dom(g) \end{cases}$

It should be clear by now that this gets us access to the set of alternatives to *John introduced* $[Bill]_{F1}$ *to Mary*: Running through the domain of individuals, we systematically change the value of g at index 1, and put all resulting propositions in a set C of alternatives. (Note that, since Bill is one of the relevant individuals, this set contains, amongst others, the proposition *that John introduced Bill to Mary*.) *Only* then is taken to quantify over this set of alternatives and to state that each true proposition in the set C of alternatives is identical to the proposition we get if we simply ignore the F-index F1 in the scope of $only_{F1}$. Thus we can essentially keep the semantics of *only* as proposed by Rooth and others (though in fact *only* now is a universal quantifier quantifying over possible values of the assignment g at index 1).

(31)   a. $[[only_{F1} \text{ } \varphi]]^g$ is defined only, if $1 \notin dom(g)$. If defined,
       b. $[[only_{F1} \text{ } \varphi]]^g = 1$ iff $\forall p \in C(p(w) = 1 \rightarrow p = [[\varphi]]^g)$

Since Wold's approach is a selective binding approach, it is able to cope both with Kratzer's Tanglewood example and with Krifka's second occurrence focus example without recourse to covert focus movement. It should be noted, however, that this approach is no longer truly in keeping with Rooth (1985, 1992), for the following reason: In Rooth's proposal, it is the F-marker on the focused constituent, and thus, in a sense, the focused constituent itself, that triggers the computation of alternatives. In Wold's proposal, however, the F-index marking the focused constituent is completely ignored, as long as it is not bound by some focus-sensitive operator such as *only*. Thus it is, in a sense, the binder, and not the bindee, that appeals to the notion of alternatives, and in the case of free focus, we are ultimately led to the conclusion that seemingly free focus is in fact bound by some covert (illocutionary) focus-sensitive operator.

2.2. Structured propositions

This is essentially what is put forward in Cresswell and von Stechow (1982) and Jacobs (1984), and what is usually called the relational approach to focus interpretation. These analyses, however, are not couched within the general framework of alternative semantics, but within the structured meanings approach as developed in von Stechow (1981, 1982) and Cresswell and von Stechow (1982), and later taken up and refined in Krifka (1991, 2001) and Reich (2003). The basic idea within the structured meanings approach to focus is that the partitioning of a sentence S in a focus α and a background β carries over to the semantic interpretation and triggers a structuring $\langle [[\alpha]] , [[\beta]]\rangle$ of the proposition $[[S]]$ denoted by S.

By way of illustration, consider (33). Interpreting the focus structure in (33a) results in a structured proposition consisting of the individual *Bill* and the property of being introduced to Mary by John; see (33b). The structuring of the proposition allows local access to both the denotation of the focus and the denotation of the background. And irrespective of whether we take this structured proposition to be computed on a second level of interpretation or whether we take it to represent the ordinary semantic interpretation of (33a), the unstructured interpretation of (32a) is always easily recoverable via functional application $[[\beta]]([[\alpha]])$.

(32)   a. *Who did John introduce to Mary?*
       b. λx. *John introduced x to Mary*

(33)   a. *John introduced [Bill] to Mary.*
       b. $\langle$ *Bill, λx. John introduced x to Mary*$\rangle$

Usually, the structured meanings approach builds on a categorial semantics for *wh*-interrogatives which interprets interrogative *wh*-words as λ-binders binding a variable of corresponding type in the position marked by the *wh*-word. Within the categorial approach, a question like (32a) does not denote a set of propositions, but a property, namely the property of being introduced to Mary by John. As is apparent from (32b) and (33b), Q/A congruence then is simply a matter of identity: A (sentential) utterance A is a congruent answer to a question Q if the semantic interpretation of the background of A matches the denotation of Q.

Interpreting focus particles like *only* appears to be just as simple. Since *only* is focus-sensitive, it operates on the interpretation of the focus structure, i.e., on the structured proposition in question; see (34b). If we stipulate the existence of an alternative function $\lambda x.\ alt_c(x)$ that provides us in a given context c with the salient alternatives to Bill in c, then *only* simply states that no alternative to Bill has the property of having been introduced to Mary by John.

(34) a. *John only introduced [Bill]$_F$ to Mary.*
      b. $only(\langle Bill,\ \lambda x.\ John\ introduced\ x\ to\ Mary\rangle)$
      c. $[[only]](\langle a, P\rangle) = 1$ iff $\forall\, x \in alt_c(a)(P(x) = 1 \rightarrow x = a)$

This, of course, raises two questions. First, how exactly do we get from the focus structure (34a) to its interpretation (34b)? And, second, is the semantics of *only* essentially equivalent to the semantics of *only* as stated within the framework of alternative semantics?

As for the first question, it seems that we are forced to assume movement of the bound focus to its binder in one way or another, either by adjoining the focus to the binder itself (35a), or by adjoining it to the binder's sister node (35b) (see also von Stechow 1991).

(35) a. *[only [Bill]$_F$] λ1 [John introduced t$_1$ to Mary].*
      b. *only [[Bill]$_F$ λ1 [John introduced t$_1$ to Mary]].*

This suggests that the structured meanings approach to the interpretation of focus is in fact a genuine movement approach (and, thus, fits nicely with, for instance, the cartographic approach). Keeping examples (25a) and (25b) in mind, this may of course cast some doubts on the viability of the structured meanings approach. On the other hand, we also saw in the last section that the island-insensitive nature of alternative semantics is in fact challenged in more complex examples (for detailed discussion, see Rooth 1996). And what is more, building on work done by Steedman (1991) and Drubig (1994), Krifka (1996) designs a semantic argument which suggests that association with focus, or to be more precise: association with focus phrase FP, does respect island constraints after all. To see this, consider example (36).

(36) *Sam only talked to [the woman who introduced [Bill]$_F$ to John]$_{FP}$*

Suppose that *only* associates with *Bill*, and suppose further the following context: Sam only talked to one person, namely Mary, and Mary introduced two people to John, namely Bill and, say, Tim. Intuition tells us that, in this context, (36) is to be judged as true. However, given the semantics of *only* in (34c), (36) comes out as false, since, by assumption, both *Sam talked to the woman who introduced Tim to John* and *Sam talked to the woman who introduced Bill to John* are true, but Bill is not identical to Tim. Does the semantics of *only* in (23c) fare better? Not really. The problem is that within alternative semantics – and this concerns all variants of alternative semantics, including the binding approach put forward in Wold (1996) (even though this variant is capable of interpreting nested foci) – we need to compare intensions rather than extensions, but the definite description *the woman who introduced Bill to John* is certainly different from the definite description *the woman who introduced Tim to John*, and, as a consequence, the resulting propositions are different, too. According to Krifka (1996) this suggests that *only* does not in fact directly associate with the focus *Bill*, but rather with the so-called focus phrase (FP) *the woman who introduced Bill to John*, which he takes to covertly move to its binder *only*. And what about the focus *Bill*, which is internal to the FP? (37) suggests, in turn, that focus interpretation within FP does not involve focus movement and that the derivation of alternatives to the focus phrase FP can proceed along the lines of alternative semantics.

(37) *Sam only talked to [the man who mentioned [the woman who introduced [Bill]$_F$ to Sue]]$_{FP}$*

As we just saw, Krifka's (1996) proposal relies on the assumption that there are two kinds of focus-related constituents, the focus and the focus phrase, which behave completely differently at the level of logical form, one being subject to covert movement, the other being interpreted in situ. Alternatively, one could think of examples like (36) as nested focus structures which are subject to a syntactically and semantically uniform treatment of the two foci in question; see (38). But what could such a uniform treatment of nested focus structures look like?

(38) *Sam only talked to [the woman who introduced [Bill]$_F$ to John]$_F$*

Suppose both foci move covertly. In such a case, movement of the internal focus *Bill* needs to target the DP *the woman who introduced Bill to John*, which is in violation of the complex noun phrase constraint. This suggests that focus, embedded or not, needs to be interpreted in situ. On the other hand, Krifka's argument shows that *only* needs access to the extension of the embedding focus, that is, some kind of structured meaning approach is called for.

The challenge then is to derive the structured meanings in question without moving the focused constituents. As is argued in Reich (2004), one solution to this challenge may be the use of choice functions. To see this, consider first the somewhat simpler example in (39a).

(39) a. *John only$_{F1}$ introduced [Bill]$_{F1}$ to Mary.*
   b. *only(⟨Bill, λx. John introduced x to Mary⟩)*
   c. *only(⟨f$_{Bill}$, λf$_1$. John introduced f$_1$(alt$_c$(Bill)) to Mary⟩)*

Suppose, following Kratzer and Wold, that F-markers come as F-indices that are bound by some coindexed focus-sensitive operator; see (39a). Within the structured meanings approach, the binding of a focus F1 is usually taken to trigger focus movement and to structure the proposition; see (39b). Alternatively, we could think of the F-index as locally introducing alternatives to *Bill*. To this effect, we make use of the context-sensitive alternative function $\lambda x. alt_c(x)$, which maps Bill to the set of its contextually salient alternatives (including Bill himself). Since $alt_c(Bill)$ is a set, there is a (minimal) choice function f_{Bill} which chooses exactly Bill from this set. The resulting proposition *John introduced $f_{Bill}(alt_c(Bill))$ to Mary* is apparently equivalent to the proposition *John introduced Bill to Mary* (for $f_{Bill}(alt_c(Bill))$ = Bill), but it allows access to the salient alternatives to *Bill* if we substitute a variable f_1 over choice functions for the function f_{Bill}. Since *only* is coindexed with the focus in question, the choice function variable f_1 can be bound by *only*, and the choice function f_{Bill} can be locally reconstructed as a definite description without covertly moving the focus to its binder. Similar to Wold's approach, the latter process requires some means of ignoring the bound focus F1 (see Reich 2004 for details).

The choice function approach to association with focus combines aspects of alternative semantics (the fact that the focus introduces alternatives and is interpreted in situ) with the general architecture of structured meanings. Within this approach, examples like (38) above can now, in fact, be analyzed in a uniform way as nested focus structures; see (40).

(40) *Sam only F1 talked to [F2 [the woman who introduced [Bill]$_{F2}$ to John]]$_{F1}$*

The basic idea is that *only* (or, more precisely, its binder index F1) binds the F-index F1 that marks the definite description *the woman who introduced Bill to John* as focus. This index (or, more precisely, its corresponding binder index F2) in turn binds the F-index F2 on *Bill*. Local binding of F2 results, as desired, in an alternative set containing structured definite descriptions of the form $\langle f_{\text{Tim}}, \lambda f_2.the\ woman\ who\ introduced\ f_2\ (alt_c(Bill))\ to\ John\rangle$.

As regards the interpretation of *only*, we may now require *only* to compare extensions of unstructured alternatives, which solves the problem raised by Krifka without stipulating the existence of a focus phrase FP (see also von Heusinger 1997 for a proposal within alternative semantics). This comes at a price, however. As is evident from the discussion above, the proposals become more and more complex, and one may wonder whether there is some simpler alternative which is nevertheless firmly grounded on intuitions about focus.

2.3. Givenness

As we saw in Section 1, the literature actually refers to two different intuitions when it comes to focus: One intuition is that focus triggers alternatives; this is the starting point of alternative semantics. The other intuition is that focus marks information as new, or, more precisely, as not being given; this is the starting point of Schwarzschild's (1999) givenness approach (see Halliday 1967, Chafe 1976, von Stechow 1981, amongst others).

Consider (41) by way of illustration. If (41a) is intended as an answer to the question *What did John's mother do?*, the object *Bill* is stressed. However, if the same question is answered with (41b), stress shifts to the verb *praise*. But why is that? The straightforward answer to this question is: because the referent of *him*, i.e., John, was already mentioned in the preceding question. Thus, in a sense, *him* is given in (40b) relative to the relevant context.

(41) *What did John's mother do?*

    a. *She praised BILL.*

    b. *She PRAISED him.*

The case is similar in (42). In (42a) the head noun *convertible* receives stress, while the attributive adjective *red* is less prominent. In (42b), however, stress shifts to the adjective *blue*, and the head noun is less prominent.

Again, it is straightforward to trace this effect back to the head noun *convertible* being given in (42b) in the context of (42a). Considered from this perspective, the contrastive interpretation of the adjective *blue* in (42b) is actually more of a side effect of deaccenting *convertible* than it is the actual reason why the adjective is stressed.

(42)   a. *John drove Mary's red* conVERtible.
       b. *No, John drove Mary's* BLUE *convertible.*

But can we determine whether the utterance of some phrase is given relative to some known context *c*? In the case of expressions of type *e* givenness boils down to coreference. But in what sense is, for example, the noun *convertible* given in an utterance of (42b)? According to Schwarzschild (1999), givenness is an entailment relation between two utterances A and U, and U is given relative to A, roughly speaking, if the denotation of A entails the denotation of U, provided we ignore the semantic contribution of the focused constituents. Reconsider (42), and suppose that in (42b) only the adjective *blue* is F-marked. Ignoring the semantic contribution of the adjective *blue* boils down to substituting the focus with a variable Q of relevant type and to existentially binding the variable. Now, since *John drove Mary's red convertible* entails that $\exists Q$(*John drove Mary's Q convertible*), an utterance of (42b) with the indicated focus structure is given relative to an utterance of (42a). But this is apparently also true of an utterance of (42b) in which not only *blue*, but also *Mary's blue convertible* is F-marked. Thus, if we want to exclude the latter as a possible focus structure, we need, in addition, some constraint that tells us to use as few F-markers as possible. This is Schwarzschild's constraint AvoidF.

The nice thing about Schwarzschild's definition of givenness is that it easily generalizes to non-sentential expressions. Suppose we want to know whether the VP *drove Mary's [blue]$_F$ convertible* is given. The first thing to do is to shift this expression to type *t*, so that it existentially quantifies over possible subjects, which results in something like $\exists x$(*x drove Mary's [blue]$_F$ convertible*). The second thing to do is to existentially close the focus *blue* within the VP, which finally results in something like $\exists Q \exists x$(*x drove Mary's Q convertible*). Apparently, the latter is entailed by (42a), and so is, by assumption, the VP.

In this vein, we can also establish the givenness of the noun phrase *Mary's [blue]$_F$ convertible* in (43c). But this comes as somewhat of a surprise, since it is frequently assumed that in an answer to a *wh*-question the constituent that corresponds to the *wh*-phrase is F-marked (too), which correctly derives the elliptical or fragment answer *Mary's blue convertible* in (43c). This suggests that the role of rhetorical relations needs to be taken into consideration here (see Reich 2002 for a detailed proposal within Schwarzschild's approach).

(43) a. *John drove Mary's red* convertible.
  b. *What did he drive before that?*
  c. *(He drove) Mary's* [blue]$_F$ *convertible.*

The crucial characteristic of Schwarzschild's proposal then is that focus is in fact not interpreted at all at the level of semantics. Rather, the set of focused constituents is restricted in a process of elimination by checking givenness relations and requiring given constituents to not be F-marked. F-markers in this approach are simply used to predict the placement of accent, to which effect Schwarzschild stipulates two more constraints (1. F-marked constituents that are not immediately dominated by another F-marked constituent contain an accent; 2. A head is less prominent than its internal argument), which are, however, not of immediate concern to us here.

Since F-markers do not play any role in interpretation, the question comes up again as to whether they are in fact needed. The (now) obvious alternative is to stipulate the existence of givenness markers G that check for every G-marked constituent whether it is given in the relevant context, or not. If it is, G-marking of the constituent is licensed, otherwise it is not. This is actually what is proposed in Sauerland (2004) and elaborated on in Wagner (2007).

In the context of the question *Who drove what?*, an answer like *John drove Mary's red convertible* is represented as (44a) rather than (44b). (Note that in this approach stress is naturally restricted to non-G-marked phrases; see Sauerland 2004 and Wagner 2007.)

(44) a. *John [drove]$_G$ Mary's red convertible*
  b. *[John]$_F$ drove [Mary's red convertible]$_F$*

None of the examples considered so far contained any focus particles, such as *only*, and this is for a good reason. Since focus is, by assumption, irrelevant to interpretation, the notion of association with focus in the sense(s) introduced above cannot play any role at all in the givenness approach (as long as we stick to the assumption that givenness is in fact sufficient to account for all relevant focus phenomena). Within this approach, any explanation of the seemingly focus-sensitive semantics of *only* needs to be stated without recourse to the notion focus at all. What is needed is a more indirect way, a (very) weak theory of the semantics and pragmatics of *only*.

(45)   *John only(C) introduced* Bill *to Mary*

Apparently, the key to an adequate treatment of *only* in the givenness approach is its restrictor C. If there is some straightforward way to require C to contain all relevant propositions of the form *John introduced x to Mary*, x being some salient individual, without resorting to any kind of focus interpretation, this allows us to retain the semantics of *only* as proposed within alternative semantics. According to Schwarzschild (1997) this may in fact be viable if pragmatic felicity conditions related to the (typical) use of *only* are taken into account (which includes, as is argued in Schwarzschild 1997, its use as a form of denial).

It should be noted here that we have, in fact, already seen a weak theory of the semantics and pragmatics of focus, namely Rooth's (1992) anaphoric version of alternative semantics. Surely, Rooth's approach *does* of course refer to the notion of alternative sets, and thus to focus; however, it does this in a rather indirect manner (though not as indirect as required by the givenness approach): The domain C of the quantifier *only* is restricted by way of anaphora, that is, by coindexing it with the anaphor Γ which relates to the squiggle operator ~. As we saw above, the squiggle operator adds the presupposition that its sister's focus value is a superset of the interpretation of Γ, thus indirectly restricting *only*'s restrictor C to a subset of the focus value of α.

2.4. Presupposition

In a way, then, the domain C of *only* is restricted by relating the relevant focus structure (the syntactic and semantic scope of ~) to a somewhat complicated presupposition. But if focus interpretation requires the statement of a presuppositional constraint anyway, why don't we adopt a simpler and perhaps more intuitive requirement, which has already been proposed by Chomsky (1977) and others. Consider, for example, an utterance of (46a) with the indicated focus structure. Suppose we first substitute each focus F with a variable x, and derive, on this basis, the presupposition skeleton of (46a) in the sense of Jackendoff (1972); see (46b). In a second step, we existentially close the variables, resulting in the case of (46a) in the proposition *that John introduced someone to Mary*; see (46c). It is this proposition that is, intuitively, made salient by an utterance of (46a). So why should we not assume that this proposition is in fact presupposed by an utterance of (46a)? This position (or, to be more precise, a somewhat weaker version of this position) has in fact been recently defended in Geurts and van der Sandt (2004a,b).

(46) a. *John introduced [Bill]$_F$ to Mary*
     b. John introduced x to Mary
     c. $\exists x$(John introduced x to Mary)

At first glance, it is, in fact, not at all clear whether the presuppositional approach is really that different from that of alternative semantics or the givenness approach. In the givenness approach, (46a) is given, if there is an utterance A in the previous context that entails the proposition in (46c). Thus, the information expressed by (46c) is required to be part of any adequate context of utterance, and in this sense (46c) is presupposed by (46a). In alternative semantics, the relevant alternative set consists only of propositions of the form *John introduced x to Bill*, the disjunction of which entails the proposition in (46c).

Still, there are important differences that distinguish the presuppositional approach from the other two approaches. Consider, for example, (47), taken from Kratzer (2004).

(47) a. *Did anybody eat the beans?*
     b. *Yes, [Fred]$_F$ did (eat the beans).*

According to the givenness approach, the verb phrase *eat the beans* is given in (47b), since there is an antecedent (*eat the beans*) in (47a), and the existential closure of the antecedent apparently entails the existential closure of the VP in question. But (47a) does not presuppose that someone ate the beans, nor does its denotation entail the proposition that someone did.

As is argued in Geurts and van der Sandt (2004a) presuppositions and focus show similar projection behavior, which indicates that there might, in fact, be some common mechanism at work here. On the other hand, the contrast in (48), due to Chris Potts, shows that the presupposition triggered by *too* in (48a) cannot be satisfied by the proposition embedded under *doubt*, but the supposed presupposition in (48b) can.

(48) a. *#Sue doubts that Ed attended the meeting, but/and we all agree that Jill attended the meeting too.*
     b. *Sue doubts that Ed attended the meeting, but we all agree that [Jill]$_F$ attended the meeting/did.*

Another characteristic property of presuppositions is that their failure typically results in a truth-value gap. However, as Kratzer (2004) argues, if we answer the question in (49a) with (49b), then its utterance is, in this context, inappropriate, but it does not lack a truth value.

(49) a. *What did Fred eat?*
      b. *[Fred]$_F$ ate the beans.*

These are three of the many arguments that suggest that, in the end, focus cannot be reduced to presuppositions. For a more thorough discussion, see, for example, Rooth (1999), the comments on the target article by Geurts and van der Sandt (2004a) in the same volume of *Theoretical Linguistics*, and more recently Abusch (2007).

2.5. Weak and strong approaches to focus

This leaves us, in essence, with two kinds of approaches to the semantics and pragmatics of focus. There are, as we saw above, on the one hand, strong approaches that start from the assumption that focus and focus-sensitive expressions are directly related by some mechanism of focus binding; see, e.g., the proposals in Jacobs (1984), von Stechow (1981), Krifka (1991), Wold (1996), and Reich (2004). On the other hand, there are weak(er) approaches that are built on a more indirect way of relating focus and focus-sensitive expressions, e.g., those of Rooth (1992), von Fintel (1994), and, in particular, Schwarzschild (1999).

However, as recent work by Beaver and Clark (2003, 2008) suggests, we may not have to choose between the two approaches. Consider (50) and (51).

(50) a. A: *Does Sandy feed Nutrapup to her dogs?*
      b. B: *Yes, Sandy always feeds Nutrapup to [Fido]$_F$,*
      c.   *and she always feeds Nutrapup to [Butch]$_F$, too.*

(51) a. A: *Does Sandy feed Nutrapup to her dogs?*
      b. B: *Yes, Sandy only feeds Nutrapup to [Fido]$_F$,*
      c.   *#and she only feeds Nutrapup to [Butch]$_F$, too.*

Beaver and Clark observe that an utterance of (51c) in the context of (51a) and (51b) is infelicitous. This contrasts with (50c), which differs from (51c) only in that the second occurrence focus is, loosely speaking, bound by *always* rather than *only*. This suggests that *only* systematically triggers an exhaustive interpretation, while *always* does not. The fact that *only* triggers an exhaustive interpretation is captured nicely in strong approaches. But what about *always*? As long as the alternative set is taken to only contain propositions of the form *Sandy feeds Nutrapup to x*, where *x* is some (salient) dog, both weak and strong theories likewise predict an exhaustive interpretation for *always*. How, then, can we account for the fact that *always* does not explicitly exclude situations in which Sandy feeds Fido together with, say, Butch? Suppose *always* does not quantify over alternatives to Fido, but over contextually relevant situations *s*. Suppose further that the focus structure in (50b) restricts this set to the set of situations *s* where Sandy feeds Nutrapup to some number of dogs. Given this, we can take *always* to require of all these contextually relevant situations *s* that they contain some situation *s'* in which Sandy feeds Nutrapup to Fido. Apparently, this is consistent with *s* itself being a complex situation in which Nutrapup is fed to both Fido and Butch.

The difference between *only* and *always* is then accounted for by appealing to a weak theory of focus in the case of *always* and a strong theory in the case of *only*. Building on work done by Bonomi and Casalegno (1993) and Herburger (2000), Beaver and Clark (2003, 2008) propose a uniform analysis in terms of quantification over events, one that attributes the observed contrast to context-sensitive properties of *always* that *only* seems to lack.

3.   Topic and comment in semantics and pragmatics

3.1. Discourse topic

In the previous section, we argued that sentences like (52b) fall into two parts, the focal part on the one hand, and the background part on the other. Sometimes, the non-focal part is also called the topic (see, e.g., von Stechow 1981).

(52)   a.   *What did you sell to Clyde?*
     b.   *I sold [my typewriter]$_F$ to Clyde.*

This topic concept relates to what is usually called a *discourse topic* in the current literature. The basic idea is that, in general, discourse is structured by explicitly or implicitly given questions, frequently called questions under discussion, QUDs for short (see, amongst others, von Stechow 1981, Klein and von Stutterheim 1987, Steedman 1990, van Kuppevelt 1991, Roberts 1996, Büring 2003, Aloni et al. 2007). In (52), for example, it is the question (52a) that structures the discourse sequence consisting of (52a) and (52b). In this sense, the question in (52a) is the topic of the discourse in (52). This discourse topic, however, is reflected in the focus structure of (52b). This is evident in the structured propositions approach to focus: The question in (52a) denotes the property $\lambda x.I$ *sold x to Clyde*, which is identical to the non-focal part of the structured proposition ⟨*my typewriter, $\lambda x.I$ sold x to Clyde*⟩ that interprets the focus structure in (52b). In this sense, the non-focal part of (52b) is, or better reflects, the topic that an utterance of (52b) relates to.

3.2. Contrastive topic

Suppose that the idea of *wh*-questions structuring discourse is on the right track, that is that each utterance in a text or discourse needs to address some implicitly or explicitly given QUD. But then, what about questions themselves? What do they relate to? Consider (53).

(53)   a.   *What did [you]$_F$ sell to Clyde?*
       b.   *[I]$_{CT}$ sold [my typewriter]$_F$ to Clyde.*

Like any other utterance, questions are also part of a more complex discourse, and thus typically relate to previous context. In particular, questions also carry focus structures; see for example (53a). Now, as we saw in (52) above, the topic an utterance relates to appears to be reflected in the focus structure of the utterance itself. With respect to (52b), we argued that the non-focal part of the answer corresponds to the topic it relates to. Since the question (53a) denotes, modulo focus, the property $\lambda x.I$ *sold x to Clyde*, its focus structure denotes the structured question ⟨*you, $\lambda y \lambda x.y$ sold x to Clyde*⟩. The non-focal part of this structured question, however, corresponds to the (unstructured) interpretation of the question *Who sold what to Clyde?* Thus, by the same line of reasoning, we are able to establish that the question in (53a) actually addresses the more general question of *Who sold what to Clyde?*. Thus, the topic that a given question relates to in discourse is simply a more general question.

What is of further interest here is the fact that the focus structure of the question in (53a) not only reflects the discourse topic it relates to, but that it also seems to have an interesting effect on the way the answer (53b) to (53a) is pronounced. Even though (53a) can be answered with the short answer *my typewriter*, the sentential answer in (53b) seems to require a pitch accent on the subject *I*. This accent differs from the pitch accent on *my typewriter* in that it is best described as a fall-rise contour. In short, this accent seems to be a B accent in the sense of Jackendoff (1972). Suppose we interpret B accents in a manner essentially parallel to A accents, as structuring meanings; then the answer in (53b) denotes the nested structured proposition in (54b).

(54) a. *[I]$_{CT}$ sold [my typewriter]$_F$ to Clyde.*
      b. ⟨*I, λy.*⟨*my typewriter, λx.y sold x to Clyde*⟩⟩

This is very much reminiscent of what Jackendoff claimed about the interpretation of A and B accents (Jackendoff 1972: 262): "The B accent occurs on the variable whose value is chosen first, the one which [the] speaker [...] is asking about. The A accent occurs on the variable whose value is chosen second, so as to make the sentence true for the value of the other variable." In other words, the interpretation of the B accent gives rise to a set of contrasting questions of the form *What did y sell to Clyde?*, *y* being some (salient) individual; see (55). All these contrasting questions address the same topic in discourse, the question *Who sold what to Clyde?*.

(55) a. *What did Bill sell to Clyde?*
      b. *What did Sue sell to Clyde?*, etc.

From this point of view, B accents simply mark contrastive focus on a higher level, namely contrastive focus in *wh*-questions (see, e.g., Romero 1998). On the other hand, it is, intuitively, the contrastive focus in the *wh*-question (53a) which determines who the "speaker [...] is asking about" in (53b). In this sense, the B accent also marks an aboutness topic. Thus, all in all, it seems justified to dub B accented constituents *contrastive topics*.

This is actually the term introduced by Büring (1997) to refer to B accented constituents, which he takes to be marked with the index CT; see (53b) above. Taking as his starting point the work of Jackendoff (1972), Büring (1997) proposes an interpretation of contrastive topics within the framework of alternative semantics along the lines sketched in the previous paragraphs: While A accents give rise to propositional alternatives (sets of propositions), B accents give rise to alternative questions (sets of sets of propositions). By way of illustration, consider once more (53b). Interpreting the focus on *my typewriter* in (53b) results in a set of propositions as indicated in (56), which (essentially) corresponds to the Hamblin denotation of the question *What did you sell to Clyde?*. If we now interpret the contrastive topic *I* using essentially the same techniques, though on a different level of interpretation, this results in a set of (contrasting) questions like (56) and (57), or, to put it somewhat differently, in a set of sets of (contrasting) propositions. This set of sets of propositions is denotationally equivalent to a set of questions like *What did y sell to Clyde?*, where y is any individual. And this higher order object is in turn equivalent to the denotation of the question *Who sold what to Clyde?* (Hagstrom 1998).

(56)   *What did you sell to Clyde?*
   a. *that I sold my typewriter to Clyde,*
   b. *that I sold my adding machine to Clyde, etc.*

(57)   *What did Sue sell to Clyde?*
   a. *that Sue sold her typewriter to Clyde,*
   b. *that Sue sold her adding machine to Clyde, etc.*

According to Büring (1997, 1999), B accents further trigger an implicature, which we could dub an *incompleteness implicature*. It basically states that B accents suggest that there is still one locally relevant QUD that has not yet been fully resolved; see (58), adapted from Büring (1999: 150).

(58)   Given a sentence A, containing a contrastive topic, there is an element Q in $[[A]]_{CT}$, such that Q is still under consideration after uttering A.

Related to this, observe that B accents may (for whatever reason) also give rise to scope inversion effects, as in the example *All (B) of my friends didn't (A) come* already discussed above.

3.3. Sentence topic

As we have seen above, contrastive topics systematically carry B accents, and may be quantificational. These properties distinguish contrastive topics from other constituents like *Mr. Morgan* in (59) (taken from Reinhart 1981) that are also usually called topics in the literature.

(59)   *Mr. Morgan is a careful researcher and a knowledgable semiticist, but his originality leaves something to be desired.*

In what sense, then, is *Mr. Morgan* or rather its referent the topic of (59)? *Mr. Morgan* certainly does not constitute a topic in the sense of a discourse topic as introduced above. This would be a QUD like, for example, *What are Mr. Morgan's scholarly abilities?*.

As Reinhart (1981) and many others argue, there is an intuitively (somewhat) different concept of topicality at stake here, namely aboutness: (59) "is about Morgan, because it predicates something about Morgan" (Reinhart 1981: 54). Since predication is a relation that holds between two parts of a sentence (or rather their denotation), aboutness topics always correspond to (the denotation of) an expression in the sentence. Let us call these topics, following Dik (1978), *sentence topics*. As mentioned above, sentence topics may also occur left dislocated or as part of the phrase *as for NP*, see (60a) and (60b), which respectively mark Felix and Rosa as sentence topic. Both are truth-conditionally equivalent to the sentence *Felix invited Rosa to dance with him*, that is, topicality has no truth-conditional effects.

(60) a. *As for Felix, he invited Rosa to dance with him.*
      b. *As for Rosa, Felix invited her to dance with him.*

Rather, as Strawson (1964) argues, topics are a means to organize knowledge and to assess the truth of a sentence. As Reinhart (1981: 60) puts it "to assess the truth of [(60a)] we are likely to search our knowledge of Felix and see if among the people he may have invited we find Rosa, while in the assessment of [(60b)] we are more likely to check if among the things that happened to Rosa, we can find an invitation from Felix". Furthermore, Reinhart (1981: 65) argues that while "quantified NPs are often hard, and sometimes impossible, to interpret as topics", specific indefinites may very well function as topics; see, for example, the specific indefinite *a child of my acquaintance* in (61) and the discussion in Endriss (2009).

(61) *When she was five years old,* a child of my acquaintance *announced a theory that she was inhabited by rabbits.*   (The New York Times)

This example also shows that topics do not necessarily constitute old information. Thus, they may, but need not, be part of the background of a sentence.

As mentioned above, Reinhart (1981: 80) sees topics as "one of the means available in the language to organize, or classify the information exchanged in communication – they are signals for how to construct the context set, or under which entries to classify the new proposition". Reinhart compares this procedure to the organization of a library catalogue. Suppose you are interested in information about Felix. In such a case, you would probably check the catalogue entry for "Felix". And if you are interested in information about Rosa, you would probably check the catalogue entry for "Rosa". In both cases you may end up with the propositional information that Felix invited Rosa to dance with him, but you would have come about it in two different ways.

Formally, the information presented by (60a) and (60b) can be represented as ordered pairs relating the topic and the proposition that are expressed by the relevant utterance; see (62a) and (62b). (Note that these representations look very much like structured meanings, but it is important to see that they are different: Structured meanings like $\langle\alpha,\beta\rangle$ can be destructed via functional application $\beta(\alpha)$ while the structured representations in (62) cannot.)

(62)   a. $\langle$*Felix, that Felix invited Rosa to dance with him*$\rangle$
       b. $\langle$*Rosa, that Felix invited Rosa to dance with him*$\rangle$

Thus, saying that an utterance of a sentence S in a context c is about a is equivalent to saying that the propositional information conveyed by the utterance is stored under the entry for a in the context c; if such an entry is not yet available, as is the case with specific indefinites, an entry for a is created first.

This notion of topicality is, in one way or another, at the heart of most approaches to information structure, including the f-structure approach in Erteschik-Shir (1997, 2007), the link/tail approach in Vallduví (1990, 1992) or the proposal put forward in Lambrecht (1994). It could be somewhat too restrictive though. To see this, consider (63).

(62)   *Körperlich geht es   Peter   gut.*
       physically goes it-EXPL Peter-DAT well
       'Physically, Peter is well.'

Intuition tells us that *körperlich* ('physically') is a topic-like expression. This is corroborated by the fact that in languages with morphosyntactic topic markers like Korean, a word like *körperlich* would be marked as a topic (see Jacobs 2001: 655). However, (63) is of course not about *körperlich* in the sense of Reinhart, rather it is what Chafe (1976) calls a frame-setter, i.e., an expression which restricts the truth of the proposition to a certain domain. Chafe (1976: 51) therefore, concludes that "'real' topics (in topic prominent languages) are not so much 'what the sentence is about' as 'the frame within which the sentence holds'".

On the other hand, it is far from clear whether the latter characterization is in fact general enough to also include Felix as the topic of (60a). This is the starting point for Jacobs' (2001) proposal according to which topicality is a prototypical concept characterized by four different properties: informational separation, predication, addressation, and frame-setting. Whether such a radical move is actually enforced by the facts is still a matter of debate.

References

Abusch, Dorit
    2007   Presupposition triggering from alternatives. *Journal of Semantics* 27: 37–80.
Aloni, Maria, David Beaver, Brady Clark and Robert van Rooij
    2007   The dynamics of topic and focus. In *Questions in Dynamic Semantics*, Maria Aloni, Alastair Butler and Paul Dekker (eds.), 123–146. Amsterdam: Elsevier.
Anderson, Stephen R.
    1972   How to get even. *Language* 48: 893–905.
Bartels, Christine
    1999   *The Intonation of English Statements and Questions: A Compositional Interpretation*. London: Routledge.
Beaver, David Ian and Brady Z. Clark
    2003   "Always" and "only": Why not all focus sensitive operators are alike. *Natural Language Semantics* 11: 323–362.
Beaver, David Ian and Brady Z. Clark
    2008   *Sense and Sensitivity: How Focus determines Meaning*. Oxford: Blackwell.
Beaver, David Ian, Brady Z. Clark, Edward S. Flemming, Florian T. Jaeger and Maria K. Wolters
    2007   When semantics meets phonetics: Acoustical studies of second occurrence focus. *Language* 83: 245–276.
Bolinger, Dwight
    1965   *Forms of English: Accent, Morpheme, Order*. Cambridge, MA: Harvard University Press.
Bonomi, Andrea and Paolo Casalegno
    1993   Only: Association with focus in event semantics. *Natural Language Semantics* 2: 1–45.
Bosch, Peter and Rob van der Sandt (eds.)
    1999   *Focus*. Cambridge: Cambridge University Press.
Büring, Daniel
    1997   *The Meaning of Topic and Focus. The 59th Street Bridge Accent*. London: Routledge.

Büring, Daniel
    1999   Topic. In *Focus*, Bosch, Peter and Rob van der Sandt (eds.), 142–165. Cambridge: Cambridge University Press.

Büring, Daniel
    2003   On d-trees, beans, and b-accents. *Linguistics and Philosophy* 26: 511–545.

Chafe, Wallace
    1976   Givenness, contrastiveness, definiteness, subjects, topics and point of view. In *Subject and Topic*, Charles N. Li (ed.), 25–55. New York: Academic Press.

Chomsky, Noam
    1977   On wh-movement. In *Formal Syntax. Proceedings of the 1976 MSSB Irvine Conference on the Formal Syntax of Natural Languages*, Peter W. Culicover, Thomas Wasow and Adrian Akmajian (eds.), 71–132. New York: Academy Press.

Cohen, Antonie and Johan 't Hart
    1967   On the anatomy of intonation. *Lingua* 18: 177–192.

Cresswell, Max J. and Arnim von Stechow
    1982   De re belief generalized. *Linguistics and Philosophy* 5: 503–535.

Dik, Simon C.
    1978   *Functional Grammar*. Amsterdam: North Holland.

Dretske, Fred
    1972   Contrastive statements. *Philosophical Review* 81: 411–437.

Drubig, Hans Bernhard
    1994   Island constraints and the syntactic nature of focus and association with focus. Tech. Rep. 51 Arbeitspapiere des Sonderforschungsbereichs 340 Stuttgart/Tübingen.

Endriss, Cornelia
    2009   *Quantificational Topics – a Scopal Treatment of Exceptional Wide Scope Phenomena* (Studies in Linguistics and Philosophy 86). Berlin, New York: Springer.

Erteschik-Shir, Nomi
    1997   *The Dynamics of Focus Structure*. Cambridge: Cambridge University Press.

Erteschik-Shir, Nomi
    2007   *Information Structure: The Syntax-Discourse Interface*. Oxford: Oxford University Press.

Fanselow, Gisbert
    2007   The restricted access of information structure to syntax – A minority report. In *The Notions of Information Structure*, Caroline Féry, Gisbert Fanselow and Manfred Krifka (eds.), 205–220. Potsdam: Universitätsverlag Potsdam.

Féry, Caroline
    1993   *The Tonal Structure of Standard German*. Tübingen: Niemeyer.

Féry, Caroline
2007   The fallacy of invariant phonological correlates of information struc-
        tural notions. In *The Notions of Information Structure*, Caroline Féry,
        Gisbert Fanselow and Manfred Krifka (eds.), 161–184. Potsdam:
        Universitätsverlag Potsdam.
Féry, Caroline, Gisbert Fanselow and Manfred Krifka (eds.)
2007   *The Notions of Information Structure.* Potsdam: Universitätsverlag
        Potsdam.
von Fintel, Kai
1994   Restrictions on quantifier domains. Ph.D. dissertation, University of
        Massachusetts.
Frey, Werner
2000   Über die syntaktische Position der Satztopiks im Deutschen. *Zentrum
        für Allgemeine Sprachwissenschaft Papers in Linguistics* 20: 137–172.
Frey, Werner
2004   A medial topic position for German. *Linguistische Berichte* 198:
        153–190.
Geurts, Bart and Rob van der Sandt
2004a   Interpreting focus. *Theoretical Linguistics* 30: 1–44.
Geurts, Bart and Rob van der Sandt
2004b   Interpreting focus again. *Theoretical Linguistics* 30: 149–161.
Hagstrom, Paul
1998   Decomposing questions. Ph.D. dissertation, University of Massa-
        chusetts.
Halliday, Michael Λ. K.
1967   Notes on transitivity and theme in English (part I). *Journal of
        Linguistics* 3: 37–81.
Hamblin, Charles L.
1973   Questions in Montague English. *Foundations of Language* 10: 41–53.
Herburger, Elena
2000   What counts: Focus and quantification. Ph.D. dissertation, Univer-
        sity of Massachusetts.
von Heusinger, Klaus
1997   Focus in complex noun phrases. In *Proceedings of the 11th Amster-
        dam colloquium*, Paul Dekker, Martin Stokhof and Yde Venema
        (eds.), 49–54. Institute for Logic, Language and Computation/Depart-
        ment of Philosophy University of Amsterdam.
Höhle, Tilman N.
1982   Explikationen für „normale Betonung" und „normale Wortstellung".
        In *Satzglieder im Deutschen*, Werner Abraham (ed.), 73–153.
        Tübingen: Narr.
Jackendoff, Ray
1972   *Semantic Interpretation in Generative Grammar.* Cambridge, MA:
        Massachusetts Institute of Technology Press.

Jacobs, Joachim
1984   Funktionale Satzperspektive und Illokutionssemantik. *Linguistische Berichte* 91: 25–58.
Jacobs, Joachim
1997   I-Topikalisierung. *Linguistische Berichte* 168: 91–133.
Jacobs, Joachim
2001   The dimensions of topic-comment. *Linguistics* 39: 641–681.
Kiss, Katalin
1987   *Configurationality in Hungarian.* Dordrecht: Reidel.
Kiss, Katalin
2007   Topic and focus: Two structural positions associated with logical functions in the left periphery of the Hungarian sentence. In *The Notions of Information Structure*, Caroline Féry, Gisbert Fanselow and Manfred Krifka (eds.), 69–81. Potsdam: Universitätsverlag Potsdam.
Klein, Wolfgang and Christiane von Stutterheim
1987   Quaestio und referentielle Bewegung in Erzählungen. *Linguistische Berichte* 109: 163–183.
Kratzer, Angelika
1991   The representation of focus. In *Semantik – Ein internationales Handbuch zeitgenössischer Forschung. Semantics* [An International Handbook of Contemporary Research], Arnim von Stechow and Dieter Wunderlich (eds.), 825–834. Berlin/New York: Mouton de Gruyter.
Kratzer, Angelika
2004   Interpreting focus: Presupposed or expressive meanings? Comments on Geurts and van der Sandt. *Theoretical Linguistics* 30: 123–136.
Krifka, Manfred
1991   A compositional semantics for multiple focus constructions. In *Proceedings of Semantics and Linguistic Theory* 1, Steven K. Moore and Adam Zachary Wyner (eds.), 127–158. Ithaca/New York: Cornell University Press.
Krifka, Manfred
1996   Frameworks for the representation of focus. In *Formal Grammar*, Geert-Jan M. Krujiff, Glynn V. Morrill and Richard T. Oehrle (eds.), 99–112. Prague: Eighth European Summer School for Logic, Language, and Information.
Krifka, Manfred
2001   For a structured account of questions and answers. In *Audiatur Vox Sapientiae. A Festschrift for Arnim von Stechow*, 287–319. (Studia Grammatica 52). Berlin: Akademie Verlag.
van Kuppevelt, Jan
1991   Topic en comment. Ph.D. dissertation, University of Nijmegen.

Lambrecht, Knud
    1994   *Information Structure and Sentence Form: Topic, Focus, and the Mental Representation of Discourse Referents.* Cambridge: Cambridge University Press.

Musan, Renate
    2010   *Informationsstruktur.* Heidelberg: Universitätsverlag Winter.

Partee, Barbara H.
    1999   Focus, quantification, and semantics-pragmatics issues. In *Focus*, Bosch, Peter and Rob van der Sandt (eds.), 213–231. Cambridge: Cambridge University Press.

Pierrehumbert, Janet B. and Julia Hirschberg
    1990   The meaning of intonational contours in the interpretation of discourse. In *Intentions in Communication*, Philip Cohen, Jerry Morgan and Martha Pollock (eds.), 271–312. Cambridge, MA: Massachusetts Institute of Technology Press.

Reich, Ingo
    2002   Question/answer congruence and the semantics of wh-phrases. *Theoretical Linguistics* 28: 73–94.

Reich, Ingo
    2003   *Frage, Antwort und Fokus.* Berlin: Akademie Verlag.

Reich, Ingo
    2004   Association with focus and choice functions – A binding approach. *Research on Language and Computation* 2: 463–489.

Reinhart, Tanya
    1981   Pragmatics and linguistics: An analysis of sentence topics. *Philosophica* 27: 53–94.

Rizzi, Luigi
    1997   The fine structure of the left periphery. In *Elements of Grammar: Handbook in Generative Syntax*, Liliane Haegeman (ed.), 281–337. Dordrecht: Kluwer.

Rizzi, Luigi
    2004   On the cartography of syntactic structures. In *The Structure of CP and IP*, Luigi Rizzi (ed.), 3–15. New York: Oxford University Press.

Roberts, Craige
    1996   Information structure in discourse: Towards an integrated formal theory of pragmatics. In *Ohio State University Working Papers in Linguistics* 49, Jae Hak Yoon and Andreas Kathol (eds.). Ohio State University.

Romero, Maribel
    1998   Focus and reconstruction effects in wh-phrases. Ph.D. dissertation, University of Massachusetts at Amherst.

Rooth, Mats
    1985   Association with focus. Ph.D. dissertation, University of Massachusetts.

Rooth, Mats
  1992   A theory of focus interpretation. *Natural Language Semantics* 1: 75–116.
Rooth, Mats
  1996   Focus. In *The Handbook of Contemporary Semantic Theory*, Shalom Lappin (ed.), 271–298. Oxford: B. Blackwell.
Rooth, Mats
  1999   Association with focus or association with presupposition? In *Focus*, Bosch, Peter and Rob van der Sandt (eds.), 232–244. Cambridge: Cambridge University Press.
Sauerland, Uli
  2004   Don't interpret focus! Why a presuppositional account of focus fails and how a presuppositional account of focus works. In *Proceedings of Sinn und Bedeutung* 9, Emar Maier, Corien Bary and Janneke Huitink (eds.), 370–384. Nijmegen: Nijmegen Centre for Semantics.
Schwarzschild, Roger
  1997   *Why some foci must associate.* Ms., Rutgers University.
Schwarzschild, Roger
  1999   GIVENness, AVOID-F and other constraints on the placement of accent. *Natural Language Semantics* 7: 141–177.
Selkirk, Elisabeth O.
  1996   Sentence prosody: Intonation, stress and phrasing. In *The Handbook of Phonological Theory*, John A. Goldsmith (ed.), 550–569. London: Blackwell.
Stechow, Arnim von
  1981   Topic, focus and local relevance. In *Crossing the Boundaries in Linguistics*, Wolfgang Klein and Willem J. M. Levelt (eds.), 95–130. Dordrecht: D. Reidel.
Stechow, Arnim von
  1982   Structured propositions. *Tech. Rep. 59 Arbeitspapiere des Sonderforschungsbereichs 99 Konstanz.*
Stechow, Arnim von
  1991   Current issues in the theory of focus. In *Semantik. Ein internationales Handbuch zeitgenössischer Forschung* [Semantics. An International Handbook of Contemporary Research], Arnim von Stechow and Dieter Wunderlich (eds.), 804–825. Berlin/New York: Mouton de Gruyter.
Stechow, Arnim von and Dieter Wunderlich (eds.)
  1991   *Semantik. Ein internationales Handbuch zeitgenössischer Forschung.* [Semantics. An International Handbook of Contemporary Research]. Berlin/New York: Mouton de Gruyter.
Steedman, Mark
  1990   Gapping as constituent coordination. *Linguistics and Philosophy* 13: 207–263.

Steedman, Mark
   1991   Surface structure, intonation, and focus. In *Natural Language and
             Speech*, Ewan Klein and Frank Veltman (eds.), 260–296. Dordrecht:
             Kluwer.
Sternefeld, Wolfgang
   2006   *Syntax. Eine morphologisch motivierte generative Beschreibung des
             Deutschen*. Band 2. Tübingen: Stauffenburg.
Strawson, Peter F.
   1964   Identifying reference and truth values. *Theoria* 30: 96–118.
Szabolsci, Anna
   1981   Compositionality in focus. *Folia Linguistica* 15: 141–161.
Vallduví, Enric
   1990   The informational component. Ph.D. dissertation, University of Penn-
             sylvania.
Vallduví, Enric
   1992   *The Informational Component*. New York: Garland.
Wagner, Michael
   2007   Givenness and locality. In *Proceedings of Semantics and Linguistic
             Theory* 16, Jonathan Howell and Masayuki Gibson (eds.). Ithaca:
             CLC Publications.
Wold, Dag
   1996   Long distance selective binding: The case of focus. In *Proceedings
             of Semantics and Linguistic Theory* 6, Teresa Galloway and Justin
             Spence (eds.), 311–328. Ithaca, NY: Cornell University.

Contributors

Rusudan Asatiani
Institute for Oriental Studies

Tbilisi State University
1, Chavchavdze Ave
0218 Tbilisi
Georgia

rus_asatiani@hotmail.com

Aoju Chen
Utrecht Institute of Linguistics OTS

Universiteit Utrecht
Trans 10
3512 JK Utrecht
The Netherlands

aoju.chen@uu.nl

Heidi Wind Cowles
Department of Linguistics

University of Florida
PO Box 115454
Gainesville, FL 32611
USA

cowles@ufl.edu

Christine Dimroth
Institut für Germanistik

Universität Osnabrück
Neuer Graben 40
49068 Osnabrück
Germany

christine.dimroth@uni-osnabrueck.de

Beáta Gyuris
Department of Theoretical Linguistics

Hungarian Academy of Science
1394 Budapest
P.O. Box 360.
Hungary

gyuris@nytud.hu

Daniel Hole
Institut für deutsche Sprache und Linguistik

Humboldt-Universität zu Berlin
Unter den Linden 6
10099 Berlin
Germany

holcdan@googlemail.com

Wolfgang Klein
Max Planck Institute for Psycholinguistics

PO Box 310
6500 AH Nijmegen
The Netherlands

klein@mpi.nl

Manfred Krifka
Institut für deutsche Sprache und Linguistik

Humboldt-Universität zu Berlin
Unter den Linden 6
10099 Berlin
Germany

krifka@rz.hu-berlin.de

Renate Musan
Institut für Germanistik

Universität Osnabrück
Neuer Graben 40
49068 Osnabrück
Germany

renate.musan@uni-osnabrueck.de

Bhuvana Narasimhan
Department of Linguistics

University of Colorado
Hellems 290, 295 UCB
Boulder, CO 80309
USA

bhuvana.narasimhan@colorado.edu

Ingo Reich
Philosophische Fakultät II: Germanistik

Universität des Saarlandes
Postfach 15 11 50
66041 Saarbrücken
Germany

i.reich@mx.uni-saarland.de

Stavros Skopeteas
Fakultät für Linguistik und
Literaturwissenschaft

Universität Bielefeld
Postfach 10 01 31
33501 Bielefeld
Germany

stavros.skopeteas@uni-bielefeld.de

Manfred Stede
Kognitionswissenschaften

Universität Potsdam
Karl-Liebknecht-Str. 24-25
14476 Golm
Germany

stede@ling.uni-potsdam.de

Reiko Vermeulen
Department of English

Ghent University
Muinkkaai 42
9000 Ghent
Belgium

reiko.vermeulen@ugent.be

Susanne Winkler
Seminar für Englische Philologie

Universität Tübingen
Wilhelmstr.50
72074 Tübingen
Germany

sekretariat-winkler@es.uni-tuebingen.de

Index of subjects

Index of persons